CONTINUOUS-PROGRESS ED[U]CATION

MAURIE HILLSON
and
JOSEPH BONGO

with a contributory chapter
on the bilingual child and
English as a second language
in continuous-progress programs
by Eliane C. Condon

Science Research Associates, Inc., College Division
165 University Avenue, Palo Alto, California 94301

A Subsidiary of IBM

CONTINUOUS-PROGRESS EDUCATION

A PRACTICAL APPROACH

The lists of materials and equipment beginning on
pages 20 and 202 are not intended to be complete
lists. Where a brand name is given, it is not to be
inferred that this is necessarily the only or the best
version of this kind of product, or that it constitutes
a recommendation by the publisher.

CONTENTS

LIST OF FIGURES, EXAMPLES, AND ADDENDA ITEMS

PART I

PART II

Addenda

A FOREWORD

This book is concerned with some practical approaches to achieving certain features that relate to continuous-progress oriented education. It presents concepts and ideas calculated to encourage educators to develop collaboratively planned and taught continuous-progress nongraded programs. This is intended to be a "how to" book. The substantive materials and suggestions are drawn from experiences and activities of the authors. We do not intend, nor do we attempt, a ringing defense of the basic need for educational innovation, invention, and implementation. The book does not deal with statistical analyses or fully documented research areas relative to change and the process of change. Many aspects of the research and the materials of research are contained in the bibliographic references. It is from the knowledge gained in using these references that we assembled various ideas, and support for other ideas found in the text. It is only in the first chapter that we deal generally with the philosophical, sociological, and psychological reasons for the need for change in education. After that we have attempted to present a collection of ideas concerned with the implementation, and attendant activity that will bring about a fundamentally different approach to the way children are organized for learning. Our desire was to create ideas that are relevant to a more precise diagnostic and prescriptive approach to learning, along with necessary supports to sustain that kind of approach.

Schools exist to provide education for children. There is no set formula for organizing teachers and groups of children to effect the best kind of instruction possible. However, there is an overwhelming amount of evidence concerning the failures of present programs to achieve the best possible education for all children. There is a need for a redirection of education toward innovative approaches to instruction, organization, curriculum building, and learning in general. The concept of grade placement (a convenient way to organize children) has received much criticism in the past several years. An increasing desire for individuality and for individual learning has, in recent years, burst forth on the educational scene with great intensity. Teachers, caught up in the daily grind of grade requirements and hamstrung by standards that are irrationally set down, are constantly frustrated by the conflict of what ought to be done and what is achievable. Many lack training in how to implement those areas of activity that need to be implemented if better education is to result.

The purpose of this book is to ease such conflict. Educational personnel should be brought up to date on developments that make the job of teaching a far more critical and more challenging endeavor than it often appears to be. They need to be shown some techniques that have helped in implementing forms of education that are more in keeping with what teachers say they want to do for children. Many educators, teachers especially, want guidance in meeting the needs of pupils. They want usable ingredients that will help them in the area of grouping, in the exploration of activities related to differentiation, the identification of cognitive and perceptual need areas, the development of programs relating to the affective concerns of children, and a host of other activities concerned with the expansion of, and study related to, the individualization of instruction.

Such ingredients are presented in the themes of this book. It is not our purpose to cite the lengthy evidence that now exists concerning whither education goeth: "self-contained classroom or redeployed team approaches." It is not the purpose of this book to make an educational presentation relative to teaching roles: "teacher specialty versus elementary school generalist." It is not the purpose of this book to present esoteric case studies or research items that indicate various and romatic notions. Rather, the purpose is to extract from experience and from activities that have proved helpful to others in solving some of the problems concerned with the way children do *in fact* live, learn, and grow.

We believe that movement toward better ways of doing things is offered frequently by the mere inspection of present circumstances rather than by large research projects aimed at establishing new procedures. We are mindful, after all, that there are no major research activities to prove that the present graded self-contained classroom is a better way than some others, of educating children. We believe that no matter how mired down one may be, the best way to dispose of confusion is to move, however little, toward solution. The main thing is to do *something*. And to keep trying. We hope this book will get people to pull out and move forward in the direction of solution.

We would like to thank the many people with whom we have worked over the past several years and from whom we have derived many of our ideas and concepts. The number is far too great for us to thank individually in a foreword to a book. We hope that if this book is influential, and if it helps people to change things, then we will have fulfilled the insight of Tolstoi who said, "The vocation of every man and woman is to serve other people." By so doing we in turn will be paying thanks to the many people who served us with ideas and encouragement. But we must single out for special thanks Mildred Dougherty and Beverley Tanis Amick, two doctoral students who worked with us on the Design for Urban Education in Newark and developed the sequences and diagnostic materials; and Phyllis Blackman, our secretary, whose olympian production over several years in great measure undergirds our peace of mind and hoped-for success. Finally, we are both sustained by our ever patient and strongly supportive wives without whom we surely could not have written a book if faced with all the details that were attended to by our helpmates. Also, we want to extend our deep thanks to Toni Marshall, our project editor for Science Research Associates, whose assistance and insight lent constant encouragement to our endeavors.

Maurie Hillson
Joseph Bongo

INTRODUCTION

Criticisms of American education
seem to grow in intensity each year,
as does evidence to the effect that
conventional procedures and arrangements are unsuitable and even
dangerous. The graded school, with
its traditions of self-contained classrooms and textbook oriented instruction, has been a prime target
of critics for at least several decades.
In fact, we can trace the search
for alternatives back to the end of
the nineteenth century, and serious
efforts at what we now call nongraded education have been underway in one place or another throughout
the past seventy years.

Yet, despite a significant burst of
effort and enthusiasm (at least in the
literature) in the period following
World War II, it is not yet possible
to say that nongradedness has
gained a strong foothold or even
caught the attention of the typical
American teacher. Numerous books
and articles, some of my own, have
been available and professional
meetings have on countless occasions
provided opportunities for information and discussion. In the schools,
however, the graded structure pre-
vails and all of its trappings (notably
the competitive-comparative report
card and the end-of-year concern
with promotion or failure) remain
as a powerful force in the psychological and educational climate surrounding American children.

One reason for this regrettable
state of affairs is that the literature
has on the whole been too theoretical and too lacking in the practical,
down-to-earth advice that teachers
apparently need in order to comprehend the idea of continuous-

progress education and make that idea work in the day-to-day life of the classroom.

With enthusiasm, therefore, one greets a volume whose avowed purpose is to fill this gap and whose pages deal with the *how* and not only the *why* of nongraded programs. Filled as it is with step-by-step suggestions and illustrative material from actual situations, the volume offers to its readers an opportunity better to know how other educators with a desire to individualize instruction and meet the varying requirements of pupils, have gone about the various functions of curriculum planning, evaluating pupil needs, implementing programs, assessing and reporting pupil progress, and obtaining community support. Certainly it now becomes much easier for teachers to visualize several types of nongradedness at work, and to select for trial adoption those ideas and procedures that appear to have practical value in their own school situation.

A glance at the table of contents will alert the reader to the practical orientation of the volume. A significant portion of the total book is given over to examples and illustrations, to "prototypes and protocols" (Part II), and to the means of implementation. An entire chapter (8), for example, deals with some twenty-five questions of the sort that invariably arise when parents and other citizens are confronted with proposals for nongraded schooling. Another chapter (9) offers detailed advice with respect to inducting the staff into the subtleties (and sometimes the mysteries) of continuous-progress education. There is, literally, *no* chapter in the book where prac-

tical operations-oriented matters are not given precedence over the theoretical.

This does not mean that the authors downgrade theory or avoid making a philosophical commitment. On the contrary, the discerning reader will note that there runs through the volume a strong commitment to those theories that have been espoused and examined by other authors in this field, including John Goodlad and myself. What Hillson and Bongo have chosen to do, rather, is to consider the possible, given the assumption that the desirable has already been made sufficiently clear.

Every reader will probably find in this volume both strengths and weaknesses. Certainly Elaine Condon's chapter on bilingual children, almost a small book in itself, will attract attention as a unique contribution to the field. The chapter on reporting will add vitality to a topic in which too many teachers have seemed to have little genuine interest. I have already referred to the many practical ideas that enliven the volume generally. Probably deserving of additional serious discussion, in the next round of books and articles in this field, will be the commitment these authors have made to sequencing and to the whole idea of levels. And yet, in the present situation it is hard to challenge the assumption they have made, regarding the needs teachers have for a simple, understandable, and functional model that permits and facilitates the kind of each-child-oriented education of which for so long we have lacked adequate models.

ROBERT H. ANDERSON

Professor of Education
Harvard University

Editor: *Toni Marshall*

Interior design and cover batik: *Barbara Ravizza*

Drawings in example 5: *Ralph Mapson*

PART ONE

INVENTIONS,
INNOVATIONS,
AND IMPLEMENTATIONS

REASONS FOR CHANGING THE EDUCATIONAL LOCKSTEP AND MOVING TOWARD INNOVATIVE FORMS COMPATIBLE WITH THE PHILOSOPHICAL, PSYCHOLOGICAL, AND SOCIOLOGICAL CORRELATES OF CONTINUOUS-PROGRESS, NONGRADED SCHOOLS

INTRODUCTION

"Words, like glass, darken whatever they do not help us to see."[1] The terminology and the plethora of words used to describe many major innovative movements in American education seldom help us to see things clearly. They cloud rather than clarify. Take, for example, the term *nongraded*. It is basically reactive in nature. The prefix *non* indicates the absence or reverse of something. Yet the word is often used uncritically to identify all the elements of a movement that is attempting to accomplish many things, in order to establish education in a continuous-progress fashion as opposed to a lock-step grade-by-grade endeavor. When people discuss nongraded schools they are supposedly talking about institutions that have done away with strictures generally found in graded schools. But the term *nongraded* in no specific way indicates some of the crucial activities and features that are needed, that must be innovated or invented, to establish and assure continuous-progress education. Some people see nongraded education as nothing more than a program of administrative tinkering. They fail to see the large number of scientific realities that require that the school organization of today be a servant to learning in general. They do not take into account the large body of research that deals with fundamental educational change. Frequently they use (so-called) nongraded activities as compensatory grouping practices in certain areas of the curriculum rather than deal with nongraded education as a basic *intervention* and change the *process* of education.

Few educational thinkers have described some of the new educational terms more succinctly and significantly than John I. Goodlad. He, along with Robert H. Anderson, gave strong impetus to nongraded educational endeavors with the publication of their book *The Nongraded Elementary School.*[2] In his paper "Diagnosis and Prescription in Educational Practice,"[3] Goodlad observes that "Human variability demands alternatives." This, of course, is realistic.

But the crucial question for educational innovators may be: "What are the alternatives?" Goodlad goes on to spell out some choices in school organizational practices. He says:

"Present patterns of school organization support common expectations for all learners, both in what is to be learned and in rate of progression through it. The graded school implies graded content specified for each year, graded materials, provision for individual differences only within limits defined by the grade, and non-promotion as an adjustment mechanism. The self-contained classroom sharply restricts the availability of resources for adequate diagnosis and prescription. Nongrading is proposed as a device for breaking the vertical lock step; co-operative teaching, for increasing the range of personnel resources available to an instructional group. Both proposals are receiving extensive analysis, support, and criticism in educational publications; both are being implemented in various forms at an accelerating pace.

"Nongrading is essentially the removal of the grade levels which have traditionally marked the upward progression of students through the school. It raises the ceilings and lowers the floors of anticipated student performance to correspond more closely with the realities of individual differences. Nongrading, in intent, sweeps away the graded superstructure, graded content, graded textbooks, graded standards, and graded nomenclature to which we have long been accustomed. It facilitates the substitution of pupil progress uninhibited by grade barriers; subject matter organized sequentially around fundamental concepts, principles, and generalizations; instructional materials distributed according to the task at hand and student readiness for those materials; excellence determined from actual performance rather than comparisons with others; and still other provisions.

"That nongrading has not always lived up to promises for it reflects, in large measure, our difficulty in envisioning fresh expectations for schooling. Nongrading is compatible with new thrusts in curricular and instructional thought; it is markedly incompatible with the traditional expectations for education discussed earlier in this paper. Nongrading removes a large part of the system to which curriculum and instruction have been adapted, leaving teachers with more degrees of freedom in seeking to diagnose and prescribe.

"Cooperative teaching is essentially an expansion of the self-contained classroom to embrace more students and more instructional personnel. It casts aside the traditional teacher-per-grade-per-subject or group-of-subjects concept of teacher use. Instead of 30 students in a self-contained classroom with one teacher for all subjects, as in a departmentalized plan with a single teacher and one subject, visualize 75 or 100 or 140 students supervised by a team of teachers and teacher aides, deployed into instructional groups of various sizes, and space provisions appropriate to these groups. Cooperative teaching, in intent, is neither a self-contained nor a departmentalized plan of horizontal school organization. Rather, it is a scheme borrowing some features from both and providing for much more flexibility in grouping pupils and deploying instructional talent. Like nongrading, it provides more alternatives in the educational pharmacy.

"Taken together, nongrading and cooperative teaching open up many alternative clusters of students to which any given pupil can be assigned following diagnosis of his needs. Traditionally, teachers simply have received the group sent on by the previous teacher and have enjoyed relatively little opportunity to predetermine the composition of a class. The criterion for placement no longer is simply pass or fail but can be the estimated "fit" of pupil and teacher or pupil and group. Individual differences are considered prior to as well as after pupil assignment to teachers and classes. A significant area of educational decision making no longer is in the realm of the routine and automatic but now comes within the teacher's span of control.

"There is little point in talking about teachers as diagnosticians unless there are alternatives from which to prescribe. Nongrading and team teaching provide organizational alternatives not available in the conventionally organized school. Teachers are virtually forced to appraise each child carefully in weighing the potential advantages of one possible placement over another. They become diagnosticians for one significant aspect of schooling even before students are assigned to them. Hopefully, the diagnostic role begun outside of the classroom is extended into day-to-day pedagogy."[4]

The desire of innovators for an educational reorganization based on the extensive reform movement in education concerning the knowledge we now have about children represents a very short history. The movement from a one-dimensional graded school to a program that makes possible more flexible school activity and better ways of dealing with pupils and their progress, is one of recent origin. The activity aimed at eliminating competitive and comparative report cards, as well as the repudiation of report cards that base the grades of children on a normative and irrational scale, is likewise one

of short history. A switch to the concept that every child should fulfill his potential is so recent that it still is in its infancy in the approximately 73,000 elementary schools in the United States; too frequently it is only verbally embraced by many in the profession. The whole arena of humanistic practices concerning the manner by which adults should deal with children is so recent that to find the exact time of its historical beginning is quite difficult for the educational researcher.[5]

Of recent vintage are the great movement toward the individualization of instruction wherein programs offer different goals for different kinds of learners; attempts to regulate timetables of learning rate in order to help children acquire material; differentiated learning materials to modify the curriculum when rate is not the only problem; schools where teachers play many different roles; and many strategies and approaches that enhance the individualized learning program by making suitable provisions for learning.

There seem, however, to be three distinctive categories of activities that describe the attempts at making adjustments and differentiations in the educational program of the child during a short history. They are (1) promotional plans, (2) differentiated schoolwork plans, and (3) administrative reorganizational plans. Reorganizational plans are the concern of many people in education who are presently involved in, and concerned with, moving toward new forms. In this category are those departures from tradition that lead to teacher-pupil collaboration, individualization of instruction, individual contract learning, independent study, programmed instruction, computer-aided instruction, unhampered limitless progress in all areas of the curriculum, as well as many other activities aimed at developing the full potential of the child.

A classic model in educational history that

illustrates a fundamental school reorganization is the Gary Plan. It conceived of a total community school, operated on an eight-hour school day, with continuation classes and recreation facilities available in the evenings and on Saturdays. The Gary Plan had great hopes of heralding a new era of education. It suffered, however, from being far in advance of the readiness of society to accept it. At this writing it is interesting to note that many elements and ideas found in the Gary Plan are now being suggested to help solve the problems of the unfortunate situations that pervade many of the inner-city schools of the United States.

There were three other significant plans for educational reorganization: the Winnetka Plan, the Dalton Plan, and the McDade Plan. These were all based on a desire to individualize instruction and learning. They all put stress on individual student contracts in two main divisions of the curriculum: common essentials and group and creative activities. However, if one had to pick the direct ancestor to the present movement of creating individualized, flexible, gradeless, continuous-progress oriented schools, the best model might be the training school of San Francisco State College, where (in 1913) Frederic L. Burk developed a truly individualized system. It was a distinctive break with tradition. Many of its concepts assumed activities that led to the progressive movement in the 1930s. Burk's insights were aided additionally by the new scientific investigation and research revelations concerning the way children actually behaved and how they learned. All this activity came to fruition at the close of the 1960 decade as seen by the energetic desire of many educators to work with forms of continuous progress, teaming, and individualization.

It could serve no real purpose in the context of this book to move into a long definitive history of nongraded continuous-progress education and attempt to draw all the lines that seemingly lead to it. The basic purpose of this book is (1) to take for granted that educators feel there is a need for doing many different things to insure better growth in learning and (2) to deal with the fundamentals of how to implement these things. To stay true to this twofold purpose, we suggest the history of this area be summed up by stating: A study of the reorganizational activities of the elementary school leads to the conclusion that all the attempted basic circumventions of the graded idea were honest attempts to eliminate the strictures and constraints that graded education insinuated on both its users and its recipients, and to treat individual differences more realistically.

Many of the extant inventions, innovations, and implementations necessary to develop capacity for, and competence in, the performance of children are backed by empirical studies as well as by highly plausible-sounding insights relative to the whole area of philosophical, psychological, and sociological activity. Benjamin S. Bloom sums it up adequately when he says:

"Each teacher begins a new term (or course) with the expectation that about a third of his students will adequately learn what he has to teach. He expects about a third of his students to fail or to just "get by." Finally, he expects another third to learn a good deal of what he has to teach, but not enough to be regarded as "good students." This set of expectations, supported by school policies and practices in grading, becomes transmitted to the students through the grading procedures and through the methods and materials of instruction. The system creates a self-fulfilling prophecy such that the final sorting of students through the grading process becomes approximately equivalent to the original expectations.

"This set of expectations, which fixes the academic goals of teachers and students, is the most wasteful and destructive aspect of the present educational system. It reduces the aspirations of both teachers and students; it reduces motivation for learning; and it systematically destroys the ego and self-concept of a sizable group of students who are legally required to attend school for 10 to 12 years under conditions which are frustrating and humiliating year after year. The cost of this system in reducing opportunities for further learning and in alienating youth from both school and society is so great that no society can tolerate it for long.

"Most students (perhaps over 90 percent) can master what we have to teach them, and it is the task of instruction to find the means which will enable our students to master the subject under consideration. Our basic task is to determine what we mean by mastery of the subject and to search for the methods and materials which will enable the largest proportion of our students to attain such mastery."[6]

Underpinning the insights of Bloom, we have "a model of school learning" developed by J. B. Carroll.[7] He says educators must be concerned with at least five specific areas to create mastery in the learning task. They are (1) aptitude: the amount of time required by the learner to attain mastery in a learning task; (2) perseverance: the amount of time the learner is willing to spend in learning efforts; (3) the ability to understand instruction: the learner's understanding of the nature of the task that he is to learn and the procedures that he is to follow in the learning task; (4) the quality of instruction: the degree to which the presentation, explanation, and ordering of the elements of the task to be learned represent the optimum for a given learner; and (5) the opportunity for learning: the time allowed by the teacher or the school for the pupil to practice, and thereby really learn to perform the task. These five elements are essential to the pupil's opportunity to become competent and to grow in achievement. They buttress the larger movements aimed at the reorganization of the school so that more flexible, inventive, and innovative directions can

be found to enable educators to provide opportunities that take into account different learning rates, styles, and modalities that are always found in any school population.

The expectations of teachers, according to much research, do fix the academic goals of both students and teachers. An impressive statement of recently collected evidence indicates that the self-fulfilling prophecy operates in all realms of education and that it results in the kind of behavior that is expected. Even though there is now an accumulation of scientific investigation of the self-fulfilling prophecy (mostly in the realms of sociology and psychology rather than education), it is not a new concept. Goethe, without the benefit of such scientific investigation, once observed, "Treat people as if they were what they ought to be and you help them to become what they are capable of being". It is quite obvious that the converse is also true. The creation of a different kind of educational program will obviously be necessary if educators are seeking the kind of performance and mastery that research contends can be attained. Generalizations in this context lead to a specific point of view: continuous-progress, nongraded, collaboratively planned and taught educational programs may be a better organizational form, as well as a more strategic approach, to the education of a child than other types or forms of programs that have hitherto marked the educational scene.

If this assumption is reasonable, then what are the inclusive parts or elements of action that lead toward the creation of newer forms? What are the inventions and innovations that have to be implemented in order to help build greater opportunities for attaining educational competence? Where should the emphasis be in changing the school context? Should it be on organization? On learning? On curriculum development? Or, are all of these fragments of a basic holistic intervention that aims at changing the total process? And, if so, what does changing the process really entail? To these questions we now turn.

It is extremely difficult to describe a model nongraded, continuous-progress oriented, collaboratively planned and taught school. Heathers observes, "While nongrading or 'continuous progress' can be accomplished by differentiating instruction within any organizational pattern, many school systems with nongraded programs make use of multiage grouping to bring together students who are at about the same level of advancement of one or more subjects. Other schools set up within-grade achievement-level grouping to facilitate differentiated pacing."[8] However, most of the attempts at nongrading aim at establishing different mechanical and curricular patterns that really explore and then try to exploit (in the best sense) the individual abilities and differences of children. Many of the models being designed try to use curricular designs and formats with some organizational flexibility that allows for the proper placement of pupils based on needs, irrespective of their age or number of years in school. The plans generally reflect attempts at appropriate placement of pupils, not only according to their learning rate, but also according to their style of learning. Rate is only one factor, and not always the crucial one. The curricula are enunciated and articulated in different ways. They are made up of learning tasks in various subject or skills areas. These are sequential, carefully planned, and developed on a continuum basis from the most simple to the most complex, or from readiness (entry) to competency (mastery). Items are identified with a sophisticated degree of precision and relate to necessities in learning that lead to mastery. For the most part, nongraded continuous-progress sequences are *concept* and *skill* oriented in both development and application. But most programs also have a due regard

for, and strong insistence on, the attitudinal aspects of life, or the affective concerns of learners in learning and living. Many nongraded, continuous-progress programs have similar features; however, all programs, to some degree, reflect the educational background, philosophy, and experience of those involved in their implementation. Despite some differences (basically not of kind or orientation but of degree and emphasis), there is commonness of fulfillment and activity.

The question one could ask is: What is the core of items essential to a well-thought-out program of continuous-progress, nongraded education? The following list is a nonexhaustive but realistic set of ideas usually found in answer to that question.

1. Each pupil is involved in a program where he actually savors the benefits of continuous progress. *He* is the baseline (it is at his performance level that he starts) and the only yardstick against which his true accomplishment is measured. His level is founded on a careful diagnosis of *his* ability to perform.

2. The activities and operational procedures in these programs completely eliminate pupil retardation, promotion, and nonpromotion. These factors are irrelevant, and the research that supports this conclusion is vast and venerable.[9]

3. A wholesome consideration is given to the entire area of readiness at every level. This is particularly so at the earliest level so that children will be able to perform with success when they move to formal learning situations. Thus they avoid establishing a habitual practice of failure because they cannot address the required skills. It has been estimated that probably 90 percent of all reading failures in the schools are due basically to the fact that many children are forced into learning how to read before they are ready. By the establishment of longer

periods of readiness based on a careful diagnosis of the child, one can immediately see how the movement to a continuous-progress, nongraded program would enhance generally the educational productivity of the children involved.

4. There are no ceilings on learning in continuous-progress, nongraded schools. Each child moves at his own pace. Schools holding this philosophy need to commit themselves to programs of actual continuous progress. There can be no fear on the part of teachers of encroachments on the materials usually reserved for later grades, since the organizing features of this orientation, and the components of the curricula, are articulated without regard to grade identification.

5. Continuous-progress, nongraded education is enhanced by the opportunity for teacher collaboration. By establishing opportunity for systematized continuous teacher collaboration, a variety of input is possible. The resulting programs (and programming) are more fruitful, and the continuing desire to upgrade the educational activities of the school is more fully realized.

6. Flexibility is achieved; differentiated pupil and teacher activities take place, the quality of which is enhanced through the use of many variables that assure creative ways of setting up activities.

By adapting the features listed above as underlying components of continuous-progress, nongraded education, a generalized description of a school in which these five elements are sensitively juxtaposed and integrated might be as follows: A school where there are no grade designations; instead there are various curricula defined in stages (or levels) of learning, specifically created, sequenced, and clearly described for learners. The aim is to develop a prescriptive approach to education based on a careful diagnostic workup derived from the various diagnostic tools that teachers have created to assess the

pupil's needs, strengths, and weaknesses. Pupils branch out to various groups for learning activities related to their specific conceptual and skill development. Teachers' activities are broadened for various reasons. Those who display strength and interest in a particular area are assigned to groups who need development in that area. Children as they progress through the program of sequential stages or levels of learning do so as they demonstrate competency or mastery in an area. Teachers (without fear of encroachment) develop the growth of a child to any level of achievement attainable. When they need to give materials to a child that hitherto were reserved for a "lower grade" of the school, they are able to take that material and make constructive use of it. Within the context of the innovated school, no pupil is ever pressed into trying to achieve a specified amount of learning in a specified amount of time, regardless of his ability. Rather, the desire is to see each child as the focus of the program, or the baseline from which to start, and from that point prescribe for him the items of learning that best satisfy his needs and lead to his heightened accomplishment. Children therefore grow more effectively at their own learning paces. Rapid learners quickly acquire the elements of a generally well-thought-out program. More deliberate learners grasp the prescribed material in a more leisurely fashion, and attain a greater degree of competence than is usually found in a graded situation. The so-called gifted children who frequently cause concern in graded schools no longer are problems in this context. Their programs are enriched in both depth and breadth. They are taught at levels that they are ready for. Children, on the other hand, who were forced to work with materials too difficult for them (because of the imposed normative standard or the year-by-year grade organization) are permitted to work with materials appropriate and pertinent to their particular needs. They build up a background of success that underpins future success at higher levels, albeit completed over a longer period of time. There are more opportunities for activities that allow for programs of educational depth as well as for longer periods of time where needed. Progress and flexibility for both pupils and teachers are healthy in nature. Likewise the sound mental health of children who are able to learn at their own rate is enhanced. The continuous-progress, nongraded school also allows for greater collaboration in both planning and teaching. Within the scheduling activities of continuous-progress, nongraded education, teachers leave the restrictive format of the isolated self-contained classroom. They branch out in more effective ways, in both planning and teaching. The collaborative planning in which teachers become decision makers in determining ways to meet the needs of students becomes a worthy and relevant part of this type of organization and it enhances the whole educational activity.

Collaborative planning and teaching activities lead to adult concern for the development of ideas that lead to the personalization or individualization of instruction and in general serve to move programs forward in the areas of curriculum development and organizational creativity.

This last concept is reflected in a major position taken by Heathers as it concerns the whole question of grouping:

"Writing an epitaph for grouping may well be the task of the reviewer of research on grouping for the 1980 edition of this encyclopedia. Even today it appears that grouping as a central theme of organization for instruction has nearly run its course and is in the process of being replaced by a familiar theme—individualized instruction—that became a focus of educational reform in the mid-1960s.

"The concept of individualization has acquired such potency that it is reducing to subordinate status even those grouping arrangements being promoted under the banners of nongrading and team teaching."[10]

With all due regard for our colleagues who hold this point of view, we feel that it is somewhat premature. The activities and insights discussed in this book are drawn from agony and action in the field. We agree rather with the situation as it is, and as it is described by Goodlad:

"It should come as no surprise, then, that comprehensive experiments in schooling are the rarest of all educational phenomena. Small wonder that teachers practice so little individualizing instruction, inductive teaching, nongrading, team teaching, or other recently recommended practices. They have not seen them. If teachers are to change, they must see models of what they are to change to; they must practice under guidance the new behaviors called for in the exemplary models. If teachers are to change, the occupation itself must have built into it the necessary provisions for self-renewal. The creation of these conditions is an important agenda item for the decade ahead."[11]

It may be that the theoretical ideas and creative concepts for programs for elementary education are worthy of continuous perusal and investigation but idealism must always be tempered by reality. The problem is here and now, and there is a distance to travel before each professional is a clinical diagnostician and a prescriptive expert. There are realities of present-day educational circumstances that must be faced in order to get to the desired levels suggested in the areas of individualization in education.

A continuous-progress, nongraded, collaboratively planned school can, through its organization and development of programs, move the perceptive educator toward a whole series of opportunities that mean better education for the children involved. There are several reasons for this: (1) The approach to education generally becomes open rather than closed. The teacher is no longer thought to be equally competent in all his daylong activities with the same group of children. (2) Teachers on a day-to-day basis, through collaborative endeavors, discuss particular diagnosed needs of their children and plan programs accordingly. (3) The constant attempt to deal with the precise and appropriate needs of children (rather than working with them in a diffuse way) is enhanced. (4) Many tensions inherent in most learning activities are lessened, because teachers teach to clearly defined needs in a context of reduced competence levels. Teachers are no longer expected to cover a large spectrum of performance levels found in the typical classroom. (5) Because of the basic grouping procedures arising out of the diagnostic activities, teachers move toward teaching specific emphases. This is a *focal point* of teaching procedure and can, if perceptively done, result in much more individualization in learning and teaching.

It is not the purpose of this chapter to support philosophically, psychologically, sociologically, and educationally why there must be an intense movement toward the creation of newer forms of education by citing an overwhelming collection of evidence that favors such a movement. Many have written about the need and the extent of the problem.[12] There is much material available to inform the reader of descriptive and empirical research to indicate that children in nongraded, continuous-progress, collaboratively planned programs perform significantly better in academic achievement than do their counterparts in conventionally graded classrooms. There is a growing agreement among teachers who have taught in innovated organizational forms concerning the values that accrue to them and to the children who are being schooled in this way.

The remainder of this book deals with the development of the ideas and activities that relate to objectives we feel are essential to the creation of continuous-progress, nongraded educational programs. They are all concerned with implementation rather than with a philosophical posture. A chapter (or less) is devoted to each objective, with a discussion of action guidelines that have proved helpful in the implementation of the objective.

To assure a greater educational opportunity for all children through the establishment of flexible models that redirect the present context by altering the process, certain commitments to fundamental ideas need to be made. These become the framework for developing the change that moves a school from a conventional form to an innovative form. The following represent components that we feel apply in the movement toward a continuous-progress, nongraded school.

1. The educational program will be arranged so that every child has the placement that reflects his educational development.

2. There will be a learning sequence of skills and concepts that states the objectives to be sought and the philosophy to be adhered to in the teaching-learning process. The sequence will be adaptable, and definable operationally as to methods and approaches.

3. There will be a collection of instruments and techniques that will be used to diagnose the pupils' competence in relation to the objectives stated in the learning sequence or curriculum.

4. There will be a learning developmental inventory or profile for the purpose of screening components of the diagnoses in order to establish a pertinent and appropriate learning stage for each pupil.

5. The learning sequences (stages, levels, or packages) will be arranged longitudinally, from simple to complex, and the organizing elements

found in these stages will be those essential educational concepts and skills needed by the learner regardless of his grade level, age, or years in school.

6. There will be a reporting and record-keeping system consistent with the sequential development in the educational areas and the operationally defined curriculum.

7. There will be an organizational framework to support the needed flexibility (as well as the educational concepts) of this operationally oriented, continuous-progress program.

In addition to the attainment of these seven objectives a public relations program is necessary and is a requisite activity in any movement toward educational change. The need to involve and educate parents and the community to accept various individualized goals on continuous-progress education must be carefully planned and carried out.

There are some obvious problems and concerns that face those who attempt to create new departures, to invent, to innovate, and to change things. But the only way to assure change is to take the first step.

The chapters that follow offer a "start now" program for the educational innovator. They deal with ways that educators can accomplish the objectives stated above.

It is our intention to provide a resource of experience and activity that will help the educator translate, within his own context, educational programs that will become courageously contemporary and superlative in every way.

SEQUENCING

Several years ago one of the authors of this book was driving along with his then very young son beside him in the car. He made a wrong turn, but realizing it would lead to the same destination he continued. As the boy kept looking out the window his face displayed a look of increasing consternation and uneasiness. The territory they were driving in was quite new to him since he had never traveled the road before, though the conventional route was familiar to him. The author wondered what was bothering his son and finally asked, "What seems to be the matter? "

He said, "Let's go away from this place and take the other road."

"Why? " asked his father.

The boy replied, "Daddy, I don't like to be where I don't know where I am."

There are many people who are involved in continuous-progress, nongraded education who are certainly in a place where they don't really know where they are. Many of them simply reorganized parts of their programs in order to regroup pupils because of scores on standardized tests. Others simply scheduled activities based on a hoped-for homogeneity in one area of the curriculum insofar as they thought they could determine it. Still others backed into some nongraded or continuous-progress activities because nonpromotion procedures in their school created various kinds of combination-graded classes. We recall a discussion with the principal of a nongraded school. When asked if he would be kind enough to send us the various curriculum materials and items he had developed, he said, "Oh, we haven't developed anything like that. What we are doing is developing the curriculum as we go along."

This educational posture is an obvious revelation of the problem that besets many people involved in conceptualization and articulation of nongraded, continuous-progress education. Robert H. Anderson has observed rightfully that, "the great majority of pilot programs have been deficient." He classifies the efforts of nongrading that took place between 1942 and the mid 1960s in four ways: "(1) Serious efforts to give the idea full-scale development in a well-conceived form; (2) serious efforts to implement one or more aspects of the nongraded idea in a well-conceived form; (3) modest efforts to achieve nongrading in an inadequate theoretical frame of reference; and (4) fraudulent or naive use of the vocabulary of nongradedness to describe what is in fact a conventional graded program."[1]

Unfortunately, if serious efforts to give the idea full-scale development in a well-conceived form are not prevalent, then the concepts and directions of nongraded, continuous-progress education will suffer. From the discussion with the principal referred to above, one can see that his activity falls more distinctly in category 4 than in any of the others mentioned.

In order to reverse this trend, which dooms by association some well-thought-out attempts at real innovation, a clearer definition of what is entailed in the change must be made. Progression from a conventional educational system to a continuous-progress, nongraded educational program insists that there be a greater consideration given to the development of learning objectives. Continuous-progress, nongraded programs do not herald the ushering in of "soft" pedagogy or educational programming that lacks standards. The contrary is true. Nongraded, continuous-progress programs represent innovated systems. They are made up of components of activity that lead toward higher and more fruitful levels of competency and performance than have been found in graded schools. Graded schools frequently have not taken into consideration the

many factors concerned with the way one learns, the approach to learning, and the many aspects of the teacher-learner relationship so necessary for the better growth of the children in an innovated and inventive climate of educational activity. The development of a program in a well-conceived form does not allow for "as-we-go-along" development. It means careful planning of what *ought* to be taught, and sequencing the "ought" so that it is taught rather than hopefully "caught."

There are various ways to begin this process of moving toward the development of well-thought-out sequences in continuous-progress, nongraded programs. Education changes in degrees from the conventional year-by-year graded school where organization of the curriculum is based on vertical grade identification as the only element that cements each of the units together, to nongraded, continuous-progress education when its vertical progression is based on the identification of essential educational organizing elements. These elements are sequential in nature, highly related, and are on a continuum basis from the most simple to the most complex in the areas where growth is desired. Generally the process can be summed up as (1) a definition of what is to be taught; (2) the manner in which one organizes what is to be taught; (3) the assessment of the learner in relation to the material to be taught, and his distance from the necessary competency in that area; and (4) a system of evaluating that particular learner to assess the degree to which he has achieved the material that has been prescribed.

We feel that the first essential requisite in the development of continuous-progress, nongraded education is the creation of a sequence in each of the areas that is to be nongraded: that is, reading, language arts, mathematics, social studies, science. Naturally, all other areas should also become nongraded.

The first objective, in a program of implementation is concerned with the development of sequences. This step can be stated as a multi-dimensional objective, since it encompasses more than one idea. The attainment of operational continuous-progress, nongraded education becomes closer to reality both in intent and action when the following objective is effectuated.

Continuous-progress, nongraded, educational programs require clearly written documents that embrace the curriculum, the objectives, and the philosophy in each particular area of education that is being addressed. These documents are learning sequences—sets of learning levels, or stages of learning. Within each level or stage, adaptable approaches, methodologies, and suggested ways to meet the needs of the various learners that will be involved in the program are set down. Other operational procedures are defined so that the teacher can make approaches to the learner within the innovative and flexible framework. And there are coded identifications of the resources and various materials to support the suggested approaches used to meet the various needs of individually different learners.

This may seem like a good deal to accomplish. It is a necessary prerequisite for any successful program. The mere revision of graded basal-reading programs into a series of small hurdles is not broadly based continuous-progress, nongraded education that is thought out to the point of being a really serious effort at full-scale development. The grouping of children based solely on results of achievement tests is not continuous-progress, nongraded education. That represents rather a partial administrative device, and only an *attempt* to implement one particular idea related to nongraded education.

The development of sequences that we suggest represents an attempt to create a curriculum orientation of skills and concepts stated in behavioral terms from the readiness stage to the stage where mastery is attained. We feel, especially in the early years of school, that content

is vehicular in nature and is used to teach skills and concepts. Also in relation to the development of sequences, we make a distinction between the primary and the intermediate areas of school in continuous-progress, nongraded programs. In the primary years we feel the emphasis should be on skill development rather than on an intense systematic study of content. Content is used to enhance skill development. Content serves as a vehicle through which skills are attained and concepts developed. In the intermediate years, one envisions a greater emphasis on the content areas. In those years children pursue more extensively their study of the content, and make applications and extensions of the skills learned in the primary areas.

In order to understand fully where one is in this whole spectrum of change, one must develop curricula wherein clear statements of goals for instruction based upon skills, concepts, and suggested content to be achieved are articulated and integrated. The mere recognition of facts, so often found as a goal in education, needs to be rejected. The levels of achievement desired within the continuous-progress, nongraded program need to be carefully described. They must be articulated internally, and soundly incorporated throughout the program to best serve the learner.

Most of the substantive content and skills development areas need to be put in the form of learning sequences. They should be rationally set down and made acceptable to key people in the program. Adherence to these patterns will allow for curricular adjustments to satisfy the learning styles of individual children. In turn they allow for rejection of setting fixed amounts of learning, over a specified amount of time, to different kinds of learners. Within the sequences teachers can alter the rate or modify the content, because they have the opportunity to be discriminative in the use of materials available to them within the levels program. Also within this context, independent study is not only encouraged but can readily take place. Related and relevant instructional materials, keyed to every level of instruction, serve as resources to be used in teaching the skills and concepts that are defined. Self-teaching and self-testing materials are also made available to children who move into independent learning phases.

One of the best ways of seeing the suggested objectives of continuous-progress, nongraded education in a total and interrelated fashion is to take one level of one particular area of the curriculum. We have selected the language-arts skill sequence to use as an example throughout the book. In each chapter it will be related to, and elaborated on, in referring to the objectives and to other material being discussed. This model can serve as a prototype for those who want to plan their own sequences in a different but related context. First, however, a short discussion regarding the manner by which decisions are made as to what is to be included in a sequence of learning stages from readiness to competency is required.

There are various ways of arriving at decisions concerning particular inclusions. The most desirable may be to call a meeting of teachers in a particular subject-matter area from the early years to the higher levels of schooling. This means that, when indicated, elementary teachers would meet with teachers of English and language arts at the middle and high school levels. Together they would define specifically the kind of student, in terms of skill performance, abilities, and competencies, they would like to see as a result of the educational program in their particular area. In a word, they would describe the *end* behavior of their program. Decisions would be made as to what segments of the school would be responsible for the various levels of sophistication related to the particular area of work. They would probably decide that the elementary years would be those in which skills would be introduced, somewhat refined,

and applied. This is a period of learning how to learn. The middle school area would likely be assigned to those skill, content, and growth areas that lead to more polished performance in the items necessary for the kind of person the group envisions as the end result of their program. The high school years could be reserved for the kinds of activities and approaches that bring about established mastery and habitual behavior relating to the prescribed goals set by the curriculum designers. Then the activity of articulation among these various levels takes place. Figure 2-1 is a schema representing articulation between three school units. The number of levels is arbitrary and does not necessarily indicate a judgment as to what the number of levels should be. The manner of this articulation is obvious.

All three units, even though having levels generally allocated to them, deal with the realities of pupil growth. In each unit it is possible to dip down or go beyond insofar as there is need to, but only in relationship to a clear analysis of the learners for whom the material is intended. Levels 10, 11, 12, and 17, 18, 19, and 20, though generally allocated to specific units of the school organization, realistically are offered in more than one unit as evidence of the reality of actual pupil growth and progress. The idea of a continuum in learning in each area is a valid one. And the reality of being "ahead" in one area of a continuum and "behind" in another area reflects the reality and reasonable aspects of what a learner actually is.

The question will always arise, Must everyone who wants to nongrade go through this kind of activity? Since there are commercially prepared curricula and the like, why not use them?

The answer to the first question is an unequivocal Yes, everyone has to go through it! Our experiences in all the places we have worked have indicated that this is the unalterable case. Many commercial materials do exist. Many sequences, suggested schema for learning, various

Figure 2-1 SCHEMA FOR ARTICULATION OF LEVELS BASED ON SKILLS, TASKS,
LEARNINGS, ETC., IN THREE SCHOOL UNITS FROM
KINDERGARTEN THROUGH TWELVE-YEAR PROGRAM

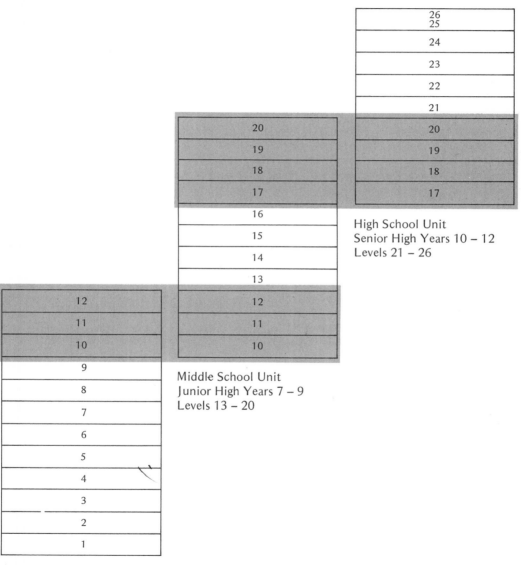

High School Unit
Senior High Years 10 – 12
Levels 21 – 26

Middle School Unit
Junior High Years 7 – 9
Levels 13 – 20

Elementary School Unit
School Years K – 6
Levels 1 – 12

manuals allied with reading programs, service tests related to basal texts do now exist. Nonetheless, actual learning, growth, performance, and upgrading of education vis-a-vis the student does not move apace.

The main reasons why teachers must develop and organize their own items and directions are these: (1) Teachers meeting together to review the material of what ought to be taught are at the same time involved in their own personal and particular review. They become aware of materials that they were not aware of before. (2) Such meetings result in sequential articulation and the elimination of much of the repetition found in many commercial sequences and in graded schools where teachers work on assumptions of what may or may not have come before or after. (3) The general activity of interacting in a professional way in identifying materials and equipment and the methods and activities to teach specific skills leads to educational activities of professional enhancement. (4) Experience and research indicate that in programs where teachers cooperate in the planning, development, execution, and production of materials, they use the materials with enthusiasm, which is usually reflected in the attitude of the children. (5) Materials constructed to meet the needs of the pupils and the school district in which they are used are more readily accepted, more precise in meeting specific needs, and more frequently used. For these reasons the planning and personalization of the curriculum to meet the needs of those involved in the innovation are crucial. No collection of material as it stands is relatable and relevant to all situations.

Let us examine a *learning stage* taken from a language-arts skill sequence. Basically a stage is made up of a general description of what the level entails, a specific statement of skills to be achieved, methods and activities involved in teaching the skills, the materials and equipment to use, and the sources of those items available to the teacher in her approaches to the teaching-learning activities.

Figure 2-2   LANGUAGE-ARTS SKILLS SEQUENCE, LEVEL 1

General Description of the Level

This is the readiness stage. It represents the period of necessary preparation prior to entry in the more formal learning that is to follow. During the readiness stage various activities that underpin growth in conceptual and perceptual experiences necessary for learning take place. Skills and concepts learned in this stage are the agreed-upon prerequisite areas needed for success in reading. They represent the fundamental areas of growth required for participation in school activities. Without the pressures of unrealistic norms, special attention can be given to a host of readiness activities, crucial in preparing for school success. During this level the teacher notes specifically (1) interest factors; (2) attitudes of children toward the school experience; (3) backgrounds from which the children come; (4) various other linguistic competencies, or lack thereof, that each child possesses.

The length of time a child spends at this level will vary with different backgrounds and different competencies. Several children in any group may need to spend a few months to a full year (or more) in this area of readiness. A careful assessment of needs will indicate the time when readiness is sufficiently established that a move to the next level of activity can take place. The basic diagnostic instruments (inventories and activities) that relate to this level are to serve as the source items from which a teacher establishes the mode of intervention and teaching approach needed to meet a child where he is. In this stage of learning a teacher will be careful to watch for the physical readiness of each child to handle and to enjoy a more formal school program. Continuing checks on adequate vision, hearing, oral language ability, and general health are important aspects of the day-to-day teaching procedure. Emotional readiness, essential to success in any school activity, is frequently assessed by the perceptive teacher as he watches to see whether a child displays anxiety, withdrawal tendencies, lack of self-confidence, or any of the various immature adjustment attitudes. In addition, the teacher observes the child's ability to make comfortable associations with others, whether he has gained acceptance, and whether he displays a sense of independence. These are requisites if the learner is to accept the responsibility for moving forward in his educational program, based on his own needs and abilities.

Figure 2-2   LANGUAGE-ARTS SKILLS SEQUENCE, LEVEL 1 *(continued)*

Skills	Methods and Activities	Materials, Equipment, and Source
I. GROSS MOTOR-COORDI- NATION SKILLS **Demonstration of agility:** 1. Catches a large ball 2. Throws a large ball 3. Walks a chalk line or balance beam 4. Runs, jumps, climbs, skips, hops, gallops 5. Jumps on one leg 6. Jumps from a crouching position 7. Displays effective coordination 8. Displays fully developed laterality 9. Displays spatial orientation	Running games as tag, jump rope, eraser tag Sing-and-do songs Relay races using balls, sticks, bean bags, and the like Classroom calisthenics and follows directions for games such as "Simon Says" Singing games as "Skip to My Lou," "Looby-Lou," "Farmer in the Dell" Refer to various sources for relevant methods—for example, Lawrence W. Carrillo, *Informal Reading-Readiness Experiences*, Chandler, 1964, pp. 47–65 Muska Mosston, *Teaching Physical Education: From Command to Discovery*; Charles E. Merrill, 1966, pp. 183–227 *A Guide to Movement Exploration*, Peck Printing. Marion Monroe, and Bernice Rogers, *Foundations for Reading: Informal and Pre-Reading Procedures*, Scott, Foresman, 1964.	Various sized rubber balls, bean bags, jump ropes Playground equipment such as: Balance bar Walking beam Ramps Rocking boat Tricycles Jungle Gym equipment Jumping boards Low bars A pole maze (labyrinth of small poles arranged over an area for hide and seek) A walking wall constructed of cement blocks An inclined jumping board Baskets, pails, and boxes Piano Phonograph As a basic source reference on suggested equipment and supplies, see: Anne Marie Evans, "How to Equip and Supply Your Pre-Kindergarten Classrooms," *Nations Schools*, vol. 77, no. 6, (June 1966)

Figure 2-2   LANGUAGE-ARTS SKILLS SEQUENCE, LEVEL 1 *(continued)*

Skills	Methods and Activities	Materials, Equipment, and Source
II. FINE MOTOR COORDINATION SKILLS **Demonstration of agility:** 1. Uses scissors 2. Uses crayons, pencils, paint brushes, clay 3. Uses paste 4. Coordinates hand and eye by tracing and drawing shapes with fingers and crayons 5. Draws simple outlines 6. Colors within defined areas 7. Displays use of fingers for grasping and holding, and demonstrates digital dexterity 8. Puts together simple puzzles in form boards 9. Displays ability to re-create and name simple shapes 10. Displays developed speech patterns 11. Displays ability to match forms in spaces shown on board	Crayons for drawing, coloring, tracing Clay modeling Finger painting Paper tearing and cutting Wooden or plastic figures to show geometric shapes Tempora painting Make and use papier-mâché Form boards—whole and divided Chalk circles Parquetry boxes Color-cubes and designs Make collages Stories illustrated with flannelboard	Crayons, finger paint, chalk, tempora, clay, scissors, paint brushes, construction paper, newsprint, glue and paste, pegs and pegboards, Tinker Toys, puzzles, tools, a playhouse, parquetry boxes, color-cubes and designs, templates, scraps of cloth, scraps of paper, wrapping paper, a shoe for lacing, beads for stringing, various teacher-made ditto materials, Holt, Rinehart & Winston *Mathematics Kit* *Monroe Reading Aptitude Tests* (Grades K–1) Houghton Mifflin, 1935 (section dealing with visual abilities) *Frostig Developmental Test of Visual Perception* Test 1 — Eye-Motor Coordination Test 2 — Figure-Ground

Figure 2-2   LANGUAGE-ARTS SKILLS SEQUENCE, LEVEL 1 *(continued)*

Skills	*Methods and Activities*	*Materials, Equipment, and Source*
III. KNOWLEDGE OF CERTAIN RELATIONSHIPS A. **Demonstration of knowledge in:** 1. Classification of objects into categories 2. Arrangement of one or more pictures in correct time sequence (left to right) that tells story of events in the pictures 3. Identification of specific human beings 4. Identification of specific actions 5. Identification of emotional expressions 6. Identification of various objects 7. Prediction of an outcome from sequence of pictures 8. Ability to explain why outcome in picture sequence did in fact occur 9. Ability to explain familial roles 10. Ability to explain teacher-pupil, pupil-pupil, and school-home role	Various role-playing activities Live case studies of incidents Prescribed situational problems Rearranging pictures in sequence in pocketchart or on flannelboard Using various materials and objects brought from home for display that begin with a certain consonant. (Make use of a different sound each week.) Flannelboard stories told by teacher with children supplying ending, altering story, developing ideas Collages to depict various collections Use of flannelboard for stories told and illustrated Multiple recorded endings of stories read by children, followed by group discussions as to which would be more realistic in terms of the facts and items	Pictures (conventional and abstract) Story sequence games Flannelboard Large pocketchart for class use Small pocketcharts for individual pupil use Scraps of cloth, paper, etc., for various uses Teacher-made ditto materials Holt, Rinehart & Winston *Mathematics Kit* *Peabody Language Kit* Various workbooks with sequenced material Various games dealing with developing classification and groupings See current catalogue of Creative Playthings, Inc., Princeton, N.J. 08540

Figure 2-2   LANGUAGE-ARTS SKILLS SEQUENCE, LEVEL 1 *(continued)*

Skills	*Methods and Activities*	*Materials, Equipment, and Source*
B. Displays the following visual memory skills:		
1. Recognizes, recalls and names colors	Various ABC books	Beginning Science Kit
2. Names objects on flash card and identifies picture from memory	Use of the *Kinder Math* charts	*Geometric Shapes*, Holt Rinehart & Winston
	Use of the commercial flash cards and color-word cards	Various shapes and collections
3. Visualizes letter from flash card and finds same letter on page in front of him	Color-word matching games	D.C. Heath Transparencies on object collections
4. Finds word visualized on flash card		*The Math Workbook for Kindergarten*, Don Suppes, et al, L. W. Singer
		Shapes-Alike Chart, Ideal Co.
5. Identifies words found in directions given to him in materials; for example, *color, make, draw, circle, underline,* and *trace*		*Size Recognition Chart*, Ideal Co.
		The Giant Alphabet Box, Platt and Munk
6. Remembers visual stimuli with increasing span and complexity		*Alphabet Flash Cards*, Kenworthy Co.
		Lower Case Matching Chart, Ideal Co.
7. Establishes perceptual ability concerning figure-ground relationships of large shapes	Refer to Frostig, op. cit., Test 2 — Figure-Ground	Games found in teacher's edition for *Ready to Go*, New York: Holt, Rinehart & Winston, 1960
8. Recognizes his name in written form		Block or sandpaper letters, lower- and uppercase, either teacher-made or commercial product.
		Typewriter (primer)

Figure 2-2   LANGUAGE-ARTS SKILLS SEQUENCE, LEVEL 1 *(continued)*

Skills	*Methods and Activities*	*Materials, Equipment, and Source*
C. Displays following auditory & perceptual development:		
1. Differentiates between words that rhyme and those that don't	Many discussion activities where children relate everyday experiences	*Advantage Workbook*, Prentice-Hall. Exercises with classification correspondence, seriation, special relationships
2. Identifies words that begin with similar sounds	Program or activities in which children follow oral directions (1, 2, and 3 parts or more)	The Judy Clock, Judy Co. Recognition of numerals
3. Differentiates words that begin with different sounds	Choral speaking	The following records:
	Rhyming word games	*Muffin in the City*
4. Differentiates words that end differently	Reading and reciting nursery rhymes	*Muffin in the Country*
5. Recognizes own name	Use of *The Language Master*	*Getting Ready to Read*, Houghton-Mifflin
6. Recognizes names of local places	Use of *Wepman Auditory Discrimination Test* (ages 5–8, 2 forms), Language Research Associates.	*Language Kit A*, Units 1, 4, 7, 9, 11, 14, Ginn & Co.
7. Recognizes classmates' names		*Language Kit B*, Ginn & Co.
8. Follows ideas being presented	Parts of *Illinois Test of Psycho-Linguistic Abilities* (ages 2.5–9, 1 form) Univ. of Illinois Press.	Teacher-made games and materials
		Stories read by teacher
9. Predicts outcome by recalling main points of story relating to details and main sequence	Oral discussion using familiar objects, names, pictures, and events	Record collection *Sounds I Can Hear*
		Talking Time, by Louise Scott
10. Understands directions (carries out two-part or more sequential direction)	Classroom projects: telling and reading stories; role playing; illustrating through actions; acting out drawings or words; creative dramatics; cutting out pictures and relating items to them	*Reading, Writing and Readiness Charts*, Ideal Co.
		Alphabet cards
11. Associates letter sound with letter form and makes sight-sound-symbol relationship		Records: *Ping*
		The Little Engine That Could
		The Red Carpet

Figure 2-2 LANGUAGE-ARTS SKILLS SEQUENCE, LEVEL 1 *(continued)*.

Skills	Methods and Activities	Materials, Equipment, and Source
12. Recites nursery rhymes (at least four alone)	Administration of digit-span test	Record and filmstrip series: *Look about You*
13. Sits for period of time and maintains attention	Drawing pictures of objects that begin with letter sound enunciated by teacher	*Listen, These Are the Sounds Around You*
		People We Know
	Children telling stories of what is happening from tapes of various sounds	*Places to Go*, Guidance Associates, Pleasantville, N.Y.
		Record and study activities: *A Child's World of Poetry*, Society for Visual Education
		Let's Listen to Sounds
		Musical and Nonmusical Activities, Classroom Materials, Inc.
		Let's Listen to Beginning Rhyming Sounds, Ginn & Co.
		Listening Time Stories and Singing Fun, Bowman Publishing Corp.
		Talking Time Filmstrips and Sounds We Hear, Louise Scott, Bowman Publishing Corp.
		Phonics We Use (Learning Kit), Lyons & Carnahan
		Spin a Sound Game
		Consonant games
		Sound and Consonant Lotto
		Reference book for all teachers: *They All Need to Talk: Oral Communication in the Language Arts Program*, Wilma M. Possien (N.Y.: Appleton-Century-Crofts, 1969.)

Figure 2-2   LANGUAGE-ARTS SKILLS SEQUENCE, LEVEL 1 *(continued)*

Skills	Methods and Activities	Materials, Equipment, and Source
IV. WORD ATTACK SKILLS **Displays ability in the following areas:** 1. Makes visual discriminations and displays perceptual competence 2. Identifies colors; brightness, light, and dark 3. Identifies likenesses and differences in shapes: circles, squares, triangles, ovals, rectangles 4. Identifies likenesses and differences in letters without necessarily knowing their names 5. Identifies numerals from 0 to 9 6. Can move from left to right in following a story 7. Displays familiarity with both upper- and lower-case letters	Coloring pictures and discussing colors Games involving naming pupils in the class Activities relating to naming members of family in reading and readiness books Use of *Monroe Reading Aptitude Tests*, op. cit. *The Gates Reading Readiness Test* (Grade 1), Teachers College, Columbia Univ. (Use of picture directions, word matching, and reading letters and numbers may be useful.) Number progression; counting objects, reading pictures, reading charts, reading picture sequences from left to right, and reading charts from left to right Inquisitive ^{TM} games, Science Research Associates Songs and rhythms Counting frame Developing a daily calendar Using left-to-right progression activities involving a flashlight	Teacher-made materials of all sorts Paper cutouts, magazine pictures, flannelboard objects Charts Names of pupils on desks, tables, and chairs Number charts showing sets of items such as animals or figures Teacher-made and pupil-made charts with quantitative pictures *Inquisitive Games* ^{TM}, Science Research Associates Lotto Games Various *Kinder Math* charts Counting frame Suggested items from any teachers manual in readiness area concerning word-attack skills readiness Refer to Monroe and Rogers, op. cit., especially pp. 53–54. Lawrence and Carrillo, op. cit.

Figure 2-2   LANGUAGE-ARTS SKILLS SEQUENCE, LEVEL 1 *(continued)*

Skills	*Methods and Activities*	*Materials, Equipment, and Source*
V. DEVELOPMENT OF ORAL EXPRESSION AND LANGUAGE GROWTH AS EVIDENCED BY AN INCREASING VOCABULARY **Displays abilities in following areas:** 1. Expresses thoughts precisely, accurately, and clearly 2. Demonstrates in expression of thoughts an increasing use of spoken vocabulary 3. Increases ability to use complete sentences and varied language and linguistic patterns 4. Selects picture that corresponds to dictated sentence 5. Indicates he knows that words stand for actions, relationships, conditions concepts, as well as things 6. Shows understanding of logical distinctions made by use of conjunctions (paper and pencil), causal connectives (*so, that, because*), prepositions (*on, in, to, for, under, above*), and comparative words (*more, less*)	*(The general method used is pupil interaction and dialogue to establish contact with functional operation.)* Making puppet shows concerning various aspects of social living and school activity Developing comprehensive sharing and show-and-tell program to elicit ideas and abilities Using records and tapes that tell stories Using Ginn *Language Kit A* (see page 291 especially for list of activities) Games in which children create an oral text for picture story Using experience charts of two and three sentences developed by children Holding discussions concerning social studies and science ideas Taking trips to places near school for vocabulary development and development of language-experience stories Flannelboard activities	Magazines and pictures of all sorts Various pictures drawn by teacher and pupils Use of Ginn *Language Kit A* Use of Peabody *Language Kit* Sufficient quantities of chart paper for language experience stories Scripts and scenarios for plays that pupils can do in puppetry activities Books of creative dramatics and plays, *The Straw Ox, The Crowded House* Story-reenactment activities from reading books Taped read-along or talk-along activities to develop expressive and vocabulary areas

Figure 2-2 LANGUAGE-ARTS SKILLS SEQUENCE, LEVEL 1 *(continued)*

Skills	*Methods and Activities*	*Materials, Equipment, and Source*
7. Uses words with common meanings and reasonably complete sentences 8. Produces speech sounds correctly 9. Exchanges ideas, translates or interprets them as information to others	Role-playing and case-study activities Developing rhythm band Developing art activities using various textured materials to stimulate articulation and discussion (See Wilma M. Possien, op. cit.) Sandbox play with defined areas of objectives for development of certain vocabulary activities	
VI. THE DEVELOPMENT OF SENSORY AWARENESS Displays sensory awareness in: 1. Knowledge of the concepts of qualities such as hardness-softness, long-short, high-low, old-new, big-little, rough-smooth 2. Knows and is aware of the use of five senses	Following directions in games that call for crawling over the table, standing up high, sitting under something, and so forth Using fabrics and textured materials to elicit assessment of their quality Various kinds of blocks for comparative situations, such as arithmetic rods Comparative activities having to do with the size of children in classroom (height, weight) Using various materials for feeling, smelling, tasting, to determine their qualities	Using teacher-made materials *Language Arts for Beginners* Units 7 and 13, D. C. Heath

Figure 2-2   LANGUAGE-ARTS SKILLS SEQUENCE, LEVEL 1 *(continued)*

Skills	*Methods and Activities*	*Materials, Equipment, and Source*
VII. CRITICAL & COGNI-TIVE LANGUAGE LEARNINGS		
A. **Displays the following oral abilities:**		
1. Produces speech sounds correctly	A program of tracing using various activities: tracing shapes and various sizes with relative firmness, tracing over sandpaper letters, tracing (on transparent plastic covering) upper- and lower-case letters, figures, and so forth, and verbalizing about them	Paper, pencils, crayons, chalk, chalkboards, water-soluble pens for use on plastic covering; *Kindergarten Math Book,* alphabet cards, and various teacher-made materials
2. Expresses himself verbally		
3. Can answer questions about himself (name, parts of his body, age, brothers and sisters)		
4. Can help compose a story chart	Drawing circles and other forms on chalkboard, draw-a-man; verbalizing the ideas	
5. Can complete a story sequence	Developing various activities found in *Kindergarten Math Book,* Science Research Associates	
	Verbalizing story ideas in sequence; articulation activities, and phonic activities	
B. **Displays the following written abilities:**		
1. Can print own name using capital and lower-case letters	Being able to print various kinds of items from a flash card, or copy from a chalkboard, or from a dictated statement	
2. Can print other letters from alphabet copy form		
3. Has developed general muscular control for written work		
4. Can draw circles, squares, lines, triangles, rectangles		

Figure 2-2   LANGUAGE-ARTS SKILLS SEQUENCE, LEVEL 1 *(continued)*

Skills	*Methods and Activities*	*Materials, Equipment, and Source*
C. Displays the following Comprehension Skills:		
1. Uses spoken context by supplying missing words in orally given sentence. (uses various linguistic patterns as suggested in the books on linguistics)	See *Language Kit B*, Ginn & Co., p. 344, for list of activities Selected parts of *Durrell Reading Readiness Test* Various sentences illustrating several sentence patterns to be used for dictation and analysis	*Durrell Reading Readiness Test* *Language Kit B*, Ginn & Co. *Getting Ready to Read*, Houghton Mifflin Various reading techniques developed in the Denver public schools by McKee and Harrison See Joseph E. Brzeinski, "Beginning Reading in Denver", *Reading Teacher*, vol. 18 (1964), pp. 16–21.
2. Uses spoken context and makes letter-sound association with first letter of printed word		
D. Displays following work and study skill learnings:		
1. Pursues work independently	(All of these skills are developed in a continuous and cohesive fashion and are observable in activities of the classroom.) Suggested activities are: assigning independent work where child makes individual learning contract and is involved in planning, following directions, and carrying through to completion; teacher-pupil relationships resulting from above Creating pupil teams with check sheets to be used in oral practice sessions	Craft paper and primer typewriter for making individual contracts Various locations for materials and equipment so that routinized behavior can take place as desired in skills listing Worksheet checklist related to manner in which child assumes increasing responsibility; chart in which he can identify himself on particular growth continuum
2. Works well in groups		
3. Gives uninterrupted attention to instruction		
4. Returns supplies and equipment to proper places		
5. Completes work he begins		
6. Directs attention to a given activity for a minimum of fifteen minutes		
7. Accepts responsibility		

Figure 2-2   LANGUAGE-ARTS SKILLS SEQUENCE, LEVEL 1 *(continued)*

Skills	Methods and Activities	Materials, Equipment, and Source
E. Displays following locational & spatial identification skills:		
1. Knows right and left, and has determined laterality 2. Identifies right and left sides of any given object, page, or place	Finger plays, singing games, calendar activities moving from left to right across top, and from top to bottom; cutting and pasting pictures or numbers in order from left to right; coloring various items on a page in various colors when identified as being on left side, right side, at top, or at bottom Making construction materials and selected items from Frostig *Intermediate Workbook*	Various poems and finger play activities Large classroom calendar Various tracking activities, either mimeographed or commercially made Refer to Frostig, Monroe, Carrillo, etc.

The opportunities for the teacher to take a variety of teaching approaches to the various learners within this context should be obvious to the reader. The creative teacher who derives from his day-to-day contact insights concerning the way the children are performing and learning will pursue many other methods and activities, and make creative use of materials and equipment. The understanding is that this learning stage, as all subsequent learning stages that follow it, does not represent something to be slavishly adhered to, but rather something that outlines, guides, and indicates (for the teacher) a developmental program that can be approached by staying with or departing from the items noted (as good practice indicates) based on the day-to-day teaching procedures taking place within the classroom. The use of various kinds of content serves as the vehicle through which these skills are taught. This is the beginning stage that will, in a fluid fashion, feed into the next stage that increases in difficulty. A higher level likewise feeds into the next higher one. The child moves through a program wherein each level, besides being cumulative, is like a ramp leading up to a highway of learning. It is spiral in nature and reinforcing in its process. We must always remember that the levels can be thought of as rungs on a ladder. A rung on a ladder is a place at which one holds his position until he is ready to move to the next height, each height being ever upward toward the goal, or top, that is sought.

This prototype of learning stage 1 fulfills the major objective stated above. The reader can readily see that a sequence is made up of a series of educational organizing elements irrespective of a grade. The sequence is longitudinal and is continuous in its progressive growth potential. There are ways, methods, and techniques of approach that are *suggested* within the sequence. They guide the teacher in achieving for his pupils those skills that have been determined. In addition, the teacher has at hand a ready resource of materials and equipment that he can draw from and that will support the endeavors in the classroom.

There is a distinct advantage to this kind of approach. The opportunity for extending readiness programs through this sequence, because there is no limit of time, staves off one of the major causes of school failure: forcing a child into formal educational activities (that is, reading) before he is ready. This particular level, when combined with the levels that follow it, offers a cohesive block of work and an open period of time that will make allowances for spurts and lags in learning. It allows a more realistic look at the child and his needs without imposing the fearful threat of nonpromotion. It allows the teacher to deal with the learner in an integrative educational fashion rather than on the one-year, one-grade basis, which is an artificial fragmentation of learning and in no way relates to the process by which children do, in fact, learn.

There has been much discussion concerning the whole conceptualization and organization related to a levels, stages, or learning sequence approach to continuous-progress, nongraded education. The discussion may be more rhetorical and representative of a fundamental semantic difficulty than substantive. Conventional schools as we know them, especially the graded schools, have for many years used the terms *scope* and *sequence* to relate to curriculum development. The essential understanding is that there are basic sequences of learnings that are unalterable, vertical in nature, that must be applied because they represent the cores of understandings or learnings that everybody needs in that discipline or subject matter area. Unfortunately, in many teachers' manuals there is frequently a prescribed sequence. In it the learnings have been set down in a way that is not sequential at all. It often reflects but one point of view. This certainly can be said of social studies, where basic arguments are raging over whether one should start with the present and be present-oriented and look to the past to establish the knowledge of the present, or whether one should be past-oriented because the contention is that no knowledge of the present can be understood until a learning of the past is well established. Any arithmetic or reading series reflects the same kind of problem. Fundamental arguments of this sort may be relatively useless. By creating systematic sequencing for a given field, one can enhance knowledge of the interrelated structure of that field. That is to say, the manner by which real understanding is gained may be through knowledge of the particular structure of a discipline because of the sequential nature of the development of the ideas, skills, and concepts of that particular area.

We feel the establishment of sequence should be seen in the following light: a sequence development and levels approach is not an unalterable system without opportunities to achieve more rapidly, or differently, when a sudden light dawns, or without opportunities to move nonsystematically through items that fit the style of the learner. We feel rather that a sequence or levels approach is made up of necessary compilations that can be arranged so that their probable or logical importance can be interrelated and more readily learned. A good teacher will adhere to or depart from a sequence as day-to-day activities indicate, the necessity to change being based on a perceptive, continuous, diagnostic approach to learning. Sequence is a plan of organization, a statement of order of presentation within a subject matter area that is helpful in teaching-learning situations. During a sequence, within levels of operation, various teaching methods will be variable. For instance, the method used will always take into consideration the abilities, experiences, and needs of the pupils involved, as well as their interests and capacities and kind of educational reinforcements they have experienced previously.

There are writers who consider learning a nonsequential, random kind of activity.[2] To a great degree we admit to the random nature and nonsequential aspect of certain kinds of learning. We are, however, more involved and more heavily committed to the idea of developing insights into processes wherein a student develops his own particular learning style. We are equally quick to note that random learning, nonsequential learning, intuitive opportunities for greater learning, the whole area of developing a process by which one learns, are necessarily built on at least the rudimentary aspects of a skills program concerned with certain functionings inherent to success in school. To that end, especially in communication arts, mathematics, and social studies, we feel the organization of those activities and materials of instruction in relation to the learner's background on a continuum from readiness to competency is essential in developing the kind of competence

that leads to becoming an ultimate learner is determined by the learner's insight into a particular style or approach to learning.

Many programs have suffered because of the administratively chaotic nature of other approaches to continuous-progress, nongraded programs. On the other hand, Tewksbury discusses six criticisms of the levels plan in nongraded schools. His summation of that analysis is revealing. He states:

"An analysis of these criticisms suggests that some are based on misunderstanding whereas others involve problems which with care can probably be . . . solved. The levels plan seems to be sufficiently flexible so that it can be modified by the staff in a school system to satisfy local needs. For this reason the plan has been found to be a workable one in many nongraded schools."[3]

With a well-conceived sequence and a philosophical commitment to a levels approach in a nongraded, continuous-progress program, the next step becomes one of finding out precisely where each child is on that continuum. The diagnostic plan is crucial in the productive operation of the innovated school. Acquiring sophistication in diagnostic procedures is the next step in a program of implementation of continuous-progress, nongraded schools.

DIAGNOSING THE STUDENT POPULATION AS A PREREQUISITE TO PLACEMENT IN THE CONTINUOUS-PROGRESS, NONGRADED SEQUENCE

3

PLACEMENT

Chapter 2 dealt with the concept of sequence and its development by stages or levels from the most simple to the most complex in the areas of curricula that are to be continuous-progress oriented. The point was made that the teachers from the various levels within the schools must be brought together to determine what the academic behavior of the pupil should be at the completion of his schooling. On the basis of these agreed-upon outcomes, curricular sequences are established that start at readiness and progress to achieved mastery.

The need to diagnose each child to find out how far he is from the desired outcome is obvious. Repetition, inappropriate work, and lack of readiness are but a few of the constantly observed problems of nondiagnostically oriented programs frequently found in the graded school.

The second step in the development of continuous-progress, nongraded education is the creation of diagnostic tools that specifically identify the strengths and weaknesses of each pupil in relation to the sequence of the curriculum. There are many things to be considered in the whole area of diagnosis. There are many levels as well as varied purposes. For example, there are very specific materials, collected and developed in inventory form, that help assess the degree of competence in certain precise items of a sequence. There are the less specific, more informal kinds of assessments that have to be collected and used in placement and grouping: cumulative records, conferences with previous teachers, oral and written work observed by the teacher, and conferences with pupils. There are the essential considerations concerned with the whole nature of the child and his relation to schooling. This represents a multifaceted approach to diagnosis and includes such things as chronological age, test scores related to ability or capacity, social maturity, basic motivational sensibilities, various needs as evidenced by the child's educational reinforcements, his family, and other items related to this, and his physical maturation. Additionally, various styles of learning related to social and economic circumstances, ethnic values, customs and mores, as well as those related to urban and rural life are considerations to be taken into account in any attempt at perceptive diagnostic practices.

The problems of diagnosis are selecting and bringing together diverse, but necessary, inventoried items into a cohesive approach that yields information essential in the establishment of the desired objective of continuous-progress education: appropriate placement of the child in a situation that relates specifically to his particular current needs and creates a climate in which ultimate learning can be addressed by him and in which he accomplishes all that he is capable of accomplishing.

The second objective one seeks to attain in implementing continuous-progress, nongraded schools is related to the crucial aspect of diagnostic practices. Stated simply:

A continuous-progress, nongraded school seeks to create in every area it nongrades well-thought-out collections of material that can be used handily and perceptibly in diagnosing a pupil's competence as it relates to the defined levels or stages of the learning sequence.

The diagnostic materials must relate to, and be representative of, the multilevel nature of a specific learning sequence. There will be diagnostic materials that are related to and derived from the sequence. These determine readiness for participation in a program of formal learning. There will be diagnostic instruments and inventories, more precise in nature, that relate to children who have been in school for a longer period of time and who need to be more carefully diagnosed because of their apparent lack of success due to weaknesses in skills that are necessary for mastery. The diagnoses will allow for sophisticated, carefully thought-out, precisely defined guidelines for pupil-teacher assignments.

The diagnostic activities here suggested bring several things into play at once. They create a more perceptive approach to placement of a pupil based on the needs and abilities for the acquisition of the skills he needs to insure his success in the sequence being considered. Such diagnostic approaches enable the educator to find the total range of competence that exists in his school. From this information he can, in a more perceptive way, control the heterogeneity within any one group relative to specific skill needs. He can narrow the ranges in any classroom so that teachers deal with a range of skill-learning probabilities that are more manageable and reasonable than those found in a graded program. These approaches to diagnosis allow for placement and flexible assignment based on the special needs of the children. Various opportunities for assignments that create ultimate learning programs can be readily made if educators have in front of them diagnostic workups that indicate more clearly the educational direction that ought to be taken.

The use of diagnostic instruments also leads to a greater opportunity for dealing with various styles of learning. By carefully watching and by carefully extracting from the diagnostic workups certain kinds of revelations, it is possible to perceptively deal with (or to identify) a particular style of the learner and with that knowledge make more appropriate and pertinent activities and placements available to him.

There are several items, periods, or times one must consider carefully in the area of diagnostic activity as the continuous-progress, nongraded program develops: (1) initial levels or stages assignment; (2) early adjustments after the initial assignments; (3) criteria and activities attendant to the movement of a pupil from level to level; (4) transitional periods between levels for an individual or special case; (5) determination concerning the extension of a time period within a level; (6) articulation between and among levels and the diagnostic activities related to that articulation. The development of this diagnostic orientation, the training of teachers to handle it well, and the creation of relevant and valid techniques and instruments are the fundamental crucial areas that separate conventional approaches from innovative continuous-progress orientations.

It needs to be mentioned very specifically that diagnosis *does not mean the mere giving of standardized tests and the restatement of assignments and pupil growth in terms of grade levels.* Most teachers are aware that frequently standardized tests are given and grade-level scores attained, but when a child is given a book related to his grade-level score he fails to achieve competently. It is apparent to all who use standard tests that it is impossible to establish one operable and consistent set of circumstances that will apply to all the aspects of a child's performance and therefore yield wholly accurate insights.

It is likewise obvious that the assignment of children to groups based on such tests is sometimes nondescript, diffuse, and frequently irrelevant as it may concern particular needs necessary for real learning. For too many years, educators have only verbally committed themselves to really dealing with the individual differences of children. They grouped them instead through similarity of chronological age. In making assignments, they set up their expectations based, paradoxically, on the very chronology that they supposedly gave verbal testimony against in their recognition of individual differences.

An acceptable process of diagnosis involves a multilevel diagnostic protocol to examine in detail those items the learner finds necessary to work with a specific situation. Diagnostic tools or surveys are attempts to create instruments to look at the component parts of the various items attendant to the performance necessary for success. Diagnostic tools are analytic in nature so that various components can be seen clearly and can yield data that will lead to a decision concerning prescription and placement.

There is no question but that proper diagnosis is an absolute prerequisite to increasing the effectiveness of instruction. Proper diagnosis, based on material found in the learning sequence, allows one to make different kinds of curriculum provisions not available under the graded program. It allows a teacher to bring into play effective instructional programs because the administrative provisions have underpinned the opportunity for a clearer approach to the real needs of the students.

We sometimes part from concepts held by others in our complete conviction that continuous-progress, nongraded education and diagnostic teaching are actually internally reinforcing concepts that lead to the greater enhancement of education.

Basically, we contend that education must be based on a diagnostic workup of each child or it remains ambiguous and serves the needs of society to a lesser degree than is demanded for survival. We liken this diagnosis to that of a competent doctor who first examines each patient very carefully. On the basis of the examination, he provides a detailed program for remedying an illness, or a regime that continues the existent good health of the patient. A doctor frequently may refer to sources that give identifications and symptoms of various diseases even though his many years of experience have allowed him to focus on many problems in a general way. The sources can be likened to the sequence of levels in language arts, or any field, that contains all the items that come together to establish a situation against which one can check an error, gain a new insight, or discover an overlooked possibility. The doctor's diagnosis, when completed, allows him to move to a prescriptive remedy.

This remedy is based on what the individual can tolerate. What an individual can tolerate is certainly not the same for every patient. Similarly in education, what each child can take or tolerate is variable. Diagnosis, therefore, is made up of many factors and is not merely an attempt to determine a grade level. A doctor doesn't give every patient with the same symptom the same treatment. Every child who measures on a standard test at the 2.0 grade level cannot always read each of the grade 2 books of every reading series. We must find out more. It is the cause of the symptom that determines the remedy. We must know why a child scores 2.0 and still reads a grade 2 book haltingly so that we can determine what to do about it.

There are several types of diagnostic tests: those that attempt to arrive at a total grade level score; those used basically in educational clinics and are semistandardized in an attempt to get a collected insight; and those that are developed by classroom teachers who have a desire to find those particular elements that seem to be retarding or influencing a child's learning behavior.

The question is often asked: Why must individual profiles and diagnoses be used by a teacher rather than standard tests only? Benjamin S. Bloom says,

"The student who completes twelve years in the public school system in a large urban community is likely to have come into contact with fifty to a hundred different teachers. Each of these teachers works with a particular group of students for one or two terms and has little to do with the student before or after this time period. Knowing little about the student before the particular term in which he teaches him, the teacher tends to look upon him as a *standard unit like every other student.* (Most teachers are likely to regard the student as totally lacking in the particular unit or subject or the specific cognitive skills and abilities which the teacher desires to develop.)

"The fallacy of such assumptions has been amply demonstrated by the work of the past fifty years in the measurement of individual differences. In practically every measurable characteristic, there is a great range of levels of performance from the highest individual in the group to the lowest—where the group is defined by age of its members or by number of years they have attended school.

"The magnitude of these differences is difficult to determine because we have very few measurements which can be expressed in absolute units such as we use in the measurement of height or weight, but a quick glance at a set of norms for the different grades on almost any standardized test will convince the reader. Inspecting the norms for a well-known and carefully developed battery of aptitude tests we notice that an average of about 40 percent of ninth grade students exceed the scores made by the lowest third of the twelfth grade students.

"It is also clear that each student brings a unique set of characteristics to the educational enterprise. If one attempts to describe an individual with a battery of tests which yield ten scores or more, it would be difficult to find two identical profiles in a group of 100 persons of the same age or grade level.

"While it is clear that there is great variation among individuals on any given characteristic and that each individual is likely to have a relatively unique distribution of characteristics, not all of this variability is directly related to education. If we can accept the assumption that knowledge of the major characteristics of an individual is better than ignorance of these characteristics, we may then ask what characteristics we should know about and what we might do with this knowledge."[1]

We contend that the use of an individual battery of tests yielding ten scores or more is impossible to use to derive an identical profile of children who could be set up as look-alike learners. On the other hand the development of clearly thought-out diagnostic instruments that are discrete in terms of what they are attempting to find or measure can bring together a group of learners who each display a lack of a particular skill or concept and who can be taught to be competent in that particular skill. (See analysis of John Gill School diagnostic experiment in part II.)

In developing a diagnostic approach, educators moving toward continuous-progress, nongraded education will find immediately that standardized and semistandardized tests are useful in some ways but insufficient to their needs. What is needed, and what must be developed, are those informal kinds of activities and diagnoses related to the learning sequence agreed upon by the professionals involved in the program. What they have spelled out in their program may be quite unrelated to the existing standard materials.

In chapter 2, learning level stage 1 of a language-arts skills sequence was fully developed. We now turn to some diagnostic items that can serve as examples in defining the actual performance level a child displays relative to that particular stage of learning. Figure 3-1 is a simple diagnostic-survey instrument in that it matches a readiness level that does not embrace some of the more sophisticated skills found at higher levels. As a child moves through the levels, paper-and-pencil performance surveys are used more frequently.

Figure 3-1   DIAGNOSTIC SURVEY RELATED TO LEARNING STAGE 1
OF LANGUAGE-ARTS SKILLS SEQUENCE, FOR ASSIGNMENT PURPOSES

Pupil_____ Teacher_____ Date_____

Directions: This survey is given in mid-May of the kindergarten year. It attempts to evaluate the level of performance in the various categories from a very adequate to an inadequate degree. Please check the competency in each of the items listed below according to the following level of intensity:

I = Inadequate
A = Adequate
V = Very Adequate

Each of the sections below has a minimum competency performance scale (MCPS). It indicates the stage of readiness in each of the categories. If the child does not achieve a level of minimum competency in the various areas, he will be assigned to the readiness program of level 1. If, on the other hand, he attains a minimum competency level in the areas herein described, he is ready for work at level 2, and should be given a diagnosis appropriate to the elements in that stage, for placement.

Inventory of Basic Readiness Skills

1. GROSS MOTOR SKILLS

	I	A	V

a) Catches and throws a large ball

b) Walks a balance beam or chalk line

c) Runs, jumps, skips, climbs, hops, and gallops

d) Jumps from a crouching position

e) Crawls forward and backward

(MCPS = 3 items of above 5)   Achieved MCPS 1: yes ( ) no ( )

2. FINE MOTOR COORDINATION SKILLS

a) Uses crayons and pencils

b) Uses scissors

c) Coordinates hand and eye by drawing and tracing shapes

d) Draws simple outlines and shapes, and colors within defined areas

e) Uses fingers and hands with dexterity for grasping and holding

f) Puts together a simple form board

(MCPS = 4 items of above 5)   Achieved MCPS 2: yes ( ) no ( )

Figure 3-1   DIAGNOSTIC SURVEY RELATED TO LEARNING STAGE 1
OF LANGUAGE-ARTS SKILLS SEQUENCE, FOR ASSIGNMENT PURPOSES *(continued)*

3. SENSORY PERCEPTION

I	A	V

   a) Can identify qualities of soft-hard, long-short, high-low, old-new, big-little, near-far

   b) Uses and describes aspects of taste, touch, sight, sound, and odor

   (MCPS = 1 item of above 2)   Achieved MCPS 3: yes ( ) no ( )

4. AUDITORY PERCEPTION

   a) Follows oral directions

   b) Identifies rhyming words

   c) Responds to his own name

   d) Identifies likenesses and differences in letter sounds

   e) Identifies various sounds of things (trains, planes, rain, wind, whistle, etc.)

   (MCPS = 3 items of above 5)   Achieved MCPS 4: yes ( ) no ( )

5. VISUAL PERCEPTION

   a) Names the primary colors

   b) Differentiates various shapes: circles, squares, triangles, ovals

   c) Identifies likenesses and differences in upper- and lowercase letters

   d) Identifies numerals 0 to 9

   e) Moves in a left-to-right progression in following a story

   f) Displays a sight familiarity with upper- and lowercase letters

   (MCPS = 4 items of above 6)   Achieved MCPS 5: yes ( ) no ( )

6. ORAL EXPRESSION

   a) Expresses thoughts verbally

   b) Uses a growing vocabulary

   c) Recites nursery rhymes

   d) Uses complete sentences and varied language patterns

   e) Demonstrates expression in the oral presentation of an idea

   f) Produces speech sounds correctly

   (MCPS = 3 items of above 6)   Achieved MCPS 6: yes ( ) no ( )

Figure 3-1   DIAGNOSTIC SURVEY RELATED TO LEARNING STAGE 1
OF LANGUAGE-ARTS SKILLS SEQUENCE, FOR ASSIGNMENT PURPOSES *(continued)*

7. CRITICAL AND COGNITIVE PERCEPTUAL ABILITIES

	I	A	V

a) Helps to compose a story chart

b) Helps to complete a story sequence

c) Prints his name using capital and lowercase letters

d) Prints other letters of the alphabet

e) Uses the spoken context to make a letter sound association with the first letter of a printed word

f) Supplies missing words in orally dictated sentences

(MCPS = 4 items of above 6)   Achieved MCPS 7: yes ( ) no ( )

8. WORKS IN STUDY SKILL BEHAVIORS

a) Pursues work independently

b) Works well in a group

c) Gives uninterrupted attention to instruction

d) Returns supplies and equipment to proper places

e) Completes work that he begins

f) Has an attention span of 15 minutes

(MCPS = 4 items of above 6)   Achieved MCPS 8: yes ( ) no ( )

MCPS scores indicate child is ready for diagnosis at level 2: yes ( ) no ( )
MCPS scores indicate child is at level 1: yes ( ) no ( )

By carefully matching the items of the inventory in figure 3-1 with the items found in the learning sequence in figure 2-2, chapter 2, one is able to see immediately the relation between curriculum objectives and diagnosed needs. The diagnostic inventory attempts to establish the level of competency of a child so that a clear determination can be made as to what prescriptive treatment is necessary in relation to his learning activities.

An additional opportunity for seeing a child in greater depth through diagnosis is offered by an End-of-Kindergarten Screening device (see figure 3-2) made up of four categories. This allows a teacher to survey quickly the extent to which he feels a child is "ready." By using this device as a gross screening instrument and getting a score that is not really binding or convertible, a teacher who knows the child can declare, in spite of the score, whether he is really "ready" or "not ready" in various categories. The use of multiple instruments helps to gain depth in diagnosis and serves in developing a clearer picture of the needs of a child.

Figure 3-2   END-OF-KINDERGARTEN SCREENING FOR INITIAL ASSIGNMENTS

Child _____ Teacher _____ Date _____

Age as of September _____   Total Score (135) _____

Basic Readiness Characteristics

Extent Displayed by Child

	Ready	Not Ready	Rating 1 2 3 4 5
1. PHYSICAL DEVELOPMENT			
a) Intensity and length of physical concentration			
Physical well-being			
Health habits			
b) Visual and perceptual			
Tracks from left to right			
Coordinates eyes			
Sees likenesses/differences			
c) Auditory			
Intensity of attentiveness			
Listening ability			
Identifies likenesses/differences in sounds			
d) Motor			
Large muscle use and control			
Small muscle use and control			
2. AFFECTIVE AND EMOTIONAL TONE			
Adjustment to school environment			
Acceptance-rejection concerning activities			
Emotional control			
Sense of self-confidence			

Figure 3-2   END-OF-KINDERGARTEN SCREENING FOR
INITIAL ASSIGNMENTS *(continued)*

Extent Displayed by Child

	Ready	Not Ready	Rating 1 2 3 4 5
3. SOCIAL READINESS			
Attitudes toward peers			
Attitudes toward adults			
Participation skills			
Responsibility			
4. MENTAL READINESS			
Expresses thoughts well			
Inquires and is curious			
Displays a good memory			
Carries out directions			
Makes intelligent responses			

Pertinent comments or unique features that will be an aid:

It becomes apparent that a child who displays a "very adequate" performance in most of these areas listed is ready for formal learning. The items represent a level of educational maturity that is necessary for success in formal learning. These elements have been agreed to by teachers and in turn represent agreed-to typicalities in behavior that can be scaled from 1 to 5. In a word, teachers established the items and objectified their judgments of them. If a child displays large gaps of competence in the items in both these rating instruments, then it is educationally sound to teach him in the level of the sequence called "Language-Arts Skills Sequence, Level 1." Here he will benefit from the kinds of approaches that are operationally defined in establishing the specific skills called for.

Diagnostic practices and activities can range all the way from "sketchy" to a level of "overkill." Many individually prescribed instructional programs now appearing on the educational scene seem to represent an acceptable middle ground. Individually prescribed instructional programs are in compatible balance with the concept of continuous-progress, nongraded education when they are not overly fragmentized, and make use of content to teach skills that are broken down and categorized. Individual prescription in educational instruction is based fundamentally on the development of sequences that list the skills much the way they have been discussed in chapter 2. Skills are fragmented so that the component areas and subskills are spread out and clearly defined within the categories decided on as making up a relevant, valid sequence.

The next step after establishing the skill categories is to find out where pupils are functioning in relation to mastery. Individually prescribed instruction has as its goal the desire to develop the mastery of skills based upon the pupil's own rate of learning. Therefore it becomes necessary, indeed mandatory, to find out exactly where intrusion should begin, or what background the pupil reveals, before intervening into his learning program. The diagnostic tests that are developed in individually prescribed instruction are in the nature of pretests. They are keyed exactly to the appropriate materials for the children.

The diagnostic activities discussed here relate only to the readiness stage. Part II gives examples of diagnostic instruments related to other learning stages. They were developed in different contexts and provide some idea of how teachers can, by drawing from various areas and by relating to their established sequence, develop a first-rate diagnostic program that will yield insight into the level of functioning of the learners involved in the programs being addressed.[2]

Once having diagnosed the school population in relation to the sequence, and once being in possession of a collection of items covering the learners, the establishment of a prescriptively oriented continuous-progress program becomes a formidable task. What is next required is a manner of categorizing and being able to deal handily with the collected material.

The method of organizing to create a set of instruments to screen out the elements of diagnosis so that they can be used readily in developing prescriptive placements and assignments is of paramount importance in avoiding getting bogged down by an overabundance of paperwork and bookkeeping procedures.

Another component that brings the reader closer to the reality of implementation of continuous-progress, nongraded education is the Learning Developmental Inventory, a set of forms used to develop a cumulative profile of the elements of diagnosis. It is from these forms and inventories that precise profiles of children are drawn that give immediate visual insight into their particular prescriptive needs. Creating learning developmental inventories is essential to continuous-progress, nongraded education. It is to these that we now turn. They relate to the concept of sequence and the concept of diagnosis discussed in chapters 2 and 3.

DEVELOPING LEARNING DEVELOPMENTAL INVENTORIES FOR SCREENING AND FOR ASSIGNMENTS TO LEARNING STAGES

4

INVENTORIES

An inventory is an objective and factual collection of items relating to a pupil's abilities or disabilities based on a diagnosis of his performance in a given area. The sequence discussed previously is a suggested skills and concepts development program. The diagnostic approach was described as a set of activities aimed at determining the actual extent to which the strengths and weaknesses related to the skills are present in an individual. Inventories serve as detailed cumulative records that are perpetual in nature and are used continuously for noting the acquisition of and growth in skills as bases for realistic grouping and for teaching-learning situations.

There needs to be a rather clear distinction made between the diagnostic practices (sometimes referred to as diagnostic inventories), which in many ways are tests of performance concerning selected skills and competencies, and the learning developmental inventories, which are checklists used to scrutinize a pupil's actual profile of performance in a given area. Besides being a checklist, the learning developmental inventories represent summaries of accomplishments at various stages throughout the area being addressed from the stage of readiness to the stage of achieved competence or mastery.

The learning sequence (LS), diagnostic inventory (DI), and learning developmental inventory or profile (LDI or LDP) represent three basic items that make up the core of essentials necessary to the development of continuous-progress, nongraded educational orientations in any area of the curriculum. No matter what area one chooses to establish as a continuous-progress, nongraded educational program, it behooves him to create (1) a learning sequence (so that he knows what is to be taught); (2) a diagnostic inventory (so that he knows to what extent the pupil is competent on a scale from readiness to mastery in the area to be taught); and (3) a learning developmental inventory (so that he knows the pupil's actual profile or status relative to the sequence and preparatory to grouping procedures and teacher assignments that are requisite to developing pertinent and appropriate learning activities for each pupil).

The learning developmental inventory is not fully diagnostic, but rather a quasi-diagnostic device used for collecting the results of the comprehensive diagnosis in a more precise and usable way. *Diagnosis* represents, in reality, those procedures used for the measurement of achievements and abilities, and the determination of the extent of learning deficiencies and difficulties. We have chosen to use the concept of a *developmental inventory* as that procedure or technique of screening out the various elements of the diagnosis so that learning profiles can be clearly established. Actually, the developmental inventories serve as feedback mechanisms from the diagnostic activities and workups, allowing the educator to use them meaningfully in reference to the pupil.

One of the fundamental activities found in continuous-progress, nongraded education that is different from the conventionally organized and taught graded school relates to this whole area of creating learning inventories that denote rather clearly the level of a pupil's prowess, or problems. From many years of experience in administration, and consultation in schools, we have the impression that a tremendous amount of "marking time" takes place in our schools. Teachers frequently are offering many things that any inventory would reveal are fundamentally already within the ability or knowledge of the children. Some educators have indicated

that many able students could complete the work of an eight-year school program in four years if they did not have to move through the constant repetitions that encumber them. Philip W. Jackson makes the observation that:

"In several ways students in elementary classrooms are required to wait their turn and to delay their actions. No one knows for certain how much of the average student's time is spent in neutral as it were, but for many students in many classrooms it must be a memorable portion."[1]

We could readily adduce further evidence to back this contention of repetition and delay. We quickly point out, however, that we are not critical of the proper kinds of educational review that reinforce or fix learning. We are critical of the unnecessary repititious use of teacher time that could be spent in taking inventories and developing clear sets of objectives based on the abilities of pupils so that they could pursue fruitful learning activities instead of unnecessary repetition. We are very much against the "more of the same" kind of activities given to children who learn fast. We feel that children who learn rapidly have a need for moving in new directions. Likewise, there is a fundamental need to allow unhampered advancement to curricula of higher levels for children who display readiness to achieve more rapidly.

Sophistication for learning based on an inventory should indicate the level of curriculum offering, not years in school, grade, or chronological age. Presumptions based on a grade or age are preconceptions that reject the scientific approach and make much of what is offered in a classroom irrelevant. Inventories bring the teacher and the taught into a meaningful relationship. They leave the often irrelevant preconceptions behind and lead to heightened critical and clinical approaches to the needs of the learner.

The third major objective is:

A continuous-progress, nongraded school seeks to create inventories that record and denote the relevant features of the diagnoses that are used to assess the learner in relation to the sequence, so that precise learning profiles of identifiable items are readily seen and readily usable in establishing relevant grouping procedures wherein the learner will be educationally employed and responsive in an appropriate and worthwhile setting.

In chapter 2 a fully developed learning stage of a language-arts skills sequence was presented. In chapter 3 the diagnostic inventory related to that level and that served to determine a pupil's relative strengths, weaknesses, or needs, was spelled out. Figure 4-1 is a learning developmental inventory, related to these two items, at the same stage or level. It is level 1 only, and each level in the sequence has a matching level in the inventory. The diagnosis and its relationship are explained in the introduction to, and directions of, the inventory.

Figure 4-1   LEARNING DEVELOPMENTAL INVENTORY RELATED
TO THE LANGUAGE-ARTS SKILLS SEQUENCE

This learning developmental inventory is made up of 200 items of behavior attendant to language-arts learning. The emphasis is on skills, abilities, and concepts related to successful mastery in the language-arts sequence. Each of the items on the inventory is stated in behavioral terms. Each item is observable; some are measurable. The use of the paper-and-pencil diagnostic inventory (DI), teacher-made worksheets, precise exercises, and various other diagnostic commercially developed items related to specific areas herein noted can be used. The behavioral existence of each item must be judged on the basis of whether the child "can" or "cannot" perform the stated task, or "does" or "does not" exhibit the stated behavior. This learning developmental inventory begins at the readiness level, level 1, and becomes progressively more sophisticated in reference to the skills-development program. Mastery is achieved by the attainment of the skills of the last level of the inventory. The LDI serves as the profile of activities from which the prescriptive approach to grouping is to be made.

The manner of the LDI's operation is simple. A minimum number of items at each level need to be accomplished before mastery of that level is attained. When that mastery is established the child progresses to the next level. He is taught those things that he cannot do from the sequence that that level relates to. When competency is established the child progresses to the next level and continues on in that fashion. The levels are seen as being prescriptively inclusive. They serve to guide the teacher in focusing on the specific skill needs of a child so that his growth will be assured. This Learning Developmental Inventory is a master screening device that relates closely to the learning sequence and diagnostic inventory. At the conclusion of each level on the learning developmental inventory the teacher adds up the number of pluses and minuses. On the basis of the suggested procedure for scoring, he then suggests the basic assignment to the level of the sequence wherein the items, skills, or concepts that need to be taught will be addressed. Comments and other pertinent information are presented at the end of each of the levels.

Figure 4-1   LEARNING DEVELOPMENTAL INVENTORY RELATED TO THE
LANGUAGE-ARTS SKILLS SEQUENCE *(continued)*

LDI – LEVEL I

Name:_____ Birth Date:_____

School:_____ Room:_____ Boy:_____ Girl:_____

Check every item below either plus (+) for yes, or minus (–) for no.

	Date: Mo/Yr			
1. Listens to stories with interest and enthusiasm				
2. Displays interest in books and in learning how to read				
3. Listens to and follows oral directions				
4. Works well in a group				
5. Works well independently				
6. Expresses himself adequately and displays use of an increasing vocabulary				
7. Displays gross and fine motor coordination				
8. Perceives likenesses and differences through visual discrimination (size, shape, color, position, etc.)				
9. Restates a story in sequence after hearing it read				
10. Separates and identifies auditory likenesses and differences				
11. Picks out details, omissions, motions, and distances in pictures				
12. Follows a left-to-right progression (things)				
13. Follows a top-to-bottom progression (things)				

Figure 4-1   LEARNING DEVELOPMENTAL INVENTORY RELATED TO THE
LANGUAGE-ARTS SKILLS SEQUENCE *(continued)*

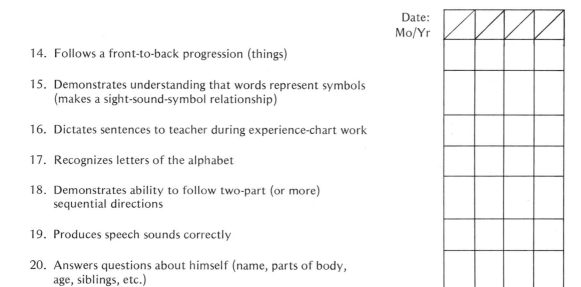

Date:
Mo/Yr

14. Follows a front-to-back progression (things)

15. Demonstrates understanding that words represent symbols
(makes a sight-sound-symbol relationship)

16. Dictates sentences to teacher during experience-chart work

17. Recognizes letters of the alphabet

18. Demonstrates ability to follow two-part (or more)
sequential directions

19. Produces speech sounds correctly

20. Answers questions about himself (name, parts of body,
age, siblings, etc.)

Note: The pupil progresses to the next level if he has 17 or more items checked plus (+). If this total is reached, continue checking on next level of the inventory.

Comments: (Directions for comments are as follows: Please state for each item any untoward or unusual kind of behavior by the pupil.)

This short presentation of elements of the learning developmental inventory level should indicate several things to the reader as he studies it more deeply and as he sees it in a longitudinally more developed manner in part II. He will see that frequently there are repetitions of particular items at various levels. He will find that there are items relating to specified activities that can be said to be learning "afresh," and items that can be said to be required "maintenance" in learning. For this reason he will sometimes find in each level similar behaviors stated in different terminology. By studying the diagnostic inventory items that relate to level 1, and the learning developmental inventory items that relate to learning level 1, the reader will see the manner by which he can precisely and quickly establish the particular learning status of a pupil relative to his strengths and weaknesses, and the things that the pupil will have to be taught.

We suggest that in the creation of a learning developmental inventory corresponding to the diagnostic inventory a small guidebook also be created to identify correlated interrelationships of the various sections of each. We suggest further that the learning developmental inventory be made up of a forced-choice collection of items wherein the teacher states that a child either can or cannot perform the item stated or does or does not display the behavior noted in the inventory. Data yielded from this procedure allows for the creation of precise opportunities to teach more meticulously particular skills whose inclusion in the inventory is an indication of a previously determined professional decision. The inventory inclusions are the relevant items that make up the area of education being addressed. The ability to perform them well will either enhance the learning activity of a child or cripple him in his educational endeavors. For that reason alone the careful attainment of competence becomes a requisite concern. The forced-choice selection for each item helps to clarify the true status of the learner.

We suggest that all areas of the curriculum that are nongraded or continuous-progress oriented likewise be translated into developmental steps that lend themselves easily to inventory form. These will offer instruments to teachers and administrators that will be valuable and will, in a coordinate way, establish a cohesive three-part approach to establishing an open, continuous-progress, nongraded program.

Most common in the area of nongrading are the arithmetic inventories and the language-learning, or reading, inventories. Many of these are readily available and can serve as prototypes for developing one's own inventory. Each school system needs to develop an inventory concerning the basic activities it wants to attend to in its recommended learning activities.

Inventories related to science and social studies learnings are still rare. The problems concerning the way that social studies and science should be taught may be the reasons why inventories, sequences, diagnoses, and other similar activities have not been developed. Until one

reaches a consensus within a school district as to what the emphasis is to be in these two curriculum areas, it is difficult to create a sequential development program, a diagnostic approach, and inventories that will help in the placement of pupils or assignment of teachers. For example, some school systems feel they could nongrade, or establish a continuous-progress program, by developing a sequence in social studies skills. They would range from the most simple to the most complex, and could be placed in various stages of learning from readiness to mastery in the context of social studies education. After the skills sequence is developed, diagnostic instruments could be created to give insight into the pupil's level of ability or competence in these skills, and a learning developmental inventory could be created to establish the status relative to the cumulative set of skills that a pupil displays, in preparation for placing him where he can be taught with others who have problems similar to his.

However, there are those who feel that methods of inquiry and discovery, or heuristic teaching, should serve as the base in social studies education. These educators contend that the teaching that has held sway in too many present-day classrooms is in disrepute and should be replaced by a concept having to do with the learning act. They likewise contend that this learning is underpinned by inquiry, discovery, and the general heuristic processes that seem more fruitful than those involved in directive skills development. We take the position that the argument or debate is a healthy one. We feel, however, that regardless of what particular position is embraced by educators, it still lends itself to a nongraded continuous-progress orientation. It is even more so in the case of discovery, inquiry, and heuristic approaches. Regardless of the material chosen for study, the concept of developing that material in a precise, sequential way, diagnosing those who are to deal with the material in order to assess the competence they display in handling it, and collecting those behaviors into a handy inventory, still serves the educator in a far better way than his reliance on the frequently diffuse, somewhat textbook-oriented, and nondescript unscientific graded approach.

Once the inventories are completed and a child is evaluated precisely as to his learning level, then these inventories serve both as forms from which placement is made and as up-to-date educational histories of the learners. For example, if the desire is to create continuous-progress, nongraded education in language arts, after the inventory has been completed with items checked at each level until the level is reached where there is an insufficient total of plus responses, then simply by taking these profiles and putting them in piles, the administrator and teachers have at hand a rather carefully diagnosed pupil population with an actual count at various levels of competence.

It is with this kind of information that the technical aspects of organization that assure continuous-progress, nongraded education are addressed. With a knowledge of the number of children who are still at readiness, as well as those who range all along a continuum to competency, it becomes a much more educationally realistic situation to deal with those children on the basis of their needs rather than on the old numerological activity where principals assigned x number of children to each teacher and then as new children entered school assigned Teacher A $x+1$, Teacher B $x+1$, and then all over again, Teacher A $x+2$, Teacher B $x+2$, ad infinitum.

Numerological assignment is probably the least imaginative and least scientific one can think of if he considers the whole area of ways that grouping can be done. But with a learning development inventory that carefully notes essential educational elements relevant to success, and individually notes a child's competence to deal with these elements, then grouping and assignment become more scientifically based. Grouping activities within the school will reflect the reality of the pupil population rather than the fiction of the conventional grade and the idea of "so many kids per classroom."

The clever and adaptive ways of dealing with this particular pupil population relate to the organizational situation in a school. Developing vehicles of organization now becomes important. The experience that is to be given to each child is evaluated. The desire to educate in a more productive way, realistically using teachers for the enhancement of learning rather than merely for the keeping of school, confronts those who have developed sequences, diagnosed, and taken an inventory in those school areas that are to be continuous-progress, nongraded oriented.

IMPLEMENTATION

DEVELOPING ORGANIZATIONAL VEHICLES TO IMPLEMENT NONGRADED, CONTINUOUS-PROGRESS EDUCATION

The organization of the elementary school can move all the way from the self-contained classroom made up for the most part of chronologically aged children working for one year with the same teacher, to fully individualized programs where each child is working on prescriptions specifically created for him and where he is guided by several teachers. If one were to plot grouping and school organization procedures (which in many instances are mutually inclusive terms) on a continuum, the left-hand side or initial point would represent the self-contained organization and the right-hand side or final point would represent the highly individualized approaches to organization. By moving from extreme left to extreme right one would see many alternatives in the area of grouping.

It is conceivable that one point on the continuum would represent an attempt at organization that tries to classify pupils (for the purpose of instruction) who display a relatively high degree of similarity of needs in reference to the skills or subject areas. This is an alteration of the heterogeneous, self-contained classroom as we know it.

Another point along the continuum may represent heterogeneous classroom organizations where children are assigned to their classrooms randomly, or on the basis of obvious dissimilarity even though the ages may be the same. In this classroom the opportunity to reassign children for part of the day into "look-alike" learning groups offers a certain control of the heterogeneity; and for part of a day children are together because of a high degree of similarity in regard to certain factors that affect learning, for example, in the areas of reading or math.

Organization represented by points on the left side of the continuum are primarily intraclass grouping procedures. Pupils are divided into instructional groups within a given class, based on the diagnosis and the inventories that show their educational status. Grouping used to be synonymous with the term *grading*, but as the term *grade* and the definition of *grade* plummet into disrepute as being nondescript and nonscientific, grouping as an activity transcends the concept of grade. The process used in developing and collecting data from inventories and observations to determine what set of learners should constitute a group for instructional purposes, shapes the organizational practices of a school. The more creative and prescriptive an educator becomes, the more definitively he will move from the far left point of the continuum to the right side (no pun intended) and toward the breakdown of the self-contained classroom, to the reassignment of children and of teachers in order to heighten the opportunities to achieve the ultimate organization that underpins programs of individualization.

One cannot carefully trace the whole process that one needs to go through. It is not always linear but reflects various factors of concern, commitment, and creativity. There are always several variables involved in grouping. It is not clear to us, at this particular writing, whether a school needs to go through all the possible steps in attempting to achieve individualization. In fact, one could say it is difficult to establish whether there are a definite number of steps that have to be gone through.

For example, we were able in several school systems to effect a change that moved from a very conventional self-contained classroom setup of chronologically aged pupils to the innovative establishment of two teams of teachers, one for language arts and one for math and science. The teachers in this new organization no longer taught all the subjects of the school day as they did previously, but only those subjects they wanted to specialize in. They had groups assigned to them for those subject areas to a much greater extent and in larger numbers than they would ever have dealt with in a self-contained classroom.

It is difficult, possibly incorrect, to say that before moving into the intensified activity of diagnosis and prescription required for individualization of instruction, along with the kinds of activity and functions required, that a school staff ought first to go through an activity where the self-contained classroom is de-emphasized and the teacher becomes a member of a team that is responsible for only part of the curriculum. What can be said, however, is that education must deliberately *start to move out of the self-contained classroom* if the desire is to achieve a nonrestrictive organization that can facilitate in developing the themes of continuous-progress, nongraded individualized instruction.

We have a fundamental opposition to several kinds of grouping and find support in the research for this opposition. For example, multi-age, heterogeneous classrooms have in many ways put a fantastic burden on the teacher, to the point that the impossibility of diagnosing and prescribing has resulted in a chaotic educational situation. Additionally, self-contained classrooms based on diagnosed homogeneity of reading ability very often create a kind of singlemindedness in the teacher which obscures real insight into individual differences and lulls him into the feeling that homogeneity in one area means homogeneity in other areas. This diminishes educational input as well as the opportunity for children to grow. There are other organizational activities that seem to support this seeking after a never-never-land of homogeneity and that counteract the desired goal of achieving the point on the right side on the continuum that represents heightened individuality.

Reports from the field indicate that continuous-progress, nongraded programs using alternative and adaptive organizational vehicles that go beyond the self-contained classroom, and that narrow the range of levels within a learning area, allow excellent teachers to become superior, good teachers to become excellent, and ordinary teachers to perform far better than they did before. This indicates to a great degree that continuous-progress, nongraded education is in many ways still true to the original but limited conception of it: that it is fundamentally an organizational situation rather than a far-reaching program of change.

But one could be trapped by that particular statement if he did not consider that organization allows a teacher to become better only if he becomes better at doing something. And the something that he is doing, of course, relates to the teaching of a curriculum in a more precise way so that an enhancement of learning takes place.

This underpins the major concept of the organizational continuum: toward the right-hand side there is a kind of organizational orientation that allows teachers to teach to their strengths in various subject-matter areas and accept assignments of students based on their diagnosed needs. It suggests to us a need for the implementation of teaching teams in the areas of reading, or the larger area of language arts (using social studies contextually to teach the skills of those areas), and math and science.

When a school has carefully created sequences in areas that lend themselves to specific sequencing and can be organized in a fashion other than by grades, developed a diagnostic system that relates to that sequence, and created a learning developmental inventory that screens out elements of the diagnosis in order to establish the precise status of the learner, it then moves to develop an organizational condition to support that growth of the continuous-progress, nongraded program.

Continuous-progress, nongraded educational programs and schools require an overall organizational framework that permits a program of flexible grouping procedures and teacher use that allows for the maintenance of programs, where each experience a child has is appropriate for him, and produces a positive response for the time he spends in getting an education. The organization encourages continuous-progress for each child, individually or in look-alike groups, based on a careful diagnosis. It allows for alternatives for the placement of a child who does not show that he is profiting from his present educational placement. Chronological placement is replaced by a program that uses a broadened class base from which the assignment of children creates a situation in which the levels in any class constitute a narrower range of learning-spread in that nongraded area. Multi-age grouping is an emergent, natural situation.

Whatever the general alteration of the concept of the self-contained classroom is, it varies, but in general it is an amalgamation of various kinds of multi-age grouping procedures, teacher teams, and agreed-upon time schedules for curriculum offerings. It allows for greater sophistication in assignment, grouping activities, and flexibility, to the degree that it is obvious the needs of children are paramount and changes can be made to meet those needs.

It should be noted that frequently flexibility may be enhanced or restrained by the school plant. Older buildings, egg-crate in structure, should not stand in the way of developing organized flexibility. There is a growing movement in educational architecture identified as open-planned school construction. The techniques and necessary arrangements for open-plan teaching and organization are compatible with the whole idea of the organization stated above. Open-plan teaching requires that there be varying kinds of grouping procedures. When open-plan schools have been constructed, but preparation for open-plan teaching has not been made, teachers have managed to create self-contained stations that are reminiscent of the self-contained classroom with its four surrounding walls. As in conventional buildings, open-plan buildings can reflect many educational situations. Even without walls, activities can range from those of the simple self-contained classroom type to the wholly innovated, team-planned and collaboratively taught programs based on an organized broadened basis.

Experiences, the growing body of descriptive narrative literature, and the empirical evidence concerning the adaptation of organization have led us to adopt a set of guidelines aimed at bringing teachers together so they can meet and plan on a regular basis during the school day.

There are several ways that this can be achieved. The fundamental purpose of collaborative teacher planning is the need for teachers to come together, to become decision makers, to develop the goals and strategies of teaching as well as the ways of evaluating children so that they can realistically create the kinds of approaches and assignments that meet specific learning needs. One way of doing this is to create a program in which teachers are teamed horizontally. Teachers of music, art, social studies, math, reading, science, and other areas team up in a horizontal arrangement. Unfortunately, from our observations it seems that too much time is spent in programs such as this in defining roles. Teachers in horizontal teams display a vested interest in their own subject-matter content. They frequently get into discussions that prevent them from focusing on the things they ought to be doing, or on the areas that concern the education of children. The horizontal team approach requires skilled leaders who know the dynamics of group rela-

tionships and can lead teachers in discussing the areas or the kinds of alternatives that need to be addressed.

Another form of teaming is vertical team organization. In it the attempt is to team for the purposes of teaching skills and concepts. It requires envisioning curricula (or substantive content) as vehicular in organization. Rather than seeking the goal of maintaining subject-matter integrity, skills are taught through subject matter. The vested interest is in teaching a child the materials, concepts, or skills at the point where he is, rather than plying him with subject-matter content per se as frequently happens in a horizontally teamed program. When organization is vertically teamed, it works across grade levels and each child begins at the skill level where he functions satisfactorily. Vertically, teams are able to move a child from one instructional situation to another without deep concern about the kinds of content that he has to be involved in. In the vertical team approach, the *process* becomes the more important element. Rather than focusing on content only, content is continuously reconstructed, torn apart, reconstituted, and tailored to meet the individual needs of the children, based on the diagnosis and prescription for learning. The grouping to meet these needs requires both pupil and teacher assignment into skill-level groups where the spans of differences are accommodated by narrowing the range of abilities within any given level.

The question immediately arises: Is it necessary to team in order to be successful at nongrading? The answer is no. But again we must reflect on a concept developed earlier in this chapter—that teacher teaming liberates teachers to a greater degree of flexibility than they could have in a nonteamed, noncollaborative atmosphere. So the point is, getting people together can very much enhance the educational program if they develop the kinds of techniques, interaction, and planning that focuses on the desired ends of continuous-progress education and leads to increased individualization and learning. The education of children is far too important to be allowed to remain in self-contained classroom rivalries. Much can be accomplished for children by teacher collaboration and the resultant multi-adult exposure in learning.

How does one move to these kinds of organizations and what kinds of schema can be established in which they can take place? One way is to look at a school with eight teachers who wanted to move in this direction (see figures 5-1, 5-2, and 5-3). We asked the teachers if they would like to move out of their self-contained classrooms and try an innovated organizational form. We demonstrated the preparation and the activities attendant to a form of team approach and the manner in which it could offer fundamental opportunities. We indicated that another advantage would be the provision for time within the school day to plan and to see demonstrations of materials as well as to spend time in the development of activities of learning.

The question then became: How do you move to a situation where you can achieve this planning *every* day within the school day? The decision was made that four teachers would teach the language arts, reading, and social studies (see figures 5-1, 5-2, and 5-3). A look at the schedule will show that these sections are identified as 1-1, 1-2, 1-3, and 1-4. This is an administrative tool to show where the sections are and to keep track of them as people are moved from place to place throughout a day. Eight teachers are programmed within this innovative schedule—four in language arts, reading, and social studies, and four in the math and science area. The specialist teachers in the

building are assigned at various times so that each of the two teams of four can be released for four out of five school days for a planning session.

Children come to school at 8:45. They go to a homeroom for a homebase period. The eight sections—1-1, 1-2, 1-3, and 1-4 in language arts, social studies, and reading, and 1-5, 1-6, 1-7, and 1-8 in science and math—represent approximately 220 pupils. The morning and afternoon programs were interchanged or substitutions were provided. For example, in the language arts, reading, and social studies schedule, there are slightly over 100 children in the morning and the same number in the afternoon, or approximately 220 children in all. Four teachers teach the language arts, reading, and social studies to these 220 children, half of them in the morning and the other half in the afternoon. Four other teachers teach the same children math and science, half of them in the morning and the other half in the afternoon. Each of the four teachers works within a large block of time. In the morning for language arts, reading, and social studies the teacher had a two-hour block of teaching time, and an equal amount of time in the afternoon. In the morning between 9:00 and 9:40 each teacher had an opportunity to plan. The whole team of four teachers met three days a week (Tuesday through Thursday). On the other days, Monday and/or Friday, two teachers met with their homebase groups and two met with the instructional specialists. By using this approach, four planning sessions per week were afforded. After the nine o'clock planning session, all teachers returned to their own homerooms. Half of the 220 pupils were then assigned to them by levels. The team of four teachers taught language arts, social studies, and reading in the two-hour block of time. Each of the four teachers in that team was teaching a set of specific levels within his classroom. The levels they started out with

Figure 5-1 READING, LANGUAGE ARTS, AND SOCIAL STUDIES
COLLABORATIVE TEACHING–PLANNING TEAM

	Teacher A Section 1-1	Teacher B Section 1-2	Teacher C Section 1-3	Teacher D Section 1-4
8:45 to 9:00	Homebase 1-1	Homebase 1-2	Homebase 1-3	Homebase 1-4
9:00 to 9:40	Mon.: Specialist T.W.T.: Team Planning Fri.: with 1-1 Home- base Group	Mon.: Specialist T.W.T.: Team Planning Fri.: with 1-2 Home- base Group	Mon.: Homebase Group with 1-3 T.W.T.: Team Planning Fri.: Specialist	Mon.: Homebase Group with 1-4 T.W.T.: Team Planning Fri.: Specialist
9:40 to 11:40	Large Block of Time Sections 1-1, 1-2, 1-3, 1-4 (in Diagnosed Assigned Levels) Reading, Language Arts, and Social Studies			
11:45	Dismissal	Dismissal	Dismissal	Dismissal
LUNCH				
1:00 to 3:00	Large Block of Time Sections 1-5, 1-6, 1-7, 1-8 (in Diagnosed Assigned Levels) Reading, Language Arts, and Social Studies			
3:00 to 3:15	1-1 with Homebase Teacher	1-2 with Homebase Teacher	1-3 with Homebase Teacher	1-4 with Homebase Teacher
3:15	Dismissal	Dismissal	Dismissal	Dismissal

Figure 5-2 MATH – SCIENCE COLLABORATIVE TEACHING–PLANNING TEAM

	Teacher E Section 1-5	Teacher F Section 1-6	Teacher G Section 1-7	Teacher H Section 1-8
8:45 to 9:00	Homebase 1-5	Homebase 1-6	Homebase 1-7	Homebase 1-8
9:00 to 10:40	Large Block of Time Sections 1-5, 1-6, 1-7, 1-8 (in Diagnosed Assigned Levels) Math and Science			
10:40 to 11:00	Mon.: Specialist T.W.T.: Team Planning Fri.: Homebase Group with 1-5	Mon.: Specialist T.W.T.: Team Planning Fri.: Homebase Group with 1-6	Mon.: Homebase Group with 1-7 T.W.T.: Team Planning Fri.: Specialist	Mon.: Homebase Group with 1-8 T.W.T.: Team Planning Fri.: Specialist
11:00 to 11:45	Homebase Group Mon., Wed., Thurs., Fri., with 1-5	Homebase Group Mon., Wed., Thurs., Fri., with 1-6	Homebase Group Tues., Thurs., Fri., with 1-7	Homebase Group Wed., Thurs., Fri. with 1-8
	Tues.: Prepare Independent Work, Worksheets, etc., for Math Team.	Wed.: Prepare Independent Work, Worksheets, etc., for Math Team.	Mon., Wed.: Prepare Science Material and Equipment for Science Team.	Mon., Tues.: Coordinate A-V Services; Equip., Film, etc. for School. Prepare A-V Material, etc. for Math-Science.
11:45	Dismissal	Dismissal	Dismissal	Dismissal
LUNCH				
1:00 to 2:20	Large Block of Time Sections 1-1, 1-2, 1-3, 1-4 (in Diagnosed Assigned Levels) Math and Science			
2:20 to 3:00	Homebase Mon., Wed., Thurs., Fri., with 1-5	Homebase Mon., Tues., Thurs., Fri., with 1-6	Homebase Tues., Thurs., Fri., with 1-7	Homebase Wed., Thurs., Fri. with 1-8
	Tues.: Prepare Independent Work, Worksheets, etc., for Math Team.	Wed.: Prepare Independent Work, Worksheets, etc., for Math Team.	Mon., Wed.: Prepare Science Material and Equipment for Science Team.	Mon., Tues.: Coordinate A-V Services, Equip., Films, etc. for School. Prepare A-V Materials, etc. for Math-Science.
3:00 to 3:15	Homebase 1-5	Homebase 1-6	Homebase 1-7	Homebase 1-8
3:15	Dismissal	Dismissal	Dismissal	Dismissal

Figure 5-3 MASTER SCHEDULE OF CLASS SECTION ASSIGNMENT
FOR COLLABORATIVE PLANNING TIME

	Assembly	*Art*	*Music*	*Library*	*Rhythms*	*Speech*
9:00 to 9:40	Tues. 1-1, 1-4 Wed. 1-2, 1-3	Mon., Wed. 1-1 Tues., Thurs. 1-2 Fri. 1-4	Mon. 1-2 Thurs. 1-1 Fri. 1-3	Tues. 1-3 Wed. 1-4	Thurs. 1-4	Fri. 1-3
9:40 to 10:20	Service to Other School Groups					
10:20 to 11:00	Tues. 1-5, 1-8 Wed. 1-6, 1-7	Mon., Wed. 1-5 Tues., Thurs. 1-6 Fri. 1-8	Mon. 1-6 Thurs. 1-5 Fri. 1-7	Tues. 1-7 Wed. 1-8	Thurs. 1-8	Fri. 1-7
11:00 to 11:40		Mon., Wed. 1-7 Tues. 1-8	Mon. 1-8	Tues. 1-5 Wed. 1-6		
1:00 to 1:40	Specialist Service to Other School Groups					
1:40 to 2:20						
2:20 to 3:00		Mon., Wed. 1-3 Tues. 1-4	Mon. 1-4	Tues. 1-1 Wed. 1-2		

initially were drawn from their homebase groups, so that there was very little movement in the morning except by children as they moved from one level to the next within the group.

Much was accomplished with this situation. By having children for two hours for three subject areas it was possible to work with them in a semi-self-contained situation. When the teachers became more secure, the four-member team regrouped in various ways with the 100 children. Any time these teachers wanted to carry on activities together, they did so. Out of team planning this coordinate teacher activity was nurtured. At noon the children were dismissed. When they returned in the afternoon, the team of teachers of language arts, reading, and social studies again had their large two-hour block of time. They taught the children who had had math and science in the morning.

These same kinds of opportunities were afforded the math and science team. The most important aspect of this kind of assignment is the master teachers' schedule. Two times a week the art teacher went to classrooms and worked with the children so the teachers were free to plan. The same kind of schedule was set up with the music specialists. Teachers were also freed to plan when pupils went to an assembly, to the library, or to physical education. A similar schedule and organization operated for the math-science team, with the exception that the math-science team was using a smaller block of time and was therefore free to plan activities and items for the whole team in an additional planning time. At 10:40 the math teachers met in the planning session. They were teaching from 9:00 to 10:40 in their own large block of time. With the children being assigned to some other place in the school the opportunity to free teachers to plan becomes obvious. Of course it requires specialist resources to do this, and the question needs to be asked: How can one achieve this without the number of specialists that were available in this situation? There are several ways to do this, wholly, or at least partially.

One possible and very probable approach is to provide professional days on which pupils are allowed to go home early. Another way is to volunteer as a team and meet briefly after school two or three times a week. As Chadwick and Anderson point out:

"There never was sufficient time for planning....However, one rather ingenious solution did evolve....All children (were) instructed to arrive at school at 9:10 A.M. on Mondays by contrast with the customary arrival time of 8:30. The time thus lost was to be made up by shortening the lunch hour on Mondays and Wednesdays by 20 minutes. This arrangement... allowed teachers to spend 8:10 to 9:00 each Monday with staff meetings in which schedule coordination and general planning were possible. One incidental benefit was that the earlier afternoon start gave the afternoon kindergarten an extra 20 minutes of class time per week, thus partially correcting the imbalance that often characterizes morning versus afternoon kindergarten programs. The success of this arrangement and the ease with which children adjusted to a timetable that varied day by day, gives rise to speculation and encouragement as to the ultimate feasibility of differentiated schedules for young children, not only day by day but child by child! Not a single parent complained when the time change took place."[1]

We found another ingenious situation for creating planning time, devised by a principal with a desire to move a nongraded team into action. His primary department was made up of a first, a second, and a third grade. They came together as a broadly based multi-aged vertical team in a continuous-progress, nongraded approach. The sequences were created, diagnostic material developed, and the inventories established, but literally out of the teachers' hides, because no planning time was available. However, the principal offered to take the three classes in physical education, for at least a forty-minute period three days a week, thus freeing the teachers to plan. They were able through that planning time to establish programs and activities, develop procedures, revise sequences, and generally deal with those concerns that enhanced the educational program to a very great degree.

Another way of creating opportunity for planning can be seen in a school that is open-plan in structure and, as a result, has a built-in supervisory activity. In the open plan, children are set off in individualized approaches to education. The teachers can pull away into areas where they are physically present but unavailable by agreement. In the open classroom, pupils pursue either generalized activities or their own individualized activities. At either end of this type of setting there are two offices—one is the principal's and the other the audiovisual coordinator's office. These two people are, at a given time during the day, both present in their offices with doors open so that they can oversee the learning activities as well as be available to pupils while the teachers have a planning session. A school with this kind of orientation and administration is very child-centered and displays a cohesiveness of purpose. Education is purposeful and relevant, and the setting and the open space add to the program.

Still another way of establishing planning time is to develop paraprofessionals so that they can serve in such a way that teachers are free at specified times during the day to plan.

We have characterized the kind of teaming and planning program that splits the school day into reciprocal halves as "flip-flop" grouping. The morning session flips over and becomes the afternoon session, and the afternoon session flips over and becomes the morning session for each of two groups or teams of teachers. Figure 5-4 indicates a way that this was achieved using two uneven teams, one in reading and language arts, and the other in math, science, and social studies.

Continuous-progress education requires a great deal of flexible grouping. Team teaching or team planning or any form of collaboration likewise requires a great deal of adaptability. Opportunities for increasing flexibility are created by adding certain features to an ongoing program. By adding the concept of pupil teaming and team learning, opportunities for individualization and educational appropriateness are greatly increased. Pupil team learning creates opportunities for individualization in several ways. In such programs children involve themselves in many activities. They organize materials, make presentations to one another, check each other's work, become in a sense creative specialists, serve as curriculum resource people in a variety of the classroom topics, and become tutors to other children.

However, the ultimate in continuous progress may be reached when educators move toward a program where individual contract learning is achieved. This allows for a heavy emphasis on individualized learning. Contracts are entered into by pupil and teacher. They are endorsed to meet specific needs and are used to carefully coordinate the diverse elements of curriculum activities. Various kinds of contracts can be arranged to develop content and activities. They can be highly innovative and process-oriented as well as oriented toward developing insights and knowledge concerning subject-matter material.

It is interesting to note that literature about current grouping in elementary education reveals that there has been no defense of the self-contained classroom by any reputable scholar. Rather, most of the material in scholarly journals discusses viable alternatives to such single-purposed orientation and organization. To adhere to the self-contained classroom organization seems a rather dangerous commitment when one admits that education and behavior can be addressed in a much more scientific manner. In view of the present situation, one can almost say that multi-age intergrade grouping procedures that were in evidence during the era of the one-room schoolhouse now return to the scene in a new scientifically supported form, and the self-contained classroom that was the major organizational program for the past several generations has persisted into a scientific arena of time that shows it to be unequivocally the least imaginative of the many approaches that could be created. It is almost impossible for teachers to be omnicompetent to do the kind of job required in this highly complex society when called on to teach equally well all areas of the curriculum.

Recently a group of teachers, evaluating what they were doing in their self-contained classrooms, came up mathematically with the evidence that made them the only group in the

Figure 5-4   ORGANIZATIONAL PATTERN: AN EXAMPLE

Time	*Team A Five Teachers*					*Team B Four Teachers*					Partial Teaming
	M	T	W	Th	F	M	T	W	Th	F	
8:30–8:45	Opening Activities and Reassignment					To Reading and Math Levels					Reading Specialist
8:45	Reading and Language Arts					Mathematics					A.M. Kindergarten 200 minutes Reassign as ready
						Health, Science, and Social Studies		Art	Health, Science, and Social Studies		
10:45						Music					
10:45	Recess									Recess	
10:55		Group Planning Team A		Physical Education		Physical Education		Group Planning Team B			
11:20	Lit.			Story Time		Story Time				Lit.	
11:30 12:15	Lunch Break					Lunch Break					
12:15 2:15	Repeat morning reading and language-arts program for Team B pupils.					Repeat morning math, science, art, and social-studies program for Team A pupils.					P.M. Kindergarten 200 minutes Reassign as ready
						Music					
2:30	Dismissal					Dismissal					
4:00	Team Planning			Ls. 1 ESL Ls. 1-2 Ls. 3-4 Ls. 5-6 Ls. 6-7-8		Team Planning					

world that was able to teach six hours in a five-hour day. But when the realities of what they were doing were opened to inspection it became obvious they were having trouble even squeezing five hours into a five-hour day. Much of the five hours was coverage, not education. When they moved to a reorganization, differentiated teach-er roles developed; teachers were reassigned according to their desired teaching activities, and a vastly different picture emerged.

The continuous-progress, nongraded school that considers the above suggestion in its development becomes a school where children are involved in a sequence that is based on continuous progress, is nongraded, and allows for un-hampered progress based on diagnostic and prescriptive needs. It is a school where horizontal grouping and vertical teaming practices are used so individual flexibility can be maintained. It is a school where for the sake of teaching economy and for focal point impact, the heterogeneity is controlled. It is a school where teachers work as a team to become decision makers, so that they can coordinate their efforts and collaborate in their planning to create greater opportunities both for themselves and for their pupils.

Under proper supervision, continuous progress for learners of vastly different abilities is capitalized on. Arrangement of classes is such that it encourages various sized groupings. There are independent study areas. There are completely open areas to serve the obvious need for inter-action and continuous growth.

In the presently innovated school, the everyday idioms that related to the self-contained classrooms are altered. As grade delineations that make vertical progress disintegrate, and individualization and individual progress become the key factors of organization, teachers deal with new vocabularies that are aimed at focusing on the child in a much more sophisticated and process-oriented way.

Several additional innovated schedules and discussions follow that broadly cover the continuum on school organization from adaptive self-containment to completely individualized approaches. Each administrator must find for himself and his teachers the spot where they are on this continuum. If he agrees that the most ideal situation to achieve is a collaboratively developed, individualized program of multi-age children working singly or in groups, and if he presently operates at a self-contained classroom level where one area of the curriculum has been sequenced and the move toward a nongraded program is tentative, then he knows the job that is cut out for him and the manner by which he

needs to proceed. He then moves his school to a point where the actual learning revolves around the student himself. In order to do this he must create an organization that is sympathetic to that point of view. It must liberate teachers in such a way that they can select various approaches from the many possibilities of activity open to them because of new found flexibility. In a word, the educator needs to adopt organizational means that insure flexibility to implement the objectives discussed. Figure 5-5 represents a master teacher schedule aimed at developing flexibility.

It was used to initiate change and to move toward a nongraded, continuous-progress program in the Nishuane Elementary School, Montclair, New Jersey. The strategy was to develop a flexible schedule that could be implemented without developing feelings of inadequacy in the teachers because of unfamiliarity with the procedures. This change was stimulated when Nishuane School was integrating 125 fifth- and sixth-grade pupils from an all-white, upper middle class school with a similar group in the then predominantly black Nishuane School. In a sense the staff developed a school organization, and some educational concepts for fifth and sixth that were different from those of kindergarten through fourth grade. This created a school within a school—each with its own organization.

The four-column headings labeled Math-Science indicate a math-science team of four teachers. Note under each heading boxes that designate which subjects a teacher is teaching. Where two or more boxes are labeled Math the team may group or regroup the children in math in any way they wish, depending on the diagnosed needs of the children. The same applies to science. Note also that a teacher has math and science "back to back." This is a technique for creating a large block of time for math and science for a group. It may be from eighty to a hundred minutes depending on the time felt necessary for these learning areas.

Figure 5-5   MASTER TEACHER SCHEDULE

Period	Math – Science	Math – Science	Math – Science	Math – Science	Lang. Arts, Reading, S.S.	Lang. Arts, Reading, S.S.	Lang. Arts, Reading, S.S.	Lang. Arts, Reading, S.S.
1	Administrative Supervisory Duties	Supervise Ind. Study	Math	Math	Team Planning for Fifth-Grade Team		L.A.	L.A.
2	Team Planning				Read	Read	Team Planning for Sixth-Grade Team	
3	Math	Science	Science	Science	L.A.	L.A.	Read	Read
4	Supervise Ind. Study	Science	Supervise Ind. Study	Math	S.S.	S.S.	S.S.	S.S.
	Lunch	Lunch	Lunch	Lunch	Lunch	Lunch	Lunch	Lunch
5	Math	Math	Math	Science	Supervise	Supervise	Read	Read
6	Science	Science	Science	Science	To Asst. Team for Regroup into Smaller Groups	To Asst. Team for Regroup into Smaller Groups	L.A.	L.A.
7	Math	Math	Science	Math	To Asst. Team for Regroup into Smaller Groups	To Asst. Team for Regroup into Smaller Groups	S.S.	S.S.
8	Activity Dismissal	Activity Dismissal	Activity Dismissal	Activity Dismissal	Activity Dismissal	Activity Dismissal	Activity Dismissal	Activity Dismissal

The numbers (1–8) represent the eight time modules, of forty minutes each, of the school day. Thus a math-science block equals eighty minutes. All four teachers on the math-science team are free everyday to plan during the second forty-minute time module. The intention of the schedule was to have one teacher teach the same group math and science. This was not possible for all groups due to problems of logistics: the desire to have the team leader assist and supervise the team, and to have teachers supervise the independent study of pupils in math and science. These four teachers were able to deal with approximately 250 pupils, plan the learning experiences more precisely and qualitatively, have more time for learning activities that need not be stopped at the end of thirty or forty minutes, and have opportunities for grouping or regrouping children for precise needs.

On the schedule six columns are headed Language Arts, Reading and Social Studies. Three teachers are designated as a fifth-grade team, and three as a sixth-grade team. During the first time module, the fifth-grade team is free to plan. The sixth-grade team is free to meet and plan during the third time module. Grade designation for these teams gives the teachers a feeling of adequacy and security, because it represents a procedure acceptable to them that is not too "far out."

However, in the second time module for the teachers of language arts, reading, and social studies, every teacher is scheduled for reading. This allows the teacher to "baffle out" the grade designation and gradedness as a reality in reading. The procedure was to give a diagnostic inventory that had been developed on the basis of a learning sequence that was acceptable to all the teachers. Following an analysis and inventory of learning status and recognition of strengths and weaknesses, the six teachers grouped children according to level of performance. Thus, for reading, all children who were look-alikes in strengths and weaknesses related to reading skills and concepts were placed in the same group. Because all reading groups were meeting at the same time, children were able to be moved from group to group on the basis of readiness to attack higher levels of learning competencies in the use of the reading skills. Each teacher taught a specific level of reading development. As children became competent in a specific level and as they moved to higher levels and there ceased to be any who were operating at the level a teacher was previously teaching, that teacher assumed the teaching of skills, concepts, and content on the next level. This gave teachers a great deal of flexibility in meeting the precise needs of children and in being able to move them along as rapidly as possible according to each child's learning rate.

Those children who were the responsibility of the fifth-grade team moved back to their homeroom teachers for the third and fourth module of time for language arts and social studies. The schedule shows that the three groups that made up the language-arts and social-studies team met at these times. The team was able to group and regroup these classes in any manner the teachers decided—that is, for special skills, projects, large and small group instruction, and so forth. The large block of time was broken up for the sixth-grade team for their planning module.

When children are not with a teacher who is in team planning, they are with other teachers in art, music, drama, independent study, the instructional-materials center, or physical education.

Time modules 5, 6, 7, and 8 occur after lunch. In the afternoon, both the fifth- and sixth-grade teams have unbroken blocks of time for language arts, reading, and social studies. In reading the procedure is the same as in the morning. Instead of six teachers for six reading groups, six teachers handle four reading groups; thus class size is controlled and made much smaller, or two teachers are released to work on specific tasks, decided on by the teams.

Figure 5-6 is a class or group schedule. At the top of each column the teacher, room, and class

Figure 5-6 CLASS OR GROUP SCHEDULE

HR	Able 210–5th	Baker 205–5th	Charley 209–5th	David 203–5th	Edwards 211–5th	Frank 201–6th	Grant 208–6th	Henry 206–6th	Ivan 202–6th	Jacks 207–6th
1	M.W. B.Gym T.Th. B. Study 202 T.Th. G.Gym F. Study 202	M.W. B.Gym T.Th. B. Study 202 T.Th. G.Gym F. Drama	M.W. B.Gym T.Th. B Study 202 T.Th. G.Gym F. Library	Math 203	Math 205	L.A. 207	L.A. 208	L.A. 206	M.F. Music T.W. Art Th. Library	T.W. Music M.F. Art Th. Drama
2	Reading 210	Reading 209	Reading 211	M.F. Music T.W. Art Th. Drama	T.W. Music M.F. Art Th. Library	Reading 207	Reading 208	Reading 206	M.W. B.Gym T.Th. B.Study.Lib. T.Th. G.Gym M.W. G.Study.Lib. F. Drama	M.W. B.Gym T.Th. B.Study.Lib. T.Th. G.Gym M.W. G.Study.Lib. F. Library
3	L.A. 210	L.A. 209	L.A. 211	Science 203	Science 205	M.W. G.Gym T.Th. B.Study T.Th. G.Gym M.W. G.Study 204 F. Library	M.W. B.Gym T.Th. B.Study T.Th. G.Gym M.W. G.Study 204 F. Study	M.W. B.Gym T.Th. B.Study T.Th. G.Gym M.W. G.Study 204 F. Drama	Math 202	Math 201
4	Social Studies 210	Social Studies 209	Social Studies 211	M.W. B.Gym T. B.Study,Art Th. B.Study 204 T.Th. G.Gym M.W. G.Study,Art F. Library	M.W. B.Gym T. B.Study,Art Th. B.Study 204 T.Th. G.Gym M.W. G.Study,Art F. Drama	Social Studies 207	Social Studies 208	Social Studies 206	Science 202	Science 205
5	Math 201	Math 202	Math 203	Reading 210	Reading 209	M.W. Music T.Th. Art F. Drama	M.W. Art T.Th. Music F. Library	Science 205	Reading 206	Reading 207
6	Science 203	Science 205	M.W. Art T.Th. Music F. Drama	L.A. 210	L.A. 209	Science 201	Science 202	M.W. Music T.Th. Art F. Library	L.A. 206	L.A. 207
7	M.W. Music T.Th. Art F. Drama	M.W. Art T.Th. Music F. Library	Science 203	Social Studies 210	Social Studies 210	Math 201	Math 202	Math 205	Social Studies 206	Social Studies 207
8	T.W.Th. Activities M. Library						F. Drama			

are indicated. Numerals 1 through 8 refer to the time modules. Each box shows location and subject of each class. For example, Miss Able's classroom, 210, is a fifth grade. Children in this classroom are scheduled as follows:

1st module:

Mon. and Wed.	Boys gym
Tues. and Thurs.	Boys supervised study
Tues. and Thurs.	Girls gym
Mon. and Wed.	Girls supervised study
Fri.	Boys and girls supervised study, room 202

2nd module:

Room 210 for reading. (Note that on the class schedule children are in homeroom 210. Initial placement in homeroom was on the basis of reading diagnosis.) Children are able to move to other reading groups when ready.

3rd and 4th module:

Room 210 for language arts. Child has same teacher for language arts, reading, and social studies. Child may eventually have a different teacher for reading, because he will be able to move to the next higher learning levels. He remains with the same teacher for language arts and social studies until fifth-grade team makes some decisions for regrouping children for large and small group instruction.

5th module:

Room 201 for math

6th module:

Room 203 for science. This is one of three groups that did not have same teacher for science and math. Math teacher was the team leader and taught only four classes.

7th module:

Mon. and Wed.	Room 204 for music
Tues. and Thurs.	Art
Fri.	Drama

8th module:

Mon. (only)	Library (instructional-materials center)
Tues., Wed., Thurs., Fri.	Activities

Note that most classes have two academic teachers during the school day. A class could have a third teacher when it moved to a new reading level, or a fourth teacher for science. Only three groups do not have the same teacher for math and science; thus these classes have one teacher for language arts and social studies, another teacher for math, and a different one for science.

Every child in the fifth and sixth grade, in addition to the academic learning area, has two modules a week of art, music, and physical education, and one module a week of drama. A child also could have two modules of activities a week during the eighth module of the school day. The other three modules were reserved for supervised or independent study. Children were given homework assignments that took an average pupil thirty minutes to complete. Homework was not assigned in more than two areas on any given day. No homework was assigned on Friday. Children, however, had individual or group projects that they worked on over the weekend.

The schedules represented by figures 5-5 and 5-6 are rudimentary and serve as beginnings in moving toward the reorganization of a school and in developing flexibility for a continuous-progress, nongraded program. Emphasis is on the improvement of the teaching-learning process through a change of organization. In these schedules no new teachers were added to the school staff. Ten self-contained classroom teachers were used in addition to an art teacher for three days a week, a full-time music teacher, a full-time librarian, a physical-education teacher for four half days a week, and a drama teacher for four half days a week. Without specialists or consultants, other devices would need to be used.

Figure 5-7 represents the kind of schedule that can be used without teacher specialists. This schedule has the same objectives as those in the schedule shown in figure 5-5. Because there are no teacher specialists available, teams of teachers cannot meet during school hours except as suggested by a few techniques discussed earlier.

In figure 5-7, columns headed "R" represent three readiness or kindergarten teachers and columns 1–10 and 1–9 represent nineteen classroom teachers, or twenty-two teachers in all. This schedule is used for the primary years but is easily adaptable for intermediate years.

There is a morning and an afternoon division of the schedule. Ten teachers teach reading, language arts, and art; nine teach math, social studies, science, music, and physical education in the morning.

Children are grouped according to fourteen learning levels in reading. The teachers using this schedule developed their own reading-learning sequence, diagnostic test, and screening device. They made a diagnostic analysis of all the chilren and grouped each according to his performance level.

Those teaching reading and language arts made ten reading groups for the morning according to the reading levels or stages of growth developed in their reading sequence. They also made ten reading groups for the afternoon. The math teachers converted the ten morning groups in reading into nine math groups and did the same for the ten afternoon reading groups. The schedule then operated in the following manner: ten groups to language arts-reading in the morning; nine to math, social studies, and science. In the afternoon the ten groups that went to reading

became the nine groups that had math. The nine groups that had math in the morning became the ten reading groups in the afternoon. This activity effectuated the following changes in approach:

1. Teachers no longer in self-contained classrooms
2. Teachers teaching two groups in two large blocks of time
3. In the morning a child could be moved to new group in reading and in math when ready
4. Child need not be with same group in math as in reading
5. Child could move as fast as his learning rate allowed and could be with several different groups in reading and math during school year
6. Learning sequences developed in reading and math effectively removed grade lines in all subjects
7. Teachers had time to focus on precise needs of children and development of quality in educational experience
8. Teacher teams were developed for groups of learners in reading and in math

This type of schedule gives much flexibility for grouping and regrouping of learners for precise needs without the use of subject specialists. One disadvantage in this schedule as related in figure 5-5 is that teachers cannot meet as teams during the school day. However, they can meet two or three days a week after school.

This schedule operated in a school that was predominantly non-English speaking. Sixteen English-as-a-second language (ESL) groups were established and each had one hour of instruction daily. The diagnosed reassignments vis-a-vis reading needs were highly correlated with the second language aptitudes of the pupils and made grouping and subsequent teaching more productive.

Unfortunately many teachers are not yet ready to leave the self-contained classroom.

Figure 5-7 SCHEDULE WITHOUT SPECIALISTS

	R 1	R 2	R 3	Reading—Language Arts											Math—Social Studies—Science								
				1	2	3	4	5	6	7	8	9	10		1	2	3	4	5	6	7	8	9
A.M.	1	2	3	ART (6 groups can be smaller groups for one hour)			Ten Groups			ESL One hour 4 Groups / One hour 4 Groups								Nine Groups MUSIC — PHYS. ED.						
								Lunch											Lunch				
P.M.	1	2	3	ART (6 groups can be smaller groups for one hour)						ESL One hour 4 Groups / One hour 4 Groups								MUSIC — PHYS. ED.						

Figure 5-8 shows an adaptation of the self-contained idea in a primary school made up of three readiness (kindergarten) teachers and nineteen classroom teachers. No teacher specialists were available, or needed, for this particular organization. In the primary years there were nine levels in the reading sequence developed by the teachers. Nineteen groups were organized into eight different levels. The kindergarten teachers worked with level I (readiness level).

Teachers had two and a half hours to devote solely to reading and language arts and supplemental experiences that reinforced the basic skills. They were able to provide quality educational experiences in this large block of time. It was possible to move a child to any reading level when he was ready for a higher-level group. Each child was able to move as fast or as slow as his learning rate would permit.

Teachers may develop teacher teams and be responsible for three or four groups of learners who are at a similar learning stage in reading and language arts. These teams can make decisions about the learning experiences and grouping of their pupils.

All the groups are initially assigned a homeroom teacher following a diagnostic analysis of each student in reading. A child may start out with his homeroom teacher but later move to other teachers for reading–language-arts experiences. He may have as many as three or four reading teachers during a school year. There are no grade designations for reading and language arts.

In the afternoon children return to their homeroom teacher for the remainder of the school day for math, social studies, and science. Art, music, and physical education are scheduled with the principal for either the morning or afternoon session. Thus each teacher teaches all the areas of the curriculum.

Figure 5-9 is similar to figures 5-7 and 5-8, with some adaptations. Many teachers want to teach all subject areas, but they also feel something must be done to individualize and differentiate instruction in realistic ways. The areas of math, reading, and language arts are critical in the primary and intermediate levels, especially in urban communities. If these basic skills are not mastered so that they can be used as tools to learn how to learn, then problems of remediation and the inability to achieve and receive satisfaction prevent many students from realizing success. The schedule in figure 5-9 satisfies teachers who want only limited differentiated teaching and are willing to make some changes. The several features it offers are:

1. It divides activities into morning and afternoon.

2. There are three kindergarten teachers and nineteen other classroom teachers. This organization serves a primary and an intermediate school. A "reading-learning sequence" that included language arts was developed into fourteen stages, from kindergarten through the seventh year of school. Eight stages of growth were for the primary, and the remaining six for the intermediate years. A math learning sequence was developed using the same concept.

3. The nineteen teachers who were previously in a kindergarten through third-grade organization grouped and regrouped their pupils on eight or nine levels of learning. Ordinarily these teachers could have, for example, three reading groups in a heterogeneous class. This would mean fifty-seven groups in reading. These groups would have nineteen groups of fast learners, nineteen of developmental learners, and nineteen slower learners. How economical, in terms of teaching and learning time, is this for quality of learning experience? We feel that making children competent in reading is a priority. Dealing with eight groups of look-alikes is more effective than dealing with fifty-seven groups.

Teachers working with the schedule in figure 5-9 have the flexibility to move a child easily from one level of performance to the next

Figure 5-8   AN ADAPTATION OF THE SELF-CONTAINED IDEA

Readiness or Kindergarten	Primary																		
3 Teachers	1	2	3	4	5	6	7	8	9	10	11	12	13	14	15	16	17	18	19
A.M. 2-1/2 hours	Reading and Language-Arts Levels Assigned to 19 Teachers																		
	Lunch																		
P.M. 2-1/2 hours	Mathematics, Science, and Social Studies Taught in Homerooms																		

Figure 5-9   A FLEXIBLE SCHEDULE

READINESS				PRIMARY — INTERMEDIATE																	
Teachers	1	2	3	1	2	3	4	5	6	7	8	9	10	11	12	13	14	15	16	17	18	19
A.M.	Reading–Language Arts 19 Groups Can Be Grouped by Levels Program for Reading — (Sequence Will Have Eight Levels) Math Can Group by Levels Developed by Math Sequence																					
	Lunch																					
P.M.	Social Studies–Science Art–Music–Phys. Ed.																					

higher one whenever the child is ready. There are several sections of any one stage of growth: six sections of level two, four sections of level three, three of level four, and so on. Teachers deal with the precise learner weaknesses and strengths as well as learning rates in reading and language arts because they are dealing with look-alikes. Thus teachers focus on what they must produce using a variety of ways to teach similar needs and to provide experiences in self-interest areas and the cooperative exploration of social problems.

4. Similar procedures and concepts are used for teaching math skills and concepts and for the reassignment of pupils and teachers. Some differences will be seen in the time module allowed for math, which is shorter than for reading and language arts. Teachers and the administration will decide on the module of time needed for each of the morning blocks.

5. In the afternoon section, social studies, science, the humanities, and physical education are taught by every teacher. These areas should be integrated with each other in dealing with social problems of the community, city, state, nation, and the world.

It must be kept in mind that the diagnostic and prescriptive approach underpins the strategy in teaching and learning. In the school organization suggested in figure 5-9, children are diagnosed for their strengths and weaknesses in the basic skills and are grouped initially in homerooms according to similarity of needs in reading and language arts. They are grouped and regrouped during the school year according to performance and readiness for new and more abstract learning activities. After two or three weeks, children are grouped in math on the basis of a diagnosis of their precise needs in skills and conceptualization. Activities are prescribed by teachers who teach at different skill levels. A child can be in a reading and language-arts stage different from the

one he is in in math. All children return to the homeroom teacher for the remainder of the day for social studies, science, the humanities, and physical education. When teachers are teamed and cooperatively make decisions concerning learning activities and are also responsible for particular groups of children, through cooperative interchange, activities can be developed for large and small group learning, along with differentiated tasks for each teacher. There are many teaching and grouping alternatives, depending on what teachers are ready for and capable of doing.

We contend that it is easy for people in education to conceptualize grand schemes of what good teaching and learning are, but it is quite another matter to carry them out or translate them into meaningful action. Many schools claim they individualize instruction in order to meet the needs of children; they say they provide differentiated teaching activities. However, from observation and evaluation of what is different in their teaching processes and in the experiences being given to children, one actually finds few real changes from the old systems. We feel that there are few basic changes because experienced teachers, and new teachers as well, are not trained for what is being theoretically proposed. The desire for educational change insists that the professional deal with reality. He must find ways to motivate teachers to try new techniques and assume new attitudes about the learning activities of children. Educators must still continue to change the teacher-education programs so that new teachers will be able to deal with new concepts of learning, with new technology of education, and with new learning-management techniques. We feel this cannot wait to happen in the schools of the future. Education must deal with the realities of today to make sure that children are able to use the basic skills competently to learn how to learn.

Any reorganizational practices that will simply let teachers do better that which they know how to do will be a worthy step. But reorganizational practices that will free teachers to deal with the realities of the pupil population, and make teachers aware of their own limitations in dealing with the realities of education may lead to a search for practices, programs, and perspectives that will enhance the whole educational tone. The development of organizational vehicles that provide opportunities to implement nongraded, continuous progress is essential. So too is the reporting of any such implementations.

RECORDING AND REPORTING

DEVELOPING APPROPRIATE, RELEVANT RECORD-KEEPING AND REPORTING SYSTEMS FOR CONTINUOUS-PROGRESS PROGRAMS

The report card in American education is in many ways the Frankenstein that was created by the educational profession. Many marking or grading systems were developed with a specificity that defies the imagination. Such excesses were seen in grades like 97½ in reading, or 68 in social studies. The adoption of the normal curve as the framework for the distribution of marks was also a roadway to delusion. As Bloom points out:

"There is nothing sacred about the normal curve. It is the distribution most appropriate to chance and random activity. Education is a purposeful activity and we seek to have the students learn what we have to teach. If we are effective in our instruction, the distribution of achievement should be very different from a normal curve. In fact we may even insist that our educational efforts have been *unsuccessful* to the extent to which our distribution of achievement approximates the normal distribution."[1]

The unreliability of teacher grading is well documented in educational literature. Unless report forms reveal distinct changes relating to the new educational setting that is suggested by continuous-progress, nongraded school orientations, it seems the whole arena of change is a contradictory one that may work against the greater enhancement of learning. Reporting should round out the total conceptualization of the kind of school programs we are advocating.

Continuous-progress, nongraded educational programs demand pertinent, appropriate, and relevant reporting and record-keeping systems consistent with the operationally defined sequences developed in the areas to be nongraded. Reporting and record-keeping systems mutually reinforce the educational orientation and become cumulative profiles of activities related to the diagnostic inventory and the learning developmental inventory.

Continuous-progress, nongraded schools require special kinds of reporting and different kinds of record keeping. They also require different kinds of correspondence and parent informational activities. We see education as the progressive development of an individual involved in the acquisition of many skills that will develop him to his most complete self-realization. To be able to mark or grade the extent of self-realization is an exercise in futility despite claims to the contrary. On the other hand, to be able to logically set down by descriptive statements a pupil's actual achievement in terms of learning outcomes is a reality that can be embraced.

Though there has long been a question concerning how, when, or whether we should revise our reporting systems, we feel that revision, if done without regard for school reorganization and curriculum development in general, is mere tinkering with the problem. It may only represent a way to get teachers off the hook and find excuses for failure to organize better education by showing, through revision of the reporting system, that various kinds of individuals exist, differences abound, and grades don't mean anything anyway. In many ways, report-card revision without school reorganization is an educational fabrication. If in actual fact a grade level doesn't exist, and if children do differ in abilities, competence, and learning rate and this is reflected on a revised report form, then how does one rationalize the elimination of the norma-tive marking system while still remaining within the graded structure? Nonetheless, to attack the existing system has always been difficult. It is still difficult in many places, not because of parents but because of teachers. There seems to be a constant desire on the part of many people in education to fit the child to the system rather than to create a system for the child. The point of view we have is that a serious and detrimental effect is imposed on the whole process of learning when a system of marking that uses symbols, such as A, B, C, D, E, and F, or percentages is employed rather than making an attempt to change to a system in which one can define, develop, and evaluate the true growth of the individual.

The nongraded continuous-progress school is based on the idea that continuous progress is not only available but is the organizing feature of that school. To accurately create a reflection of that activity, several things must be considered. The following areas seem relevant to the development of individual growth records that would help in revealing the progress of each child:

1. Knowledge of where a child is or at what level he operates presently.
2. Knowledge of what a child is ready for at the moment.
3. Knowledge of the quality of a child's performance in relation to his seeming ability to perform.
4. Knowledge of whether or not he is putting forth the kind of effort that reflects the kind of performance that can be expected of him.
5. Knowledge of his basic background.
6. Knowledge of his native endowment insofar as it can be ascertained.
7. A basic estimation of the starting point for a child in any given area of work.
8. Records of his previous history of achievement in relation to present achievement.

There are many forms that report cards can take, and any number of books carry forms or formats that seem pleasing to a host of varied groups of people. But it is not the format that is important, even though a pleasing format might help. Rather it is what is contained in the format. What is reported and in what form must of necessity reflect the ideational aspects of the program. This ideational area of agreement must be attained before the establishment of a system that will reveal progress and growth.

The continuous-progress, nongraded school sees process as the fundamental emphasis. This is different from content, which has been described as "a related body of facts, laws, theories, and generalizations, as in a traditional science course, or a description of events, as in a history course, or in any other predetermined arrangement of a particular segment of man's knowledge."[2]

Process on the other hand "can be associated with knowledge and with human activities." And process can also be described as encompassing those activities "for utilizing knowledge and communicating it (along with being) involved in arriving at decisions, evaluating consequences, and in accommodating new insights."[3] To grade realistically or assign marks to process involvement (a growing, dynamic, and frequently intuitive thing) is to court the disaster of trying to reach the never-never land.

Usually the schools develop programs where the taking and giving of examinations is the whole orientation. In such situations one frequently finds the desire of teachers is not really one of assessing the extent of learning that has taken place. Rather it is a program of building up a case for or against a pupil; to find out how badly off he is so parents can have that revealed to them in such a way that the teacher gets off the hook.

The reporting activities of most schools have become systematic programs that catalogue the student and help create situations that insist he fit into the system, or else. Report systems have imposed programs of conformity, so that students are forced either to fit the predetermined situations or face failure. For many years report systems have been created for the convenience of the instructor and the administration. Their purpose has not been one of revelation as much as one of obfuscation.

Without a new conceptualization of the school, without a basic intervention that leads to new directions, it becomes difficult to support some of the changes in marking procedures and basic grading programs. The reason for this is simple. Parents ask, and rightfully so, "Why, suddenly, do you want to change the grading system when nothing else is being changed?"

After all, it has taken educators almost a century and a half to fix firmly in the minds of parents the myth that accuracy has been achieved in the way they grade and mark. It has taken more than a hundred years to establish with professional intensity the fact that education organized in a graded fashion is beneficial. Now most of the studies reveal how wrong this may have been. Instead of trying to establish programs that eliminate the problems and strictures, and intervene in order to develop new systems, educators too frequently develop activities that serve as excuses for not coming to grips with the real problems. Reporting or report-card revision is an excellent case in point. Through new reporting forms and adaptations of an already archaic and educationally disreputable system they attempt to rationalize what is fundamentally an indefensible organization. So organization must change and reporting to parents likewise must change.

At this point we make the assumption that some agreement exists between the authors and the reader concerning the major objectives stated in the preceding chapters. Hopefully, the reader feels that these objectives are to be attained to varying degrees in varying ways in any movement toward continuous-progress, nongraded schools. The remainder of this chapter is a discussion of creating the means for informing parents of the progress their children are making within the newly achieved school context. Even though we feel the word *report*, as it concerns report cards, has now served its time historically and needs replacement, pragmatic considerations more or less insist that we use the term in trying to elaborate the movement from older to newer forms. This movement is not abrupt and may require gradations, as shown in figure 6-1.

It should be noted that the report form for relating pupil progress to parents is part of a larger record-keeping system. The system includes the following:

1. Individual pupil progress forms sent to parents whenever a child moves from one level to another in a nongraded area.

2. A periodic statement of status that relates the general progress of a child in the total schooling scheme (a report form).

3. Documents, simplistic in nature, that indicate movement of a child from level to level or assignment to assignment throughout the school year.

4. A cumulative record system with behaviors noted on checklists or profile statements that allow teachers a quick overview of an in-depth analysis of a child.

5. A guidebook relating to the above that explains the system, directed to teachers, parents, and the administration.

It is apparent from the many observations we have made concerning "models" that we do not have a *pure* model report and record system for a continuous-progress, nongraded school. Our contention is that there are no single models but rather various components that are relevant to the creation of continuous-progress, nongraded school report and record systems.

The development of systems for showing pupil progress and ways for relating such progress to parents are in an aspirational state. The ultimate is yet to be achieved. Crystalization of one model is an anathema rather than a help. It is wiser to establish clearly some of the components that need to be considered, and to suggest formats related to the concepts agreed upon.

Ruth Strang[4] has several relevant suggestions that are helpful in developing reporting systems. She indicates that parents, teachers, and pupils should study the problems cooperatively and involve as many of the specialists of the school personnel as possible. She suggests that improvement of marking and reporting begin with a study of the existing system. Reaction of the group to the usefulness of the information of the old form as compared to the stated objectives of a new program will be an important step in evaluating whether objectives are being

Figure 6-1   MOVEMENT OF REPORT-CARD FORMAT FROM OLD TO NEW

1 — Old forms adapted; marks or percentages in use

2 — Old form, some new terminology; some marks or qualitative words

3 — Combination of old and new items; no marks or percentages

4 — Adaptive new form; more checklist(s) of behavior-oriented material

5 — Ultimate new form; graphic measure of child's progress only

achieved or whether the teaching relation to these objectives should be reconsidered. Strang also indicates that a determination as to what marking and reporting should accomplish will arise out of a study of the present reporting system and the group discussions. This requires a host of decisions, since nongraded activities are based on sequential growth and therefore require a new method of annotation rather than the simplistic system of A through F, numerical, or percentage rankings. She suggests collecting some of the marking and reporting systems that have been employed by other schools. It is relatively simple now to get school systems to share this kind of item. Many educational texts in general methods have sample items and activities as well as formats of reporting.

The preparation of a preliminary form and setting up a way of getting a continuous feedback is the next step in the program. Then the form should be made available to representative groups, to pupils, teachers, parents, and the public so they can raise questions and indicate their feelings about it. This should lead to a revised and acceptable generalized form that can be used and accepted on a trial basis in terms of its strengths and weaknesses and its relevance in the whole area of reporting. Revisions based on these evaluations can then take place. Evaluation of whether educational objectives have been reached, whether information flow between the school and the parent has been enhanced, whether the revelation of the child's progress is fruitful and meaningful, and other concerns, will lead to a functional system of reporting.

Regardless of the ideas involved here which all may use to guide their efforts, the commonality of activity rarely leads to a single system that is the best for every type of school. The differences of philosophy attendant to the working out of continuous-progress programs will indicate various approaches and many and different

techniques will be needed. It seems obvious that the greatest possible participation of parents in all aspects of school life underpins successful school programs. We want to emphasize this as it concerns the changes necessary in developing an adequate system of reporting and record keeping: one that is relevant, precise, and appropriate in the whole arena of continuous-progress, nongraded schools; one that emphasizes the individualization and heightened personalization of inststruction and learning.

One of us, writing in a different context, has indicated that in his

"considerable experience in meeting with teacher groups throughout the United States concerning school organization, the nongraded school in particular and the attendant features of aspects of nongrading . . . he . . . found that many of the things . . . he speaks about seemingly received acceptance according to a scale that could be marked from *intensely ready acceptance* to almost absolute fear of acceptance. Toward the bottom of the scale at the level of *absolute fear of acceptance* the whole matter of reporting progress and report cards in general vis-a-vis nongrading can be placed. It is not that the teachers and the school administrators alike do not realize that there are better ways of reporting pupil progress. Rather it reflects the problems and intensity of feelings which are evoked that they have already experienced in situations concerning report card changes and other procedures of reporting the progress of pupils' work to the patrons of the schools—the parents."[5]

He felt that had other things been done, then the natural evolution of reporting to parents in a more meaningful way and the development of record keeping and evaluation forms would have been achieved in a far more receptive and responsive climate. The natural outgrowth (a new report card) of the attained objectives of innovative programs would have been more readily seen.

The irritation usually generated by confusion and lack of insight would have been minimized or eliminated altogether.

We suggest dealing with a combination of concerns in a somewhat linear fashion in developing directions toward nongraded, continuous-progress education. First, look back to the sequence and its development in chapter 2, the diagnostic inventory and its development in chapter 3, the learning developmental inventory and its relationship in chapter 4, and the suggested organizational schema discussed in chapter 5. A progressive kind of program becomes evident. Developing better, more relevant ways of reporting can also be seen as a progressive developmental program. The first new form can be one based on the sequence and issued to parents at any time a child moves from level to level within the program.

Figure 6-2 is a language-arts skill-development progress chart. The selected competencies described are drawn from a learning developmental sequence. Note that on the right side under Present Attainment a star represents level completed and a diamond the level of present work. This form is sent home at any time and may be retained by the parents. By reading from top to bottom, one can see the level of accomplishment a child achieves from beginning readiness to competence, the last level on the chart. Space to indicate a desire for a conference and for comments is included on the form.

Coupled with this progress report is the language-arts levels accomplishment permanent record card (figure 6-3). Each accomplishment level has page numbers that refer to the pages of the sequence that have been developed. Along with the date that the work was completed, the manner in which it was completed is recorded according to the code shown in the report. Space for notes or comments and the teacher's signature are included. A parent, on receipt of the progress report, can go to school and confer with the teacher, who has his copy of the progress report to use along with the permanent record card. Then parent and teacher can discuss in a meaningful way the extensiveness of the report, the progress of the child, and his relationship to other areas of the curriculum. This kind of cohesive, planned approach makes it possible for a parent to see more fully what a situation really is.

Figure 6-2   A LANGUAGE-ARTS PROGRAM OF CONTINUOUS-PROGRESS EDUCATION

Language-Arts Progress Chart: Levels I Through IV

(This progress report need not be returned. Any questions concerning your child's progress will be welcomed by his classroom teacher.)

☆ Level Completed   ◇ Level of Present Work

Level	Description of Selected Competencies	Present Attainment
I	The period of preparation in language development and reading. Learns to follow directions; reads pictures from left to right; listens to and recalls material; associates meanings with symbols; enunciates and pronounces clearly; distinguishes shapes and forms; and distinguishes differences in sounds.	
II	The initial experiences in language development. Learns to acquire and use sight words for reading; reads phrases; recognizes capital and lowercase letters; recognizes letters of the alphabet; recognizes words from context clues; identifies rhyming words; substitutes consonants and uses word form clues in reading; enjoys the reading activities and experiences.	
III	Creating the desire to discuss, talk, and read. Learns to select main ideas from a story; recalls and states a sequence of ideas; draws conclusions; uses context clues; substitutes initial and final consonants; uses configuration clues; uses word form clues; substitutes long and short medial vowels; recognizes digraphs and compound words.	
IV	The advanced language activities and reading in story books. Learns to read silently without lip movement; uses and reads longer units of material; uses phonetic analysis on unknown words using sight words as a base; uses structural analysis for prefixes, suffixes, and roots; and readily uses books for seeking information.	

Figure 6-2 A LANGUAGE-ARTS PROGRAM OF CONTINUOUS-PROGRESS
EDUCATION *(continued)*

Language-Arts Progress Chart: Levels V Through IX

(This progress report need not be returned. Any questions concerning
your child's progress will be welcomed by his classroom teacher.)

☆ Level Completed   ◇ Level of Present Work

Level	*Description of Selected Competencies*	*Present Attainment*
V	Steady growth in language arts and reading independence. Learns to read longer material; reads more critically; increases his rate of reading; reads with expressive skill; differentiates between a sentence and a line of print; uses phonetic and structural skills, the silent *e* rule and the vowel digraph principle; and shows increased skill in syllabification activities.	
VI	Sustained language usage growth and transitional reading. Grows in independence and use of interpretive skills; establishes the concept of reading as a thinking process; applies the hard and soft *c* and *g* rule; learns the three-letter consonant blends; becomes competent in the short and long vowel sounds and uses them as an aid in syllabification skills; and recognizes root words and words with added variant endings.	
VII	Stressed language-arts independence and reading in a wide variety of materials. Increases rate of reading; reads with expression; varies style of reading for work with various materials; uses glossaries and dictionaries for establishing precise meanings; and gains full interpretation. Learns the principles of the schwa, digraphs, diphthongs, prefixes, suffixes, compound words, variants, and syllabification.	

Figure 6-2   A LANGUAGE-ARTS PROGRAM OF CONTINUOUS-PROGRESS
EDUCATION *(continued)*

Language-Arts Progress Chart: Levels V Through IX *(continued)*

Level	Description of Selected Competencies	Present Attainment
VIII	Stressed language independence and sustained application of skills for longer and more difficult reading material. Establishes greater competency in interpretive skills; identifies synonyms, homonyms, key ideas in a story; draws conclusions and makes relationships of cause and effect; skims; applies all word-analysis skills; learns nuances in sounding; and learns the principles of syllabification.	
IX Independent or Enrichment Level	Individualization language-arts activities and self-selection in reading. Uses various reference materials; reads periodicals and current-events materials; and moves deeply into the vast resources of literature for children. Perceptively applies various learned skills.	
Additional Observations Concerning Progress		

Conference Requested to Discuss the Following:

Figure 6-3 LANGUAGE-ARTS ACCOMPLISHMENT PERMANENT
RECORD CARD (PRIMARY)

Name _____ Birth Date _____ Code for Manner Completed:

Address _____ School _____

1—Fully accomplished
2—Mostly accomplished
3—Specific needs as noted
(Use (x) in appropriate box)

	Language Arts	Date Comp.	Manner Completed 1 | 2 | 3				Notes or Comments	Teacher
pp. 18–20 of curriculum	**Level I** Period of preparation in language development and reading. Learns to follow directions; reads pictures from left to right; listens to and recalls material; associates meanings with symbols; enunciates and pronounces clearly; distinguishes shapes and forms; and distinguishes differences in sounds.							
pp. 21–23 of curriculum	**Level II** Initial experiences in language development. Learns to acquire and use sight words for reading; reads phrases; recognizes letters of alphabet; recognizes words from context clues; identifies rhyming words; substitutes consonants; uses word form clues; enjoys reading experiences.							

Figure 6-3   LANGUAGE-ARTS ACCOMPLISHMENT PERMANENT
RECORD CARD (PRIMARY) *(continued)*

	Language Arts	Date Comp.	Manner Completed			Notes or Comments	Teacher
			1	2	3		
pp. 24–27 of curriculum	**Level III** Creating the desire to discuss, talk, and read. Learns to select main ideas from a story; recalls and states a sequence of ideas; draws conclusions; uses context clues; uses configuration clues; uses word form clues; substitutes initial and final consonants; substitutes long and short medial vowels; recognizes digraphs and compound words.						
pp. 31–36 of curriculum	**Level IV** Advanced language activities and reading in story books. Learns to read silently without lip movement; uses and reads longer units of material; uses phonetic analysis of unknown words, using sight words as a base; uses structural analysis for prefixes, suffixes, and roots; and readily uses books for seeking information.						

Figure 6-3 LANGUAGE-ARTS ACCOMPLISHMENT PERMANENT
RECORD CARD (PRIMARY) *(continued)*

Language Arts	Date Comp.	Manner Completed 1	2	3	Notes or Comments	Teacher
Level V Steady growth in language arts and reading independence. Reads longer material; reads more critically; increases rate of reading; reads with expressive skill; differentiates between a sentence and a line of print; uses the phonetic and structural skills, the silent *e* rule and the vowel digraph principle; and shows increased skill in syllabification activities. *pp. 37–42 of curriculum*						
Level VI Sustained language usage growth and transitional reading. Grows in independence and use of interpretive skills; establishes concept of reading as a thinking process; applies hard and soft *c* and *g* rule; learns the three-letter consonant blends; becomes competent in short and long vowel sounds and uses them as an aid in syllabification skills; and recognizes root words and words with added variant endings. *pp. 43–48 of curriculum*						

Figure 6-3 LANGUAGE-ARTS ACCOMPLISHMENT PERMANENT RECORD CARD (PRIMARY) *(continued)*

Language Arts	Date Comp.	Manner Completed 1 | 2 | 3			Notes or Comments	Teacher
Level VII Stressed language-arts independence and read-in in wide variety of materials. Increases rate of reading; reads with expression; varies style of reading for work with various materials; uses glossaries and dictionaries for precise meanings; and gains full interpretation. Learns principles of schwa, digraphs, diphthongs, prefixes, suffixes, compound words, variants, syllabification.						
Level VIII Stressed language independence and sustained application of skills for longer and more difficult reading material. Establishes greater competency in interpretive skills; identifies synonyms, homonyms, key ideas in a story; draws conclusions and makes relationships of cause and effect; skims; applies all word-analysis skills; learns nuances in sounding; and learns the principles of syllabification.						

pp. 49–53 of curriculum

pp. 54–58 of curriculum

Figure 6-3   LANGUAGE-ARTS ACCOMPLISHMENT PERMANENT
RECORD CARD (PRIMARY) *(continued)*

	Language Arts	*Date Comp.*	*Manner Completed*			*Notes or Comments*	*Teacher*
			1	*2*	*3*		
pp. 59–63 of curriculum	**Level IX** Individual language-arts activities and self-selection in reading. Uses various reference materials; reads periodicals and current-events materials; and moves deeply into the vast resources of literature for children; perceptively applies various learned skills.						
	Additional observations concerning progress.						

Figure 6-4 is essentially a periodic rather than a progressive report. It is issued on a specific date at each third of the year. It is an adaptive form in that the language-arts skills program and the math skills program are nongraded, while the other areas of the curriculum are not. A parent has an opportunity to see the progression on a continuum from the beginning to the end and can place a child in relation to his own accomplishment. The opportunity to state whether a pupil needs to improve or whether his work is satisfactory is made possible in the other areas of the activity. For example, under reading-language arts and arithmetic levels on the inside front page of the report card is a statement in parentheses that says "see level explanation." Under the reporting periods of

1, 2, and 3, a teacher will also put either S (Satisfactory) or N (Needs Improvement). Therefore, a parent reading this report card will know whether his child, who is working at level 4, is doing satisfactorily or needs to improve his effort because he has the potential to do better. This gives a teacher the opportunity to use several ideas that were alluded to at the outset of this chapter. Also a teacher can state the quality of a child's performance rather specifically at his present level. The assessment of quality may indicate whether a child is doing as well as can reasonably be expected of him. We feel that every teacher should have an opportunity to make a comment on this. The ways this idea was created are discussed under "Developing a Primary Report to Parents."

Figure 6-4   PROGRESS REPORT

Name _____ School Year_____

School_____ Principal _____

This report to parents will be given to your child to take home three times. It is designed to give you a more complete account of your child's academic performance and behavior. This report is being used for eight classes only. Its purpose is to find a better way to report to parents.

Your child's personal development, cooperation with others, work habits, sense of responsibility, and well-being are the school's everyday concern. Your continuous personal interest and understanding of the development of your child are highest among the factors that will influence his achievement. You are urged to become acquainted with your child's teachers and to seek personal conferences several times during the year.

This report of achievement is based on the new continuous-progress program started this year in the school. You will note that grades are no longer used to designate your child's placement and learning. Levels are used to indicate the placement and learning activities of children. Eight levels are used in reading and arithmetic. It takes the same length of time to go through the eight levels as it does through four years of school.

	Report Period		
Social Habits	1	2	3
Conduct: self-control			
Cooperates; works well with others			
Respects rights and property of others			
Work Habits			
Begins work promptly			
Works independently, quietly			
Completes class assignments on time			
Follows directions			
Listens attentively			
Academic Progress			
Reading–Language Arts (See level explanation)			
Arithmetic (See level explanation)			
Social Studies			
Science			
Health and Safety			
Art			
Music			

Explanation of Marks   S = Satisfactory   N = Needs Improvement

Figure 6-4   PROGRESS REPORT *(continued)*

Your child is learning the skills and ideas at the level checked (x) for him in Reading–Language Arts.

Level 1   ☐   Follows directions; reads pictures from left to right. Listens to and recalls material, associates meaning with symbols; distinguishes shapes and forms; knows differences in sound.

Level 2   ☐   Knows and uses sight words; reads phrases, recognizes capital and small letters; knows letters of the alphabet; identifies rhyming words. Enjoys reading activities and experiences.

Level 3   ☐   Selects main ideas from a story; states a sequence of ideas; draws conclusions; is learning initial and final consonants; uses consonant blends.

Level 4   ☐   Reads silently without lip movement; is continuing phonetic analysis of unknown words by knowing consonants; is learning long and short vowels and vowel sounds; is using compound words.

Level 5   ☐   Reads independently; reads longer material; reads more critically and with expression, using and learning more word-analysis skills; is showing greater reading performance.

Level 6   ☐   Uses reading as a thinking process; uses three-letter consonant blends, becoming competent in short-long vowel sounds; recognizes root words and words with different endings.

Level 7   ☐   Has increased rate of reading; reads with expression; uses a variety of reading material; is learning to use glossaries and dictionaries for precise meanings of words.

Level 8   ☐   Applies skills for longer and more difficult reading material; shows greater comprehension in material read and use of reading skills, learning to identify synonyms, homonyms, and key ideas in a story; makes relationships of cause and effect; vocabulary is expanding.

Figure 6-4   PROGRESS REPORT *(continued)*

Your child is learning the skills and ideas at the level checked (x) for him in arithmetic:

Level 1 ☐ Learning the meaning of numbers; writing numerals; can identify numbers of items grouped together.

Level 2 ☐ Learning the meaning of zero, ones, and tens in counting; counts in order; learning addition and subtraction.

Level 3 ☐ Continuing to learn use of numbers and number ideas; learning more addition and subtraction skills and mechanics; introduction of the whole and parts of a whole.

Level 4 ☐ Learning more facts in addition and subtraction and is beginning to know facts and ideas of multiplication; understanding the fractional parts of a number and of things.

Level 5 ☐ Learning multiplication and carrying with tens and ones; associating multiplication facts with corresponding division facts.

Level 6 ☐ Working with whole numbers and fractional parts of whole numbers; relating multiplication to division; using common fractions in addition and subtraction.

Level 7 ☐ Can do more difficult addition, subtraction, multiplication, and division; working with fractions and decimals.

Level 8 ☐ Learning to work with whole numbers of addition, subtraction, multiplication, and division by two and three place numbers and by working with fractions in multiplication and division; working with measurement problems.

Figure 6-4   PROGRESS REPORT *(continued)*

	Sept.	Oct.	Nov.	Dec.	Jan.
Attendance —					
Days Absent					
Times Tardy					
	Feb.	Mar.	Apr.	May	June
Attendance —					
Days Absent					
Times Tardy					

Please check (x) the box for each report period following each skill area if you desire a conference with the teacher.

	Report Period		
	1	2	3
Reading–Language Arts			
Math–Science			

First Report Period _____

Parent's signature _____

Parent's comments _____

_____

_____

Second Report Period _____

Parent's signature _____

Parent's comments _____

_____

_____

_____

In recent years educators have been encouraging the use of more and more parent-teacher conferences to report pupil's academic and social growth. Some school districts have renounced the use of report cards entirely and have substituted parent conferences at least twice a year. Other districts have attempted a combination of report card and parent conferences to report to parents who could not always come for conferences.

Where parent-teacher conferences are held, there are problems concerning: What do I report? How do I report so parents can understand? Do I give letter or numeral grades? How concrete should I be with a parent concerning academic and social problems? Do I report a child's progress in relation to his potential? Do I report his progress in comparison with that of his peers and with national norms? How honest should I be concerning his progress? Many school districts that have parent-teacher conferences still report in a manner similar to a report card except that it is verbal. Figure 6-5 represents an attempt to break with that activity and to be more creative.

Some districts have combined two factors related to parent-teacher conferences. They have created a progress report that is sent home two or three times a year. It deals with the evaluation progress based on a child's intellectual potential. This potential is determined by the teachers' subjective opinion of past classroom performance, by observation, or by using a combination of I Q and achievement-test results and teacher-subjective opinion. At least twice a year these districts also report achievement results as demonstrated in the classroom. This report compares a child with his peers in terms of letter or numerical grades.

Many districts also report progress by using standardized achievement tests such as the Iowa Test of Basic Skills (I T B S), the California Achievement Test (C A T) or the Metropolitan Achievement Test (M A T). These are only a few of the procedures available and represent an honest attempt by educators to report pupil progress.

It is fair to say that such reporting is not easy. One can never please all parents or all teachers with procedures. We believe that reporting academic and social growth is one of the critical areas for the school to be accountable to parents, pupils, and community for the educational program. We believe that what the teachers and the school state they are teaching should be reported to parents and pupils in substantive terms—that is, if the school states that reading is being taught, then it must report specifically what is being taught and why. Reporting should not be in generalities such as, "John is making progress in reading and is keeping up with his peers." "Maria has received a 'satisfactory' in reading," or "Ruth has received a B in reading." The same holds true for other learning areas of the educational program.

Also, consideration must be given to situations that demand new procedures and alternatives in reporting pupil achievement and social growth. Some of those situations are programs of individualized instruction, independent learning, continuous-learning progress; differentiations in the instructional tasks of the school as suggested by McKenna, Joyce, Grannis, and Meil; independently prescribed instruction (I P I); and other changes relating to assignment of students for specific purposes within a school.[6]

Following are two prototypes that relate to some relevant procedures for reporting pupil achievement and social growth to parents.

In September 1965 the Montclair (New Jersey) Public Schools made a decision to initiate an intermediate-school program that could be articulated with a proposed middle-school development. This included a program of development of quality educational experiences for black and white fifth- and sixth-grade students who were

Figure 6-5   GUIDE TO PARENT–TEACHER CONFERENCES

"The Key to Mutual Understanding"

Your conference is scheduled for:

Date _____ Time _____ Room _____	
Teacher _____	

Conference Notes:

A Message to Parents

Dear Parent:

   The parent-teacher conference we have planned is an important part of our school's reporting and evaluating process. We hope this pamphlet will assist you in preparing for your conference. Please read it carefully, and list any questions you may want to ask.

   During the past few months, I have been preparing information and materials about your child's progress. We will discuss his social, emotional, physical, and academic growth. I am sure this will be helpful to you. I hope that our conference will be a "key to mutual understanding."

Your child's teacher

A Parent Asks:	*A Teacher Learns:*
What is my child working on now?	To know you as a parent.
Does he contribute to class activities?	About your child's playmates, family, and out-of-school interests.
What does he do easily and well?	
What does he do poorly? Why?	What your child tells you about school.
Does he complete his work correctly?	How he accepts directions and responsibilities at home.
Does he listen and follow instructions?	
Does he get along well with others in school?	What you think of his health.
How can I help my child at home?	How your child uses his free time out of school.

Other questions I want to ask:

newly integrated. The educational program and school organization attempted to—

1. Develop a flexible schedule for assigning pupils and teachers in more effective ways to improve teaching and learning.
2. Make use of diagnostic and prescriptive approaches to teaching and learning.
3. Encourage more participation on the part of black parents.
4. Build trust among black and white parents.
5. Encourage white parents to participate in school activities.

In the process of implementing these goals, a flexible schedule was developed along with learning sequences in reading and math. These sequences emphasized the teaching of skills and concepts rather than content. It was felt that if teachers knew which skills and concepts they were to teach they could make better decisions concerning content and activities needed to achieve prescribed goals. This also would encourage the use both of relevant content and activities in the teaching process. Diagnostic tools were developed that related to the skills and concepts to be learned in reading and math. They did not take the place of standardized tests, but they gave feedback on how well a child could perform and at what levels of learning he was operating.

These procedures made it quite obvious that if there were changes in the way one conceived of the curriculum and in addressing reading and math, then new ways of reporting to parents and children were needed.

The first step taken by the teachers following the acceptance of a learning sequence in reading and math and a diagnostic workup for the fifth and sixth grades, was to develop an individual profile in reading and math for each child (figures 6-6 and 6-7). Teachers recorded pretest and posttest diagnosis results to show where a child started and how far he had progressed in relation to the skills to be learned.

The individual profile in reading was divided into five major areas: (1) phonics, (2) word structure, (3) reading comprehension, (4) vocabulary, (5) dictionary skills. The first three categories were further subdivided into specific skill areas. Each of these profiles indicates the major skills found in the learning sequences. This forces attention on which skills a teacher is responsible and accountable for teaching. In a discussion with the school staff it was found that their concerns about the reporting system then in use were:

1. Parents did not understand the progress report and were upset by the achievement report.

The progress report was intended to state what the progress of a child was in relation to his potential. For example, if a child received 1 in reading, it indicated that he was working up to capacity; 2 indicated he was not progressing up to his potential and could improve; 3 indicated great improvement was possible and needed. Most parents interpreted 1 as academic achievement comparable to an A. Of course this was not so, but that is what it meant to them. Both parents and children became upset when the achievement (not progress) report went home. A child who received 1 in reading progress may have received C in reading achievement. Parents questioned this: "How can my child get 1 in reading progress but C in achievement?" They reasoned that he should receive an A if he was working up to his potential. The parents thought the teacher was evaluating a child's academic growth in terms of his potential. Therefore, if a child was working up to his potential, he should be given an A. They thought the philosophy espoused by the school and the teacher meant that a child was not to be compared with his peers. Of course this was not the case. The school then attempted to interpret the purposes of the progress report and the achievement report which were two different things. But still parents and children did not understand; they continued to be confused.

Figure 6-6 INDIVIDUAL READING DIAGNOSTIC RECORD AND PROFILE

Student's Name _____

Teacher _____

Grade _____

School _____

Year _____

Diagnostic Area		Pretest (date: _____)				Posttest (date: _____)				Percent Correct (Pre: = Red; Post = Blue)									
		# P	# C	Specific Weaknesses	Other Comments	# P	# C	Specific Weaknesses	Other Comments	10	20	30	40	50	60	70	80	90	100
Phonics	Beginning Consonants																		
	Final Consonants																		
	Consonant Blends																		
	Digraphs																		
	Long Vowels																		
	Short Vowels																		
	Vowel Teams																		
Word Structure	Syllables																		
	Prefixes																		
	Suffixes																		
	Roots																		
Reading Comprehension	Outlining																		
	Sequence																		
	Main Ideas																		
	Comprehension																		
Vocabulary																			
Dictionary																			

General Basic Skills Tests

(Grade Equivalent Scores)

Fall, 1966 (V-_____) (R-_____)

Spring, 1967 (V-_____) (R-_____)

Fall, 1966 (V-_____) (R-_____)

Spring, 1967 (V-_____) (R-_____)

Other Information:

Figure 6-7   NONGRADED MATHEMATICS PROGRESS RECORD AND PROFILE

Name _____

Teacher _____

Diagnostic Area	Pretest First Administration			Posttest Second Administration			Percent Correct (Pre: = Red; Post = Blue)										
	Dte	# P	# C	Comments (strengths, weaknesses, etc.)	Dte	# P	# C	Comments (strengths, weaknesses, etc.)	10	20	30	40	50	60	70	80	90	100
Number System																		
Common Fractions																		
Ratio-Proportion																		
Decimal Fractions																		
Percent																		
Interest Discount																		
Installment Buying																		
Geometrics																		
Measurement																		
Algebraic Symbols																		
Simple Equations																		
Equations: 2+ operation																		
Directed Numbers																		
Graphing																		
Statistics																		
Insurance																		
Sets																		

General Basic Skills Test
(Arithmetic Grade Equipment Scores)

Fall _____ Spring _____

Recommendations:

Often in interpreting reporting procedures, schools emphasize the desire to have children work up to their potential. They indicate concern about competition among peers, but fail to emphasize equally that children compare themselves with other children.

2. Teachers had a difficult time interpreting to parents the validity and reliability of the way they decide what a child's potential is.

3. Most of the time allocated to parent-teacher conferences was spent in explaining or clarifying the reporting systems, and dealing with the hostility that developed. This left little time to deal with the issues of achievement and social growth.

Teachers and principal finally agreed to develop a pilot reporting system based on what they said they could teach, and should be held accountable for. They conducted a survey of parents to see which of two reporting systems they thought was the more effective. The report in figure 6-8 is a simple explanation addressed to parents and signed by the principal. In announcing this new procedure, a letter was sent to all fifth- and sixth-grade parents stating that this was an experiment to find ways to give a more complete and relevant report on childrens' learning activities. The letter also indicated that the school would welcome parent opinions and recommendations regarding ways of reporting meaningfully to them.

This report has an evaluation key. There was much discussion and exchange of views as to what this key should be. Many teachers were concerned as to whether parents would accept anything but a letter grade. Some thought that excellent (E) should not be used. It was finally agreed that excellent (E), satisfactory (S), improving (I), and unsatisfactory (U) would be used for evaluation of learning areas. Teachers also felt that an evaluation of pupil behavior should be used; S, I, and U were agreed on.

The school staff decided it should emphasize four skills and understandings: reading, social studies, language arts, and mathematics. Since they were to teach skills and concepts, they needed to be specific in each of the areas being emphasized as to what major skills were being taught. They stated what they were teaching, and evaluated it in precise terms.

Teachers also agreed to state the present instructional level for each of the four areas. This level was arrived at by indicating the specific grade achievement level attained in a general test of basic skills or by the graded book in which the child was reading successfully. We believe this is an important step towards honesty and accountability. We are sure all educators recognize that a child in the fifth grade may not be learning fifth-grade skills and content. Hence, on the report, in the area of reading, a teacher could note with relative simplicity the child's instructional level for three reporting periods. If a child progressed to a higher level during a school year, it could be indicated, thereby representing one way of denoting growth that is immediately visible to both parent and child.

Under reading skills and understandings, six items are listed. This set of categories is followed by two others: total achievement evaluation in reading; and classroom behavior. The headings listed as 1, 2, and 3 indicate the reporting periods of ten weeks each. Similar headings were developed in social studies, language arts, and math, along with the specific skills being taught.

Several things became apparent in this form of evaluation. First, teachers were able to evaluate the specific skill they were working on in each of the reporting periods. Second, it was possible to show satisfactory progress in some skills and unsatisfactory progress in others. This was more realistic and precise than had been possible on previous report forms. A child could have some satisfactory items and some unsatisfactory items, and yet receive "satisfactory" in total progress and achievement in relation to his learning level rather than in comparison with his peers. Third, it was possible to indicate a child's

Figure 6-8 INTERMEDIATE SCHOOL REPORT OF ACHIEVEMENT

Name_____ Grade_____ Homeroom Teacher_____

    This Report of Achievement will be given to your child to take home every ten weeks. It is designed to give you a more complete account of your child's academic performance and behavior. It is being used only at Intermediate School, and only for the fifth and sixth grades.

    Your child's personal development, his cooperation with others, work habits, sense of responsibility, and well-being are the school's everyday concern. Your continuous personal interest and understanding of the development of your child are highest among the factors which will influence his achievement. Therefore you are urged to become acquainted with your child's teachers, and seek personal conferences several times during the year.

Principal

Evaluation Key

Separate areas (skills) in each subject are marked, as well as the total evaluation of these areas.

E = Excellent	S = Satisfactory	I = Improving	U = Unsatisfactory

A mark for classroom behavior is also given by each teacher:

S = Satisfactory	U = Unsatisfactory	I = Improving

Reading: Your child's present instructional level in the classroom is _____ grade in Reading.*

1	2	3

Reading Skills and Understanding	1	2	3
1. Beginning and final consonants, consonant blends, and digraphs			
2. Long and short vowels and vowel teams			
3. Syllables, prefixes, suffixes, and root words			
4. Outlining, sequence, and main ideas			
5. Vocabulary and dictionary use			
6. Comprehension			
Total achievement evaluation in reading			
Classroom behavior			

This means the level at which the teacher is instructing the child and the level at which the child is performing in the classroom.

Figure 6-8 INTERMEDIATE SCHOOL REPORT OF ACHIEVEMENT *(continued)*

Social Studies: Your child's present instructional level in the classroom is ＿＿＿＿＿ grade in Social Studies.

	1	2	3

Social Studies Skills and Understanding

	1	2	3
1. Locating and organizing information			
2. Map reading			
3. Understanding and interpreting concepts and facts			
Total achievement evaluation in social studies			
Classroom behavior			

Language Arts: Your child's present instructional level in the classroom is ＿＿＿＿＿ grade in Language Arts.

	1	2	3

Language Arts Skills and Understanding

	1	2	3
1. Grammar			
2. Oral usage			
3. Written communication			
4. Penmanship			
5. Use of resource materials			
6. Spelling			
Total achievement evaluation in Language Arts			
Classroom behavior			

Figure 6-8   INTERMEDIATE SCHOOL REPORT OF ACHIEVEMENT *(continued)*

Mathematics: Your child's present instructional level in the classroom is _____ grade
in Mathematics.

	1	2	3

Mathematics Skills and Understanding	1	2	3
1. Understanding of number system			
2. Working with whole numbers			
3. Working with measurement problems			
4. Common fractions			
5. Using comparisons–ratio and proportion			
6. Working with decimals			
Total achievement evaluation in mathematics			
Classroom behavior			

	Grade	Behavior	Grade	Behavior	Grade	Behavior
Science						
Health						
Art						
Music						
Physical education						
Dramatics						

Attendance:* Days Absent   1   2   3   Times Tardy   1   2   3

	1	2	3

*Days absent and times tardy are cumulative from September to June. Pupils absent or tardy are
required to bring a written statement from their parents giving cause of absence or tardiness.*

Figure 6-8   INTERMEDIATE SCHOOL REPORT OF ACHIEVEMENT *(continued)*

*Please check the box for each report period following each subject if you desire a personal confer-
ence with the teacher. If a subject is checked, the teacher will call you or notify you for an
appointment.*

	1	2	3
Reading			
Language Arts–Social Studies			
Math–Science–Health			
Art			
Music			
Physical Education			

Parent's signature: _____

1st Report Period	2nd Report Period	3rd Report Period

behavior in class that may have had an effect on his participation and performance. We are quick to state, however, that if the program is relevant, concerted, and involves children actively, classroom behavior will not be a problem to learning. As relevance increases aberrant behavior decreases. And finally, reporting in this manner forced teachers to teach what they were going to evaluate and report to parents.

A basic concern of teachers was that parents would not understand the report. They thought that, since parents were used to older reporting practices which had become acceptable through habit, the new report card might cause them to ask for clarification and thus come into schools more often for conferences. However, this was counteracted by the hope that parents could be helped to understand the new nomenclature and also more specifically what the teacher was teaching. Teachers hoped they could explain how they were teaching as well as what the specific strengths and weaknesses of a child were. They could also interpret the alternative ways they were attempting to teach. Finally, the use of the report as a guide for parent-teacher conferences where teachers could show their expertise and training more effectively was anticipated.

Consensus was finally reached that the school would initiate this pilot reporting procedure. Parents were asked to check for each report period if a conference was desired and for what area of study. It served teachers in setting up appointments with parents and guided them in what to prepare for the conference. If no conference was requested, it was a cue to who needed prodding. Names of noncooperative parents were referred to the principal who found several ways to bring them to the school for conferences.

Did this strategy of reporting work? Over 90 percent of the parents of fifth- and sixth-grade children participated in parent-teacher conferences. They were held during five specified afternoons during each semester. Teachers were released from classes for this purpose. Conferences were also held during and at the close of the school day. Two evenings during each semester were made available for parents who found it impossible to come during school hours. Also the differentiated teaching tasks allowed many conferences to be held by two or more teachers with the same parent.

We feel it obligatory to report that the biggest problem in developing this new reporting procedure was with the teachers themselves in their adjustment to and implementation of the procedures that made the system a reality. Children, oriented to the new procedure, readily accepted it. In fact, representatives from the student government of the fifth and sixth grades wanted to know why science, health, art, and music were not evaluated in the same manner as the other subjects.

The Nishuane School Report-Card Questionnaire (figure 6-9) indicates the degree of parent acceptance of the new reporting procedure. There was better than a 75 percent response to questionnaires sent to all families of children in the school. The intensity of response was equally representative of both black and white parents. Many comments were made by parents—too numerous to list in detail. Several are shown here.

"Keep up the good work."
"For the first time I really feel I know what is going on."

"This is the clearest picture I've ever had."
"Can't you extend this to all other areas? "
Now, some four years later, a Report of Progress has evolved for use at Nishuane School that clearly realizes their hopes for an individualized approach to reporting pupil growth. Figures 6-10, 6-11, and 6-12 are facsimilies of forms in current use.

Developing a Primary Report to Parents (Refer to figure 6-4)

This report of progress was initiated in the Camden Street School of Newark, New Jersey, following the development of a continuous-progress, nongraded program for the primary years. The program involved the development of learning sequences in reading and the language arts, and math; diagnostic tools related to the sequences; a screening learning developmental inventory to assist in moving children from level to level in their learning experiences. Figure 6-4 shows eight levels of growth in reading and language arts. Each level states succinctly the major emphasis of skills being taught. The teacher in reporting merely places an X in the box next to the level designation. An X at level 1, means a child is working on these skills. An X at level 5 means a child has mastery of the skills described in levels 1, 2, 3, and 4. Similar procedures are used to report math progress. Other areas of evaluation such as the social growth, habits, and content areas are evaluated in a more customary manner.

Similar problems to those discussed previously were encountered in making this simple change to new reporting procedures. One of us met during each school day with two teams of teachers. These teams decided that this form was more positive than evaluating children by letter grades. It was more specific and would cause teachers to be specific in parent conferences. It would cause parents to come to the school and ask for clarification. It would create a program where teachers would have to help

Figure 6-9   NISHUANE SCHOOL REPORT CARD QUESTIONNAIRE

To: Nishuane Parents

During previous school years, you as parents received two achievement reports for your child—one in November and one as a final report card.

Early in January, Nishuane School began to explore a different achievement report to parents. This report was sent home on two occasions since January and will also be sent home as a final report with letter grades.

We are anxious to receive some evaluation from you concerning this exploratory reporting procedure. Therefore, would you please rate this new report card by placing one check mark (✓) in the box which indicates your reaction to various qualities of the present report card compared with those in previous years.

Please have your child return the completed questionnaire to his or her homeroom teacher.

Composite Results

This Year's Report Card is:

	Number Family Returns	Better Than Last Year's		Similar to Last Year's		Not as Good as Last Year's		No. Ans.
		%	#	%	#	%	#	
1. Overall effectiveness— provides more information	83	87.9	72	6.0	5	7.2	6	
2. Evaluation key	82	74.7	62	18.1	15	6.0	5	1.2
3. Reading report	81	81.0	68	8.4	7	7.2	6	2.4
4. Social studies report	80	80.7	67	8.4	7	7.2	6	3.6
5. Language arts report	79	80.7	67	6.0	5	8.4	7	4.8
6. Mathematics report	79	80.7	67	8.4	7	6.0	5	4.8
7. Reports for other educational areas	77	71.1	59	14.5	12	7.2	6	7.2

8. Do you feel too many aspects of reading are being evaluated?   YES 12% $\overline{(10)}$ NO 87.9% $\overline{(72)}$ (82)   NO ANS: 1.2%

9. Do you like the manner in which your child's instructional level in the classroom is indicated for each report?   YES 87.9% $\overline{(73)}$ NO 8.4% $\overline{(7)}$ (80)   NO ANS: 3.6%

10. Do you feel more aspects of the science area should be evaluated?   YES 44.6% $\overline{(37)}$ NO 45.8% $\overline{(38)}$ (75)   NO ANS: 9.6%

11. Do you like the way absences and times tardy are being recorded?   YES 87.9% $\overline{(73)}$ NO 2.4% $\overline{(2)}$ (75)   NO ANS: 9.6%

If you have any additional comments regarding this new report sheet, please use the back side of this questionnaire to record these comments.

Figure 6-10   REPORT OF PROGRESS

REPORT OF PROGRESS
PRIMARY GRADES (K-4)

THE PUBLIC SCHOOLS
MONTCLAIR, NEW JERSEY

To the Parents:

This report offers the teacher's best professional judgment of your child's progress in school. It will be reviewed with you twice each year at parent-teacher conferences and mailed home in January and June. It consists of four parts:

1. **Language Arts—Mathematics—Science**

   In each of these subjects the skills we teach the younger elementary school children—ages five through nine or ten—are listed on separate profile sheets. The skills that your child has mastered will be marked on the profile. In the conference the teacher will indicate the next areas of concentration for your child.

2. **Social Studies—Physical Education—Music —Art**

   The mark in these subjects will indicate that the child is making satisfactory progress or that improvement is needed. A more detailed evaluation will be included in the teacher's written comments or in the oral report at the conference.

3. **Habits and Attitudes**

   The teacher's comments indicate those areas that need to be brought to your attention. They are based on her observation of the child's habits and attitudes in the school setting.

4. **The Teacher's Written Comments**

   We are confident that these written reports, in conjunction with parent-teacher conferences will give a comprehensive evaluation of your child's progress during the school year.

   Later in the year we will be seeking the comments and suggestions of parents with respect to the new reporting approach.

Paul A. Shelly
Superintendent of Schools

9/69

Pupil _____ School _____

Teacher _____ School Year _____

SCHOOL SUBJECTS

Marking Key	REPORT PERIOD			
S—Satisfactory	1	2	3	4
✓—Improvement is needed				
I—Is improving				
Social Studies				
Physical Education				
Music				
Art				

ATTENDANCE	Sept.–Dec.	Jan.–June
Days Absent		
Times Tardy		

HABITS AND ATTITUDES

Healthful Living

Relationship With Others

Work Habits

Sept. 19 _____ Child reports to Room _____

COMMENTS AND SUGGESTIONS

1st Conference held _____

JANUARY REPORT

Teacher's Signature _____

2nd Conference held _____

JUNE REPORT

Teacher's Signature _____

PUPIL _____ SCHOOL_____

LANGUAGE ARTS AREAS	LEVEL A	LEVEL B	LEVEL C
AUDITORY DISCRIMINATION	Recognizes: Sounds, Rhyming words	Hears: Consonants in various positions in words, consonant combinations. Matches sounds to symbols	Hears consonant combinations. Identifies sounds in words. Distinguishes vowel sounds
VISUAL DISCRIMINATION	Matches. Recognizes likenesses and differences. Moves eyes from left to right. Identifies objects	Identifies and matches: Upper and lower case letters, color words	Discriminates between similar symbols. Recognizes: Common components, plural endings
LISTENING	Knows sounds. Reacts to games and stories. Follows simple directions	Gives reasons for reactions to stories, recordings. Follows 2-step directions	Replies and reacts to questions. Follows 3-step directions. Forms visual images
ORAL EXPRESSION	Avoids immature speech. Organizes ideas. Enjoys and participates in speaking activities	Retells, in sequence, short stories heard	Retells, in sequence, stories heard and read
MOTOR SKILLS AND HANDWRITING	Traces, copies and draws basic shapes. Handles materials properly. Recognizes writing as a form. Copies name correctly.	Writes: Names, letters, *ITA characters, *words	Writes: Short words, simple sentences, *stories. Copies: Simple sentences, Short stories
WORD ANALYSIS		Uses picture and letter clues to identify words	Matches pictures and beginning sounds. *Uses consonant clues to identify words. *Blends symbols to form new words
WORD STUDY	Develops vocabulary through listening and speaking	Displays curiosity about words	Uses picture dictionary. Identifies similar words quickly. Recognizes words rapidly. Understands meanings of words
ORAL READING			Reads in phrases. Reads with expression. Answers questions
SILENT READING AND COMPREHENSION	Arranges pictures in sequence	Interprets pictures	Thinks critically about pictures. Understands and reacts to stories. Reads to answer specific questions
WRITTEN EXPRESSION		*Writes simple sentences	*Writes short stories
MECHANICS			
SPELLING			
STUDY SKILLS	Classifies shapes	Classifies objects and pictures	Classifies objects and pictures in several categories
INTEREST AND APPRECIATION	Enjoys library	Shows interest in books. Works independently. Completes tasks on time	Pays attention. Creates stories. Evaluates endings. Shares reading experiences

*I.T.A. 9/69

Figure 6-11   LANGUAGE ARTS PROGRESS REPORT *(continued)*   109

TEACHER _____   CONFERENCE DATES _____

LEVEL D	LEVEL E	LEVEL F	LEVEL G
Hears: Differences between single consonants and blends, parts in compound words	**Hears:** Vowel digraphs, phonograms, "r" influenced words, contractions, triple blends	**Hears:** Vowel digraphs, Schwa sound, Syllables	**Hears:** Multi-syllables in words, accent
Recognizes: Vowels, compound words, prefixes, blends, *common components. *Makes transition to T.O.	**Recognizes:** Vowel digraphs, "r" influenced words, word parts, contractions, triple blends, prefixes and suffixes	**Recognizes:** Parts of words, syllable patterns	**Recognizes:** Common components of words, syllables
Comments to others. **Gets** meaning from context or voice. **Reacts** to speaker. **Retells** main ideas	**Follows** 4-step directions. **Respects** ideas of others. **Answers** questions. **Retells** story in sequence	**Follows** 5-step directions. **Shows** adequate concentration. **Evaluates** critically. **Listens** with responsibility for facts, ideas, etc.	**Adapts** skill to purpose. **Recognizes:** Sound pattern, important ideas
Shares and **interprets** information. **Role plays** in small groups. **Applies** acceptable speaking standards	**Uses** acceptable speaking standards. **Recounts** in order. **Shows** vocabulary growth. **Participates** in oral activities.	**Selects** topics and **plans** talks. **Gives** book reports from simple notes. **Develops** ideas and keeps to subject. **Respects** opinions of others	**Keeps** interest of audience. **Speaks** in complete, concise sentences. **Keeps** talks within a time limit. **Chooses** variety of sentence beginnings. **Includes** necessary and correct facts in proper sequence. **Gives** report which develops one main incident or character
Attempts to write legibly	**Writes** neatly and legibly. **Slants** and **spaces** letters and words properly and uniformly	**Makes** clear distinction between capital and lower case letters	**Applies** standards for good writing to daily classroom and homework assignments
Uses phonics to attack words. **Sounds** compound words	**Uses:** Vowel digraphs "r" influenced vowels. **Sounds** word parts. **Attacks** words independently	**Uses** schwa sound. **Divides** words into syllables. **Accents** words	**Unlocks** multi-syllable words. **Applies** rules of accenting. **Changes** meaning through use of prefixes and suffixes
Identifies and **uses** comparison words. **Understands** some antonyms and synonyms	**Makes** personal dictionary. **Selects** words precisely. **Understands** some multi-meaning words	**Uses** exact descriptive words. **Understands** homonyms. **Gets** meaning from contextual clues. **Builds** words from common components	**Understands** syllabication. **Builds** words from less regular components. **Substitutes** descriptive words for dull, neutral words
Understands material read **Re-reads** for information. **Recalls** details. **Observes** punctuation. **Understands** 's and quotation marks	**Reads** in thought units. **Enunciates** clearly	**Reads** expressively poetry and parts in plays. **Adapts** voice to reading situation	**Interprets** meaning through punctuation. **Reads** fluently. **Dramatizes** characters in play
Rereads to locate information. **Follows** written directions. **Recalls** in sequence. **Expresses** opinion about materials read	**Distinguishes** between fact and fiction. **Chooses** correct meaning from context	**Reads** for detail. **Interprets** figures of speech. **Understands** meaning of different type. **Understands** informative material. **Notes** sequence.	**Understands** pattern of material. **Selects** main ideas. **Understands** sequence of time, place and events. **Reads** critically
Composes simple sentences. **Develops** simple topic **Creates** own stories	**Distinguishes** between statement and question. **Places** sentences in logical order. **Identifies** sentences which do not belong. **Writes** original stories and poems. **Participates** in group letter writing	**Writes** complete sentences and questions. **Develops** proper paragraph. **Writes** creatively. **Knows** parts of letter. **Applies** correct standards for writing letters, notes and reports	**Understands** sentence structure. **Uses** more complex sentences. **Writes** creatively in a variety of forms. **Writes** acceptable reports from outlines
Punctuates simple sentences	**Capitalizes** proper nouns. **Punctuates** statements correctly. **Uses** comma in date. **Uses** irregular verbs correctly. **Uses** subjects and verbs that agree	**Applies** basic rules of capitalization and punctuation. **Recognizes** and **uses** parts of speech in building sentences	**Applies** more complex rules for punctuation, capitalization and usage
Understands concept of spelling. **Spells** phonetic words correctly	**Spells** weekly unit words correctly. **Shows** positive carry over in written work. **Uses** simple dictionary to confirm spelling	**Spells** abbreviations and contractions. **Spells** homonyms at level. **Shows** increasing ability to spell words not previously learned	**Shows** mastery. **Spells** plurals and possessives. **Identifies** change in root before addition of suffix. **Takes** dictation.
Classifies words. **Keeps** simple records	**Arranges** words in alphabetical order by first letter. **Selects** titles for stories. **Uses** table of contents	**Alphabetizes** by first 2 letters. **Begins** steps in outlining. **Uses** parts of books	**Uses** reference skills. **Alphabetizes** by first 3 letters. **Uses** outlining skills. **Knows** techniques for correct informational reading
Reads in spare time	**Makes** use of library	**Reads** voluntarily. **Discusses** books read with others. **Reads** variety of material. **Appreciates** vivid language	**Enjoys** reading for information and recreation. **Appreciates** different forms of literature. **Reads** widely. **Motivates** self voluntarily.

Figure 6-12   MATHEMATICS PROGRESS REPORT
The Montclair Public Schools, Montclair, New Jersey

PUPIL _____   SCHOOL_____

MATH AREAS	LEVEL A	LEVEL B	LEVEL C	LEVEL D
NUMERATION	Recognizes: size, patterns, numerals 0-12, numbers 0-12, cardinals 0-12, ordinals 1st-5th. Compares sets according to value. Matches sets one-to-one	Uses symbols (>, <) to 100. Identifies: positional relations, odd & even numbers, ordinals to 12th. words as number names to 12. Counts, writes numerals to 100. Skip counts by 5's, 10's	Uses symbols (>, <, =) to 200. Orders numerals. Identifies: ordinals to 20th, words as number names. Counts, writes numerals. Counts, writes numbers before, after, between. Skip counts by 2's, 5's, 10's	Uses symbols (>, <, =) to 500. Identifies: ordinals to 50th, words as number names. Counts, writes numerals
PLACE VALUE		Identifies: sets of 10 to 100, meaning of symbol "10", numeral for the number, place value of tens ,ones. Uses: expanded notation, symbols (>, <)	Identifies place value to 200. Uses: expanded notation, symbols (>, <)	Identifies place value to 500. Uses: expanded notation, symbols (>, <)
ADDITION and SUBTRACTION	Identifies: number in pictured set & number in combined sets, number of a set & various subsets, numerals 0-12	Identifies: symbols (+, —, =), sums & differences thru 12, subtraction as an inverse operation. Uses: equations & vertical notation, commutative & zero principles	Identifies sums & differences through 18. Checks addition & subtraction. Uses symbols (>, <) to compare equations. Finds missing addends. Adds & subtracts through 99 (no regrouping). Solves word problems (no regrouping)	Adds & subtracts through hundreds (regrouping). Solves word problems (regrouping)
MULTIPLICATION and DIVISION				Identifies: equivalent sets & states total, total set & divides into equal subsets
COMBINATION of PROCESSES				
FRACTIONS and DECIMALS	Identifies: wholes halves	Identifies & divides objects & sets into: halves thirds fourths Uses word names	Identifies: numerals 1/2, 1/3, 1/4, meaning of fractions. Solves word problems	Identifies: numerals 1/5, 2/3, 3/4, numerator & denominator
MONEY	Recognizes: penny nickel dime	Identifies: numerical value of penny, nickel, symbol (¢). Counts pennies	Identifies: numerical value of a dime, coin collections to 99¢. Solves word problems	Identifies: numerical value of quarter, half dollar, symbols—decimal point (.), dollar sign ($), symbols (>, <, =, ¢). Skip counts
TIME	Reads numerals to 12 on clock face	Tells time to the hour. Identifies: days, weeks, months	Tells time to the 1/2 hour. Solves word problems	Tells time in: 15 minute intervals, 5 minute intervals. Solves word problems
SYSTEMS of MEASUREMENT		Uses arbitrary units of length. Reads thermometer	Identifies: centimeter, decimeter, meter, inch, foot, yard, cup, pint, quart. Solves word problems	Identifies: half gallon, gallon
GEOMETRY	Identifies plane figures: square, rectangle, circle, triangle, elipse	Identifies solid shapes: cone, cylinder, cube, sphere, pyramid, elipsoid, rectangular prism. Identifies plane & bilateral symmetry	Identifies: angle, vertex, ray	Identifies: open & closed curves, straight lines, line segments, points
SPECIAL TOPICS			Identifies: Roman numerals to XII. Constructs bar graphs	Identifies: Roman numerals to XX. Uses bar graphs. Identifies vocabulary for bar graphs

9/69

_____ TEACHER _____   CONFERENCE DATES _____

LEVEL E	LEVEL F	LEVEL G	LEVEL H	LEVEL I	LEVEL J
Identifies words as number names to 1000. Counts, writes numerals	Identifies words as number names to 10,-000. Counts, writes numerals. Skip counts by 3's, 4's	Identifies words as number names, 100,000 -1,000,000	Rounds numbers to nearest designated value		
Identifies place value to 1000. Uses: expanded notation, symbols (>, <)	Identifies place value to 10,000. Regroups in expanded notation through hundreds	Identifies place value to 100,000 and 1,000,-000			
Adds & subtracts through thousands (regrouping). Adds single digits in equations & vertical notation. Uses associative principle	Adds columns (regrouping). Solves word problems (regrouping)				
Identifies: symbols ×, ÷, principles, missing factors & products. Uses terms: factor, times, product, divided by. Multiplies & divides through 5 x 5. Solves word problems	Identifies: Mult. as repeated addition, div. as repeated subt. symbol ⌐. Uses terms: divisor, dividend, quotient. Uses vertical notation. Multiplies & divides: through 9 x 9, with one-digit multiplier and divisor (no regrouping)	Uses term "remainder" Multiplies & divides: with one- and two-digit, multipliers and divisors (regrouping). Uses mult. & div. algorithm. Checks multiplication & division. Solves word problems	Multiplies & divides with two or more digit multipliers & divisors Solves word problems	Estimates quotients	
Identifies missing symbols (+, −, ×, ÷). Solves equations	Identifies: symbols (>, <, =, ≠). Solves: problems (no regrouping), word problems	Solves: problems (regrouping), word problems	Solves word problems		
Identifies fractions thru tenths. Solves word problems	Identifies: common fractions, equivalent fractions. Uses: symbols (>, <, =). Adds like fractions to make a whole. Orders sets of fractional numbers	Identifies: equivalent fractions in lower & higher terms, whole numbers as fractions, improper fractions, mixed numerals, principles, fractional parts of whole numbers with whole number answers	Adds & subtracts: like fractions, mixed fractions. Writes fractions as decimals with tenths, hundredths. Solves word problems	Adds & subtracts: unlike fractions, mixed fractions. Writes fractions as decimals with thousands. Identifies place value of decimals	Multiplies fractions. Divides fractions. Adds decimals. Subtracts decimals. Solves word problems
Identifies numerical value of bills. Makes change. Solves word problems	Adds dollars & cents. Subtracts dollars & cents. Solves word problems	Multiplies dollars & cents with 1-digit multiplier. Divides dollars & cents with 1-digit divisor. Solves word problems	Multiplies dollars & cents. Divides dollars & cents. Identifies relationship between money & decimals. Solves word problems		
Tells time in minute intervals. Identifies: A.M. P.M. Solves word problems	Adds time units. Subtracts time units. Solves word problems	Identifies: decade, score, century, time zones	Solves word problems		
Identifies: ounce, pound. Converts to larger or smaller units. Solves word problems	Identifies mile. Measures to nearest specified unit. Constructs scale drawings. Uses F and C thermometers	Estimates measurements of length. Finds: perimeter, area, volume	Identifies: grams, kilograms. Adds measurements. Subtracts measurements. Solves word problems	Multiplies & divides measurement. Finds diameter & circumference of circles	Uses decimals in measurement. Solves word problems
Identifies plane figures for solids	Constructs solid figures	Identifies polygons. Solves word problems	Identifies: edges & faces of geometric shapes, terms used with a circle. Uses a compass	Uses a protractor. Compares angles. Finds sums of angles	Draws parallel & perpendicular lines. Distinguishes between congruent triangles & similar triangles
Identifies: Roman numerals to L. Graphs data	Identifies: Roman numerals to C. Graphs number pairs	Identifies: Roman numerals to D. Solves word problems using line graphs. Uses base 5	Identifies: Roman numerals to M. Uses negative numbers & quadrants in graphing. Uses base 3. Adds & subtracts in base 3 & 5	Identifies: dates using Roman numerals. Uses base 2	Uses other bases

Figure 6-13 PRIMARY CARD

PRIMARY CARD

Pupil Progress Profile

Student's Name

PALM BEACH PUBLIC SCHOOL

PALM BEACH, FLORIDA

William R. Swyers, Principal

This report is the teachers' summaries of your child's efforts to achieve. It is NOT a comparison with the achievement of any other child. It emphasizes not only his scholastic achievement, but also worthwhile habits, attitudes, and skills necessary for his full development.

This report reflects whether, in the opinion of teachers, your child is working satisfactorily.

Palm Beach Public Elementary School is a Continuous Progress School, and because there is no academic lid put upon any of its pupils, each child advances as he achieves, regardless of his chronological age.

It is essential that Parent-Teacher Conferences supplement this card at the close of each nine week period. Your child's teacher will contact you concerning these conferences.

CITIZENSHIP

The qualities checked (√) are areas where improvement is needed.

Demonstrates self-control					
Listens and follows directions					
Completes work					
Works well independently					
Works well in group activities					
Makes wise use of time					
Makes wise use of materials					

Teacher Comments:

Date of Progress Profile

Parents may arrange for a special teacher conference by calling the school office, 832-0112.

Figure 6-13 PRIMARY CARD *(continued)*

	School Citizenship	Reading	Language Arts	Mathematics	Social Studies	Science	Art	Music	Physical Education	Spanish	Band
Efforts are Satisfactory											
Must Improve Efforts											

TEACHER COMMENT

TEACHER COMMENT

Figure 6-14   INTERMEDIATE AND JUNIOR HIGH CARD

INTERMEDIATE & JUNIOR HIGH CARD

Pupil Progress Profile

Student's Name _____

PALM BEACH PUBLIC SCHOOL

PALM BEACH, FLORIDA

ROBERT W. FULTON   WILLIAM R. SWYERS
Supt. of Schools   Principal

"A Continuous Pupil Progress School, 1 thru 9"

This report is the teachers' summaries of your child's efforts to achieve. It is NOT a comparison with the achievement of any other child. It emphasizes not only his scholastic achievement, but also worthwhile habits, attitudes, and skills necessary for his full development.

This report reflects whether, in the opinion of teachers, your child is working satisfactorily.

Palm Beach Public School is a Continuous Pupil Progress School, and because there is no academic lid put upon any of its pupils, each child advances as he achieves, regardless of his chronological age.

Date of Progress Profile _____

Parents may arrange for a special teacher conference by calling the school office, 832-0112.

We believe:

Each child differs in physical and mental growth patterns.

Each child should be allowed to develop at his own rate physically, mentally and socially in an atmosphere uncharged with stress and pressure.

Each child should have opportunities to work in a stimulating environment and at a level at which he can be successful.

Each child should be provided with experiences that will encourage him to desire and love learning that stems from real and definite needs.

Each child shall be taught to live democratically and the spirit of self direction and problem solving shall be a part of his school life's experiences.

Each child shall be taught to think rather than rote-learn and recite facts of little relevance.

The children in our school are grouped subject-wise according to their progress on our skill charts, records on standardized achievement tests and teacher judgments. In our plan, we have 26 levels of learning in years one thru nine. We have three divisions:

1. Primary   —levels 1 thru 12
2. Intermediate—levels 13 thru 20
3. Junior High —levels 21 thru 26

Most children will advance from Primary to Intermediate in three years, from Intermediate to Junior High in three years, and complete Junior High in three years. However, a few may take as long as ten years instead of the normal nine. No child will leave before nine years, as we have two enrichment and exploratory levels, one in the 6th year and one in the 9th year.

RECORD OF ATTENDANCE

	1st 9 wks.	2nd 9 wks.	3rd 9 wks.	4th 9 wks.	Total
Days absent					
Days present					
Days tardy					

SUBJECT AREA PROGRESS EVALUATION

The profile line under this heading indicates to you, at a glance, just what subject (and specifically what part of the subject) your child is above or below his area potential.

TEACHER COMMENTS

STUDY, SOCIAL AND OTHER HABITS

An (✗) in any of these columns under a specific teacher's name indicates each item in which improvement is needed. The characteristics listed are considered necessary for the proper development of the pupil.

Figure 6-14 INTERMEDIATE AND JUNIOR HIGH CARD *(continued)*

SUBJECT
AREA
PROGRESS
EVALUATION

Exerts extra effort
Efforts are satisfactory
Must improve efforts

Teacher's name

COMMUNICATIONS ARTS — Listening skills, Speaking skills, Reading skills, Spelling skills, Grammar skills, Handwriting skills, Composition skills, Literature skills — Wolf, Toms

SOCIAL SCIENCE — Knowledge of content, Resource and research skills, Geographical understanding, Cultural appreciations — Case

MATHEMATICS — Basic math skills, Computation skills — Gold

SCIENCE — Problem solving skills, Basic science concepts, Laboratory techniques, Research skills — Singh

MUSIC — Basic music skills, Participation, Appreciation — Bass

ART — Basic art skills, Participation, Appreciation — Fritz

PHYSICAL EDUCATION — Physical fitness, Participation, Sportsmanship — Perry

LIBRARY — Research skills, Use of time — Michel

HOME ECONOMICS — Methodology, Cooking skills, Clothing skills, Homemaking skills — McKay

GENERAL SHOP — Tool skills, Product quality, Shop concepts — Robles

BUSINESS EDUCATION — Typing skills, Business concepts, Other machine skills — Fields

FOREIGN LANGUAGES — Verbal skills, Reading skills, Writing and grammar skills — Dick

INDEPENDENT STUDY — Project formulation, Research skills, Use of time — Arroz

SOCIAL HABITS Teacher:
Courteous in speech and habits
Exhibits self control
Observes school rules
Is cooperative
Respects others' property
Respects rights of others
Controls talking
Cares for school property

STUDY HABITS
Makes good use of time
Produces neat and careful work
Responsible in group work
Plans and evaluates own work
Submits work on time
Works independently
Listens and follows directions

OTHERS

parents to understand the more positive approach to evaluating children; and because of specificity it would force teachers to focus on skills.

Teachers felt more secure with the new procedure after the first report was sent home and people began to call for appointments and to react positively. In fact, teachers who had worked in the school for twenty years said it was the best experience they had ever had with parents. This was true in spite of the fact that this school was in the heart of the Newark riot areas of 1967. The clientele was a minority, low socio-economic group, consisting of some Puerto Rican but predominantly black children.

Forms used at one time in a few of the nongraded schools in Palm Beach County, Florida, are shown in figures 6-13 and 6-14. This type of reporting form provides a basic and simple continuum that indicates in all areas of the curriculum whether a child is or is not doing satisfactory work. Before one can arrive at this form, it has to be understood that every child has been diagnosed within the sequence and is in an appropriate and pertinent place in the educational scheme. In addition, other continuous-progress reports have been sent home. They show where a child is on the various continua that give brief descriptions of the competencies attendant thereto. (Refer to figures 6-2 and 6-4.) The Palm Beach form reports realistic progress and shows that the bar graph should be right at the middle for all subjects. It shows definitively to the parent who reads it that his child has been appropriately and pertinently assigned to a program in the school system and is responding to that environment; and that he is operating with satisfaction at his particular level in all areas noted on the card. When a parent reads "satisfactory" but feels the need for more information, he simply goes to the school. A teacher with various sequences, diagnostic instruments, inventories, and a cumulative record system,

meets the parent who through discussion becomes fully aware of the child's individualized progress and prowess in all educational areas. A parent can come away with knowledge of the exact performance of his child at that moment. He has a fairly adequate knowledge of pace and rate. He knows or feels the assignment is based on the performance and the growing ability of his child. He knows the prognosis in terms of rate and content of continued academic growth. This windfall of knowledge is a far cry from the nondescript single-purposed letter grade.

It is a very far cry from a percentile-rank system of marking that gives only the percentage of the class that is excelled by any one student in the class. What good is it for a parent to know that when there are ninety-eight students in a class, the fiftieth percentile is the point below which forty-nine of the students will fall, and that his son is now fifty-first or therefore forty-nine below the top student? The elements of a nongraded, continuous-progress program record and progress relating system are likewise a far cry from the percentage marking wherein theoretically one is perfect if he gets a mark of 100 percent. The 100 percent varying with the concepts held by the teacher or the requirements of the subject matter, but in no way replicating an individual's competence and ability to achieve or other elements attendant to real growth in education.

Continuous-progress, nongraded reporting practices are certainly different from the concept of an educational record and progress relating system dealing with "standard" scores. If the class distribution is approximately normal (and this is always open to question, because normal means different things, and distributions differ), the standard score is fairly easy to use. However, rarely have we found such a distribution, and therefore the standard score usually requires the development of a whole program of statistical analysis and the use of standard deviations above and below the mean to show the range of marks over the whole distribution. When one starts to involve teachers in reporting to parents grades based on that kind of measurement, then the schools are caught up in the gobbledegook and mumbo-jumbo of irrelevant ideas that frequently provide parents more consternation than clarity.[7] We feel that the Palm Beach Public Schools developed pupil progress profiles that are excellent in their reflection of a continuous-progress orientation. Both the philosophy as stated, and the continuum idea based on the individual progress of a child indicate what can be achieved as an ultimate program of reporting in a meaningful and educationally significant way.

COMMUNITY RELATIONS

DEVELOPING COMMUNITY INFORMATION AND RELATIONS PROGRAMS TO ASSURE THE SUCCESS OF INNOVATIONS AND CHANGE

"Tell it like it is, man!" This is the demand heard in the inner city from people caught up in the life of the ghetto. Its main characteristic is directness. Low-income people omit the circumlocutions and verbal niceties of middle-class language patterns. Their language requires the kind of directness that is frightening, yet so real in its honesty that it might well serve as a model for others. We feel that in community relations much of the difficulty that confronts educators and the acceptance of new educational programs is a result of this middle-class inability, or unwillingness, to tell it like it is. The unsureness of results and reactions in human behavior seems to keep administrators from dealing in a direct way with many ideas. The feeling that anything they say may be used against them also keeps them from being candid and from making available to the public ongoing information that allows for an understanding of programs that children are involved in. Many people have indicated to us that it is almost impossible to find out what is really going on in the schools. They have neither the time nor the energy nor the wherewithal to monitor programs and find out things that are important to them in the learning activities of their children. Many of them are angered by this lack of communication and unhappy with the circumstances that surround it.[1]

This need not be. A school that obscures rather than informs, or is inarticulate concerning its programs and activities, is marked by educational defilement rather than political sagacity. It usually indicates that the schools are "plain unsure" of what they are doing, or not truly committed. The unfortunate outcomes of such behavior are suspicion and uneasiness, which work to the detriment of developing first-rate practices. Innovative programs can never be conceived, mounted, funded, and supported without a broadly based backing of the community. The schools, after all, belong to the people. In most instances the voters have the final say concerning support of budgets, bond issues, and candidates for the school board. The behavior of board members for or against things that the school wants to do is reflected in the parents who elected those members and who frequently find it difficult to understand what the schools are trying to do. This results in the conflicts, attacks, and retrenchments that are too often apparent in many communities. This is a lamentable situation, especially since it is usually avoidable.

We believe the best way to develop an informative community-relations program relative to educational change is to tell it like it is. All techniques and activities should lead directly to the attainment of this objective.

Lawrence D. Fish observes:

"Three groups with important abilities and responsibilities play significant roles in the curriculum development process: a) children, b) parents, and c) professional educators. . .there is only one way in our society to insure the success of the revolution that is upon us in education. Involvement, consultation and continuing dialogue among all concerned groups is the necessary way. The responsibility for an effective school curriculum for children from infancy to adulthood lies with all members of our society. Parents, least of all, can escape this responsibility."[2]

It is our contention that parents and teachers are natural allies in the education of children. All too frequently a lack of communication has resulted in suspicions in both groups that set up a tug of war that often requires mediation by a principal. By telling it like it is, cooperative endeavors in moving toward a program of change are usually possible.

We were recently speaking to a man who was recovering from a serious operation. He said that the whole experience was "a process of involvement." Beginning with the admittance procedure, which was kindly and carefully done, every activity was explained so it did not seem to be a mystery. He was involved in explanations relevant to his particular illness, his care, and the various roles of people who treated him so that he understood procedures and developments. The secure mental health with which he faced his surgery and recuperation, he said, was enhanced by the knowledge and awareness of what was involved.

We believe that similar kinds of involvement would be helpful in the development of curriculum and educational changes. The responsibility of being involved assures the kind of development and insight that creates a mind-set leading to the support and suggestions necessary for the success of whatever change is taking place. For this reason the community and the parents of any school system need to play a major role in determining the manner by which schools will become what they want them to be.

Parents, however, tend to operate between two extremes—either strongly for, or suspiciously against, based on the information they have. It is natural to be suspicious about the unfamiliar. People are usually suspicious when they feel they are being put upon. They are suspicious when there is a seeming lack of commitment or sureness about the person who is suggesting the innovation.

We suggest you test your own feelings in a critical situation. Would you go to a surgeon who was known to be "fast with the knife" rather than one who felt that before any decision was reached a careful workup and diagnosis should be completed and a second or even a third opinion secured? Or less dramatically, would you take your car for a major checkup to a mechanic who seemed to be unsure of where to begin and how to proceed?

Parents should have an impact on the whole area of school program development. Such impact can be seen in several ways. (1) It can be a support program to the rest of the community based on information given to them by a professional group whom they trust. (2) It can be a program of change that seeks their individual competencies or contributions, based on their varied backgrounds. (3) It can be a role of continually informing the community through the PTA or similar groups of the professional activities of teachers and the growing betterment of the school system. (4) It can be a program to mollify controversies that frequently arise within basic school communities. (5) It can be a project that helps in promoting programs and getting support from school boards for school programs. However, if a community feels it is being "had" and is treated by the professionals in an aloof manner that projects the idea that parent judgments and insights are not relevant to the professional activity, then none of the activities listed above are possible. A community can never be convinced of educational purposes and changes until educators, acting professionally, are reasonably sure about the kinds of changes that should be attempted. A process of self-education by the professionals is a prerequisite to a total community program that will support new forms of continuous-progress, nongraded education.

No amount of enthusiasm can carry through a program that does not have the hard data or demonstrable underpinnings of success. The job of creating community support for educational change should not be seen as a selling job. It should be an experience of bringing diverse elements of the community together and arranging for communication that can bring about a con-

sensus concerning the directions, adaptations, or adoptions of new or different programs. Gloria Dapper makes the following observation for all who are concerned with developing a more fruitful and informational program in educational change.

"In a sense, everybody is part of our school system, just as everybody is part of the government. But it is important to delineate some lines of responsibility and to suggest some working relationships, or what is left for everybody to do will wind up being done by nobody.

"Broadly speaking, the four principal actors on the school stage are the school superintendent, the board member, the citizens' committee member and the school reporter. The audience is the general public whose interest varies considerably from complete apathy or even genuine antagonism to wholehearted enthusiasm for everything that happens on stage. As with most audiences, the greatest number are people of good will who are willing to be convinced.

"In the school drama, the actors are not type cast but are human beings whose special faults and virtues can influence the script. The cast is, therefore, different in each community. Even so, there are some general truths that can be stated about the various school dramas being enacted throughout the country."[3]

She observes that school boards are "bowing to the public's wishes and holding open board meetings." Superintendents are meeting problems by making staff members aware of and a major part of the public relations program so that they can answer requests for parental information.

However, before one can move to this reality the total staff must examine the program in a professional way. Then the responsibility to develop strategies for the involvement of the public becomes paramount.

The first thing that needs to be done is to study the educational needs and involvement that lead to the establishment of major objectives of particular ideas stated in the preceding chapters. Through teacher workshops, studies, and programs of analysis on how to better deal with the needs of children, there arise obvious desires to create new or different components. Before getting parents involved, there needs to be an adequate level of commitment on the part of teachers.

The educational staff should undertake a program of study and analysis that will lead to some tentative adoptions of the kinds of procedures and teaching strategies that they think will better serve their pupils. They should bring together a rather large collection of materials concerning the whole area of change so they can evaluate what others have done in a similar context. (See list of places to write to in the Addenda.) Their commitment to developing a philosophy with a basic rationale for creating programs that better meet the needs of individual differences will, of course, be a part of this study.

Arising out of such activity should come insights concerning (1) various kinds of innovations that would best serve the needs of their pupils; (2) problems involved in creating this innovation within the present context and the extent of dislocation that may take place in the process; (3) a timetable for adoption from introduction to completion of the components of innovation they feel necessary; (4) the manner by which others can be brought into a program of constant reappraisal to support and maintain the impetus for worthwhile change. At this point the development of a carefully spelled out parental information and involvement program should take place. The security of teachers, backed by study, permits them to function in a truly professional role as they become involved with parents.

The quicker parents participate, the better the opportunity for support in a program of change. Parent involvement can take place very early in workshops, institutes, or teacher meetings.

We have participated in many workshops throughout the United States and Canada where parents were involved. They were eager to be informed and to serve on committees to bring about change. We found the least difficult problem in bringing about change is readying, convincing, and moving parents toward acceptance and support for continuous-progress, nongraded education. Parents generally, when involved in workshops that are relevant and deal with the solution of problems, have been caught up in the enthusiasm of a professional staff on the move.

Continuous-progress, nongraded educational programs require that there be plans for involving, informing, and including people of a community in such a way that they will be able to become advocates who help others adjust to and accept the various individualized goals of a program, its organization, and growth.

The first thing that must be done is to involve interested people in a program of local research. A simple reflection of the situation within the school concerning the status of the learners is the most important of all aspects. The mere collection of raw data from any set of standardized tests related to any set of mental maturity or IQ tests will reveal extremely varied achievement patterns within a grade. The reality of the learner's capacity as marked by a test and his performance as noted by actual grade-level score achievement is frequently so contradictory and diverse that it shocks the observer. An additional reality is that a learner can differ in performance from subject matter to subject matter and is therefore being categorized in a most inefficient and nonscientific way.

Other factors and learning styles that create marked differences from area to area concerning learning can also be seen. They have to do with a host of activities that cannot be accounted for

Figure 7-1   RANGE OF ACHIEVEMENT ON STANDARDIZED TEST—GRADES 2, 3, AND 4

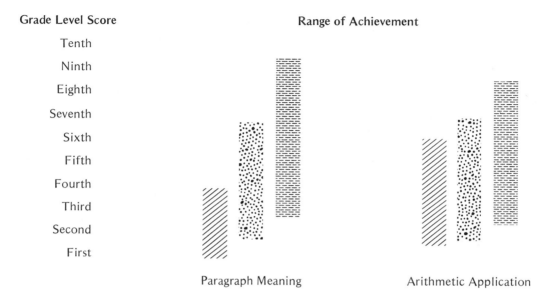

within the present graded system. Figure 7-1 indicates this situation dramatically. It represents the results of a frequently used elementary school achievement test battery. This particular battery was administered in the fall of the year to grades 2, 3, and 4. We have selected two items—paragraph meaning and arithmetic application—to illustrate our point concerning grade level performance and expectancy, and real performance and mastery. All other sections of the battery yielded similar results and showed that the wide range of achievement in pupil performance does not support grade-level classification, unrealistic expectancy standards, and other activities attendant to graded organization and

curricular design. It becomes obvious that this evidence relates the reality of pupil differences in a most marked way. It is this kind of reality that not only is true in the school system represented by figure 7-1, but can be replicated over and over in school systems throughout the United States and Canada that use standardized tests both for achievement and for the measurement of intelligence.

Local research, of course, yields data that raise some fundamental questions. Who is really a first-grader, a second-grader, a third-grader, or a fourth-grader? What criteria are employed to account for varying differences of performance among these children? If some pupils are cutting across as many as four grades, then isn't the attempt to apply a grade level to these varying kinds of learners ludicrous? And isn't this approach to education at such a level of intellectual impoverishment that it is impossible to rationalize its continuance even to the most uninformed layman?

Figure 7-2 should be helpful in developing community relations to effect educational changes. Activities must be thoughtfully planned and sequenced. Then the people to be involved at each step can be determined.

Involvement of parents, as noted in figure 7-2, comes early in the program and requires careful planning. Any movement toward change and innovation needs to deal with the area of educational research and experimentation. This is frequently not within the ken of lay personnel. Some findings may be too technical to be understood by nonprofessionals. Committees that include parents should be planned so that the areas of activity are carefully delineated and are worthy of their insight and energy but not encumbered by the technical aspects of education.

There are several areas where parents can serve particularly well by providing competencies helpful in the development of programs—for example, (1) in establishing the basic philosophy of the local school system as they see it; (2) in evaluating the present reporting system and its relevance to the knowledge they desire; (3) in developing ways by which technical terms can be restated in common, more understandable lay terms; (4) in the development of a series of questions in anticipation of what the general community will ask.

As members of a professional group, educators frequently feel they have a monopoly on the knowledge of the profession. It has become increasingly clear in recent years, however, that the professionals want to share their responsibilities. For example, the NEA code indicates that the profession wants to "share the respon-

sibility for improving the educational opportunities for all. . .and share with other citizens the development of sound public policy. As educators we are particularly accountable for participating in the development of educational programs and policies and for interpreting them to the public." But the street runs both ways. It is important that parents indicate that they, too, because they sustain the cost of teacher training (which is for the most part public) and because they sustain the cost for public education in general, have not only the desire but the absolute right to participate in the development of programs of educational change.

We feel that the problem of public support for change is basically summed up in the worry of parents that their children are being experimented with. This concern can be overcome by assuring the community that no program will ever be pursued with such intensity that it cannot be changed immediately if this seems best for the pupils. The desire, it should be noted, is to make any innovation a matter of research rather than opinionated debate. But it should also be added that when one accepts this point of view he accepts the formalities that govern it. They are: (1) Any component set into action will receive continuous evaluation from which alternative suggestions can be made when evidence dictates a need for further change. (2) Evaluation of the program is not an unalterable experimental period but one of contextual evaluation that allows the people involved to adhere to, or depart from, practices as collected evidence dictates. (3) Educational innovation is a humanistic endeavor in which a professional staff is not to be thought of in a challenging way, but rather as a group committed to developing a better organization and better programs for the enhancement of education.

The innovative program must be put into operation without undue emotion. Nongraded, continuous progress should not be sold to the public as a remedy for every deficiency found

Figure 7-2 STEPS IN DEVELOPMENT OF COMMUNITY-RELATIONS PROGRAMS
ATTENDANT TO EDUCATIONAL CHANGE

Step	Suggested Activities	Persons Involved
1.	Year-long program of study involving released-time and/or workshops and institutes relative to need for educational change in school orientation and organization.	Professional staff and selected laymen.
2.	Development of relevant documents concerning status of educational progress vis-a-vis pupils at local level; case studies of pupils; charts of individual differences from standardized tests, etc.; feedback information from pupils who have gone through school system and are presently in higher education.	Professional staff and selected laymen.
3.	Arriving at basic commitment to different kind of educational program.	Professional staff and selected laymen.
4.	Securing support of Board of Education for intensification of study, and adoption of programs revealed by study.	Superintendent of schools, operating on his conviction gained from the professional staff and selected lay personnel in steps 1, 2 and 3.
5.	Creation of a strong informational and involvement program of total community.	Professional staff, selected laymen, and expanded lay involvement through organizations.
6.	Basic program aimed at readying community for change.	Members of professional staff and laymen who are good at public relations; regular public-relations media, newspapers, television, radio, etc.
7.	Developed program of public and community relations.	Members of professional staff and lay committees to develop informational sources.
8.	Suggested educational format for change.	Total professional staff and selected personnel from lay groups.
9.	Inception and continuation of innovative program.	Total professional staff and a lay advisory committee to help in evaluation and interpretation.
10.	Continuous orientation plans relative to progress and evaluation of program.	Superintendent, his total professional staff, and various informational sources of the community.

in schooling and in life. The movement toward newer forms should not indicate that it is simply the outgrowth of criticism of what the schools have been doing in the past. The idea should be that as scientific investigation takes place an up-to-date school system is open to the adoption of new forms. "Change" is what a first-rate school does. It *must* change. Just as in medicine the adoption of a new drug or technique represents change to a new cure, so too in education do the creation of innovative and inventive forms represent change toward new ways for learning.

Organization for change, and the study for change need to be planned carefully. There should be a lead-in program where tentative goals are established so that it will be understood that the process of change takes place over a series of steps and is never achieved completely and ultimately overnight. Priorities must be established as to which changes take place first and the sequence of those that follow. The desire may be to move from a conventional to a nominal continuous-progress oriented program, to a more fully expanded continuous-progress program, and finally to the whole area of individualization. Realization of the ultimate program may take a period of years to achieve. As each aspect of the tenative program becomes obviously successful and offers activities that can be expanded, the movement toward other aspects for full adoption will take place.

Desired change will never happen unless all who are involved, the full professional staff and parents, are willing to participate in continuous evaluation, interpretation, and study that make for a sensible, cohesive approach toward developing plans of positive value for the child. After all, educational change is desirable only because it focuses on the child and develops those things that enhance his learning and life.

It should be a matter of immediate concern and understanding to all involved that change from a conventional system that has held sway for the last 130 years will not go unchallenged. Dislocation of firmly entrenched ideas sometimes generates strong emotion and uncritical and unhealthy reactionary postures. After all, most parents are products of graded education and may think: Look how well we've turned out!

It behooves those who study and work for change to avoid creating the intensity of feeling that allows them to become a rallying point for dissident people who frequently stand ready to attack the schools no matter what they do. Careful evaluation, reasonableness, honest development of research, anticipation of questions, willingness to be flexible, and all the other attendant items of good judgment are necessary if communities are to develop first-rate educational programs.

Activities that deal with human affairs are risky, but we can say that the era of the seventies that was introduced on July 19, 1969, by a man walking on the moon, will insist that the often discussed objectives that for many years have marked educational dialogues will become implemented realities. The existence of objectives for the instruction of individual learners, the development of diagnostic procedures to establish the status of learners, the creation of curriculum resources and organizational forms to support that kind of instruction are all necessary. These innovative directions will revolutionize the whole process of education just as it is thought the knowledge of the universe gained from the technological achievements of the Apollo missions will alter the lot of mankind for the good of mankind.

QUESTIONS AND ANSWERS

The following selected questions and answers are drawn from our experience in working with teachers and parents in continuous-progress education. We found that even though we deplored the concept of nonpromotion, parents still tended to equate schooling and progress within the school with their own backgrounds, which made use of promotion, nonpromotion, acceleration, skipping, and similar techniques. The newer generation of parents, however, seems to have come through a basic educational pattern that allowed automatic or social promotion, with a resultant weakening of the concept of nonpromotion. They therefore see nongraded, continuous-progress as being similar to automatic or social promotion. It is wise in making a presentation, to create a distinction between automatic promotion (simply moving a child on whether or not he is ready for the materials of the next grade, and hoping the teacher will instruct him at the level of his achievement) and continuous progress (the continuous growth of a child based on his competency to perform in the area specified as nongraded and continuous-progress oriented). The education professional has talked much about the slow learner and the gifted child and thereby given parents terminology they can use in their understanding, perceptions, and descriptions or definitions of programs. Frequently, in question-and-answer periods these terms crop up and obscure because they contribute to closure rather than exposition. Our desire is to eliminate such terminology. In our answers we indicate that *slow* in the context of nongraded, continuous-progress education has to do basically with rate and not with intellect. *The Parent's Guide to Nongraded Schools* (Wildwood and Lake Drive Schools, Mountain Lakes, New Jersey) is a helpful booklet for a study of various questions addressed in a direct and meaningful way. Certain aspects, considered to be relevant, are posed as questions that might be raised by parents.

From our list of questions and answers that follow, some may be selected to present in a booklet for parents as an explanation in anticipation of an innovative program.

Question: We notice you recommend stages or levels of learning. What is the difference between the concept of a grade and level or stage?

Answer: A grade refers to a set of items that must be covered or accomplished within a certain time; for example, in 180 to 190 days of a school year, and upon which promotion or nonpromotion is established. A level or stage is a statement of skills and competencies a child must achieve before educational progress can take place. Levels are achieved and each stage of learning successfully dealt with on the basis of competence displayed in relation to specific items. This is done without limit of time. Material can be adjusted to various styles of learning that best suit the child. Learning is made possible through a variety of techniques and materials based on the needs of the individual learner.

Question: How do you determine what a level is, and what is included in a level of work?

Answer: A level of learning is a carefully thought-out grouping of related skills and concepts. A variety of subject matter can be used to teach these skills. Material found in the level is primarily concerned with the development of the process of learning. A child is expected to make applications rather than try to jump over hurdles to complete a year's work or cover a set of principles that all students supposedly should cover at a given time.

Question: How do you know when children are ready to move from one level to another?

Answer: A sequence consists of a series of learnings to be achieved during that level. Each teacher has checklists and inventories for each child so that he can note the status of the child's performance level. A child's ongoing accomplishments indicate that the requirements of successful performance have been achieved by him. In due time he continues into the next level with the material becoming progressively more difficult.

Question: How long do you keep a child on a level if he is not able to do the work?

Answer: This is decided on an individual basis. The uniqueness of a child and the fact that he is a unique learner is taken into account. The flexibility of the system, however, offers various alternatives when a child is not making progress in a particular situation. When it is determined that he is no longer profiting from work at a certain level he is moved into one that is more appropriate for his needs. It may be a different approach to learning. It may be to a group where he can become a leader. It may be an assignment to different kinds of materials because of a learning block he has. It may be to a training program geared to improving certain basic habits or attitudes that are not learning skills but that affect learning.

Question: What assurance do we have that a child is placed at the proper level?

Answer: Diagnostic instruments, inventories, and screening devices used to identify the status of a child in his ability to perform skills that will make him a competent learner give the teacher an understanding of the proper performance level for him. Because a continuous-progress, non-graded program has instruments and documents to aid a teacher in his observation, we can be assured that each child can be appropriately placed. With the opportunity to move at any time children who are not getting the most out of school, the need to stay with any group that may be inappropriate for a child is greatly lessened, and the opportunity for a proper assignment heightened.

Question: Are children generally moved individually or in groups?

Answer: The desire is to eventually make it possible for all children to become individually involved learners. The first step in introducing continuous-progress education may require the development of groups of similar students and assurance that the group is teachable, and cohesive in terms of its present needs. In general children are moved in groups, though not infrequently individuals are moved or sent into other experiences. They are moved on the basis of certain situations; for example, when someone has been absent due to prolonged illness and his group has gone beyond the area he was working in, he can be placed in a different situation. Where a child makes a growth spurt he may be moved up. Individual contracts are frequently developed with pupils who are self-propelled learners. Pupil teams of related learners may be set up with checklists and curriculum material to pursue activities that contribute to the individualization of the program.

Question: How do parents know at what level of operation a child is performing?

Answer: The system of reporting indicates to parents the level of operation of a child. The progress report is made up of a series of statements from readiness to competence. This allows parents to see the skills and growth, on what we call a continuum basis, that is, points of growth that are continuous from introduction to competence. A parent will see the place marked where his child is performing, and can read descriptions of the areas he has already covered. In this way a parent can observe the distance a child has moved. The progress report is related to the sequence of skills. A parent conference or report form will reveal whether this level of progress is satisfactory or if the work needs to improve. For the most part the information given to parents in a program such as this is far more accurate, far more precise, and far more informative than the kind of reporting found in most conventional schools that utilize a single grade, mark, or percentage figure.

Question: Do children in this kind of program move very often?

Answer: The physical movement of children should not be a predetermination of any school program. If we are committed to developing individualized programs of learning and creating groups that are at problem-solving levels in keeping with their needs, then a predetermination of the amount of movement that will take place in the development of concepts and skills cannot be made.

Often children move within their group from level to level without a change of teacher. Teachers take children through the levels as they progress throughout the year. Or it can happen that children who have growth spurts can be moved to another teacher during the year. Those who lag can be moved horizontally to other teachers for a more appropriate situation related to their particular needs. The problem of moving pupils becomes less and less as we realize that physical movement itself does not harm them. It is what happens to them after the movement is made that counts. Research now points to the fact that very young children can move quite a good deal without confusion and, indeed they enjoy it. The need is to develop programs that are appropriate for them and to have specific reasons for a move. The idea that all children should have one teacher all day long, in a room they call their own, is more mythologial than educational. However, there is no question that children do have varying kinds of problems, and if for some reason it is not wise to move a child from one teacher to another then that will not be done. All changes are based on the knowledge of what will be good for, or detrimental to, a child. Where changes are not made, then varied activities can be used.

Question: In view of the fact that you are grouping this way, won't there be children who are unhappy when they find they are in the slow group?

Answer: There is no slow group. The concept of slowness in continuous-progress, nongraded education is one of rate not intellect. Slowness in relation to intellectual ability is simply not basic to most of the grouping procedures in continuous-progress education. The analysis of skills brings about reassignment of children on the basis of their skill needs. Some children need to work at a very elementary level because of their obvious incompetence in a particular area. Within any group there may be children who are incompetent in a particular skill; there may also be those who are more gifted intellectually than others. Nonetheless, at that particular moment in their growth, the development of skills is a fundamental concern. The desire to develop groups in light of specific needs, skills, and concepts is a sound one. It means that all children involved will be able to participate according to what their particular skill needs are. Those who are intellectually more deliberate learners may need to spend more time on the skills to become competent. That opportunity should be given and the alteration of both the rate and the modification of the material decided on in relation to the particular needs of the learners.

Earmarking groups as slow, dull, or in other negative ways is removed from nongraded, continuous-progress education. Such education is based on the ability to perform rather than on intellectual capacity as measured by tests. Under this system teachers doubt the tests used to measure, rather than the child who is measured.

Question: What happens to a gifted or superior child in a continuous-progress program?

Answer: Because this education is continuous-progress oriented it is based on growth that is vertical so that every upward step moves into material formerly reserved for upper grades. Material is made available to a child when he needs it. Rapid learners are able to move ahead continuously in an ever-growing opportunity to achieve real depth in the area they are working because they are in a nongraded situation. There are also enrichment opportunities that give a rapid learner who has successfully and competently established himself in the needed skills an in-depth program that will make him a well-rounded as well as a competent learner. This kind of program recognizes students who learn quickly. The idea really is not to move children up to higher levels but to move the curriculum down to those who are quick and who frequently could cover much of the material in half the time that is normally planned in a graded school.

Question: What about a child who comes from a graded school into a nongraded program? What do you do with him?

Answer: Because a continuous-progress program is geared to the individual, it allows for an appropriate assignment to the level of operation where a child can function best. All good teaching requires that a child be taught at a level where he can best achieve. When a pupil is transferred into the school, he will be diagnosed immediately in terms of his performances on the materials at the level of his operation. He is then placed on a trial basis and carefully watched for the first several days or until further information indicates reassignment in order to fill his particular needs.

Question: What do you do for a child who may have to leave a nongraded school and move to a graded program?

Answer: When a child is being transferred to another school, his placement there will, of course, be according to that particular program. However, the nongraded school also sends with a child a statement that shows his level of competence in all areas where he is presently working. The receiving school will know a lot more about a child when he comes to them than they would if he were from a school where cumulative records give grade level and little else.

Question: How will we refer to the setup of the school when we no longer say a child is in first, second, or third grade?

Answer: The school will be called a continuous-progress school. All classes will be designated by room number or by the teacher's name. The term *grade* must be dropped. All attempts to relate progress in a continuous-progress nongraded school to a graded progress is harmful because it does not reflect all the other changes that are taking place within the new system. For this reason it is wise when one moves toward continuous-progress that sequences be developed all the way from the first year in school to the completion of elementary school education. In developing a program, indication should be made that the organization (and facilities) will require a three-year primary and a three-year intermediate program. From the time a child begins school to what would usually be the beginning of the fourth year, there is no designation of grade. Rather it is a three-year block of time in which a child progresses through various levels of learning. Neither promotion nor failure takes place, and most children will enter the fourth year or grade (if one continues to operate a fourth grade) after four years of school, which includes kindergarten. Some children may require an additional year to become competent in the basic skills.

Question: What do you mean by "require an additional year"? Isn't this the same as non-promotion?

Answer: The additional year relates to *time* and is not a term of reproach as it is in promotion and nonpromotion programs. What we are talking about is an extended readiness program, or a program that gives a child greater opportunity to develop himself before he is placed in formal learning, and this may require an additional year. If he were moved to formal learning and was not ready, this could lead to habitual failure. By extending readiness activities the building of skills brings a child to the level of operation that he normally would not have achieved had he been kept back in a conventional school. This is a far more healthy kind of activity, since it does not denote failure. A child makes continuous progress at his own rate without being retained. The probability is that he will achieve a level of intellectual competence higher than he would have otherwise, if nonpromotion had been used. The facts are well known now that nonpromotion and its distasteful features actually interfere with learning. Slow-learning children who are automatically promoted in spite of their lack of achievement do better than they would if they were made to repeat the same material. In continuous-progress education, *competence*, then, becomes the basis for movement. It has proved to be a more successful way of dealing with the sound mental health of children as well as with their overall academic success.

Question: Is the way you group children more or less "tracking" and therefore undemocratic and unfair?

Answer: No, it is just the opposite of tracking or undemocratic grouping that assigns children to various levels on the notion that they have intellectual capacities to learn in a certain way—that is, slow, average, above average, or fast. The grouping used in continuous-progress education is based on a child's diagnosed readiness and ability to perform. It would be very undemocratic if we attempted to treat unequally ready children as learning equals by giving them all the same basic program that is supposed to meet the needs of everyone at the same time. Our desire is not to fit the child to a preconceived system, but to develop a system that fits a child and meets his needs. We should not treat all children as if they are academically alike because they are not alike.

Question: Does this reorganization or approach alter the manner or method of teaching?

Answer: Continuous-progress, nongraded education starts with reorganization of the setting in which educational activity takes place. Almost immediately flexibility, increased opportunity for individualization, diagnosis, and prescription lead to different methods and means of teaching that mean better education. A nongraded organization immediately allows teachers to use more effectively a variety of methods.

Question: If this type of program is so good, why wasn't it adopted long before now?

Answer: The movement toward this kind of education does not imply an unrestricted condemnation of the activities that presently exist in our schools. It is, however, a step toward making school organization a reality that works for a child involved in the kinds of things that we know will best serve him. It is not a criticism of the school staff. It is rather a compliment to

them that they want to move toward a more realistic set of procedures aimed at the greater good of children generally. Widespread acceptance of this type of program is now beginning to take place. Many years of graded education are difficult to change. It is as we move into the decade of the seventies that the scientific findings and greater sharing resulting from better communication will accelerate changes.

Question: Is team teaching a part of a continuous-progress, nongraded program?

Answer: The growing desire for teaming in teaching generally works well with continuous-progress, nongraded programs. Team planning, coordinated teaching activities, and other ventures that lead to a greater cooperative endeavor on the part of the teaching staff generally tend to become an important aspect of continuous-progress, nongraded education.

Question: What does one do with an atypical child in a program such as this? For example, a child with an emotional or psychological problem?

Answer: Grouping that makes learning in the levels more comfortable for a child also brings about lessening of behavior that we now classify as psychologically and emotionally difficult. With rare exception, research shows that there is a great reduction in the problems of an atypical child when he is fitted into the kind of program we are discussing. The intensely atypical child, of course, still has to be dealt with in a unique fashion.

Question: What about the general turnover of teachers? Most systems have a turnover of about 20 percent. Doesn't this affect the progress and success of a program such as this?

Answer: No. As a matter of fact, new teachers are greater educational casualties in the traditional kind of school. In a well-developed program of continuous-progress, nongraded education, where inexperienced and new teachers are given guidelines, sequences, suggested teaching procedures, and the like, then the opportunity is afforded for them to make a more intensive and better impact sooner. With narrow ranges within classrooms, specified levels to be taught, materials to use at those levels, diagnostic instruments aimed at developing teacher insight and revealing learner needs, a kind of clinical approach is established that will lead inexperienced teachers toward greater and more immediate success than has usually been possible with other systems.

Question: How do you train teachers to do all this?

Answer: Actually, the training of teachers right now is sufficient for them to perform better in this kind of a program than in others. Insufficient training has been compounded because teachers are confronted immediately after their training with impossible situations involving wide differences in learning, and the problem of developing individualized programs. They have been given ideas on how they should perform, but have not been educated or teamed to create the reality for such performance. In a continuous-progress program, where a broad base of learners is used to diagnose similarity and then develop precise learning levels, and where the range of performance is far narrower than in conventional grades, even an inexperienced teacher can develop the kind of educational input that was suggested in his theoretical training in college.

Question: Are there enough materials to serve different kinds of groupings effectively?

Answer: Rarely do we have sufficient materials for everything, but many well-thought-out, creative materials and approaches at many levels are now available. The real problem becomes that of selecting and evaluating to determine those that are most usable and appropriate in a continuous-progress program. Also teacher-created materials are now widely used, and with planning time can be readily developed.

Question: Is this an experimental program and can it harm our children?

Answer: No, this kind of education is no longer experimental. Programs of a similar nature are constantly being put into operation. We can trace the beginning of this type of activity back to 1939. However, the decade of 1960 to 1970 saw a marked speed up of the activity. In the *Encyclopedia of Educational Research* (published in 1960), there is an article on the nongraded school and an indication that it is a program very worthy of consideration. In the most recent *Encyclopedia of Educational Research* (published in 1969), not only is a significant amount of space devoted to the concept of nongraded education, but it is obvious from the number of articles cited that the movement is well established and is well beyond the experimental stage. Actually, nongraded continuous-progress education and its various suggested forms are aspects of good learning procedure that have been attempted in some ways in the organizational pattern of the graded school. It was during the last decade that an intensive move was made to alter the structure or framework so more of the aspects of this kind of education could be used to aid the learner.

Question: Is there any one model that parents and teachers could readily adapt for our school system and all agree to as the best way of doing things?

Answer: The various elements that are basic to continuous-progress, nongraded education have to be thought through and adapted to a variety of situations. The superstructuring of a program developed elsewhere onto an ongoing program may prove unworkable. There are many approaches to individualization, even though by sequencing one can develop a clear set of expectations that will be achieved by the end of a given period of time. There are a variety of approaches that need to be used in trying to develop activities where learning basic concepts and processes can be achieved by other than rote repetition.

Question: All of this sounds good, but there must be some problems or bad features. What are they?

Answer: There are shortcomings in any kind of innovation. In a survey we conducted we asked that same question. One respondent in a system that developed a program of continuous-progress, nongraded education over a period of ten years replied: "Nothing is bad if we attend to all of the problems as they occur." However, there are certain kinds of things that we must be concerned about and contend with. First, there is some difficulty in changing into more meaningful sequences. Most schools are organized around topics covered in certain grades and depend heavily on graded textbooks and graded mate-rials. Basic changes in the curriculum and the school structure need to be made. Creating sequential learning in all subjects requires time and effort by the faculty in reorganizing and establishing different patterns. Second, teachers and parents are generally familiar with the graded system and have a strong tendency to continue their grade-mindness. Third, the teaching, even though more challenging, is frequently more taxing. Fruitful educational challenge and teaching to meet the challenge are hard work, but they are rewarding. Fourth, this program calls for new reporting practices, new systems of record keeping, and the like. The planning and involvement in these new activities is an added burden for the already heavily burdened faculty. And finally, there is always the grave danger that establishing continuous-progress, nongraded programs without creating curriculum reform may simply result in replacing grades with levels that are set up to be hurdled, or covered, replete with all the shortcomings and problems of graded education. However, it should be noted that none of the problems we have listed are insurmountable. They can be overcome.

WAYS OF ORGANIZING
INSTITUTES AND WORKSHOPS,
AND ONGOING ACTIVITIES
THAT LEAD TO
IMPLEMENTATION OF
CONTINUOUS PROGRESS

9

WORKSHOPS AND INSTITUTES

Many people have come to us with the question: Can we implement programs such as you have described without the aid of consultants and without intensive workshop activities? The answer varies. Some school districts, under good leadership, have been able to read the materials of others and conceptualize the directions they could take. This was done without the aid of consultants. This book may serve some schools in such a manner. Some school districts have achieved change by having selected members of their staffs attend workshops outside the district, then let those people assume leadership in the implementation of ideas.

Programs have also been developed in conjunction with universities, which served as a spark to ignite change. Such arrangements brought together the leadership of both groups and the impact of the program was carried into the school district where the ideas were translated into action programs.

We have been involved in all of these kinds of situations, though we have worked essentially in two broad areas of activity: general consultancy and specific consultancy. General consultancy involved programs in which we helped to develop, within workshops, the broad-based ideas and activities concerned with educational change. Specific consultancy was related to particular activities relevant to continuous-progress, nongraded programs that we were asked to help activate within school districts.

What follows is a suggested set of activities relating to organizing and implementing for change. These plans are derived from actual renditions of what took place in various districts. For the purpose of this presentation we have adopted the pseudonym *Prototype School District, Anywhere, U.S.A. or Canada.*

The Year-Long In-Service Elementary Curriculum Workshop Approach

The year-long in-service elementary workshop that we suggest as one approach entails the following: The superintendent and his in-service curriculum committee determine that a year will be devoted to a series of workshop meetings concerned with innovation and change. The superintendent obtains from his board a commitment to provide funds for a consultant and workshop program, plus a series of released-time periods, at least one a month, for the ten-month period so that the program can be developed. Setup of the sessions and their presentation are made, and a program of study is undertaken. Figure 9-1 is a memorandum from the superintendent of Prototype City to his school board for such a workshop.

Figure 9-1   MEMORANDUM TO: MEMBERS OF THE BOARD OF EDUCATION

Memorandum to: Members of the Board of Education,
Prototype City, Anywhere, U.S.A. or
Canada

From: The Superintendent of Schools

Date: June 15, 1969

RE: Curriculum Workshops

The superintendent of schools recommends that the board of education enter into a contract with William Smith and John Jones to conduct a series of curriculum workshops for all the teachers in the present grades kindergarten through six. The sessions will be held in Memorial Park School on Mondays from 1:30 to 5:00 P.M. on the following ten days: September 15, October 20, November 10, December 15, January 12, February 9, March 9, April 13, May 11, and June 8. In addition to these ten dates, there will be a public presentation to the board of education at one of their regular monthly meetings in January or February, when the progress will be evaluated and future directions discussed as the final five meetings are being readied. At that meeting, the superintendent, principals, teachers, and consultants will be present.

Also there will be scheduled, before the close of the school year, a public meeting inviting the parents of the community to a presentation of the workshop, its development, and its future course. By inviting the community at this stage, the workshop and the school system as a whole invites community participation and approval of the direction in which we are moving.

What follows is an outline of the first five sessions of the workshop. The remaining five sessions that will round out the total workshop program will be structured and planned on the basis of the insights gained and the directions established in the first five programs.

Figure 9-1   MEMORANDUM TO: MEMBERS OF THE BOARD OF EDUCATION *(continued)*

First Session—September 15

Recapitulation of present trends in basic educational movements.

Analysis of concept of continuous-progress education.

Presentation of various aspects of organization: how it underpins student behavior, growth in the academic areas, curriculum revision.

Analysis of vehicles of organization for education of children in the elementary years.

Second Session—October 20

In-depth discussion (with film strips and tapes) of individualization in education.

Analytical and diagnostic approaches to teaching and learning.

Techniques, approaches, and manners of individual diagnosis and analytic teaching.

Evaluation of some techniques for using available materials to insure differentiation of instruction.

Third Session—November 10

Presentations and various approaches to selected learning problems in the elementary school.

Exploration of activities relating to extension and differentiation of in-school learning readiness.

Activities necessary to identification of specific needs of pupils (cognitive and perceptual) and kinds of activities necessary to assure a different setting for individual growth. Partial list of items that will be discussed are: continuous-progress format, in-school team planning, oral-paired practices, and various regrouping patterns.

Fourth Session—December 15

Various kinds of process vehicles.

Activities necessary for creating desired goals of learning program in which the learner is central to the learning process. Establishing a program where focus is on the individual child.

Areas to be considered if teaching and learning are to coalesce into a program that uses a range of methods and techniques resulting in growth of
1. individual instruction
2. self-directed learning
3. self-mastery
4. individualization in general

Presentation and analysis of case studies.

Ways that educational problems can be handled.

Presentation and discussion concerning prescriptive and analytic teaching based on concept of mastery in all areas of the curriculum.

Regrouping into heterogeneous classroom activities with differentiation within classroom to assure democratization as well as individual growth according to individual needs of learner.

Fifth Session—January 12

Immediate in-service education needed to create a different kind of educational format.

Various activities of bringing together necessary materials for success.

Activities that underpin creation of particular written documents that will guide teachers in the learning process.

Series of discussions to indicate guidelines necessary for translating various activities into classroom action involving patterns of grouping that have been successful in other school systems. From these discussions ideas as to the next directions will be gathered.

Basic determinations concerning the following:
1. next steps in total program
2. priorities concerning next direction
3. timetable of desired achievements and plan
4. needed materials for effecting change
5. subgroup meetings vis-a-vis specific items of concern: sequences, diagnostic items, inventories, and grouping; coding materials; reassignment and specialization procedures; suggesting curricula emphases; and other concerns as they arise

Figure 9-2   PROGRESS REPORT ON THE CURRICULUM WORKSHOPS FOR
THE SUPERINTENDENT OF SCHOOLS

The job of the school is to organize in such a way as to capitalize on the realities that exist in any group of learners or in any individual learner.

This is our charge—to accept the realities and use them as the impetus for finding better ways for the organization of learning. As teachers we have preached individual differences, yet we have not truly provided for the child who is capable of reading well beyond his level, or the child who, because his level of achievement is below the norm, is frustrated in areas where reading is vital. We have spelled out areas of study in each subject, but have not provided a sequential program of basic skills and concepts essential to true understanding of the content. We cannot rely on incidental learning but must provide a structure of levels of attainment with built-in diagnostic materials.

The five Monday afternoon meetings that have been held since the inception of the program in September have addressed three particular areas.

The first consisted of discussions of the various kinds of innovations that are taking place in education, especially in elementary education. A definitive statement was made of the nongraded, continuous-progress program throughout the United States. Various materials were shown and discussed. Aspects of collaboration as they concern continuous-progress programs and the involvement of teachers in the clearer knowledge of where pupils stand, what programs are needed, and the direction that should be taken were also discussed. After sufficient information was gathered by the teachers, and various questions were answered, differences between what our system has and what reasonable steps could be taken were studied; then the second large segment of the program took place.

This part of the program relates to the implementation of those ideas that relate specifically to upgrading and enhancing our system. Questions we are presently addressing and will continue to address before arriving at a mode of operation include the following:

What are better organizational schedules for assigning teachers and students so that they can teach and learn in a more effective manner?

What instruments and vehicles are available that allow for a careful diagnosis of students?

What subject-matter areas as well as methods of inquiry and discussion can be put into sequential levels of learning to help teachers bring children through a program based on diagnosis of needs to a level of achieved mastery?

The third area is the phase that we now move into. Teachers in groups within their area of competence will create the sequences needed in various areas of the curriculum: reading and language arts, mathematics, social sciences, and science. (These statements of educational objectives will help broaden the bases which can be used for pupil classification in terms of learning needs. In developing these levels we will provide a guide for teachers and for students; we will also provide parents with explicit information concerning a child's progress.) These sequences will then be dovetailed to establish a smooth operational program of levels in each of the curriculum areas. The next step will be to determine which of the teacher collaborators will address each area in the program. At this time we have some teachers who want to build a skills program and a teaching competency for themselves in the area of language arts and social studies, with emphasis on reading. Others prefer to teach mathematics and science.

The remaining weeks of the workshop will be devoted to the development of sequences and the

Figure 9-2   PROGRESS REPORT ON THE CURRICULUM WORKSHOPS FOR
THE SUPERINTENDENT OF SCHOOLS *(continued)*

training of teaching personnel to diagnose and prescribe learning activities so that greater growth can be established. Eventually we expect that several documents will be created. They will be the guidelines for applying the materials to the teaching-learning activity in an articulated fashion from kindergarten through the sixth year.

In summary, our workshop has emphasized the necessity of providing a child with the settings, the structure, and the stimuli which will give him a realization of his capacities at his own pace. Our staff is excited and we look forward to the next five sessions.

An interim report was made to members of the school board. Figure 9-2 indicates the result of the first five sessions, outlined in the memorandum.

The format shown in figure 9-2 provides a fairly adequate picture of the type of in-service workshop activity that takes place over a six-month to a year period that brings the resources of experienced consultants to bear on problems of teaching and learning. It becomes obvious that this kind of workshop program has lasting value only when it is translatable into action within the school system. The orientation of a workshop is always to establish a very strong teaching group committed to educational innovation and change. It must be stressed that a workshop is pragmatically oriented. There is, of course, a study and research period, but this period has immediate relevance for the operation of a classroom. The workshop really attempts to create opportunities for teachers to gain insight into those activities that will be helpful in the administration of programs within their own classrooms and within their own schools. It is not an attempt to find a particular kind of program, but rather an attempt to be eclectic in approach so that teachers in a workshop can determine the kinds of programs that most naturally fit their needs and their aspirations in teaching.

There are no single model programs that all others should copy. In keeping with the con-

cept of this book, that the aspects of change will differ from school system to school system, so too workshop formats and programs will differ from situation to situation. Therefore the workshops should be made up of experiences that involve participants in the investigation of the many ways that individualization of instruction leads to the creation of better programs. Workshop activities should be based on insightful assessments that will be studied, addressed, and adapted for classroom use. Workshops should establish guidelines and criteria for innovations and changes, and should point up what ought to be done and what can be achieved in a school system.

University–School District Program for Educational Change through Summer Workshop, Plus Continuing Consultancy Relationship

A school and university relationship directed toward educational change is probably one of the most fruitful approaches. One such experience in which we participated was the development of a program under the joint auspices of four school districts in the Fresno County School System and the State College of California at Fresno. Financial support came through tuition and a contribution by the four districts for a four-week course, for which credit was given. All participants were to implement within their own school districts those programs they became familiar with, studied, and decided upon during the workshop. The consultants were available throughout the workshop program, as were the principals of the ten schools who were to innovate and their instructional specialists. What was created during the twenty sessions of the workshop was a document, a blueprint for change, and a plan of action based on a timetable.

The procedures were pragmatic in nature, oriented toward practical implementation. The consultants highlighted specific concerns. The production and creation of material for use in the fall was the basic goal of the workshop.

Pragmatic and practical implementations are necessary; otherwise the more difficult but worthy theoretical ideas die. We contend that educational research should move apace in developing the theory and the insights concerned with the theory of organization. But we likewise believe that there must be intensive activities in the whole area of implementation if schools are to be successful in upgrading programs.

The Fresno Project READ (Reading Excellence Advanced and Developed) met from 8:00 A.M. to 1:00 P.M. daily for twenty sessions. The staff consisted of a director and seven additional consultants who highlighted specific areas. The whole orientation aimed toward—

1. A careful definition of what was to be immediately implemented in the schools.
2. Creation of various but precise experimental designs for the collection of data helpful in yielding insights.
3. Creation of materials, methods, and techniques to be used by teachers.
4. Agreement on the inventive and innovative organizational vehicles to be used by various schools.

A second workshop was held during the following summer in which an advanced approach to many of the concepts developed and elaborated on during the first session was attempted.

Figure 9-3   DAILY SCHEDULE FOR 20 SESSIONS

Session	General Topics
1	1. Introductions
	2. Workshop conception and keynote
	3. Basic workshop overview: dimensions and goals
	4. The purpose-product conflict in education. (Discussion of organizing participants in defined areas of need, re changes of teaching-learning processes and their relation to achieving goals of improved reading.)
2	1. Based on Discussions of Session 1: Groups of 10 participants each will meet to define the following areas:

	a) Concerns in relation to reading
	    b) Concerns re teaching of reading
	    c) Concerns of learning problems
	    d) Problem of materials
	    e) Situation concerning services
	    f) Concerns re organization vis-a-vis reading and learning
	    g) Help needed to resolve these and other problems

	2. Plenary report session for classification and categorization of concerns
	3. Presentation of ideas re categories of concern. Diagnosis and prescription—underpinning correlates that lead to reading improvement
	a) Developing a learning sequence b) Developing a diagnostic survey
3	1. Prototypes that employ diagnostic and prescriptive approaches to learning; examples of selected programs; components and various elements of programs. (Presentation with transparencies, filmstrips, and materials.)
	2. Relation between prototypes and categorized concerns evidenced by discussion groups. (Possible adaptations, whole or partial, of prototypes to children. Teacher needs and problems.) Discussion.
	3. Establishment of groups to address defined areas.
	NOTE: Beginning with session 4, the five-hour work day will be split into two major time blocks. One block will be devoted to presentations by consultants in areas that dovetail with and further the attainment of the general goals of the workshop. The other block will consist of work sessions in which teachers will develop materials, approaches and methods, new ideas, various types of organization, and ways of implementing activities for operation in September. There will be a daily evaluation session. Recapitulation and definition of assignments will be ongoing.

Figure 9-3   DAILY SCHEDULE FOR 20 SESSIONS *(continued)*

Session	General Topics
4 5 6 **7 8**	Areas to be covered in the time block for presentations for the week: 1. School organization that creates opportunity for flexibility a) Mechanical schedules b) Teacher-utilization procedures 2. School organization that creates opportunity for flexibility a) Teacher collaboration in teaching b) Collaborative teacher team-planning activities c) Pupil-reassignment procedures 3. School organization that creates opportunity for flexibility a) Procedures for individualized learning; individual timetables b) Pupil teaming and oral pairing c) Individual contract learning 4. School organization that creates opportunity for flexibility a) Large and small group instructional activities b) Programmed approaches c) Peak lesson strategies d) Instructional-materials resource centers 5. Changing the whole school climate for learning by increasing educational relevance for the learner a) Various settings for learning (classroom and schoolwide) b) Learning styles and pupil reassignment c) Teaching styles and pupil reassignment d) Contract or functional curriculum approach e) Elements of a relevant developmental curriculum f) Elimination of purpose-product conflict through changes in the process (Areas to be addressed in work-session time blocks will be concerned with methods, materials, approaches, and implementations based on readiness to achieve goals of input sessions. Study of materials, meaningful adaptations, creative or innovative departures, etc., relative to implementation will be discussed daily.)
9 10	Presentation time blocks in each of these two sessions will be concerned with English as a second language. Insights and guidelines that underpin the bilingual approach to solutions to inadequacies of foreign-language speakers in their needed English-language competence will be presented. The concept of primacy of spoken language and knowledge related to cultural context as a determinant of motivation and communication will be included.

Figure 9-3   DAILY SCHEDULE FOR 20 SESSIONS *(continued)*

Session	General Topics
	Work-session time blocks will be used to develop a variety of materials and ideas attendant to the bilingual approach. These activities will be for foreign-language speakers and educationally disadvantaged learners who have a nonstandard language pattern. There will be a demonstration lesson by a consultant.
11 12 **13**	Presentation time blocks for these three days will be concerned in depth with reading diagnosis based on the evaluation and assessment of perceptual quality and its relation to learning. Insights concerning primary perceptual development from visual recognition to higher cortical functions will be discussed. Perceptual activities and devices, and various approaches and methods of teaching will be included. During workshop sessions children will be present for demonstrations. They will be assigned to learning stations where teachers will use the instruments and materials and apply the techniques and methods. Teachers will make assessments and diagnoses of learning problems in reading.
14 15	Presentation time blocks for these two days will address development of relevant curricula and relationship to finished products we hope to achieve. a) Revised mechanical flexible schedules for each of schools b) Learning sequences for primary and middle schools c) Diagnostic inventories and their relation and conformance with sequences d) Learning developmental inventory (LDI) and diagnostic inventory (DI) Work session time blocks will deal with polishing and editing, as well as establishing ways of coding materials to create relationships to learning sequences, manner of establishing and using an instructional-resource center, and development of resource material.
16 17 **18 19** **20**	For these five sessions the whole area of reporting and evaluation, and techniques for data collection and record keeping will be presented. Concepts of the teaching-learning performance will relate to previous presentations. Two sessions will be devoted to language of the classroom, teacher-learner interaction, nature and nurture of classroom activities, and possible frameworks for interaction. Focus will be on language of the classroom as it improves teaching and learning. A seven-part program of involvement of participants in simulated classroom analysis will be developed as follows: 1. Search for meaning in the classroom 2. Pedagogical, substantive, and logical meanings 3. Types of questions, responses, reactions, and structurings 4. Patterns of classroom discourse 5. Data on student-teacher interaction

Figure 9-3 DAILY SCHEDULE FOR 20 SESSIONS *(continued)*

Session	General Topics
	6. Flow models of classroom teaching 7. Relationship of one model of analysis to others Last two sessions of the workshop will be used to do several things concomitantly: 1. Research design and educational research specialists will be used to create viable designs for upcoming year so that data collection can be precise, variables controlled, and quantitative analysis made of the pilot year. Help will be provided to establish forms and record-keeping devices and other relevant materials. 2. Consultants in specified areas will meet with principals, consultants, and teachers. Roles of participants will be analyzed, guidelines for performance created, task orientations clarified, and applications and implementations carefully scrutinized and readied. 3. Parent orientation and community-involvement techniques, including kinds and types of meetings, will be discussed and planned. 4. All members will be involved in recapitulations and assessments of materials, ideas, and directions that are to be used in the coming year. Assignment for participants: From all the components, elements, and concepts presented and discussed, workshop participants will develop a relevant and implementable package for their own schools, including techniques, timetables, and administrative and teaching concerns. The procedures, forms, and format will be discussed and elaborated on during an early session.

Colleges are not always available for the kind of joint relationship that existed in the Fresno program. However, opportunities are available for bringing together organizations other than colleges that offer consultants to school districts under a contractual obligation. One such program was developed jointly by the Bridgeport (Connecticut) Public Schools and Science Research Associates, under the auspices of the Bridgeport Title I ESEA Project. A summer program was developed in which continuous-progress and instructional activities related to continuous progress were investigated and developed for disadvantaged learners.

The staff for this workshop consisted of a director-consultant, five subject-matter consultants, a project director, and a coordinator. Sessions were held from 8:00 to 1:00 over a three-week period. The schedule for the fifteen-day program is shown in figure 9-4.

Figure 9-4   SCHEDULE FOR A FIFTEEN-DAY PROGRAM

Session	General Topics
1	Recapitulation of continuous-progress, nongraded pilot program in Bridgeport.
	Areas of concern and aspects of program will be explored. Expansion of program, needed materials, grouping movement, concept of mastery, evaluation, individualization, and definition of precise needs to be attacked during workshop periods will be discussed, analyzed, readied.
2	Diagnostic approaches to teaching and learning situation.
	Use of materials, techniques, and ways individual diagnosis can be undertaken using various instruments and devices, and available materials for differentiation of instruction.
3	Presentations and discussions of approaches to various selected learning problems. Exploration of activities attendant to extension and differentiation of in-school and reading readiness.
	Identification of specific need areas, both cognitive and perceptual.
	Aspects of affective learning procedures necessary to underpin in-school success in nongraded, continuous-progress education.
4 5	These two days will be made up of demonstration of activities of the whole area of perceptual problems, reading success and diagnosis, evaluation, assessment, and correction attendant to perceptual and cognitive problems.
	Perceptual activities and use of materials, devices, and instruments allowing for greater insight into perceptual difficulties will be discussed, explained, and used by various people of the workshop.
6	Program of exposition, explanation, and definition of activities related to each area of specialty being handled by consultant. Consultants will discuss ways they can serve in relation to continuous-progress education in general, and nongrading in particular, by presenting various activities, insights, and programs, and the way they can best be made to operate in the schools. Presentations will be followed by small group meetings (throughout remainder of workshop period) with staff to determine schedules, roles, and activities necessary for smooth operation and for use of consultants in Bridgeport schools.
7 8	Program of filmstrips and activities re teaming, collaborative and associate teaching, and ways reorganization can help to enhance the process and thereby create a better product in education.
	Educational objectives will be dealt with very specifically.
	The whole area of diagnostic and prescriptive approaches to learning will be discussed.

Figure 9-4   SCHEDULE FOR A FIFTEEN-DAY PROGRAM *(continued)*

Session	General Topics
9 10	Problems attendant to educationally disadvantaged, Spanish-speaking child will be discussed. Latin American culture and its relation to in-school success in American society will be considered. Consultant will elaborate on strategies, insights, methods, and approaches to teaching Spanish-speaking child and low-income child who has culturally different background. Consultant will talk about cultural dissonance and give specific instances on ways to ease areas of conflict so that more success can be achieved in working with children of different cultures.
11 12	These two days will have a full discussion, by consultants, of expansion of nongraded education in large city operations. Problems of supervision of in-service education, bringing together necessary materials for success, specific aspects of translating particular written documents into classroom action, patterns of successful grouping that have to do with predominantly large city schools and large city problems will be addressed.
13	Program of discussion, films, and slides relating to development and statement of educational objectives; manner by which language of classroom aids in creating objectives; knowledge of ways to see objectives more precisely.
14 15	Consultant will discuss language of classroom, and activities of direct observation of teaching; nature of activity involved in observation in classroom; possible frameworks that orient observation; and classroom discourse related to observation. Development of seven-part program to get participants in workshop to involve themselves in simulated observation. Seven items as follows: 1. Search for meaning in classroom 2. Pedagogical, substantive, and logical meanings 3. Types of questions, responses, reactions, and structurings 4. Patterns of classroom discourse 5. Data from a study of high school students 6. Flow model of classroom teaching 7. Relation of this kind of observation to other kinds of schemes

All the workshop activities were specifically aimed at aspects of the program of the Bridgeport nongraded pilot activity. Report cards and record keeping, displays of items, creation of materials for poorly prepared groups or for children requiring extended readiness, and reading-readiness problems were discussed. A program for developing a specific course of study for primary reading was also addressed. Activities of evaluation, and the manner by which readiness of a child to move to the next difficulty level were discussed. Throughout the workshop groups of children were brought in for small demonstration lessons on some of the newer aspects of educational strategy. For example,

there was a demonstration of the method of inquiry in the area of social studies at the very earliest school level.

Additionally, wherever feasible, administrators met with the consultants in small groups to discuss the needs of their schools for the coming school year vis-a-vis the program.

Arrangements were made to have materials available throughout the workshop so that teachers could become familiar with them as a means of bolstering classroom activity. Following the workshop, participants drafted a memorandum of recommendations to the superintendent and members of the board of education, part of which is given in figure 9-4a.

Figure 9-4a SOME RESULTS OF THE FIFTEEN-DAY PROGRAM

Part I

This report stems from a series of recommendations from several groups of teachers and principals who met during the last two days of the summer workshop program. After three weeks of discussion and input from consultants, they were faced with several questions, as follows:

1. What is the fundamental problem that seems to face Bridgeport as it moves from what it now has into the next steps of continuous-progress, nongraded education?
2. What concrete recommendations can be made to the administration that can be turned into a policy to aid in the movement toward continuous-progress, nongraded education?
3. In view of the tasks that face Bridgeport (as evidenced by the discussions and presentations of the visiting consultants), what needs are apparent and what needs must be envisioned concerning the following areas:

   a) In-service education of staff
   b) Use of consultants to both staff and administration
   c) Opportunity for released time for continuous-program development
   d) Mustering and acquisition of materials necessary for carrying out the expanded program
   e) Necessary materials and instruments for measuring whether Bridgeport is moving on the right track

4. What would be a meaningful list of all the items that at this moment seem to be necessary for success in the program? (It is assumed that one realizes that all these items may not be available; hence there should be an assessment of priorities as to those most needed.)
5. Any other concerns that are germane or would be helpful in creating a successful program.

Part II

The steering committee of the Bridgeport Nongraded Pilot Program met and discussed the findings and concerns growing out of group discussions. It established a set of recommended priorities based on the immediate needs for success.

The steering committee, and the workshop in general, recommends the following as being necessary requisites leading to ultimate success in continuous-progress, nongraded education in the Bridgeport schools. These recommendations concern the pilot programs and the expansion of those programs to other schools.

1. Provide an unassigned teacher (one without classroom responsibility) who will serve in a variety of roles, to work among the nongraded or continuous-progress units so that aid in progress, analysis, diagnosis, assessment, and so forth can be given to assure continuous success of children in the program.
2. Create a program of in-service activities (with released time) to instruct teachers how to teach in a diagnostic and analytic way.
3. Create a program of sharing and communication between the various units within a school as well as from school to school to assure that activities are articulated and transmitted.
4. Create a program of greater specificity in the use of subject-matter specialists in the various schools.

Figure 9-4a   SOME RESULTS OF THE FIFTEEN-DAY PROGRAM *(continued)*

5. Get a definite commitment of budgetary considerations from the board of education so that the aspects of the nongraded program can move ahead with materials, personnel, evaluation, and other relevant items.
6. Create an intensive workshop schedule throughout the school year in the area of continuous-progress education different from that of the traditional workshop. (Possibly eight days, made up of half-day sessions where intensive workshops in specified areas could be conducted by experts and consultants.)
7. Create a team of teachers within the school system to visit other schools and give demonstrations of techniques.
8. Bring in experts, especially in the area of language development, chart reading, and English as a second language.
9. Rethink and create a new report form in keeping with the concepts of education being propounded. Use a foreign-language report card for parents who do not read English so that they will be as well informed as the rest of the parent body.
10. Provide a Spanish-speaking teacher or aide for each of the buildings concerned with Spanish as a second language.
11. Provide a specific budget for the purchase of materials so that principals and teachers can make decisions at their level of in-school needs.
12. Create a program of intensive screening prior to kindergarten entrance (such as the ABC test or some other instrument) so that immediate grouping can take place and success can be more readily assured through diagnostic procedures and analytical teaching.
13. Create an eleven-month teacher year (with extra pay for the eleventh month) and a ten-month pupil year.
14. Create an opportunity to have some small workshops where consultants are brought into each school to serve a specified need and deal with the particular problems confronting that school.
15. Create an opportunity for collaboration and teaming so that longer planning periods can take place within the school day rather than after school or at lunchtime.
16. Create a budget for visits by teachers to other programs to gain knowledge of what is being done in other systems.
17. Consider buying individual, movable, study carrels for use in some buildings, especially older ones, where there is corridor space but little privacy.
18. Make more use of audiovisual facilities and define the activities, nature, and capabilities of the department.
19. Create movement toward continuous-progress, nongraded education at the higher grade levels.
20. Arrange for instructional-materials centers in each building to allow for incorporation and collection of multilevel material and various media in the continuous-progress program.
21. Use specialist teachers in primary areas to carry through some of the programs where extra help is needed.

This is by no means an exhaustive list. There are other requisites, but these are the priority concerns.

If it is not possible to develop a workshop with a university, various school districts could encourage their universities to hold week-long institutes so that there could be an intensive amount of input for a specified group. This group could take back to the school districts ideas to translate into practical activities. For example, an institute on the Continuous-Progress, Nongraded School could be held for a week in June for leadership people. Those people could go back to their communities and involve them in developing the kind of workshop program referred to at the beginning of this chapter. Such an institute on a college campus was developed somewhat as follows: one consultant with lectures from 9:00 to 11:45 and from 1:00 to 3:00 for five days. See figure 9-5.

Some Suggestions for Workshop Program Irrespective of Format Used

There are several items one should consider in working with teachers regardless of the format of the workshop:

1. Be sure the staff is compensated by being given released time, extra pay, or some other form of incentive.
2. Be sure that, early in the planning, members of the program elect the areas of responsibility for tasks they want to be involved in.
3. Move toward the area of production. It is easier to write things down and correct them after they are stated than to continue to discuss what ought to be done. Participants should produce their ideas as rapidly as possible. Editing can always make them more precise.
4. Let the group select the area they really want to work on. Their concerns should be paramount in focusing on the activity that should be selected. To that end, it may be wise to simply put people into small groups and have them talk about general concerns with regard to education. Out of this discussion the group will select a problem they feel needs working on.
5. Keep meetings short. Don't work long hours in the productive phase. As hours increase, production decreases.
6. Set a timetable. Develop within it goals that need to be addressed and try to adhere to the schedule, but with a sense of flexibility.
7. Get clerical help. Many great projects have died for lack of a typist or secretary.
8. Finally, produce a blueprint for immediate action, and with recommendations so everyone knows what the immediate goal is and what is envisioned for the long-range goal.

In-service study activities, opportunities to see other programs in action, and having experienced people work with those who want to innovate are all important factors that lead to the implementation of ideas. At this level of activity it is wise to forgo the large and theoretical orientations and stay with actual implementation procedures. There are many components to change, and careful attention must be given to each.

Figure 9-5   TOPICS FOR DISCUSSION

Monday A.M.

1. Elementary School Organizational Vehicles and Processes: Present Trends, Particular Aspects, Some Achieved Models
2. The Nongraded School: A Philosophy and Working Definition

Monday P.M.

Diagnosis and Prescription as Underpinning Correlates of Nongraded, Continuous-Progress Education

a) Learning sequences
b) Diagnostic inventories
c) Learning developmental inventories
d) Specific learning-stage inventories
e) Continuous diagnostic feedback based on individualized worksheets to ascertain established competence

Tuesday A.M.

School Organization to Assure Flexibility

a) Mechanical schedules
b) More effective teacher utilization and assignment
c) More creative use of specialists in instructional enriching areas: libraries, music, art, physical education
d) Necessary commitments for pupil reassignments and assignments based on learning-teaching styles

Tuesday P.M.

An Analysis of Three Prototype Programs, Using Filmstrips and Transparencies to Describe the Situation

Wednesday A.M.

Developing More Expansive Programs and a Scheme for Moving from Limited Nongraded Programs to Well-Planned Attempts at Multidimensional Activities

a) Paradigm of various levels of operation in nongraded education
b) Comparison of several models of school organization

Figure 9-5 TOPICS FOR DISCUSSION *(continued)*

Wednesday P.M.

Small Group Sessions to Develop Relevant Questions Concerning Needed Knowledge, Aspects, and Techniques for First-Step Implementations to be Dealt with in Other Sessions

Thursday

Collaborative Teacher Planning as an Adjunct to Continuous-Progress Education

a) Establishing objective strategies and activities concerning decisions of diagnosed needs of children
b) Establishing evaluative criteria necessary for ascertaining growth
c) Teacher concerns and activities and curricula revision
d) Teacher concerns and activities vis-a-vis grouping and programs dealing with social and emotional problems

Friday A.M.

1. Developing Community and Teacher Readiness for Change; Approaches of Study, and Analysis and Discussion of a Case-Study Approach to Educational Innovation
2. Aspects of Record Keeping and Reporting Growth and Pupil Performance in the Nongraded School

Friday P.M.

Panel Discussion on Various Aspects of Educational Innovation and Change
a) The instructional-materials center
b) Dealing with selected learning problems
c) Individual contract learning and independent study
d) Teacher styles and learning styles
e) The necessary commitments attendant to nongraded, continuous-progress education and innovation in general

NONGRADING THE BILINGUAL CHILD

CONTINUOUS-PROGRESS EDUCATION AND THE FOREIGN-LANGUAGE SPEAKER

There is much concern in education today for the child from a foreign background involved in a program using communication codes that are unfamiliar to him. The foreign-language speaker is lost when he is unable to participate in class. Frequently he is penalized because of his linguistic inability, even though he is otherwise quite an able learner. The *Bilingual Act* (1967), an amendment to the *Elementary and Secondary Education Act* (1965), makes dramatic note of this problem. Results of the early studies of schools participating in the Act show that children do not progress in the existing structure and approach to education unless their language and background are used by teachers who are aware of the problems attendant to their language conflicts and cultural differences.

With an average student population of native speakers, continuous-progress, nongraded education has been found to result in more and better learning, as well as sounder mental health. Such education is even more crucially needed for foreign-speaking children who must master the language in addition to the academic skills and knowledge usually assimilated by their peers. More often than not, the learning potential of these children is hampered by the straitjacket of a lockstep education, which fails to take into consideration the vital factor of individual differences in language and other aptitudes.[1] Time and time again, foreign students are placed in English classes to sink or swim in the alien stream of instruction, under the erroneous assumption that they will absorb the "correct" language through osmosis. Under such conditions, a few linguistically gifted individuals do manage to acquire a functional command of the tongue, but the majority struggle hopelessly against the barrier of communication, only to be branded with the unfair label of slow learner.

The problem is that all cognitive processes must be activated through the use of language, and each specific language represents a structure of mental habits, conditioned and organized unconsciously within the mind of the native speaker, but which must be learned consciously by a nonnative *before* they can serve as a means of acquiring knowledge.[2] The ability and length of time needed to construct a new linguistic framework varies from one individual to the next, according to a great many variables such as cultural background, motivation, aptitude, innate mental and physical skills (memory, learning rate, analytical perception, auditory and visual discrimination, and vocal flexibility), and to a minimal extent, intelligence. (The correlation between IQ and foreign-language achievement is only .38.)[3]

For these reasons, the current practice of segregating foreign students into special classes at each grade level is unsound, although it is admittedly preferable to the policy of letting the children flounder in conventional classes. No attempt at homogeneous grouping of any kind has the power to counteract the rigidity of gradedness or rectify the fallacy of its basic concept – that children are robots who can be programmed with the same amount and type of knowledge, in the exact same length of time. And nowhere is the lockstep system of education more destructive to academic potential, or more contradictory to psychological principles of human behavior, than in the specialized realm of language learning, where equal opportunity for achievement depends on the use of flexible grouping, founded on individually rated performance and progress. Unfortunately also, nowhere are the misconceptions of traditionalism more stubbornly entrenched in classroom practices than in language classes, where written expression and grammatical terminology still take precedence over oral considerations.

However, rather than dismiss traditional language teaching in such a summary manner, let us first examine its past record in terms of long-range effects on the acculturation of immigrants, whose livelihood depends on their ability to function adequately in an alien culture. Then let us consider the advantages of continuous-progress education for language-handicapped students. For practical purposes, both theoretical discussion and examples of demonstrated application will refer to speakers of English, French, or Spanish in a new cultural and linguistic environment.

Traditional Education and the Foreign Speaker

From an educational viewpoint, foreign students offer to the schools the challenge of both familiar and unfamiliar problems. Within their ranks, as within those of native speakers, there will be found a similar range of abilities, IQ, personality, motivation, aptitudes and attitudes – and disabilities: physiological, psychological, and emotional disturbances. All these factors affect (positively or negatively) the individual learning rates in any circumstances. However, in the case of immigrants, normal learning conditions are complicated by the interference of alien patterns of language, thought, and culture, which short-circuit the pursuit of educational goals: socialization of immature human beings, communication of knowledge, and development of individual skills. The dilemma thus faced by teachers and administrators is the question of how these objectives may be achieved with a minimum of fuss and a maximum of results, without sacrificing quality education.

To what extent have the schools succeeded in performing their task? The answer is discouraging. So far, experience has shown that educational aims have not been, and apparently cannot be, accomplished within the rigid channels of graded curricula, at least as far as the children of minority groups are concerned.[4] One glance at the achievement scale of foreign-speaking students educated in traditional institutions located in the focal areas of immigrant population—in California, New York, or the Southwest, for instance—will attest to the dismal fact that the schools have failed to prepare these children adequately for survival in a competitive society. A study conducted in 1960 to identify current levels of formal education in New York City revealed that "only 13 percent of Puerto Rican men and women 25 years of age and older in 1960 had completed either high school or more advanced education . . . more than half (of them) had less than an eighth grade education. . . ."[5] Another survey, completed one year later in the same location, discovered that "fewer than 10 percent of Puerto Ricans in the third grade were reading at their grade level or above. . . . By the eighth grade the degree of retardation was even more severe, with almost two-thirds of the Puerto Rican children retarded more than three years."[6] Significantly, this tragic situation can be depicted for nearly every substantial minority group of alien origin now residing in this country. Detailed information on these conditions is available in any recent United States Census Report.

The revelatory statistics indicated in the previous paragraph will shock dedicated educators. These figures, however, cannot portray the mental suffering and frustration of unsuccessful school years, nor the inevitable defeat of dropping out of the academic race, nor the heartbreaking corollaries of economic deprivation and social ostracism, nor the ultimate bitterness of second-class citizenship in the midst of an affluent society.

The human beings who are these statistics have no recourse against their fate. Neither they, nor the schools, are aware of their predicament until it is too late, for the deteriorating effects of an inappropriate education are not immediately noticeable. By the time they become evident, the results are usually attributed to other causes. This insidious process starts on the first day a foreign child enters a classroom. In the beginning, there are instinctive reactions to a strange environment: the alienation of being different from the rest of the class, the fear of appearing ridiculous to classmates, the dread of not knowing what the teacher expects. A few years later, these feelings are no longer linked to new experiences; the child knows that he cannot measure up to anyone's standards, and he accepts the label of slow learner. Sometimes a well-intentioned instructor withholds a child's promotion to the next grade (where he belongs, at least chronologically). Instead of helping him, the teacher's decision burdens him with the emotional problem of adjusting to a different maturity level, and it condemns him to the trauma of reviewing subject matter already associated with failure. For each year that he manages to complete under such conditions, he is rewarded with consistently low marks and negative comments on his learning ability. This damning record seals his fate for years to come. Even assuming that such a child should somehow succeed in obtaining a high school diploma, there is little chance of his climbing further on the educational ladder. His low grade-average bars him automatically from college.

The consequences of scholastic failure extend far beyond the realm of academic circles into the very web of daily existence. Indeed one may predict, with an almost invariable accuracy, that those individuals who rank lowest in education, also rank lowest later on in occupation and income. This fact is substantiated in the following excerpt from figures comparing the occupational distribution of Mexican-American and Anglo-American males in five southwestern states:[7]

Occupation	Mexican-Americans	Anglo-Americans
Professional	4.8%	15.9%
Managers, proprietors	5.1%	15.4%
Clerical	5.8%	8.2%
Sales workers	4.2%	9.7%
Craftsmen	19.2%	22.5%
Operatives	26.8%	16.6%
Service workers	8.8%	5.7%
Farm laborers	7.7%	0.6%
Other laborers	16.7%	4.6%

A superficial interpretation of these statistics could lead an uninformed observer to the conclusion that Mexican-Americans are less capable than Anglo-Americans and that they are best suited to perform menial jobs. But a more thorough investigation would reveal a striking correlation between the occupational status and the educational background of the groups, for the median years of school completed by "white persons of Spanish surnames in five Southwestern States (aged 14 and over) are 8.1."[8] Even if this figure must be considered high, since it is inflated by the inclusion of college years, presumably accumulated by the 4.8 percent of Mexican-American professionals, the fact remains that 8.1 does not even represent the minimum ten years of compulsory education required in this country. Taken all together, the statistics on this minority group alone seem to constitute a sufficient indictment of the schools for educators to do a little soul-searching and ask: "What are we doing wrong? What can we do about it? Who else is suffering from this situation?"

People who convince themselves that the adverse effects of lockstep education are restricted to immigrants should know that they are blinded by their prejudices. They should realize how the presence of foreign children in regular classes (which they cannot follow) triggers inevitably a chain reaction of emotional attitudes that interferes with learning, and strains the climate of class relations for all.

Under present conditions, teachers and administrators experience endless frustration at coping with an impossible instructional situation which nothing in their professional background has prepared them to meet. Their plight cannot be described within the confines of this chapter, for even a superficial discussion of the problem would cover a considerable number of pages. However, information on the subject may be found in an article which is included in a text of readings on education in urban communities.[9] Three major points are brought out in this article: (1) *Language inadequacies cannot be handled in a regular classroom.* (2) *Traditional curricula are inappropriate to meet the needs of foreign speakers.* (3) *Teachers should not be made the scapegoats for these failures.* Actually, even an inexperienced observer is able to see how mixed-language conditions are bound to slow down the learning rate of all the children, since neither the subject matter, nor the method, nor the medium of instruction can be geared to reach everyone in the class at the same time. It is equally clear that the cultural strain underlying such a situation must lead to the kind of misunderstandings that foster or reinforce those misconceptions known as national stereotypes. Thus, in the end, no one in the school can be said to thrive on mass-tailored activities that form the graded curriculum and are geared to the needs of the mythical average learner.

Toward a Nongraded Curriculum Sequence for Foreign Speakers

Until a flexible learning sequence is formulated to help each child develop necessary academic skills and knowledge, emergency measures may be taken to facilitate the adaptation of foreign speakers to the regular course of study, and to neutralize some of the stigmas imposed on them by the combined misconceptions of traditional thinking and ethnocentric misinformation. Suggestions concerning this temporary course of action are listed here. They are separated into two groups and are organized in descending order of importance. The measures contained in the first category are essential to the educational welfare of nonnative children; they also have the advantage of requiring very little money, time, or effort. The second set of recommendations is somewhat more onerous to implement but is considerably more effective in terms of positive results. All these procedures may be integrated later in a nongraded program.

1. Primary Requirements

a) Academic placement at nearest level, according to maturity, language proficiency, and academic background (if available). (The practice of assigning a ten-year-old child to a second-grade class because he does not understand the language will not make him learn it faster. Instead it will decrease his chance of acculturation by isolating him from his peers who would encourage him to talk.)

b) Academic placement in average class, if homogeneous grouping is in force at the school, until actual learning abilities may be truly assessed. (The practice of assigning a foreign child to the slow group in the appropriate level does not facilitate his learning the language. Instead it brands him with a label he may not deserve. Ignorance of a language should never be equated with mental inferiority.)

c) Temporary elimination of certain subject matter requiring particular knowledge of the medium of instruction in order to be understood. Time spent in hearing a meaningless stream of sounds is wasted. (Foreign speakers should be excused from regular language, reading, and social-studies classes. They should receive special language instruction, preferably from a teacher trained in foreign-language techniques.)

d) Daily language instruction for foreign speakers: one to two hours, during regular language, reading, science, or social studies periods. Instruction to be given by a foreign-language teacher or one similarly trained.

e) Establishment of separate evaluative criteria for foreign students in all subject matter. They should be based strictly on content knowledge and not on linguistic expression. Language progress should be rated as all foreign-language learning: according to oral and written mastery of appropriate utterances, sound sequences, and structural patterns. (All failing marks to be withheld until a child is able to communicate adequately in the language.)

f) Elimination of all standard tests, unless especially prepared by trained teachers for foreign-speaking children. (With the best intentions, uninformed personnel may develop what they consider erroneously to be culture-free diagnostic tests. These attempts often yield distorted results. In arithmetic, for example, division problems are styled differently in Anglo-Saxon and Romance cultures, and each is confusing to the other.)

2. *Desirable Procedures*

a) In-service training of staff on methods of teaching their native tongue as a foreign language. All trained teachers to take charge of foreign students for a regular period of time every day.

b) Scheduling of special language classes according to language proficiency; initially, elementary and intermediate sections to be set up; later on, extension into advanced sections as needed. One section of each for every level, or every group of three levels, according to total number of students. Assignment of students to appropriate language section should *not* be made on the basis of their length of stay in the country. Some individuals know more after six months than others can learn in two years.

c) Simultaneous bilingual instruction when enough students possess a similar language background. Science and social-studies instruction to be given in the students' native language. Periods corresponding to language and reading to be used for special language classes. All other subjects to be taken with regular classes.

d) Purchase of texts and materials designed to teach English as a foreign language.

e) Reinforcement of language instruction for foreign speakers in all subjects through the following devices:

Individualized instruction via ability grouping.

Tutoring by volunteer native speakers.

Use of electronic devices: language laboratory, tape recorders, language masters, and so forth.

Foundations of a Nongraded Program for Foreign Speakers

The execution of educational innovations is hampered by the unconscious resistance of those staff members who stress the passive role of the schools (preservation and transmission of cherished cultural values and knowledge) over its active one (leadership in the search for progress). Some educators even tend to equate any deviation from the practiced norm as a betrayal of tradition. Thus the heresies of scrambling the neat compartments of a familiar curriculum sequence and of eliminating the pigeonholing process of a known marking system may antagonize experienced teachers who feel threatened by the prospect of abandoning time-tested modes of operation. When such a situation exists, there is no better way of converting potential adversaries into willing supporters (or at least innocuous bystanders) than to involve them directly in program development by means of an in-service workshop consisting of the following:

Exposure to a shock language and culture.

Instruction in basic principles of contrastive linguistics and cultural anthropology.

Detailed language study (structural analysis of oral and written native language).

Study of psycholinguistic principles of language learning.

Instruction in basic principles of nongrading, with emphasis on adaptation to foreign-language situation.

Demonstration and practice of foreign-language teaching techniques. (For this purpose, groups of foreign children should be brought in to receive instruction for one hour daily.)[10]

This kind of training program has already been run successfully for several years by a cooperating group of public schools in northern New Jersey. A model nongraded program for native-born pupils and a parallel one for Spanish students are now operated in the Roosevelt Elementary School of Union City, New Jersey.

It is not necessary in this discussion to provide a description of the conditioning process teachers need to be exposed to in creating a successful nongraded sequence, since the details would be essentially the same as those covered in previous chapters. However, certain preliminary questions usually raised by administrators whenever nongrading or continuous progress is mentioned will be answered at this point.

Ten Key Questions and Answers on Continuous-Progress Education for Foreign Speakers:

1. Why set up a continuous progress, nongraded program?

Because traditional school programs have failed to equalize life opportunities for nonnative speakers.

Because continuous-progress programs have already proved successful with native speakers, and because they provide an ideal framework within which language instruction may be individualized to accommodate diverse linguistic aptitudes.

2. What kind of school will thrive on a continuous-progress orientation?

Any school will benefit from it—elementary, secondary, or any combination thereof.

3. How long does it take before a full-scale continuous-progress program operates effectively?

It depends on the number of grade levels to be reorganized. At any rate, one full year (academic and summer) of planning and preparation should be anticipated before actual implementation begins. After the initial program has been in operation for a year, plans should be made to reorganize an additional grade level every year until the system is extended to the entire school.

4. What size program should be considered initially and at what level?

Ideally a continuous-progress program should begin with the reorganization of grades one, two, and three, but practically speaking, the starting level should be determined by the largest concentration of foreign students. If most of them are at the junior high school level, then logically nongrading should begin there (at least for foreign speakers). Afterwards the program can be extended downward as well as upward, one grade at a time.

5. Which, and how many, staff members should be involved in setting up a program?

Everyone who is expected to implement the program should be involved in the planning. Administrators and teachers should participate actively in all phases of the operation. Parents should be kept informed of the goals to be achieved and the manner in which they will be carried out. Students should know that they are to share an experience with the school.

6. What kind of outside help is needed to initiate a program, and to what extent is it required?

Expert consultation is needed in two fields: foreign-language teaching and nongraded organization. Each consultant should be at least acquainted with the other's field of specialization, for teamwork is essential to the successful development of a learning sequence appropriate to the specific needs of foreign speakers.

7. Are ready-made nongraded, continuous-progress sequences for nonnative speakers available? If so, could they be implemented directly, thereby eliminating the time and cost of training the staff and developing the materials?

The answer is no on all counts as elaborated in chapter 2.

8. Should an entire school be nongraded, or should a program be set up strictly for foreign speakers, to the exclusion of native children?

The entire school should be nongraded with continuous-progress orientation, since all students will profit from the experience. While a curriculum is worked out for native children, an emergency plan of the kind mentioned previously should be set up to increase the effectiveness of language instruction for the foreign-born.

9. What sorts of materials need to be developed for an ideal program aimed at foreign speakers?

Assuming that a regular learning sequence is being developed for native speakers, the following materials need to be prepared for foreign students:

a) A language-learning sequence parallel to a regular reading or language sequence that will develop necessary linguistic skills in appropriate stages. All other skills *must be subordinated* to the development of a functional command of the language. This often requires an internal reorganization of learning-skills sequencing.

b) A sampling of language units centered on activities normally used in the regular curriculum. A good choice for primary grades would be units on food and meals, family, houses, school workers, and so forth.

c) A range of audiovisual materials illustrating these activities, to be used in conjunction with the sample units.

d) An appropriate skills inventory to be used as an evaluative instrument in the identification of learning progress and individual problems. Modified nongraded records suited to the requirements for foreign learners.

e) In the event that circumstances do not permit the use of bilingual education, two

other sequences must be adapted to the needs of foreign students (social studies and science) in terms of vocabulary range, structural control, conceptual knowledge, cultural adaptation.

10. On what basis should a budget be established?

The total expenditure will vary according to the current financial policies of the community, the extent of the anticipated program, the availability of consultant help in the vicinity, and the degree of staff competence in the realm of foreign-language teaching and nongrading. On the basis of total inexperience, for instance, intensive training in language teaching may be provided in an eight-week period during one summer.

Guiding Principles for the Development of a Continuous-Progress, Nongraded Program for Foreign Speakers

The aims of a continuous-progress, nongraded program for foreign speakers are three in number: first, to insure continuous-progress education for every child regardless of his learning abilities and cultural background; second, to equip him with the normal linguistic skills needed to function adequately in school and in society; and third, to provide him with the physical, emotional, and cognitive skills that will enable him to become a productive and well-adjusted member of the community. The successful achievement of these goals may often depend on a skillful compromise between the ideal circumstances seemingly required by theoretical principles (in pedagogy, psychology, linguistics, cultural anthropology) and the practical realities of the situation at hand. The latter should undoubtedly outweigh the former, because concepts worked out under controlled laboratory conditions are not always readily brought down to the classroom level; because the tenets of allied disciplines may sometimes conflict with one another,[11] and because even the axioms of each particular field are always subject to change.

While it is useless to make predictions on the kinds of decisions that will have to be made to insure a balanced compromise between recommended theory and desirable practice, it is possible to set forth the important facts that must guide the development of a nongraded, continuous-progress program for foreign speakers:

1. The concepts of continuous-progress and nongrading are the same, whether they apply to native speakers or to foreign students. The only difference is found in the internal organization of skills that must revolve primarily around language-learning sequences.

2. It is quite possible, according to research, that the stages of a child's intellectual development will occur in the same sequence, regardless of cultural context.

3. All children need to acquire the same basic skills and knowledge if they are to survive in society. In order to gain these essentials, foreign students must master the language of the host culture as a tool of learning.

4. Special problems, stemming from differences in language, thought, and culture, must be anticipated and accounted for in the selection of subject-matter content, classroom techniques, and evaluative criteria. Conflicts arising from these three interference points must be resolved by the school, not by the children.

5. Neither total segregation from, nor complete participation in, the regular stream of school activities offers an ideal solution to the problems of foreign-speaking students. The answer lies in a mixture of regular and special instruction to be eventually superseded by participation in the normal study program.

Cognitive Development and the Language-Learning Sequence for Foreign Speakers

It is fairly easy to prepare an adequately concrete elementary-reading sequence for native children, based on a consideration of the physical and conceptual skills needed for fluent and meaningful reading. But the task of designing a parallel sequence for foreign speakers brings into play the additional linguistic and emotional problems of pronunciation, structure, vocabulary, and acculturation. Let us consider, for example, the situation faced by a first-grade teacher placed in charge of a foreign-language-speaking class during the first few weeks of school.

He cannot test the children's coordination in gross motor skills until they understand his instructions. He cannot check their fine motor skills until they know the meaning of such basic items as scissors, paper, color, crayon, and so forth. He cannot teach them classification of sizes and shapes until they have learned both the concept and the oral expression of *like* and *different*. He cannot even operate normally in the classroom until the children have been drilled in the routine and emergency measures of the school such as knowing the verbal cues and proper behavior during dismissal, fire drills, going to the bathroom, and so forth.

If children already possess a functional command of the language, these problems are largely solved and instruction can be centered specifically on linguistic problems: proper enunciation, appropriate use of grammatical structures, and acquisition of an extended vocabulary. But even in this situation the children's limited capacity for reasoning—strictly on a concrete level—imposes certain limits to the range of subject-matter content.

On the other hand, the intellectual capacity of high school students does permit the inclusion of hypothetical reasoning in a secondary language sequence. In this case, linguistic proficiency alone will determine at which point difficult items, such as subjunctive and conditional structures, may be safely introduced. This restriction does not mean that imaginative problem-solving situations cannot be used to motivate the spontaneous use of language in classroom discussions. On the contrary, nothing is more likely to stimulate creative thinking and speech practice than the selection of an interesting contemporary topic for a unit of work—space travel, for instance. An example of the manner in which this particular subject may be treated to negotiate the hurdles of varying proficiency levels in oral expression will be found in figure 10-1 at the end of this chapter.

A Continuous-Progress, Nongraded Program for Foreign Speakers

The establishment of a continuous-progress, nongraded program, restricted exclusively to foreign students, is not recommended; it is not sound policy, either psychologically or financially. A split-curriculum arrangement may awaken or strengthen ethnocentric feelings in the community. Parental resentment, expressed by both sides (native and foreign) of the population, would justifiably accuse the schools of either segregating immigrant children or showing favoritism toward them. Finally, a full measure of educational returns on time, money, and effort spent on the organization of a gradeless sequence will be secured only through the development of a comprehensive plan, diversified to meet the needs of both native and foreign students.

Before actual work on this modified curriculum can begin, decisions must be made concerning grouping policies and scheduling. For maximum flexibility of operation, it is advisable to group children according to their maturity and oral-language proficiency, over a range of what would normally be three grade levels. However,

while kindergarten and first grade may be combined, they should not be mixed with other classes where reading and writing skills have already been introduced. Ideally, there should be three linguistic-proficiency levels; an elementary section (for all newcomers with minimal or zero knowledge of the language), an intermediate section (for all students able to communicate in the language, but with considerable inaccuracies in pronunciation and use of structures), and an advanced section (for children who know the language, but need more work in isolated sounds and patterns). In the beginning, efforts should be concentrated primarily on the first two language levels, since the initial stages of language learning are the most crucial for the proper instillation of nativelike speech habits. The third group may be entirely omitted in the primary grades, where advanced learners may be expected to fit comfortably in the regular program. Not only do very young children assimilate a foreign tongue quite readily and accurately, but they are also exposed, at that level, to a restricted subject-matter content which will not overtax their mental capacity.[12] A model grouping might be arranged as shown on page 163. This organization must be kept flexible, for a student should remain assigned to a particular language level only as long as he profits by the experience. Accordingly, provisions should be made for periodic reviews of individual progress to insure the continued development of the learner's linguistic and other abilities.

One important factor of success in language learning is class size; this should be kept in mind when language sections are organized. The acquisition of oral skills (more essential to a foreign speaker than written skills) is best achieved in small classes of twelve to twenty students. At the same time, some arrangements need to be made for the education of newcomers who enter the school during the year and have received little or no previous language

Present Grades	Reorganized Sections
Kindergarten and 1	elementary intermediate
2, 3, 4	elementary intermediate advanced (if needed)
4, 5, 6	elementary intermediate advanced
6, 7, 8	elementary intermediate advanced
8, 9, 10	elementary intermediate advanced
10, 11, 12	elementary intermediate advanced

training. If the administration anticipates a steady or intermittent stream of new arrivals throughout the year, the situation warrants the organization of an intensive language-orientation course, lasting approximately six to eight weeks and repeated if needed, to prepare these students for entrance into the regular sequence for foreign speakers.

Once the overall grouping system has been outlined, there still remains the question of deciding on what basis a student will be assigned to a particular proficiency level. The problem is best solved by the use of an evaluative instrument. A standardized test is not needed at this point; it would be less reliable than a diagnostic test tailored to local conditions, provided the latter is prepared by someone trained in foreign-language techniques, and according to the following directions:

Preparation of an Individual Diagnostic Test of Oral-Language Proficiency

Timing   Three to five minutes per student

Kinds of Test   One for primary students
One for older students

Materials Needed   Tape recorder and tapes
Test forms and pencil
Visual aids referred to in test questions (all used by tester)

Physical Facilities   Quiet room where tester will interview individual students without interruptions

Contents
Part I   Informal interview (five common questions asked in everyday life)

Part II   Questions centering on basic interference points (pronunciation and use of structures) between native and target languages

Part III   Spontaneous descriptions of pictures

Purpose of Content
Part I   To eliminate children who have no knowledge of the language

Part II   To check isolated sounds and use of common language patterns

Part III   To evaluate fluency and melody of connected speech

Test Administration   Anyone may administer the test by following directions accurately. The entire test is recorded on tape for additional reference; the student's answers are noted on the test form. The tester's accuracy may thus be verified by a language expert later on.

Evaluation of Results   Students will be assigned as follows:
Section E (Elementary)   Anyone who cannot answer two out of five questions in part I, or who fails more than 70 percent of the test

Section I (Intermediate)   Anyone who fails 40 percent to 70 percent of the test

Section A (Advanced)   Anyone who fails less than 40 percent of the test

Uses of Test   For initial placement of students in language sections
As a guide to instruction (information on individual language problems)

There is no need to give a written examination. Experience has shown that an oral test provides sufficient information on language proficiency to select an appropriate language section. It is also useless to evaluate the students' native-language knowledge; the results do not predict achievement in another idiom.

The specific points evaluated in the test should form the nucleus of the intensive language-orientation course for incoming students without previous training, since the test items represent the most common linguistic pitfalls faced by foreign learners.

A sample diagnostic test is included at the end of this chapter in figure 10-2. It is geared to the evaluation of English listening and speaking abilities on the part of Spanish speakers.

Once a student has been assigned to his proper section, the introductory phase of language learning can begin. During this time all the children in each section will receive the same instruction in basic skills for two consecutive periods during the day, through a selected number of standard units prepared in advance for each proficiency level. At the end of this observation interval, the progress of each learner will be evaluated by the teacher who will, accordingly, prescribe courses of study tailored to the specific needs of individual students. The individual achievement levels identified at this point will probably range from children in need of special assistance, to those

requiring additional work on basic linguistic concepts, to a few who are ready for independent study. Differences in oral and written abilities will also become noticeable, sometimes within the same individual.

On the basis of these findings, oral and written instruction can be organized into fifteen-minute modules, each of which may be doubled or tripled according to need. These modules will be taken up by a series of activities, from which selections will be made to form individual study programs designed to offset the difficulties and match the interests of the learners. A suggested range of activities could be set up as follows:

1. Large-Group Instruction (Oral or Written)
   To introduce new material
   To provide pattern practice
   To view language-teaching films
   To test achievement
2. Small-Group Instruction (Oral or Written)
   To work intensively on basic skills
   To apply content to life situation
   To vary the use of familiar material
   To go on field trips
3. Individual Study (Oral and/or Written)
   a) For highly gifted students (enrichment)
      Oral work with tape recorder
      Library research
      Work on a selected project
   b) For students in need of special assistance
      Tutoring sessions with volunteers
      Oral work with language master
      Programed reading
4. Language Laboratory Work (Oral Emphasis)
   To provide listening exercises (native voices)
   To provide language practice
   To improve specific points of pronunciation
   To automatize the use of specific structures

The selection and combination of modules assigned to a child in each of the above instructional categories should be determined by his past performance in terms of language-skills achievement and learning style. However, the amount of time allotted to individual study should be kept at a minimum during the elementary and intermediate phases of language learning, where progress depends considerably upon the acquisition of good pronunciation habits through guided imitation of a model. Under the circumstances, the Trump plan recommendation for a blend of 10 percent study in large lectures, 45 percent independent work, and 45 percent in small-group instruction cannot be used, at least in the initial stages of language learning.[13] Nevertheless, its basic principle is retained, since optimum learning conditions are insured by a mixture of educational ingredients: student, teacher, subject matter, and instructional strategy. The effect of this prescribed combination on learning progress must be reexamined periodically. After each successive six-to-eight-week period, the personal record of each child is reviewed and a new study plan worked out on the basis of his achievement. Such a flexible system allows a student who forges ahead in oral expression, but trails behind in written language, to work with level I material in the latter and at the same time with level II or III material in the former—a possibility unheard-of in traditional language classes, but a common occurrence in a nongraded school, where knowledge is personalized instead of being regulated by chronological standards.

A Language-Learning Sequence for Foreign Speakers

This sequence should be parallel to the regular reading or language sequence for native speakers in primary grades. It should be based on the latter's content, and suitably adapted to the requirements of foreign-language study. These objectives can be reached through implementation of the following procedures:

1. Preparation of a sequential list of language structure and pronunciation features to be taught. Order of presentation will be determined by linguistic principles and practical considerations (high frequency of usage and usefulness in daily life).

2. Analysis of regular sequence in terms of learning skills, topics, situational activities, and general content.

3. Comparison of basal readers (used in the regular reading sequence) and linguistic readers (selected for foreign speakers) from the point of view of situational, vocabulary, structural, and conceptual content.

4. Integration of information gathered from steps 1, 2, and 3, but with modifications of the last two lists in accordance with language-learning principles.

5. Elaboration of final product with appropriate list of language-learning activities and notations on cultural similarities or differences, to be presented with the subject matter.

6. Development of sample units for each level with auxiliary audiovisual material.

7. Preparation of appropriate skills inventory to record students' progress, with separate notation for oral and written language abilities.

8. Creation of a curriculum-prescription form to guide pupil study during each of the six-to-eight-week learning phases.

9. Preliminary outline of format to be used for all achievement tests given at the end of each six-to-eight-week cycle. For this purpose, figure 10-2 may serve as a partial guideline (it includes only a few basic oral skills). Actual performance tests will be designed cooperatively by teachers when the nongraded program is in operation; reliability and validity will be verified by qualified personnel.

10. Organization of a materials center where cooperative and individual work of teachers will be assembled and classified for instant retrieval.

The basic foreign-language primary sequence

will be first designed for elementary language-proficiency classes, but its overall plan is equally valid for intermediate sections, with suitable vocabulary enrichment, emphasis on appropriate pronunciation and structure problems, and elimination of basic language concepts already mastered by the learner. All other language-learning sequences (beyond third grade) may be developed in a similar manner, including their intermediate and advanced language-proficiency adaptations. As an illustration, level I of a model elementary-English primary sequence for Spanish speakers is provided at the end of this chapter in figure 10-3.

Nongrading a Foreign-Language Program for Native Students

Although the primary intention of this chapter has been to establish guidelines for the initiation of a nongraded program for foreign speakers, a logical extension of this objective points to the need for a few suggestions concerning the applicability of continuous-progress education in foreign-language classes offered to native students. So far, very little has been written by educational experts in this area, mostly because knowledge of the nature of second-language learning is not readily available outside this specialized field; and, conversely, information on nongrading principles seldom reaches foreign-language teachers in a meaningful way.

Actually, an entire text could be written on the strategies and problems of doing away with lockstep instruction in the French, Spanish, German, and other foreign-language departments of elementary and secondary schools. Basically the steps to be followed in pursuit of this aim are not very different from those already discussed in the preceding pages.

The first three years of study should be organized exactly along the lines described earlier, and a learning sequence encompassing this period should be developed within the general framework proposed by Nelson Brooks several years ago—the stream-level concept.[14] Each level may be divided into cycles (three, or more if desired) and according to staff preferences. The entire course of study may be based on selected texts, or may lead to the development of new materials. Both diversified instructional categories and diagnostic tests should be modeled after those already described in this chapter, and individual study plans prescribed for each student in the recommended manner. Thus each child will be able to progress at his own rate until he has mastered the essential foreign-language skills—in other words, until he has completed the last cycle for level III. Everyone will receive credit for the exact number of years spent in language study, regardless of the amount of content "covered" by the individual, for in such a program an accumulation of superficial knowledge is considered less important than a mastery of basic foreign-language concepts. Thus, it does not matter that gifted students will complete the sequence in two years, and others may require as many as four to five years of steady work.

Level III marks the end of language study as a basic tool of communication, and the beginning of its consideration and appreciation as an expression of human beliefs, attitudes, and emotions. Consequently, there will be a corresponding change of orientation in the curriculum development at this point. Henceforth the foreign-language program will conform to the nongraded pattern of a conventional language and literature course of study. All the conventional designations of French IV, Spanish V, or German VI will be dropped. Instead students will be offered a choice of concept-centered courses, illustrating similarities and differences in the native and target cultures through the study of literary selections. The degree of linguistic difficulty and the proportion of oral and written phases will continue to be graduated carefully to accommodate the diverse proficiency achievement of individual students. The contents of these courses arranged in order of increasing difficulty might be as follows:

Teacher	Concept	Literature	Emphasis
A	Man and Nature	Mass media selections (TV, radio, songs, films, etc.)	Oral skills
B	Man and Man	Mass media selections (magazine and newspaper articles, etc.)	Written skills
C	Man and Self	Theater selections (chronological development)	Oral skills
D	Man and God	Essays, stories, novels	Written skills

The flexibility of such a program will be maintained in two different ways: first, through the organization of individualized module-cycle combinations; and second, through the diversification of course offerings involving a yearly regrouping or substitution of concepts, literary selections, and linguistic emphases. With this arrangement, an uninterrupted stream of motivation will be guaranteed to students who plan to extend their foreign-language and literature studies beyond the intermediate level, through a constantly renewed selection of topics suited to their interests and linguistic abilities. The favorable learning conditions in such a program not only will insure continuous-progress education for all participants, but also will result in larger foreign-language enrollment, thus exposing more children to the benefits of a greater perceptual and cognitive versatility, through the acquisition of new language-thought-culture patterns.

From the preceding discussion, it is clearly evident that the rationale for a foreign-language learning sequence remains basically unchanged, whether the course of study is planned for naturalization purposes (for immigrants) or for college-entrance requirements (for native students). Because the attainment of linguistic skills is a cumulative process, operating through successive stages all the way to bilingualism, it must be oriented toward certain reference points (cycles, levels, or the like) corresponding to certain achievement levels. The learner's progress toward these checkpoints is assessed at periodic intervals in terms of the four skills he is expected to master: listening, speaking, reading, and writing. Each successive period of study is programed by the teachers in accordance with their evaluative findings, in much the same way that a course of treatment, prescribed at first by a physician on the basis of his initial diagnosis, is later altered by him to match the patient's changing condition.

The multiple advantages of such a system of individualized instruction are self-evident. There is no interference with the learning process and no pressure from arbitrary standards; consequently, the stigma of failure is eradicated for underachievers, the frustration of boredom is banished for gifted learners, and the nightmare of multilevel language classes is eliminated for the instructor. Only under such conditions will natural learning leading to meaningful education prevail, and genuine motivation resulting in a self-generating desire to study, flourish.

Figure 10-1   VARIED APPROACHES TO A SECONDARY UNIT ON SPACE TRAVEL

This unit is planned for the following bilingual situations in secondary schools:

1. Native speakers of English and parallel track of French-speaking students in the process of learning English. Adaptations are provided for elementary and intermediate levels of English proficiency.
2. Native speakers of French and parallel track of English-speaking students in the process of learning French. Adaptations are provided for elementary and intermediate levels of French proficiency.

(For practical purposes the adaptation examples offered here are restricted to the introduction only.)

A Unit on Space Travel

Situation:
The first astronauts land on Mars

Background Information:
Location of planets Mars and Earth
Concept of space travel
Transportation of astronauts
Materials and equipment needed by
astronauts during travel

Motivation:
Timeliness of subject
Speculation: What if there is life on Mars?

Central Concept:
The future of mankind; the unknown in
terms of—
Sensory perception (color, landscape, life
forms, etc.)
Emotional reactions (excitement, fear,
curiosity, etc.)
Communication problems (sounds, gestures,
thoughts, etc.)

Use of Language:
1. Native Speakers:
Conditional tense and subjunctive mode
Unrestricted use of space-age vocabulary
Spontaneous discussion; narration by
students

2. Foreign Speakers:

a) Elementary language level: High-
frequency verb form (present progressive in English, simple present
in French)

Selected vocabulary

Model narration by teacher, learned
verbatim by students

b) Intermediate language level: Regular
past tense(s) (preterite in English,
imparfait and *passé composé* in French)

Selected vocabulary

Collaborative narration (controlled by
teacher)

Preliminary Work:

1. All students:
Ask them to collect photographs of moon
landings.

2. Native speakers:
Ask them to look up information on space
travel and on Mars.

3. Foreign speakers:
Assign groups of five or six students to

Figure 10-1   VARIED APPROACHES TO A SECONDARY UNIT
ON SPACE TRAVEL *(continued)*

describe different aspects of imaginary Martians and Martian life. (Type of data accumulated will refer to contents of familiar units—on parts of the body, clothing, housing, meals, etc. Each group will select one specific topic.)

Sample Introductions of Unit (to set structural framework)

1. Native speakers:

   a) English-speaking students:
   "We are now in the year 2001, the night before the launching of a new spaceship, destination Mars. If you were the astronauts selected for this exploration, what would you think about on the eve of departure? What do you think Martians would look like? Would you expect them to be dressed like you?" Etc.

   b) French-speaking students:
   "Nous sommes en 2001, à la veille d'un voyage interplanétaire. Si vous faisiez tous partie de l'équipe des astronautes qui allaient explorer la planète Mars, quelles seraient vos pensées à la veille du départ—par exemple, au sujet de leur apparence? Vous attendriez-vous à ce que leurs vêtements soient semblables aux vôtres?" Etc.

2. Foreign speakers:

   Intermediate Level

   a) Intermediate English proficiency:
   "We are now in the year 2001. You are all astronauts who have just returned from Mars. Tell us what you saw." (The teacher stimulates conversation by asking specific questions on the physical appearance of the Martians, such as their size, shape, color, etc.

Each student provides at least one complete answer, using the correct past tense).

   b) Intermediate French proficiency:
   "Nous sommes en 2001. Vous êtes tous astronautes, et vous venez d'explorer Mars. Qu'est-ce que vous avez vu au cours de votre voyage? (The teacher uses the same procedure—questions and answers. Each student must use the appropriate past—*l'imparfait* or *le passé composé*—in his answer.)

   Elementary Level

   a) Elementary English or French proficiency: Suggested visual aids:
   Atlas view of the planets.
   Photograph of an astronaut and a spaceship.
   Colored illustration showing weird creatures in front of astronauts.

   NOTE ON TEXT: The linguistic content will be strictly controlled, and it will be taught verbatim by the teacher. Each lesson of the unit will be centered on a specific aspect of space travel. For instance, one day may be spent on the setting (location of Mars, the astronauts, their vehicle, etc.); another on the normal needs and activities of the travelers; the next few on imaginary descriptions of Mars and the Martians.

   b) Elementary English proficiency (the basic text): "This is a story about space travel. In the year 2001, a group of adventurous men leaves the planet Earth in a spaceship to explore a new planet—Mars. The men are called astronauts and their ship is called Apollo 707 . . . We are now in 2001—in imagination—and we are watching the adventures on television . . . What are the astronauts

Figure 10-1   VARIED APPROACHES TO A SECONDARY UNIT
ON SPACE TRAVEL *(continued)*

doing now?'' (This creates an opportunity for the class to review familiar vocabulary and structures by transposing normal daily activities into an imaginary setting).

c) Elementary French proficiency (the basic text): "Voici l'histoire d'un voyage interplanétaire. C'est l'année 2001, et une équipe d'hommes aventureux quitte la terre pour explorer une nouvelle planète, la planète Mars. Ces astronautes voyagent dans un vehicule interplanétaire, l'Apollon 707. Nous sommes maintenant en 2001—en imagination—et nous suivons les aventures des astronautes à la télévision. . . Qu'est-ce qu'ils font?'' (The same procedure described above in paragraph b).

Central Idea to be Used in Culminating Activities:

How does man visualize the unknown? In what ways must he be prepared to meet it on favorable terms?

Figure 10-2   SAMPLE DIAGNOSTIC TEST OF ORAL-ENGLISH PROFICIENCY
FOR SPANISH SPEAKERS

This test was prepared for students in the intermediate grades (4–8). Form A was used as a pretest for academic placement in an elementary, intermediate, or advanced English section. Form B served as an evaluation of language progress at the end of a six-week intensive training period. Both forms contain questions designed to assess a student's knowledge of stereotyped expressions (used in a regular school situation) and of basic structural and pronunciation patterns. These content items were included in the six-week curriculum taught by teachers trained in foreign-language techniques–in this case, English as a second language. They are an attempt to organize language terms based on frequency of use and aspects of what are termed linguistic interferences (between the English and the Spanish languages), before selecting the topical content (which will also be structured on the basis of high frequency occurrence and usefulness).

North Hudson Language Development Center — Title III

Summer 1969

ORAL ENGLISH PROFICIENCY TEST FOR SPANISH-SPEAKING STUDENTS

(Grades 4 through 8)

Prepared by:

Eliane C. Condon, Consultant

Hunter College
New York City

Doris Wadsworth, Project Director

Union City Schools
Union City, New Jersey

Form A: For Placement
Form B: For Evaluation

Form B — Results

Total Score (Parts I and II)   ☐

Overall Rating (Part III)

    Good   ☐

    Average   ☐

    Poor   ☐

Figure 10-2 SAMPLE DIAGNOSTIC TEST OF ORAL-ENGLISH PROFICIENCY
FOR SPANISH SPEAKERS *(continued)*

Form A

CURRICULUM CONTENT OF A SIX-WEEK INTENSIVE ENGLISH COURSE[15]

Note: Unlike most foreign language curriculum outlines, the present plan does NOT initiate learning from the standpoint of topical content or situational activities. Instead, it stresses mastery of common grammatical and sound patterns selected for their usefulness, and sequenced according to linguistic principles.

Grammatical Structures

1. Word Order:
   a. articles, adjective, noun
   b. article, adjective, noun, verb
   c. article, adjective, noun, verb, direct object
   d. statement and negative statement of *to be*
   e. statement and negative statement of present progressive
   f. Optional: questions (*to be,* present progressive of other verbs)

2. Word Form:
   a. present progressive inflection (-ing)
   b. regular plural inflection (all three pronunciations: $/s/$ $/z/$ $/Iz/$)
   c. regular past inflection (all three pronunciations: $/t/$ $/d/$ $/Id/$)
   d. simple present inflections

3. Function Words:
   a. articles (*a, an, the*)
   b. subject pronouns
   c. question words (*who, what, where*)
   d. locational prepositions (*in, on, of, to*)

Pronunciation

1. Connected Speech:
   a. general melody
   b. rhythm
   c. stress pattern
   d. intonation pattern

2. Isolated Sounds:
   a. $/ŋ/$ (as in ri*ng*)
   b. $/ð/$ (as in *th*e)
   c. $/ə/$ (as in b*u*t)
   d. $/s/$ and $/z/$ in contrast
   e. $/i/$ and $/I/$ in contrast

Figure 10-2   SAMPLE DIAGNOSTIC TEST OF ORAL-ENGLISH PROFICIENCY
FOR SPANISH SPEAKERS *(continued)*

List of Visual Aids Used in the Diagnostic Test

Page of Test	*Picture Number*	*Content*
5	77	Five green ties
	73	Red skirts
	104	A loaf of bread
	121	Bread, sugar, coffee, etc.
6	169	A father, a mother, and children
	172	A lady, a boy, a girl
	152	A sandwich
7	305	People on a bench, in a park
	139	A girl closing a door
	136	A boy opening a window
8	155	A man
	31	A car
	96	A house
9	129	A girl washing her face
	214	Boys and girls eating in a cafeteria
10	54	Boys standing
	70	Skirts
	164	Cars
	3	Dresses
	4	Hats (man's)
	C	Glasses full of water
11	129	Shoes on a box (shoes in a box) (a, b)
	80	Man's trousers (a)
	150	A teacher and a girl in a classroom
	216	A rocket being launched
12	D	A girl asking the teacher for a pencil. (Teacher pointing and saying "There's the pencil.")
	E	A boy asking a question and pointing to a box. (Father holding the box, saying "It's a hat.")
	F	Mother looking into a classroom, pointing to teacher and asking who it is. (Girl saying "It's the English teacher.")

Figure 10-2 SAMPLE DIAGNOSTIC TEST OF ORAL-ENGLISH PROFICIENCY
FOR SPANISH SPEAKERS *(continued)*

Page of Test	Picture Number	Content
13	166	A rainy landscape
	142	Children asleep in bed
	126	A boy reading a book
	141	A teacher teaching a class
14	213	A family seated at a table and eating dinner
	217	A boy getting up in the morning
	172	A street scene

Form B

ORAL ENGLISH PROFICIENCY TEST

Instructions:

1. The purpose of this section is to identify the student's ability to understand functional English and to give appropriate responses.

The Answers Must Be Given in Standard English

2. Do not ask the questions more than once.

3. Indicate the total score of correct answers in the box, at the end of part I.

Part I — Informal Interview

Check if Correct

1. Tester: Good morning.
   Student: Good morning. ☐

2. Tester: How are you?
   Student: Fine, thanks. (any acceptable answer) ☐

3. Tester: What's your name?
   Student: My name's _____ . ☐

4. Tester: How old are you?
   Student: I'm _____ . (any acceptable answer) ☐

5. Tester: Where do you live?
   Student: I live _____ . (any acceptable answer) ☐

Total Correct Answers (Part I) ☐

(Do not continue the test if the score is 2 or less.)

Figure 10-2 SAMPLE DIAGNOSTIC TEST OF ORAL-ENGLISH PROFICIENCY
FOR SPANISH SPEAKERS *(continued)*

Part II — Basic Language Skills

Instructions:

1. The purpose of this section is to rate the student's performance concerning specific interference points.

2. Test forms are enclosed in the folders.

3. Each question is based on a visual aid which will be found in a folder.

4. For each question, there is a separate folder bearing the same number as the question. For example, Question 1, Folder 1.

5. Indicate the total score of correct answers at the end of part II.

6. Add: Total Score Part I and Total Score Part II. Write the total in the box on first page of test.

7. Transfer the overall rating of connected speech from Part III to the proper boxes on first page.

Question 1 Word Order

Note: Partial answers are not *acceptable. If necessary, tell the student you want a complete answer.*

Check if Correct

a. Picture 77
   Tester: How many green ties are there?
   Student: There are five green ties.   ☐

b. Picture 73
   Tester: Are those red skirts or blue dresses?
   Student: They're red skirts.   ☐

c. Picture 104
   Tester: What is it?
   Student: It's bread.   ☐

d. Picture 121
   Tester: What's on the table?
   Student: There are _____ .   ☐
             (any acceptable answer including *three* items)

Figure 10-2   SAMPLE DIAGNOSTIC TEST OF ORAL-ENGLISH PROFICIENCY
FOR SPANISH SPEAKERS *(continued)*

Question 2   Use of *A*: Pronunciation of /ə/

	Check if Correct	
	Article *a*	*Sound* /ə/

a. Picture 169
 Tester: What's this?
 Student: It's a family.

_____ _____

b. Picture 172
 Tester: Here are three people. Who are they?
 Student: It's a woman and a boy and a girl.
 (any acceptable answer that includes a)

_____ _____

c. Picture 152
 Tester: What is it?
 Student: It's a sandwich.

_____ _____

Question 3   Use of *the*: Pronunciation of /ð/

	Check if Correct	
	Article *the*	*Sound* /ð/

a. Picture 305
 Tester: Where are they?
 Student: They're sitting on the bench.
 They're sitting in the park.
 (any acceptable answer using the)

_____ _____

b. Picture 139
 Tester: What's she doing?
 Student: She's closing the door.

_____ _____

c. Picture 136
 Tester: What's he doing?
 Student: He's opening the window.

_____ _____

Figure 10-2   SAMPLE DIAGNOSTIC TEST OF ORAL-ENGLISH PROFICIENCY
FOR SPANISH SPEAKERS *(continued)*

Question 4   Use of *it*:   Use of Negative

(Note: The child must *use a negative in order to be correct. Any standard negative form is acceptable.)*

	Check if Correct	
	it	*Negative*
a. Picture 155		
Tester: Is it a girl?		
Student: No, it isn't.		
No, it's not.	____	____
b. Picture 31		
Tester: Is it a bus?		
Student: No, it isn't.		
No, it's not.	____	____
c. Picture 96		
Tester: Is it a school?		
Student: No, it isn't.		
No, it's not.	____	____

Question 5   Use of Present Progressive: Pronunciation of /ŋ/

	Check if Correct	
	Verb Form	*Sound /ŋ/*
a. Picture 129		
Tester: What's she doing?		
Student: She's washing her face.	____	____
b. Picture 214		
Tester: What are they doing?		
Student: They're eating.	____	____
c. (Tester picks up book and reads.)		
Tester: What am I doing?		
Student: You're reading.	____	____
d. (Tester tells student to get up and walk.)		
Tester: What are you doing?		
Student: I'm walking.	____	____

Figure 10-2   SAMPLE DIAGNOSTIC TEST OF ORAL-ENGLISH PROFICIENCY
FOR SPANISH SPEAKERS *(continued)*

Question 6   Use of Plural: Pronunciation of /s/ /z/ /ɪz/

	Check if Correct	*Circle if Correct*
	Use of Plural	/s/ /z/ /ɪz/

a. Picture 54
    Tester: Who are they?
    Student: They're boy<u>s</u>.
	_____	/z/

b. Picture 70
    Tester: What are these?
    Student: They're skirt<u>s</u>.
	_____	/s/

c. Picture 164
    Tester: How many cars are there?
    Student: There are two car<u>s</u>.
    (If student says there are two, ask two what?)
	_____	/z/

d. Picture 3
    Tester: What are they?
    Student: They're dres<u>ses</u>.
	_____	/ɪz/

e. Picture 4
    Tester: What's in the picture?
    Student: Hat<u>s</u>. (any acceptable answer)
	_____	/s/

f. Picture C
    Tester: Where's the water?
    Student: In the glas<u>ses</u>. (any acceptable answer)
	_____	/ɪz/

Question 7   Use of Function Words

	Check if Correct

a. Picture 129 (a)
    Tester: Where are the shoes?
    Student: They're <u>on</u> the box.
	_____

b. Picture 129 (b)
    Tester: Where are the shoes?
    Student: They're <u>in</u> the box.
	_____

c. Picture 80 (a)
    Tester: What is it?
    Student: It's a pair <u>of</u> pants.
	_____

Figure 10-2   SAMPLE DIAGNOSTIC TEST OF ORAL-ENGLISH PROFICIENCY
FOR SPANISH SPEAKERS *(continued)*

Check if Correct

d. Picture 150
   Tester: Who are they?
   Student: The teacher <u>and</u> a girl. (any acceptable answer using <u>and</u>)   _____

e. Picture 216
   Tester: Where is it going?
   Student: It's going <u>to</u> the moon.   _____

f. Picture D
   Tester: What's the girl asking?
   Student: <u>Where's</u> the pencil?   _____

g. Picture E
   Tester: What's the boy asking?
   Student: <u>What's</u> in the box?   _____

h. Picture F
   Tester: What's the mother asking?
   Student: <u>Who's</u> that?   _____

Question 8   Pronunciation of /i/ /I/

(Circle /i/ or /I/ if correct, in text)

a. Picture 166
   Tester: What's it doing?
   Student: <u>I</u>t's rain<u>i</u>ng.

b. Picture 142
   Tester: What are they doing?
   Student: They're sleep<u>i</u>ng.

c. Picture 126
   Tester: What's he doing?
   Student: He's r<u>ea</u>d<u>i</u>ng.

d. Picture 141
   Tester: Who's she?
   Student: She's a t<u>ea</u>cher.

Total Correct Answers Part II   □

(Add score to score of Part I. Transfer total to box on first page.)

Figure 10-2 SAMPLE DIAGNOSTIC TEST OF ORAL-ENGLISH PROFICIENCY
FOR SPANISH SPEAKERS *(continued)*

Part III — Connected Speech

Tester: What do you see on this picture (tell me about this picture).
Student Responses (4 per picture):

	Fluency			Rhythm			Stress			Intonation		
	Gd	Av	P	Gd	Av	P	Gd	Av	P	Gd	Av	P
A. Picture 213												
B. Picture 217												
C. Picture 172												
Totals												

TOTAL #: Over-all Rating: Good ☐   Average ☐   Poor ☐

(Transfer scores to boxes on first page.)

Figure 10-3 LANGUAGE-LEARNING SEQUENCE FOR NON-ENGLISH SPEAKERS

Primary Grades—Level I

This primary sequence for foreign students was prepared by teachers who were trained in English as a second language techniques during the 1968 summer session of the North Hudson Development Center in Union City, New Jersey. It was developed to parallel the regular reading sequence already established for English-speaking students. The adaptation thus takes into consideration the normal curriculum and content of each level, as well as the functional language requirements and linguistic content intended for foreign children. In this manner, the new sequence is designed to facilitate the transfer of foreign children to the continuous-progress, nongraded curriculum as soon as they have achieved an adequate command of English. This is made possible by the fact that all students are taught basically the same academic content and the same learning skills, since the "foreign" program integrates the following elements:

Figure 10-3 LANGUAGE-LEARNING SEQUENCE FOR
NON-ENGLISH SPEAKERS *(continued)*

Situational content of Miami Linguistic Readers
Selected situations of *Dick and Jane* series

Linguistic content of Miami Linguistic Readers
Selected vocabulary of *Dick and Jane* series

Language-learning activities of Miami Linguistic Readers

Learning skills outlined in regular reading sequence

Materials and visual aids designed for foreign-language teaching

Standard materials used in primary education

Additional factors:

Control and sequencing of content

Sequence of language skills:
listening
speaking
reading
writing

Cultural information

Although the regular reading sequence covering the first three years of elementary school contains nine levels, the parallel plan for foreign students calls for only six at the present time. It is assumed at this point that the last three levels may not require any special treatment, and that language-handicapped children may then be able to function in a regular class situation. The program has not been in operation long enough to verify this hypothesis.

Materials included in this section are: Level I—Readiness, taken from the Language-Learning Sequence for non-English speakers. A song can be written especially for teaching English as a second language. Music and verses should comply with the following requirements:

1. The melody matches the rhythm, stress, and intonation of spoken English. There is no distortion.

2. The verses are not rhymed; they match the text taught in language classes.

3. The text is written in standard spoken English (including normal contractions).

4. The content is controlled to reinforce the commonly used sentence structures; for example, "It's a _____."
A vocabulary dealing with desserts.

Figure 10-3   LANGUAGE-LEARNING SEQUENCE FOR NON-ENGLISH SPEAKERS *(continued)*

Primary Grades — Level I — Readiness

Skills	*Grammatical Patterns*	*Pronunciation*	*Vocabulary*
Recognition of own name and names of classmates and teacher	Greetings Question: What's your name? My name is _____	/m/ in final and initial position e.g., name	morning, afternoon, evening Mr. Mrs. Miss teacher's name pupil's name hello goodbye
Familiarity with important school facilities	It's the _____	/m/ cont.	bathroom: boy's girl's nurse office gym library music room playground janitor's room
Ability to follow and give simple directions	Commands	Stress final intonation– rising and falling.	Please. Stand up. Sit down. Raise your hand. Get in line. Be quiet.
Identifying qualities such as softness, hardness; long and short; high and low; old and new; rough and smooth; big and little.	Word order statement: It's a(an) _____ _____ . (adj.) (obj.)	initial /s/	Familiar objects in classroom environment soft — hard long — short old — new rough — smooth big — little

Content	Activities	Materials	Cultural Adaptation
Classroom orientation	Teacher-made name tags Good morning song Name song	Oak-tag strips	American culture: *no* hand shaking. Spanish culture: always done.
School locations	Tour of building Cardboard replica of various facilities seen.	Oak-tag	Most Spanish schools *don't* have offices, nurses, gyms, libraries, etc.
Classroom procedures	Simon Says game Simon Says song Teacher-pupil demonstrations.		Spanish children speak out more freely and more loudly. But they are taught to respect teachers. (They look down, not at teacher, to show respect.)
Qualities	Grab bag game Guessing game Grouping big and little objects Draw big and little, long and short objects.	Large box with assorted objects	In Spanish, gender concept applies to all nouns and affects articles and adjectives.

Figure 10-3 LANGUAGE-LEARNING SEQUENCE FOR NON-ENGLISH SPEAKERS *(continued)*

Primary Grades — Level I — Readiness *(continued)*

Skills	Grammatical Patterns	Pronunciation	Vocabulary
Self-awareness of body parts Identifying personal traits	Quantitative adjectives Adj. complement, word order; e.g.: Sparky is big. "I have_____."	review final /s/ /z/	nose eyes mouth ears head body feet hands
Distinguishing similarities and differences	It's_____. It's not_____.		same different like
Ability to ask simple questions	Polite question form: May I_____?	stress rising intonation	Go to the bathroom. Go to the nurse. Get a drink of water.
Familiarity with class-room procedures	I'm_____ He's_____ She's_____ It's_____ (negative)		present, absent; firebell Gesture: pledge allegiance to flag. _____here _____not here
Recognition of and familiarity with class-room objects Use of scissors, crayons, and pencils. Tracing and drawing	Question form: What is it? Statement: It's a(an)_____. Simple commands (passive): Give the_____ to _____. May I have_____?	initial /p/ initial /b/	*Active vocabulary:* pencil, pen, paper, eraser, book, desk, chair, crayon; light, cut, paste, color, draw, trace, write, fold *Passive vocabulary:* blackboard, scissors, chalk, notebook, closet, door, window Give _____ A piece of_____ Thank you

Content	Activities	Materials	Cultural Adaptation
Body parts	Make face masks Simon Says game Chalkboard drawings Self-portraits Flannelboard faces Segmented body parts to be put in place.	Magazine pictures Flannelboard	In Spanish: possessive objects are seldom used. (Put *the* hand on *the* heart.)
Class objects		Box of assorted objects	
Classroom procedures	Role-play actions of going; using cardboard replicas of various places. Pictures illustrating pupils asking questions.	Oak-tag representations of bathroom, nurse, etc. Pictures	American polite form: May I. Greater freedom for American students in class.

Morning exercises:
  attendance
  flag salute
  inspection
  fire drill
  end of day
	Demonstration and role playing of exercises.
	
	Show a film or filmstrip.
		Film or filmstrip on fire drills	Some Spanish cultures salute flag on Fridays. No fire drills due to differences in building construction.

Classroom objects	Blindfold game Guessing games Drawing objects Grab bag game Coloring, drawing, pasting, cutting, tracing Papier mâché Clay modeling	Scissors Brushes Construction paper Newspaper Paste Scraps of cloth and paper Wrapping paper Bags Sticks Finger paints	

Figure 10-3 LANGUAGE-LEARNING SEQUENCE FOR NON-ENGLISH SPEAKERS *(continued)*

Primary Grades — Level I — Readiness *(continued)*

Skills	*Grammatical Patterns*	*Pronunciation*	*Vocabulary*
Drawing simple outlines with crayons. Coloring defined areas. Finger dexterity.			Review
Gross Motor Skills: (Follow directions) Catching large ball Walking a chalk line Running, skipping, hopping, climbing, marching Crawling forwards and backwards Jumping	Commands		*Active vocabulary:* ball, jump, block, catch, walk, run, stop *Passive vocabulary:* skip, hop, climb, march, crawl, forward, backward, chalk lines, build
Left to right progression Distinguishing left & right			Left)) Passive Right)

Auditory discrimination:
Numerals 1–10
Recognition of color
Coloring defined areas
 	
Manipulating writing instrument
 	
Distinguishing different shapes
	Question:
	How old is _____ ?
	                    (name)
	Short response (no)
	Statement:
	I'm _____ years old.
	
	Question:
	What _____ is it?
	     (color, shape)
	Statement:
	It's _____ .
	     (color, shape)
		initial /t/ /s/
		
		final /s/ /z/
		
		review final /m/
			one green
			two black
			three brown
			four orange
			five white
			six circle
			seven square
			eight triangle
			nine
			ten
			red
			yellow
			blue

Content	Activities	Materials	Cultural Adaptation
	Copying simple shapes Collages Making puppets: bag, stick, finger Finger plays Finger painting	Clay Tempera paint Chalk	Same
Physical activities	Relay races using sticks, bean bags, etc. Running games such as tag Skipping rope Calisthenics within the classroom Singing games Hide & Seek game	Bean bags Large ball Small ball Sticks Large blocks	Same
	Activities in *Before We Read* Board work Cutouts Tachistoscopes Show a film Make chain bracelets	Mimeographed sheets Oak-tag Filmstrip *Before We Read*	Same
Numbers Colors Shapes Age	Count various objects on chart and in classroom. Draw circle, square, triangle. Color objects. Cut out. Identify shapes in classroom. Make booklets of shapes with colors.	Readiness chart Construction paper Art supplies	Spanish: (Possession) I *have* 6 years. American: (state of being) I *am* 6 years old. Spanish 7 = 7 American birthday party.

Figure 10-3 LANGUAGE-LEARNING SEQUENCE FOR NON-ENGLISH SPEAKERS *(continued)*

Primary Grades — Level I — Readiness *(continued)*

Skills	Grammatical Patterns	Pronunciation	Vocabulary
Recognition of family members.	Adjective: He's *my* _____ . She's *my* _____ .	initial /t/ /d/	mother　　　my father brother sister baby boy girl
Classification	Question word: 　where: Where do you 　　　　　live? Simple present, regular verb (live) 1st, 2d per- son singular. Long response: "I live in(on) _____ ." Short response: 　(in _____) 　on Prepositions: in, on.	/I/ as in *live* /i/ as in *sheet*	city country name of city, state house apartment farm street in on where

Content	Activities	Materials	Cultural Adaptation
Gender (sex)	Point to family members on chart. Identify by name. Draw family portraits. Tell class about same.	Readiness Chart 4	Spanish: extended family American: nuclear family
Location	Dramatization of meeting in a school. Draw city scene and country scene. Cut pictures out of magazine for classification. Preposition game. Draw pictures of where pupils live.	Readiness Chart 5 Art materials Pictures relating to vocabulary	Spanish: *en* may be used for *in* or *on* in English (one concept). American: two distinct concepts: *in, on.* Spanish: more empty space than in America. Spanish apartments and farms are constructed differently; no barns.

NOTES

Chapter 1

1. Joseph Joubert
2. John I. Goodlad and Robert H. Anderson, *The Nongraded Elementary School* (New York: Harcourt Brace Jovanovich, 1959).
3. John I. Goodlad, "Diagnosis and Prescription in Educational Practice," in *New Approaches to Individualizing Instruction*, pp. 34–36. (© 1965 by Educational Testing Service, Princeton, N.J. All rights reserved. Reprinted by permission.)
4. John I. Goodlad, op. cit., pp. 27–37.
5. Discussion of historical movements in elementary education from the colonial period to the present movement of "Nongraded Organizational Arrangements" is found in: G. Wesley Sowards, "Elementary Education," *Encyclopedia of Educational Research*, Robert L. Ebel, editor, 4th edition (New York: Macmillan, 1969), pp. 420–35.
6. Benjamin S. Bloom, "Learning for Mastery," *Evaluation Comment*, vol. 1, no. 2 (May 1968), UCLA Center for the Study of Evaluation of Instructional Programs, p. 1.
7. J.B. Carroll, "A Model of School Learning," *The Teachers College Record*, vol. 64, no. 9 May 1963, pp. 723–33.
8. Glen Heathers, "Grouping," *Encyclopedia of Educational Research*, Robert L. Ebel, editor, 4th edition (New York: Macmillan, 1969), p. 563.
9. See the following for a discussion of promotional problems:
   a) Robert H. Anderson and Cynthia Ritsher, "Pupil Progress," *Encyclopedia of Educational Research*, Robert L. Ebel, editor, 4th edition (New York: Macmillan, 1969), pp. 1050–62.
   b) Leonard P. Ayers, *Laggards in Our Schools* (New York: Charities Publications Committee, 1909).

c) William H. Coffield and Paul Blommers, "Effects of Nonpromotion on Educational Achievement in the Elementary School," *Journal of Educational Psychology*, 1956, 47:235–50

d) John I. Goodlad, "Some Effects of Promotion and Nonpromotion upon the Social and Personal Adjustment of Children," *Journal of Experimental Education*, 1954, 22: 301–28.

e) Henry J. Otto and Ernest O. Melby, "An Attempt to Evaluate the Threat of Failure as a Factor in Achievement," *Elementary School Journal*, 1935, 35: 488–96.

f) Walter W. Worth, "Promotion or Nonpromotion?", *Educational Administration and Supervision*, 1960, 46: 16–26.

10. Glen Heathers, op. cit., p. 568.

11. John I. Goodlad, "The Schools vs. Education," *Saturday Review*, April 19, 1969, p. 61. (Copyright 1969 by Saturday Review, Inc.)

12. See two recommended volumes on this whole area: Leslie Hart, *The Classroom Disaster* (New York: Teachers College Press, 1969).
Philip W. Jackson, *Life in Classrooms* (New York: Holt, Rinehart & Winston, 1968).

Chapter 2

1. Robert H. Anderson, *Teaching in a World of Change* (New York: Harcourt, Brace & World, 1966), p. 51.

2. See a discussion of this in Leslie A. Hart, "Learning at Random," *Saturday Review*, April 19, 1969, pp. 62–63. (Copyright 1969 by Saturday Review, Inc.).

3. John L. Tewksbury, *Nongrading in the Elementary School* (Columbus, Ohio: Charles E. Merrill Books, 1967), p. 61.

Chapter 3

1. Benjamin S. Bloom, "Testing Cognitive Ability and Achievement," *Handbook of Research on Teaching*, N.L. Gage, editor (©1963 by Rand McNally, Chicago), p. 382.

2. One of the most succinct items dealing with this whole area is *A Guide to Assessment and Evaluation Procedures* (Providence, R.I.: New England Educational Assessment Project, 1966).

Chapter 4

1. Philip W. Jackson, *Life in Classrooms* (New York: Holt, Rinehart & Winston, 1968), p. 15.

Chapter 5

1. Ruby Chadwick and Robert H. Anderson, "The School Reorganization Project in Newton, Massachusetts," in *Perspectives on Educational Change*, Richard I. Miller, editor (New York: Appleton-Century-Crofts, Educational Division, Meredith Corp., 1967), pp. 298–99.

Chapter 6

1. Benjamin S. Bloom, op. cit., p. 2.

2. Cecil J. Parker and Louis L. Rubin, "Process as Content," in *Process as Content: Curriculum Design and the Application of Knowledge* (Chicago: Rand McNally, 1966), p. 1.

3. Ibid. p. 2.

4. Ruth Strang, *How to Report Pupil Progress*. Copyright 1955, Science Research Associates, Chicago. By permission of the publisher. Pp. 15–17.

5. Maurie Hillson, *Hillson Letter #13: The Nongraded Elementary School*, "The Nongraded School: Record Keeping, Evaluation, and Reporting Individual Progress," ©1967, Science Research Associates, Chicago. Reprinted by permission of the publisher.

6. Alice Miel, "Elements and Structure: A Design for Continuous Progress," in *A Curriculum for Children* (Washington: ASCD–National Education Association, 1969), p. 124.

   Bernard H. McKenna, *School Staffing Patterns and Pupil Interpersonal Behavior: Implications for Teacher Education* (Burlingame, Calif.: California Teachers Assoc., 1967), p. 14.

   Bruce R. Joyce, *The Teacher and His Staff—Man, Media and Machines* (Washington: National Committee on Teacher Education and Professional Standards and Center for the Study of Instruction, National Education Association, 1967), pp. 21–23.

   Joseph C. Grannis, Teachers College, Columbia University, in a discussion, November 1967.

7. Recommended reading on the whole area of conferences is found in *Conference Time for Teachers and Parents: A Teacher's Guide to Successful Conference Reporting* (Washington: National School Public Relations Assoc. and Dept. of Classroom Teachers, NEA, 1961).

Chapter 7

1. A recommended discussion of this is found in Leslie A. Hart, *The Classroom Disaster* (New York: Teachers College Press, Columbia Univ., 1969).

2. Lawrence D. Fish, "Curriculum Change Involves People," *Educational Leadership*, vol. 23 (October 1965), pp. 49–51.

3. Gloria Dapper, *Public Relations for Educators: A Handbook for the Administrator— How to Prepare and Release Information about the School Activities* (© 1964 by The Macmillan Company, New York), p. 6.

Chapter 10

1. Frank Brown, *The Nongraded High School* (Englewood Cliffs, N.J.: Prentice-Hall, 1963), pp. 35–36.

2. A complete description of language learning mechanisms is found in the following text: B.V. Belyayev, *The Psychology of Teaching Foreign Languages* (New York: Macmillan, 1964), pp. 194-205.

3. Robert L. Thorndike and Elizabeth Hagen, *Measurement and Evaluation of Psychology and Education* (New York: Wiley, 1967), p. 247.

4. Maurie Hillson, "The Reorganization of the School: Bringing about a Remission in the Problems Faced by Minority Children," *Education and the Urban Community*, Maurie Hillson et al, editors (New York: American Book Co., 1969), pp. 446–58.

5. Francesco Cordasco, "The Puerto Rican Child in the American School," *Journal of Negro Education*, vol. 36 (Spring 1967), pp. 181–86.

6. Ibid., p. 90.

7. Salvador Ramirez, "Employment Problems of Mexican American Youth," *The Mexican American* (Testimony Presented at the Cabinet Committee Hearings on Mexican American Affairs at El Paso, Texas, Inter-Agency Committee on Mexican American Affairs, Washington, 1967), p. 78.

8. Ibid., p. 79.

9. Eliane C. Condon, "English as a Second Language: A Bilingual Approach to a Practical Solution of the Inadequacies Found in

194

Foreign Language Speakers and Educationally Disadvantaged Learners," Maurie Hillson
et al., editors, *Education and the Urban Community* (New York: American Book Co.,
1969), pp. 279–94.

10. See organization of this timetable in chapter 5.

11. Robert L. Politzer, "Toward Psycholinguistic
Models of Language Instruction," *TESOL
Quarterly*, vol. 2, no. 3 (Sept. 1968), p. 151.

12. Eliane C. Condon, "Foreign Languages in the
Elementary School: Past, Present, and
Future," Maurie Hillson, editor, *Elementary
Education: Current Issues and Research* (New
York: Free Press, 1967; © 1967 by the Free
Press, a Division of the Macmillan Company),
pp. 145–60.

13. B. Frank Brown, *The Nongraded High
School* (Englewood Cliffs, N.J.: Prentice-
Hall, 1963), p. 70.

14. Nelson Brooks, "Learning a Modern Foreign
Language for Communication," *Teacher's
Notebook* (New York: Harcourt Brace
Jovanovich, 1961), p. 3.

15. Eliane C. Condon and Doris Wadsworth,
*Curriculum for Teacher-Training Program—
English as a Second Language* (Union City,
N.J.: North Hudson Language Development
Center, Summer 1969). This curriculum
was taught to Spanish students by teacher
trainees under the supervision of ESL
specialists.

PART TWO

PROTOTYPES
AND PROTOCOLS

This section consists of materials that have been developed for the purpose of implementing practical approaches to continuous-progress, nongraded programs. Some programs do not have titles in common use, because a label may often create more misunderstanding than understanding of what the innovator is trying to accomplish. However, careful perusal of the documents reveals that philosophically and operationally all are similar to those we have discussed previously.

It is impossible to be anything but highly selective in choosing examples that will be helpful in developing specific programs. To reprint complete sequences, complete diagnostic instruments, complete learning developmental profiles, and so forth would yield a volume so large and so unwieldy it would be impracticable to publish. Hence we have selected sections and aspects of materials in the hope that presentation of a broadly scattered but well-thought-out selection will serve as a base from which to develop programs to fit the needs of a particular school or system.

Chapter 1 is a self-contained presentation of reasons why educators must break the lockstep and move forward to newer forms. Additional support for the points of view expressed are found in references in the chapter itself as well as in the bibliographic materials.

Chapter 5, 6, 7, 8, and 9 are self-contained units in that all of the prototypes, protocols, and examples are presented with the narrative in part I.

Chapter 10 is also a self-contained unit, since it carries all of the items related to the chapter with sufficient examples to elaborate the whole area of continuous-progress education and the foreign language speaker, bilingualism, and the problem of English as a second language.

What follows here, then, is related material for chapters 2, 3, and 4, plus an addenda of material relating to all ten chapters of part I.

RATES OF PROGRESS OF SEVERAL KINDS OF PUPILS IN A CONTINUOUS-PROGRESS PRIMARY PROGRAM

HOW WILL A CHILD PROGRESS THROUGH THE NONGRADED PROGRAM?

CONTINUOUS-PROGRESS DEVELOPMENTAL READING-LEARNING SEQUENCE

LEVELS OF PROGRESS IN MATHEMATICAL ELEMENTS

MATERIAL RELATED TO CHAPTER 2

Because many continuous-progress programs move first from a basal graded reading program into a basal nongraded program, a realistic approach is to show the progression through a basal reading program with its expansions as suggested by a continuous-progress program, and then relate to several levels in that program.

Example 1 indicates the rates of progress of several kinds of pupils in a continuous-progress primary program. This is what traditionally is the first through third year of school, but in continuous-progress terminology is from *readiness* at level 1 to *competence* at level 8, which is: the ability to perform with success in a "fourth grade" reading book. The progress of a child through this set of levels represents continuous progress in that he is assigned, is working at, or is working on a certain body of material that he masters as readily as his ability permits. This activity is compared to what would happen in a grade where he would be assigned certain material to master in a specified

Example 1   RATES OF PROGRESS OF SEVERAL KINDS OF PUPILS IN A CONTINUOUS-PROGRESS PRIMARY PROGRAM

(Levels 1–8 represent *readiness* to *competence* in skills at the beginning level of the conventional 4th grade.)

Student	First Year	Second Year	Third Year	Fourth Year
Generally average	Levels 1–4	Levels 5–6	Levels 7–8	4th grade or Intermediate Unit.
Superior	Use of independent work, contracts, and enrichment activities.			
Slow starter due to absence or initial immaturity.	Level 1 Level 2 Level 3	Level 4 Level 5	Level 6 Level 7 Level 8	Move to 4th grade (primary substantially completed).
Immature at entrance. Matures, then proceeds normally.	Level 1 Level 2	Level 3 Level 4	Level 5-6-7 Level 6-7-8	Level 7 Level 8 or Move to 4th grade with primary substantially completed.
Lower ability range. Rate and gait problem.	Level 1 Level 2 (Modification of curriculum called for)	Level 3 Level 4	Level 5	Level 6 To 4th grade based on seniority alone.

Example 2 HOW WILL A CHILD PROGRESS THROUGH THE NONGRADED PROGRAM?

Level	1	2	3	4	5	6	7	8	9	10
Type of Child	Orientation & Readiness	Readiness	Pre-Primer	Primer	First Reader	Second Reader 1	Second Reader 2	Third Reader 1	Third Reader 2	Enrichment
Average	1		2			3		4		
Average Immature	1	2			3			4		
Slow	1	2			3		4		5	
High Ability Mature	1					2		3		4
High Ability	1	2				3			4	
Exceptional Physically Mentally Emotionally Mature			1					2		

In the chart above the numbers between the heavy lines stand for one year periods. Therefore:

1 – stands for the 1st year in the program
2 – stands for the 2d year in the program
3 – stands for the 3d year in the program
4 – stands for the 4th year in the program
5 – stands for the 5th year in the program

You can see from the chart how children of different abilities and maturity will progress in the Nongraded Program. Some will take longer to get started but will complete the work in 4 years. Still others will take 5 years and some will cover the required materials in 2 years.

(Set-up shown on the chart above are possible child progressions—only examples of what could happen.)

period of time. The example shows a series of items in a content area, separated into small steps of sequential levels of development. Most school districts choose reading to start with because it is the foundation subject of the elementary school program.

Example 2 shows a similar kind of progression, used at Williamsville Central Schools, Williamsville, New York. It is a ten-level program (including an enrichment level) as against the eight of example 1.

Since level 1, the readiness level, was presented in chapter 2, we have selected levels from another program to show progression over a period of years. Levels from *The Continuous-Progress Developmental Reading-Learning Sequence*, created by primary teachers of Roosevelt School, Union City, New Jersey, are shown as example 3. It is immediately apparent from looking at levels 3, 6, and 9 that they are in operationally defined terms according to suggestions made in chapter 2.

In addition to the area of reading, many school districts have developed programs in mathematics. One such program was developed in the Design for Urban Education, a program of the Newark Board of Education and Rutgers-The State University of New Jersey. They adapted a program originally conceived in North Rockland Central School District, Stony Point, New York, and developed a math program with fourteen levels that would represent a three-year program replacing what were normally grades one through three. Example 4, made up of levels 1, 4, 8, 11, and 13, shows the range of the continuum of skills-development from readiness to mastery.

These fourteen levels of progress present a combination of mathematical elements. Modern approaches to a meaningful understanding of both concepts and computation are shown in this small-step approach to learning. These levels are a spiral approach leading from readiness to the upper levels of math mastery. At each level the basic curriculum and the suggested teaching procedures combine to give the teacher a full opportunity to bring about a consolidation of skills through presentations, as well as practice, necessary for understanding.

The levels also represent a well-structured contiguous set of ideas and concepts. This allows for a careful diagnosis of the learner and reveals both weaknesses and strengths from which a prescriptive approach to individual needs can be made.

By using these levels as guides, and by using the suggested teaching procedures, a teacher will readily arrive at other approaches that will lead to many productive learning activities. Many items in these levels are not new. Rather the ideas and concepts are more meaningfully sequenced to lead realistically to better learning. The hope is that teachers will continue to investigate ways and styles appropriate to the goals of the math program.

Example 3 CONTINUOUS-PROGRESS DEVELOPMENTAL · READING-LEARNING SEQUENCE

Levels 3, 6, and 9

The reading levels program is designed to offer the teacher an opportunity to gauge class progress along more realistic lines that are more commensurate with actual pupil growth rates, rather than allotting work loads to children on a time basis, regardless of ability or maturity levels.

These levels are divided in such a way that materials designed for the graded classrooms can be adapted to the levels program with very little difficulty, and supplementary materials added and subtracted where necessary. The kindergarten will begin with level 1 and progress through the skills as fast as the children master them, not as time dictates. As the child progresses from one level to the next, it is well for the teacher to refer back to previous levels and make sure the skills already introduced are maintained and strengthened. Where these skills are repeated in successive levels, the increasing difficulty of the materials designated for use on the higher levels make strengthening and extending these same skills possible. Much teacher-made material is advocated in this program, for this is one way a teacher is able to match the materials used with the skills and necessities of the class being taught. These materials have the added advantage of being more vital to the pupils, since they are able to sense when a teacher is concerned sufficiently to make exercises especially for them.

As pupils finish level 1 and progress toward level 9, the emphasis shifts from learning to read to learning to learn. Study skills are an important part of the second half of elementary school. During this period, pupils should feel comfortable enough with reading to make it a source of enjoyment as well as a school activity used solely for the acquisition of knowledge.

LEVEL 3

Level 3 includes the language activities and word knowledge associated with the primer or what is usually the child's first hardcover book. At this level much more supplementary material is generally available and this can be found in other reading series as well as a great many trade books available through libraries and supermarkets as well as book stores. These have much the same vocabulary with variations occurring in the form of nouns and naming words, which are the easiest for children to remember. Children should be told these words when doing supplementary work so they do not become overburdened by word-attack problems and lose the thought and enjoyment these books are intended to give.

Practice with the initial consonants should go on and the consonant digraphs, introduced earlier, should be mastered. Pupils should learn to transpose consonants in the initial position to make other words.

Some reading with expression should be in evidence at this level. Complete ease in handling the sight vocabulary is necessary for this.

Example 3   CONTINUOUS-PROGRESS DEVELOPMENTAL
READING-LEARNING SEQUENCE *(continued)*

LEVEL 3 *(continued)*

Skills	Methods	Materials	Suggestions
VISUAL AND AUDITORY DISCRIMINATION			
Mastery of the sight vocabulary of the basal readers, primer level (at least 70 words)	Lessons from basal readers	*Fun with Our Friends*	Use of stories told and written in the class-room
SIGHT WORDS	Use of reader, manuals, and workbooks	Dolch Word List	
		Think-and-Do Book for *Fun with Our Friends*, pages 6, 20, 10, and others	Have children set up library corner in room
cake grandfather	Use of experience charts		
park grandmother			
pony your	Children read stories from library books	Miami Linguistic Readers:	
white wanted		*On the Rock in the Pond*	
black after	Workbook exercises	*The Picnic Ship*	
pretty soon		*Hot Corn Muffins*	
duck saw am	Teacher-made exercises	*The Camping Trip*	
try them		*The Magic Bean*	
got walk	Listening to stories and predicting outcomes		
let chickens			
rabbit hens			
her boots			
looked barked			
back so			
him pig			
came cows			
new fire			
toy laughed			
farm day			
games pet			
clowns children			
had zoo			
called hop			
yellow tails			
Mastery of Dolch List		*Phonics We Use,* Book B, pages 1, 6, 7, 8, 14, 15, 16, 22, and others	

Example 3   CONTINUOUS-PROGRESS DEVELOPMENTAL
READING-LEARNING SEQUENCE *(continued)*

LEVEL 3 *(continued)*

Skills	*Methods*	*Materials*	*Suggestions*
Ability to predict outcomes	Experience charts	*Phonics We Use,* Book C	Phonic games
Increased listening ability	Reading to the children	Dittoed exercises	Choral speaking
		Phonic games	Listening to poetry
Understands the purpose of the story	Use of words from many books in reading lessons		
Can use a table of contents	Limited spelling of regular, one-syllable words		
Is able to use consonants and consonant digraphs in their initial positions as clues to word recognition: p, b, m, wh, w, f, th, t, d, n, l, r, d, z, sh, ch, j, v, k, s, h	Workbook exercises Teacher-made exercises Exercises made by teacher to provide practice where needed Nursery and other rhymes	*Our Poetry Book* *Time for Poetry* (Arbuthnot)	
Continues to hear and see similarities and differences in words	Say rhymes and sentences singularly and in choral speech Oral practice in the form of discussions and story material related by pupils		Phonic games Word games
Enunciates clearly	Experience charts	Social studies topics and others as basis for discussions	
Ability to use oral language	Pupil participation in stories Dramatizations	Social studies charts and pictures	

Example 3   CONTINUOUS-PROGRESS DEVELOPMENTAL
READING-LEARNING SEQUENCE *(continued)*

LEVEL 3 *(continued)*

Skills	Methods	Materials	Suggestions
Ability to write original stories of one to two sentences	Pupils may use primers as source of words for original writing Writing of short letters	Picture dictionaries *My Little Dictionary*	
Understands basic rules of conversation, allows others to finish speaking, refrains from interrupting, states ideas clearly	Class discussions Experience charts Story plays and dramatizations	Word lists	Social studies discussions

LEVEL 6

Level 6 encompasses skills and vocabulary associated with the second half of grade two in the basal readers, and a command of the supplementary material on this reading level. Phonetic skills learned in the first five levels should be sufficiently understood to enable students to spell regular words of one and two syllables.

Comprehension skills should include the meaning of punctuation, and children should be able to use commas, periods, apostrophes, question marks, exclamation marks, and capital letters in their own written compositions. Summaries, main ideas, and inferences are to be developed as skill areas during this stage.

Skills			Methods	Materials
Has mastered sight vocabulary of second-grade readers:			Second-grade basal reading lessons	*More Friends Old and New*
nails	whispering	wear	Supplementary reading	*Think-and-Do Book* to accompany *More Friends Old and New*
enough	sitting	floor		
cart	opened	yet	Library books	
handy	quiet	second		
useful	dime	elephant	Booklets written by pupils and as pupil-teacher projects	Social studies charts and booklets
ice	bank	reply		
flyer	rainy	replied		Basal readers
valentines	shake	we'll		
kitchen	really	bus	Social studies material development	Supplemental readers
smile	save	gloves		
giving	mean	stand		*What Next?*
happened	sure	corner		Teacher-made exercises

Example 3   CONTINUOUS-PROGRESS DEVELOPMENTAL
READING-LEARNING SEQUENCE *(continued)*

LEVEL 6 *(continued)*

Skills			Methods	Materials
living	pennies	toward		
what's	sunny	waved		
while	parade	young		
wrote	feet	stepped		
rest	hi	wooden		
note	pretending	gate		
decided	marchers	through		
reach	trunks	rags		
hole	these	hold		
low	deep	finally		
we'd	kicked	close		
friendly	short	fair		
bikes	seven	coax		
rode	breakfast	offer		
riding	drive	lifted		
wet	hand	kept		
race	few	easily		
racing	knew	trotted		
pointing	quickly	free		
hose	porch	camping		
drop	even	bait		
interesting	love	pail		
glass	flag	ate		
teacher	trouble	grabbed		
paw	wild	churn		
drink	bushes	surely		
care	hare	earth		
I'd	hedgehog	queer		
since	turnips	life		
slowly	angry	voice		
most	wife	below		
hit	row	king		
river	bottom	lion		
meeting	popped	myself		
ahead	dashed	shall		
grin	full	hung		
led	boast	supper		
pat	quarrel	bite		
loud	proud	wide		
bright	owl	grew		

Example 3   CONTINUOUS-PROGRESS DEVELOPMENTAL
READING-LEARNING SEQUENCE *(continued)*

LEVEL 6 *(continued)*

Skills			Methods	Materials
rushing	fruit	poor		
ladder	crossing	part		
roared	tall	crawl		
burning	forest	squeaky		
above	skipped	warmer		
against	evening	geese		
felt	also	returned		
word	wolf	straight		
cage	great	cook		
spoke	foolish	cream		
number	sting	terrible		
alone	pot	stamping		
flew	chimney	draw		
learned	middle	leaned		
chance	sing	rope		
garage	sly	roof		
joke	pile	bridge		
sound	chin	horns		
grunting	third	gruff		
chasing	build	ugly		
ought	straw	troll		
beside	knocked	trap		
fox	huff	gobble		
stronger	blew	frightened		
act	begged	bit		
grow	bricks	hardly		
might	buttered	seeds		
done	fall	plants		
held	country	woods		
eye	taken	seemed		
ago	wonderful	raccoon		
remembered	eight	peanut		
forgot	crowded	leap		
brought	grass	landed		
tomorrow	block	yell		
afternoon	track	shirt		
unhappy	belonged	wrong		
pink	following	stood		
together	oak	huge		
pockets	branch	rock		

Example 3   CONTINUOUS-PROGRESS DEVELOPMENTAL
READING-LEARNING SEQUENCE *(continued)*

LEVEL 6 *(continued)*

Skills			Methods	Materials
carry	excited	mouth		
owns	shut	eaten		
real	katydids	bars		
across	table	such		
city	caught	blueberries		
engine	writes	nodded		
hoped	filled	cupcakes		
almost	certainly	pan		
summer	covered	oven		
pool	lake	hot		
swim	rowing	cool		
week	feathers	sudden		
clock	oil	bad		
arms	carefully	supposed		
lucky	believe	curly		
wiggle	lass	itself		
clever	least	instead		
fierce	lad	hunt		
snapped	lay	swooped		
empty	heavy	prince		
bag	tonight	roast		
market	kettle	swiftly		
set	husband	deer		
obey	iron	kill		

Uses context clues with phonetic clues to gain
word meaning

Continues to gain proficiency in use of consonant sounds in initial, medial, and final
positions

Oral and written
phonics lessons

Reading independently
and in groups

Gains proficiency in use of following consonant digraphs and blends:

Substitution in oral
lessons

   ch, wh, sh, th, ph, gh, br, cr, dr, fr, gr, pl, cl,
   fl, gl, bl, sl, sp, sm, sn, sc, sk, sw, st, tw

Practice with work-
books and teacher-
made materials; i.e.:
*r*ag to *fl*ag
      *br*ag
      *sl*ag

Example 3 CONTINUOUS-PROGRESS DEVELOPMENTAL
READING-LEARNING SEQUENCE *(continued)*

LEVEL 6 *(continued)*

Skills	Methods	Materials
Review c and g in variant positions and soft and hard sounds	*George—face* Encourage children to think of other examples	Phonics exercise books Basal reader exercises Teacher-made exercises
Teach the three letter blends: spr, str, scr, squ, thr	Substitution in words pupils are familiar with; i.e.: *r*ing to *spr*ing	Teacher-made materials Chart work
Silent consonants: *w*rong g*h*ost lam*b* *k*nife rig*h*t	Lead child to look for sounds he already knows and tell him which are silent. Illustrate with similar words and explain certain letters are silent. (These are left-overs from Old English when all letters were sounded and the language was quite different from what it is today.)	Social studies reading material
Teach similarity of sounds of: x and cks ng and nk	Substitution in known words Explanation when pupils encounter these in basal lessons Refer to *-ing* and *-ink* as phonograms: -ink, -ank, -onk, -enk, -unk -ing, -ang, -ong, -eng, -ung Use words which contain phonograms	Basal readers Workbook exercises Teacher-made exercises Oral lessons and teacher-made exercises Teacher-made practice phonics strips

Example 3   CONTINUOUS-PROGRESS DEVELOPMENTAL
READING-LEARNING SEQUENCE *(continued)*

LEVEL 6 *(continued)*

Skills	*Methods*	*Materials*
Review alphabetical order	Teacher-made exercises	Alphabet: upper and lowercase, mounted in the room
Variant sounds of r, ar, or, er, ir, ur	Substitution in known words	Social studies material and pictures
	Teach as similar sounds and point out differences where they occur; i.e., or and ir	Basal reading
	Associate these with words familiar to children	
a as it sounds before *l* and *w*: also all saw paw	Use known words and make sure at least half of exercises are oral	Workbooks Teacher-made exercises
Vowel combinations, again using: ai, ea, ee, oa, ay	Substitution in known words as: ran to rain bat to boat and others	
Vowel diphthongs: ou, ow, oi, oy, ue, ew	Teach as you would long vowel sounds, pointing out specific sound for each unit	*Time for Phonics,* Book C Teacher-made exercises
	Oral exercises	
Word Variants: s, es, ed, ing (change *y* to *i* before ending; drop the final *e* before ending)	Words from basal reader used in oral lessons	Reading workbooks Teacher-made exercises
	Allow pupils to volunteer other examples	

Example 3   CONTINUOUS-PROGRESS DEVELOPMENTAL
READING-LEARNING SEQUENCE *(continued)*

LEVEL 6 *(continued)*

Skills	*Methods*	*Materials*
Other variants, applying above rule where necessary: er, est, ly, y	happy to happier and happiest Use examples such as this involving class in oral practice before written practice	Reading workbooks *Phonics We Use* Teacher-made exercises
Knows common phonograms: are up et ar ound ame old ill at un as own oat ed und ate ack ot ig ut en an oy ing ute ight ast all og	Spelling practice Teacher-made exercises for directed practice in work areas	*Phonics We use* Phonics charts
Recognizes meanings in words with like sounds but different meanings: hear buy their here by there	Oral work with sound and sentence clues to meaning Workbook Teacher-made exercises	*Think-and-Do Book* Ditto sheets from spelling, phonics, and reading Basal readers
Reinforces ability to anticipate words that complete meaning of sentence	Have children supply missing words in a paragraph Workbook Teacher-made exercises	Basal readers *Think-and-Do Book*
Is able to interpret and give significance to main ideas and details Makes judgments, draws conclusions, recognizes implications and inferences Uses the picture dictionary		

Example 3   CONTINUOUS-PROGRESS DEVELOPMENTAL
READING-LEARNING SEQUENCE *(continued)*

LEVEL 6 *(continued)*

Skills	*Methods*	*Materials*
Can identify and use units, chapters, titles in a table of contents	Develop through oral discussions and reading in group; then practice individually in workbook and teacher-made exercises Help children recognize units and chapters when reading other books	Basal readers Library books Other textbooks
Can identify how, who, when, where, and why in stories Makes judgments and draws conclusions	Read story, discuss, answer specific questions	Basal readers Teacher-made exercises
Organizes thoughts and expresses himself well in writing. Uses complete sentences and is familiar with significance of paragraphs and how they are used to divide meaning units Can use proper punctuation in writing, and does so	Composition which is criticized constructively by teacher Extensive oral and silent reading	Workbook to accompany basal reader *Phonics We Use,* Book D Teacher-made exercises

Uses punctuation as a clue to meaning and oral expression	Oral reading by children and by teacher to use punctuation clues taught in basal readers and other materials	Workbooks
		  Spelling
		  Phonics
		  Reading
		
		Teacher-made exercises

Ability to do independent book reports	Use class or school library	Library books

LEVEL 9

In this level skills are reviewed, reinforced or strengthened, maintained, and refined. The pupil uses the skills acquired to learn independently, to increase his knowledge, and to develop reading in those areas he is interested in. Reading will serve as a tool as well as for pleasure.

Example 3   CONTINUOUS-PROGRESS DEVELOPMENTAL
READING-LEARNING SEQUENCE *(continued)*

LEVEL 9 *(continued)*

Skills	*Methods*	*Materials*
VOCABULARY		
Mastery of vocabulary in reading material used on other levels	Word Bingo	Basal readers
	Use of dictionary	
Strengthen use of phonetic and structural skills to attack unfamiliar words independently	Basal readers and other texts	
Dolch List	Supplementary readers	
PHONETIC ANALYSIS: Review and reteach where necessary		
Vowels—assure knowledge by continued review	Dittoed exercises (Word lists; pupils mark the vowels)	Teacher-made F.G. 0017 vowels T.O. 0001 s. vowels T.O. 0005 l. vowels
1. Short—one vowel in the middle of a word One vowel at the end of a word		
2. Long—one vowel at the end of a word Two vowels—one is final silent *e* Consecutive vowels	A-V materials	

3. Variant sounds—
   a) Influence of r (ar, ir, er, ur, or)
   b) au, al, aw, ou, oy, oi, ow
   c) oo, ae
   d) ow
   e) ue, ew
	Spelling Lessons	*Spelling Goals,* Book 3

Consonants—		
1. Beginning, medial, and final 2. Blends—two letter, three letter 3. Unpronounced 4. Variant pronunciations—c, g, s, gh 5. Digraphs—ch, wh, sh, tr, ph, ng 6. Same sounds but do not look alike—x, ks	Teacher-made exercises—substituting consonant with blend: cake – snake song – strong	Single consonants, T.O. 0040 Initial consonants T.O. 0039 Phonics L.M. 0016 Consonant Blends L.M. 0003 F.S..0195
STRUCTURAL ANALYSIS		
Recognition of root words: un-clean, destroy, fanc*i*est, circling	Teacher-made exercises (oral and written)	Accompanies basal reader *Uncle Funny Bunny*

Example 3   CONTINUOUS-PROGRESS DEVELOPMENTAL
READING-LEARNING SEQUENCE *(continued)*

LEVEL 9 *(continued)*

Skills	Methods	Materials

Review making plurals
  elf   — elves
  story — stories
  dish   — dishes
  song — songs
	Workbook exercises
	
	Spelling lessons
	
	Charts	

Possessive forms—
  his, hers, its, ours
  Jane's
  the boys'		

Review contractions—n't: would, are, is, have		

Prefixes and Suffixes
 	
1. Review those taught on previous levels
2. Teach meaning and usage of
    prefixes: in-, de-, im-, un-, dis-, re-, a-,
    con-, el-, up-
 	
    suffixes: -able, -en, -ese, -ish, -ward, -ness,
    -ment
	Word games: See who can find the most word beginnings	Use available textbooks

Comparisons extended:
  bad, worse, worst
  good, better, best
	Compositions	

SYLLABICATION: Review and extend skills learned		
Hearing syllables and dividing words 1. Review the generalizations 2. Use visual and auditory means to deter- mine syllables	Workbook exercises	Workbook of basic readers *Just Imagine* Wk.
Strengthen recognition of prefixes, suffixes as syllables (exception: -ed)	Oral chalkboard lessons	Teacher-made exercises
Recognition of accented and unaccented syllables	Oral reading	Supplementary readers
1. Word endings in -le—that syllable is never accented	Workbook pages	*Think-and-Do Book*

2. Words having a prefix or suffix, root word
    receives accent
3. Letters ck never separated (usually ends first
    syllable, which is accented)
	Chalkboard exercises	T.M. of basal readers

Example 3 CONTINUOUS-PROGRESS DEVELOPMENTAL
READING-LEARNING SEQUENCE *(continued)*

LEVEL 9 *(continued)*

Skills	*Methods*	*Materials*
4. Primary and secondary accent in multi-syllable words: situa*tion* 5. Compound words—usually first word receives accent: some'where; school'room (exception: when-ever')	Spelling lessons Dictionary lessons	
WORD MEANING: Strengthen independent skills		
Teach multiple meanings of words	Word-attack lessons orally	Teacher-made lessons
Extend word relationships: antonyms; synonyms; homonyms	Spelling lessons Use of dictionary	*Spelling Goals,* Book 3
Develop use of and appreciation for figurative language: metaphors; similes	Oral and silent reading Chalkboard exercises Workbooks	

Interpret uses of certain punctuation marks:
  exclamation
  quotation
  comma
  semicolon and colon
  parentheses
  apostrophe
  review use of question mark and period
	Reading for pleasure
	Reading for information
	
	Experience charts
	Oral chalkboard exercises
	
	Practice exercises in punctuating sentences
		Language textbooks of this level
		Teacher-made exercises
		Spelling text
		T.M. of basic reader
		Workbook

Extending capitalization		
Extension and mastery of essential vocabulary in content areas of science, social studies, math, health, and music	Reading and spelling books Oral and silent reading	
DICTIONARY SKILLS: Extended and strengthened		
Locating entries	Use of dictionary and glossaries	
1. Alphabetical order to 3d and 4th letters; snow, snore 2. Using the guide words 3. Identifying root words in inflected and derived forms	Worksheets made of pages from these Workbook exercises	

Example 3   CONTINUOUS-PROGRESS DEVELOPMENTAL
READING-LEARNING SEQUENCE *(continued)*

LEVEL 9 *(continued)*

Skills	*Methods*	*Materials*
Selecting the appropriate definitions in multiple-meaning words through context		
Pronunciation of words	Using various dictionary and glossary keys	
1. Extending and strengthening use of diacritical markings 2. Practice in interpreting phonetic spellings		
COMPREHENSION SKILLS		
Review skills of Level 8	Oral and silent reading	*Just Imagine* Wk.
Strengthen ability to identify main idea and supporting ideas	Workbook	
Understanding and noting analogous relationships (comparing one story with another and comparing lessons they teach)	Teacher-made exercises	
Recalling details	Discussion groups	
Notes specialized vocabulary	Using newspapers and periodicals	
Forms generalizations (by adding together ideas from more than one selection); extrapolation		
Distinguishes between fact and fiction	Dramatizations; puppet plays	
Summarizes		
CRITICAL READING SKILLS		
Extends and develops skills of Level 8		
Compares ideas and information		
Develops ability to differentiate between a fact and an opinion		
Responds to quality of words; intonation and tempo	Oral readings Dramatizations Puppet shows	
Makes judgments	Makes personal judgments from story characters	
Follows oral and written directions		

Example 4   LEVELS OF PROGRESS IN MATHEMATICAL ELEMENTS

LEVEL 1   Language and Nature of the Number System

Basic Curriculum	*Suggested Materials and Procedures*

**THE ORDER AND
PATTERN SEQUENCE
OF THE NUMBER
SYSTEM**

Reinforcing the
concept developed
previously of
cardinal numbers and
numerals through ten

Count the number of objects and draw a ring around the
correct numeral.

○ ○○ ○○○ ○○○○	△△△ △ △ △△△	○ ○ ○ ○ ○ ○	□ □ □ □ □ □ □	△ △ △ △ △ △△△△	○ ○	□ □ □
8 9 10	8 9 10	7 8 9	6 7 8	8 9 10	0 2 4	3 6 9

   Introducing the con-
cept of zero as a place
holder

Look at the first box. How many tens do you see? How many
ones? What number is 1 ten and 2 ones?

⊦⊦⊦⊦⊦⊦⊦⊦ ‖ □ ___tens ___ones ‖‖‖‖‖‖‖‖‖ ‖‖‖‖‖‖‖‖‖ ‖ □ ___tens ___ones	⊦⊦⊦⊦⊦⊦⊦ ⊦⊦⊦⊦⊦⊦⊦ ‖□ ___ tens ___ones ‖‖‖‖‖‖‖‖‖ ‖‖‖‖ □ ___tens ___ones	⊦⊦⊦⊦⊦⊦⊦ ⊦⊦⊦⊦⊦⊦⊦ ‖‖□ ___tens _____ones ‖‖‖‖‖‖‖‖‖ ‖‖‖‖‖‖‖‖‖ □ ___tens _____ones

Look at the bars. How many white squares and dark squares add
up to 10 in number 1 etc.

10 is 9 and _____

10 is 8 and _____

10 is 7 and _____

10 is 6 and _____

10 is 5 and _____

10 is 4 and _____

10 is 3 and _____

10 is 2 and _____

10 is 1 and _____

10 is 0 and _____

LEVEL 1   Language and Nature of the Number System *(continued)*

Basic Curriculum	*Suggested Materials and Procedures*

Reinforcing the concept of zero as nothing

Circle the numeral showing the correct number of objects.

□ □ □ □	△ △ △		□ □	○	□ □ △ □ □	△ □ ○	
2 3 4	2 3 4	0 1 2	1 2 3	0 1 2	3 4 5	1 2 3	0 1 2

Introducing the concept of zero as a starting point

Find on the number line the answers to all of the questions.

0   1   2   3   4   5   6   7   8   9   10   11   12

The number line shows:

3 + 1 =   7 + 2 =   8 + 1 =
6 + 0 =   5 + 3 =   9 + 2 =

e.g.   Draw a ring around the correct answer:

6 is more than 5?	Yes	No
3 is less than 6?	Yes	No
4 is more than 5?	Yes	No
5 is less than 3?	Yes	No

e.g.

Can you take 4 from 5?	Yes	No
Can you take 1 from 3?	Yes	No
Can you take 3 from 2?	Yes	No
Can you take 6 from 6?	Yes	No
Can you take 5 from 3?	Yes	No
Can you take 8 from 5?	Yes	No

LEVEL 1 Language and Nature of the Number System *(continued)*

Basic Curriculum	*Suggested Materials and Procedures*
THE 1-10 PATTERN RELATIONSHIP OF THE NUMBER SYSTEM Continuing the understanding of the relationship between and among digits	Have children draw circles (O), squares (□), (X's), and so on, in a square or set corresponding to the number within the set.

e.g.

Assist children in understanding that one number is more than (>) another number.

   e.g. Draw a circle around the number in each set which is greater than the other.

     [4 9]   [6 3]   [5 7]

Have children perform the reverse of the operation outlined above.

Draw a line from the set in column A to the corresponding number in column B.

A	B
[O O O]	5
[+ + + + +]	4
[X X X] + [X X]	6
[3 + 1]	3

LEVEL 1   Language and Nature of the Number System *(continued)*

Basic Curriculum	*Suggested Materials and Procedures*
SYMBOLS USED IN ESTABLISHING THE RELATIONSHIP BETWEEN AND AMONG NUMBERS LEADING TO SENTENCES OR STATEMENTS	
Introducing the meaning of the equality sign =	Give pupils an opportunity to discuss sets that are divided into pairs of subsets by color, position, type of objects, and so on. Have them identify the obvious combination. For example, present them with a set of three triangles and two circles and have them identify the three and two while you exhibit the symbols 3 + 2. Then ask, "How many in all?" Exhibit the numeral 5. This time, when you comment that 3 + 2 represents the same number as 5, place an equality symbol between 3 + 2 and 5, and tell the children that this is the way to show that 3 + 2 and 5 represent the same number. Read with them now, "Three plus two equals five." Do this several times, giving the children the opportunity to read the equation together. If plastic numerals are available, have the children use them at their desks to form equations.

$$\triangle \, \triangle \, \triangle \; + \; \bigcirc \, \bigcirc$$
$$3 \quad + \quad 2 \; = \; 5$$

Introducing the meanings of the symbols > and <	Draw a set of five objects and a set of three objects on the chalkboard. Ask a child to write the numeral for the number of each set below the set. Draw a □ placeholder between the two numbers and explain that this is a placeholder and it is used to show that there is a missing symbol of relation. Introduce the symbol > and explain that it may be placed between two numerals to show that the first number is *greater than* the second number. Use various sets that are not equivalent to reinforce the greater than concept. Introduce the less than concept and the symbol < in a similar manner.

$$\triangle \, \triangle \, \triangle \; > \; \square \, \square$$
$$3 \quad > \quad 2$$

$$\begin{bmatrix} \times \times \times \end{bmatrix} \; < \; \begin{bmatrix} \bigcirc \\ \bigcirc \;\; \bigcirc \\ \bigcirc \;\; \bigcirc \;\; \bigcirc \end{bmatrix}$$
$$3 \qquad < \qquad 6$$

LEVEL 1   Language and Nature of the Number System *(continued)*

Basic Curriculum	Suggested Materials and Procedures
FRACTIONS	*Note: It is not necessary to introduce symbols for fractions or give detailed meaning of fractions. Explanations should be intuitive.* Materials: Apples, candy bars, pieces of string, cardboard, scissors, pencils, erasers, chalk, paper clips, and so on. Sets of 4, 6, 8, and 10 objects.
Understanding number concepts other than whole numbers	
Understanding the idea of one half of a given collection	Have children manipulate materials to make halves. Have children manipulate the halves back together to make the whole.
Separating groups and sets into halves and realizing the two parts as equal to the whole	

LEVEL 1   Computations and Operations

Basic Curriculum	Suggested Materials and Procedures
THE ADDITION OF NUMBERS	
Introducing the concept of addition	Use sets of objects varying only in color. Children select 2 sets of different colored objects. They count total number of objects to add to sets. Give children experiences with set unions in both class demonstrations and individual work situations. Exhibit on the flannelboard a set of 3 objects and a set of 1 object. Push the two sets together and ask how many objects are in the new set. Following this demonstration give the children an opportunity to form the union of sets with their own collections (beads, counters, coins, discs, and so on). Relate these experiences to the abstract symbolism of mathematics by discussing the number combinations involved, keeping in mind that we form the union of two sets and we add pairs of numbers.

LEVEL 1   Computations and Operations *(continued)*

Basic Curriculum	*Suggested Materials and Procedures*
Learning the many possibilities when numbers such as 5 are taken apart and put together. Use small numbers (up to 10) repeatedly. Use of sets	e.g.　$1 + 2 + 1 + 1 = 5$ $1 + 2 + 2 = 5$ $2 + 1 + 2 = 5$ $2 + 2 + 1 = 5$ Use of appropriately sized blocks to find a relationship. Use the number line.
THE SUBTRACTION OF NUMBERS Introducing the concept of subtraction	Use sets of objects varying in color. Children select 2 sets and find total number of objects. Remove one set and find the number of objects remaining.
Developing situations involving the subtraction of numbers	Begin by giving the children a set activity. Exhibit a set of 5 objects on the flannelboard. Ask how many. Remove 2 objects. Ask how many objects are taken away. Ask how many are left. Display the symbols $5 - 2$. We read this as "5 minus 2." Invent story problems. Children work with sets, on their own desks, removing objects.
Adding and subtracting numbers; one less or one more	e.g.　5　6　1　4　1 　+1　+1　+3　+1　+8 　9　5　3　2　4 　−1　−1　−1　−1　−1

LEVEL 1   Geometry

Basic Curriculum	*Suggested Materials and Procedures*
Work for recognition of squares, rectangles, circles, and triangles	For an enrichment activity have pupils make designs using various patterns e.g.　▯ – ▭ – ▯ – ▭ – ▯ 　○ – □ – ○ – □ 　▷ – ▭ – ▷ – ▭

LEVEL 1 Measurement

Basic Curriculum	*Suggested Materials and Procedures*
The development of understanding the value of a penny, a nickel, and a dime	Discussion: A penny is a coin worth 1 cent; a nickel is a coin worth 5 cents; a dime is a coin worth 10 cents. Show each coin.

Give each child a supply of play money. Use various possible relationships (size and value). Example: A dime is smaller than a penny but is more money.

With the play or real money, give the children an opportunity to count various coin collections. Have them state in cents the total number for a given collection.

e.g.   Find the value of each collection:

(one cent) (5)   (5) (5)   (10) (10) (10)

(10)   (5) (5)   (10) (10) (10)

— ¢   — ¢   — ¢

(5)   (5) (5) (10) (10)   (10)   (10)

(10)   (5)

(1) (1)   (5) (5)   (10)   (1)

— ¢   (1) (1) — ¢   (1) (1) (1)   (5)

— ¢   — ¢

e.g.   Have children show different collections for the given amount.

7¢   __ nickels and __ pennies

13¢   __ nickels and __ pennies
__ nickels and __ pennies
__ nickels and __ pennies

LEVEL 1 Measurement *(continued)*

Basic Curriculum	*Suggested Materials and Procedures*

22¢   2 dimes,__ nickels,__pennies
1 dime, 1 nickel,__pennies
1 dime, 0 nickels,__pennies
__ dimes, 3 nickels,__pennies

e.g. Have children color coins to total the given amount.

e.g. Have children find the number of coins needed to buy each item.

___ dimes and 1 penny   ___nickels and 2 pennies

e.g. Mark the collection which is worth more; then tell how much more.

Example 4 LEVELS OF PROGRESS IN MATHEMATICAL ELEMENTS *(continued)*

LEVEL 4 Language and Nature of the Number System

Basic Curriculum	*Suggested Materials and Procedures*
THE ORDER AND PATTERN SEQUENCE OF THE NUMBER SYSTEM Reinforcing the concept developed previously of cardinal numbers and numerals through ninety-nine	Write the number names that are missing.

e.g.

0	1	2		4	5	6			9
10	11	12	13			16	17	18	
20		22		24	25			28	29
	31		33			36	37		
40			43		45	46		48	
50	51	52		54			57		59
		62			65	66		68	69
	71		73	74			77		
80		82	83		85		87	88	
	91	92			95			98	

e.g. Write the missing numerals.

a. 14 __15__   f. __17__ 18
b. 52 _____   g. _____ 85
c. 74 _____   h. _____ 34
d. 49 _____   i. _____ 99
e. 37 _____   j. _____ 67

Reinforcing the concept of zero as a place holder

This picture shows 5 tens and zero ones. We may write the numeral 50.

In 50, the 5 shows there are five _____ , and 0 shows there are zero ___ .

φ φ φ φ φ

5 tens and 0 ones
50

LEVEL 4 Language and Nature of the Number System *(continued)*

Basic Curriculum	*Suggested Materials and Procedures*
	Finish the work below. Write 0 to show no other ones.
	30 means _____ tens and _____ ones
	80 means _____ tens and _____ ones
	40 means _____ tens and _____ ones
	54 means _____ tens and _____ ones
Reinforcing the concept of zero as nothing	Have the pupil find the set in each row that contains the number of objects shown by the numerals to the left.
	3
	2
	1
	0
	Tell pupils the numerals indicate the number of boxes to color.
THE 1–10 PATTERN RELATIONSHIP OF THE NUMBER SYSTEM.	
Continuing the understanding of the relationship between and among digits	Review concepts previously taught.
Developing and building understanding of place value concepts by grouping by tens	

LEVEL 4   Language and Nature of the Number System *(continued)*

Basic Curriculum	*Suggested Materials and Procedures*
Introduce hundreds in the place value scheme	Grouping by tens, then by hundreds 9 tens 10 tens We write <u>90</u> We write <u>100</u>
Place value meaning of three digit numerals	e.g. Fill in the blanks: 362 means _____ hundreds, _____ tens, and _____ ones 100 means _____ hundreds, _____ tens, and _____ ones 609 means _____ hundreds, _____ tens, and _____ ones e.g. Write the numerals: 5 hundreds, 9 tens, and 6 ones _____ 2 hundreds, 1 ten, and 0 ones _____ 9 hundreds, 0 tens, and 2 ones _____
Teaching inequalities	e.g. Use as a guide, the number before or the number after the symbol. $\underline{4} <$ _____ _____ $> \underline{60}$ $\underline{10} >$ _____ _____ $< \underline{84}$ _____ $< \underline{20}$ $\underline{73} <$ _____ _____ $> \underline{139}$ $\underline{199} >$ _____ $\underline{329} <$ _____ $\underline{200} <$ _____ e.g. Put $>$ or $<$ in each circle. 7 ◯ 10 84 ◯ 74 750 ◯ 746 9 ◯ 14 124 ◯ 121 407 ◯ 704 62 ◯ 69 679 ◯ 597

LEVEL 4 Language and Nature of the Number System *(continued)*

Basic Curriculum	*Suggested Materials and Procedures*

SYMBOLS

Reviewing the operational symbols + and −

Have the children use plastic numerals and other symbols at their desks to build the equation 12 △ 3 = 15.

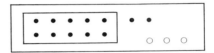

Hold up a picture card showing a set illustration of the number combination. Ask the children to tell what they think was done with these sets in order to make a set of fifteen objects. Have them place the correct operational sign in the triangle in their equation and read the completed statement.

Have the children place the equation 18 △ 2 = 16 on their desks. Hold up a card showing a set illustration related to the subtraction combination. Ask them to tell what action they think took place in order to have sixteen objects. Have them place the correct operational sign in the triangle and read the completed equation. Continue in this way to work with sets and equations in which the operational sign is required.

e.g.   18 △ 6 = 12   3 + 12 = 10 △ 5

             13 △ 4 = 17   14 + 3 = 19 △ 2

Use for supplementary activity, if so desired:

Place the numeral 9 followed by the equal sign in the center of the flannelboard. Under these symbols scatter a plus sign, a minus sign, and the numerals 0 through 9. Ask a child to use them to construct a numeral representing the number 9.

```
         9 =
   +  −     0  4  2
   1  9  7  8  6  3  5
```

He is to place it to the right of the equal sign and read his equation. The activity allows children to construct equations using different numerals for the numbers one through ten.

	LEVEL 4 Language and Nature of the Number System *(continued)*
Basic Curriculum	*Suggested Materials and Procedures*
Introducing the symbol X as meaning "times"	(Use concrete objects to demonstrate the concept of joining equivalent sets.) The picture shows 3 sets of 2. There are 6 circles in all. We know: 3 sets of 2 each are 6. We say: 3 times 2 equals 6. We write: $3 \times 2 = 6$. When we know *how many equivalent sets there are* and *how many objects* are in *each set*, we *multiply* to find the number of objects in all. The symbol X tells us to multiply.
Introducing the symbols for dollars and cents: $ and .	$ This is called the *dollar sign* 1 The numeral after $ tells us how many dollars . This is called the *cent point* 0 The first 0 after the cent point tells us there are no dimes 0 The second 0 after the cent point tells us there are no cents (pennies) e.g. Write amounts below using the $ and . : 2 dollars and 7 cents ($2.07) 6 dollars and 13 cents ($6.13)
Working with parentheses ( )	Write on the chalkboard: $3 + (6 + 2) = \square$. Review the use of parentheses. Point out that the figures in the parentheses should be considered as a name for one number and that the children must first add 6 and 2 before adding the 3. That is, $(6 + 2)$ is 8 and $3 + 8$ is 11. Therefore, $3 + (6 + 2) = 3 + 8 = 11$. Provide several other practice situations such as: $4 + (5 + 3) = 4 + 8 = 12$ $(4 + 4) + 3 = 8 + 3 = 11$

LEVEL 4 Language and Nature of the Number System *(continued)*

Basic Curriculum	*Suggested Materials and Procedures*
FRACTIONS Review concepts previously taught	Supplementary Material Have students fold pieces of paper into thirds as follows:

$\frac{1}{3}$'s $\frac{1}{3}$'s

Have pupils cut along the crease of each fold and then lay one piece over the other to see if the pieces fit each other exactly. (The *a*'s should all fit equally and the same with the *b*'s.)

Emphasizing the concept of a fraction as part of either a *whole* or a *group*

MATERIALS: region areas, pies, checkers, blocks, sticks, pencils, crayons, and so on. (Use wide variety of materials.)

Much work with concrete objects should precede any semiconcrete or written practice.

Giving experience with unit fractions $\frac{1}{2}$, $\frac{1}{3}$, $\frac{1}{4}$

Mark those objects divided into halves $\left(\frac{1}{2}\right)$.

e.g. There are two of each item below (2 boxes, 2 sets of circles, 2 sets of lines.) Circle $\frac{1}{2}$ of the objects in each set or group.

e.g. Mark those objects divided into thirds $\left(\frac{1}{3}\right)$.

LEVEL 4   Language and Nature of the Number System *(continued)*

Basic Curriculum	*Suggested Materials and Procedures*
	e.g. Ring $\frac{1}{3}$ of the objects in each set.

e.g.   Ring the correct fraction

$$\frac{1}{4} \quad \frac{1}{3} \quad \frac{1}{2} \qquad \frac{1}{4} \quad \frac{1}{3} \quad \frac{1}{2} \qquad \frac{1}{4} \quad \frac{1}{3} \quad \frac{1}{2}$$

e.g.   Color $\frac{1}{2}$ red   Color $\frac{1}{4}$ blue   Color $\frac{1}{3}$ orange

Color $\frac{1}{2}$ red   Color $\frac{1}{3}$ Color $\frac{1}{4}$

Understanding that a fractional value must be related to some *whole* to have any significance

Emphasizing that a common denominator means common-sized part.

e.g.

$$\frac{1}{2} \quad \text{not equal} \quad \frac{1}{2} \quad \text{not equal} \quad \frac{1}{2} \quad \text{not equal} \quad \frac{1}{2}$$

All the shaded areas are $\frac{1}{2}$'s, but are not equal as they refer to different wholes.

e.g.

$$\frac{1}{4} \quad \text{not equal} \quad \frac{1}{4} \quad \text{not equal} \quad \frac{1}{4} \quad \text{not equal} \quad \frac{1}{4}$$

All the shaded areas are $\frac{1}{4}$'s, but are not equal as they refer to different wholes.

LEVEL 4 Language and Nature of the Number System *(continued)*

Basic Curriculum	*Suggested Materials and Procedures*
	e.g. $\frac{1}{2}$ lb. butter + $\frac{1}{2}$ of a pie do not equal 1 whole. These $\frac{1}{4}$'s are equal and can be used in comparison. The $\frac{1}{4}$'s come from the same whole. These $\frac{1}{3}$'s are equal and can be used in comparison. The $\frac{1}{3}$'s come from the same whole.

LEVEL 4 Computations and Operations

Basic Curriculum	*Suggested Materials and Procedures*
THE SUBTRACTION OF NUMBERS Developing subtraction with and without renaming	e.g. Without renaming: $$27 - 12 = 15$$ or $$\begin{array}{r} 19 \\ -8 \\ \hline 11 \end{array}$$ or $$38 - 21 = 17$$ With renaming: $$27 - 8 = (20 + 7) - 8$$ $$8 = (7 + 1)$$ $$27 - 8 = 20 + 7 - 7 - 1$$ $$= 20 - 1$$ $$= 19$$ Renaming is done in terms of 10's and 1's. $$\begin{array}{ccc} 27 & 27+0 & 17+10=27 \\ -8 & -\ \ 8 & -\ \ \ \ 8 = -8 \\ & & \hline \ \ \ 17+\ \ 2 = 19 \end{array}$$

LEVEL 4   Computations and Operations *(continued)*

Basic Curriculum	Suggested Materials and Procedures
EXPLORING INEQUALITIES IN NUMBER SENTENCES	e.g. $3 + 4 > 3 + 2$ and $3 + 2 < 3 + 4$ $3 + 4$ and $3 + 2$ do not name the same number $6 - 2 > 3$ $27 - 9 < 20$ · $7 - 3 < 2 + 1$ $3 + 7 < 12 - 1$
THE BASIC LAWS OF OPERATION	
Commutative property of addition	$4 + 2 = 2 + 4$ $4 + 2 = 6$ $2 + 4 = 6$
Associative property of addition	$2 + 9 = \square$ $2 + (8 + 1) = \square$ $(2 + 8) + 1 = \square$ $10 + 1 = 11$

It is suggested that *order* and *grouping* should be used because these are names that will prove most effective in the classroom. You should, however, be familiar with the technical names should you do further reading in the literature of mathematics.

LEVEL 4   Measurement

Basic Curriculum	Suggested Materials and Procedures
The introduction of linear measure involving the idea of approximation with respect to linear measurement	Demonstrate on the chalkboard how to measure a given line segment. Tell the children to place their rulers on the first line so the zero mark is on the left side of the line, and then read the scale where the line ends on the right. Have them measure various line segments using inch and centimeter rulers. Be sure they all understand the color coding (color the inch scale black and the centimeter scale red). Stress the fact that units given on the black scale are called inches and those on the red scale are called centimeters.
The introduction of liquid measurement	Provide classroom experiences using liquid measure. Measure water using cup, pint, quart, and gallon containers. Demonstrate that two pints are the same as one quart by pouring water from two pint containers into one quart container. Have children participate actively in this demonstration. Do this with cups and pints, cups and quarts, quarts and gallons and so on.

LEVEL 4   Measurement *(continued)*

Basic Curriculum	*Suggested Materials and Procedures*
The introduction of measuring masses with the use of balances	Learning to use a balance. Experiment for the balance: Balance some sawdust and a large balloon. Then inflate the balloon and place it back on the balance. Let the children observe the result: add more sawdust to balance the balloon. Then deflate the balloon and observe the result once again. Take a series of objects and weigh them by gram and ten-gram weights and also by the pound.

LEVEL 4   Geometry

Basic Curriculum	*Suggested Materials and Procedures*
Teach sphere, circle, rectangle and rectangular solid, triangle and triangular prism. Also teach the names.	Use these particular two- and three-dimensional objects for set demonstrations. Point out *differences* and teach the names of the various objects.
Classification of geometric figures; at least triangle, quadrilateral, and polygon	Draw these shapes in various sizes and positions, giving the children experience in the recognition of them. Have children cut out triangles and quadrilaterals of *varying sizes.*
Locate key geometric points	Use exercises to find the midpoints of various lines. Demonstrate how an angle is formed by two straight lines. Show how a triangle and a quadrilateral are formed by line segments.

Example 4   LEVELS OF PROGRESS IN MATHEMATICAL ELEMENTS *(continued)*

LEVEL 8   Language and Nature of the Number System

Basic Curriculum	*Suggested Materials and Procedures*
THE ORDER AND PATTERN SEQUENCE OF THE NUMBER SYSTEM	

THE ORDER AND
PATTERN SEQUENCE
OF THE NUMBER
SYSTEM

Reinforcing the concept
developed previously of
cardinal numbers

e.g.

| 10 | 10 | 10 |
| 10 | 10 | 10 | 10 |

| 1 | 1 | 1 | 1 | 1 |

7 tens, 5 ones; 75; seventy-five

| 100 | 100 | 100 | 100 |

4 hundreds, 0 tens, 0 ones; 400; four hundred

| 1000 | 1000 |

| 100 | 100 |
| 100 | 100 |

| 10 |

2 thousands, 4 hundreds, 1 ten, 5 ones; 2415; two thousand four
hundred fifteen

e.g.

? ? ? ?

2, 3 4 5   3, 2 5 1

LEVEL 8   Language and Nature of the Number System *(continued)*

Basic Curriculum	*Suggested Materials and Procedures*
Introducing zero as a starting point	Write the missing numerals in each of the following number patterns.
Stressing the concept of zero as a place holder	e.g. 0,_____ , 2,_____ , 4,_____ , _____ 87, 88,_____ ,_____ ,_____ , 92,_____ _____ , 1,_____ , 3,_____ , 5,_____ _____ ,_____ ,_____ , 17, 18, 19,_____ _____ , 58,_____ ,_____ , 61,_____ ,_____ _____ ,_____ , _____ ,_____ , 4, 5,_____ In what case is zero a place holder, an arbitrary starting place?

Hundred Thousands	Ten Thousands	Thousands	Hundreds	Tens	Ones
	/ / /	/ /	/ / / /	/ /	/ / /
	3	2	4	2	3
/ / / /		/ / /	/ / /		/ /
4	0	3	3	0	2

Review concepts of cardinal numbers previously established	
Cardinal number names through nine thousand, nine hundred and ninety-nine.	
Cardinal number names through ninety-nine thousand, nine hundred and ninety-nine.	
THE 1–10 PATTERN RELATIONSHIP OF THE NUMBER SYSTEM	
Continuing the understanding of the relationships between and among digits	Provide experiences for using the abacus. Devise several kinds of abaci—horizontal, vertical. Stress the abstract idea of place value and its concrete relationship.
Develop and build understanding of place value concepts	
Continuing to emphasize grouping by tens	

LEVEL 8 Language and Nature of the Number System *(continued)*

Basic Curriculum	*Suggested Materials and Procedures*
Two-digit numerals	Give the number for each set:

(24)   (36)

e.g. Write the two-digit numeral for each exercise:

(1) 5 tens and 2 ones   (3) 80 + 3
(2) 7 tens and 5 ones   (4) 60 + 9

e.g. Write the correct digit for each ☐

62 means ☐ tens and ☐ ones
94 means ☐ tens and ☐ ones

Give the largest two-digit number that has 8 as one of its digits. (98)

Give the smallest two-digit number that has 2 as one of its digits. (12)

(We are talking about positive, whole numbers.)

Three-digit numerals

e.g. Write the numeral for each exercise.

(1) four hundreds, three tens, nine ones (439)
(2) three tens, four ones, and six hundreds (634)
(3) five hundred fifty (550)

e.g. Give the missing digits:

(1) 492 means ☐ hundreds, ☐ tens, ☐ ones
(2) 783 means ☐ ones, ☐ hundreds, ☐ tens
(3) 900 means ☐ hundreds, ☐ tens, ☐ ones

e.g. Solve the equations:

(1) $568 = 500 + 60 + \square$
(2) $961 = \square + 60 + 1$
(3) $409 = 400 + \square + 9$

Prepare for grouping by hundreds.

Re-establish concept of hundreds place.

LEVEL 8	**Language and Nature of the Number System** *(continued)*

Basic Curriculum	*Suggested Materials and Procedures*
SYMBOLS USED IN ESTABLISHING THE RELATIONSHIP BE-TWEEN AND AMONG NUMBERS LEADING TO SENTENCES AND STATEMENTS Reviewing the use of the equality sign =	For example, when we write $$5 + 2 = 8 - 1$$ we assert that the symbols 5 + 2 and 8 – 1 are each names for the same thing, the number 7. In general, when we write $A = B$, we do not mean that the letters or symbols A and B are the same. They very evidently are not! What we *do* mean is that the letters A and B are synonyms. That is, the equality $A = B$ asserts precisely that the thing named by the symbol A is *equivalent to* the thing named by the symbol B. The equals sign always should be used only in this sense. <div align="center">Supplementary Material</div> <div align="center">5 + 2 4 + 3 2 + 2 5 - 1</div> Complete: <div align="center">3 + 4 __ + __ 4 + 5 __ - __ 7 - 2 __ + __ 5 - 1 __ + __</div>
FRACTIONS Understanding that a fractional value must be related to some whole to have any significance (understanding that a common denominator means common-sized part)	e.g. All the shaded areas are $\frac{1}{4}$'s, but are not equal as they refer to different wholes: <div align="center">$\frac{1}{4}$ $\frac{1}{4}$ $\frac{1}{4}$ $\frac{1}{4}$</div>

LEVEL 8 Language and Nature of the Number System *(continued)*

Basic Curriculum	*Suggested Materials and Procedures*
	e.g. All the shaded parts are $\frac{1}{2}$'s, but are not equal as they refer to different wholes:

The whole depends on halves being of the same whole:

$$\frac{1}{2} \text{ lb. butter} + \frac{1}{2} \text{ dollar} \neq 1 \text{ whole}$$

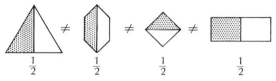

e.g. $\frac{1}{8} = \frac{1}{8}$

These $\frac{1}{8}$'s are equal and can be used in comparison.

e.g. $\frac{1}{6} = \frac{1}{6} = \frac{1}{6}$

These $\frac{1}{6}$'s are equal and can be used in comparison.

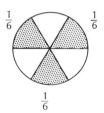

LEVEL 8   Language and Nature of the Number System *(continued)*

Basic Curriculum	*Suggested Materials and Procedures*

Understanding fractional concepts

Understanding that a fraction is a number pair

We see	We think	We write	We say
	3 black parts 4 parts in all	$\frac{3}{4}$ of region is black	three-fourths of the region is black
	2 black balls 7 balls in all	$\frac{2}{7}$ of the balls are black	two-sevenths of the balls are black
	4 black parts 6 parts in all	$\frac{4}{6}$ of the region is black	four-sixths of the region is black

Understanding the concepts of fractional parts of an object and the fact that when speaking of one-fourth of an object, we are referring to one of four parts of the same size (we are not just dividing the object into 4 parts but into 4 equal parts)

Objects *not* divided into the same size

not halves

not fifths

not sixths

Objects divided into the same size

halves

fourths

eighths

e.g.

9 of 12 squares are black
$\frac{9}{12}$ of the squares are black
3 of 4 columns have black squares
$\frac{3}{4}$ of the columns have black squares

therefore $\frac{9}{12} = \frac{3}{4}$

e.g.

$\frac{2}{4}$ of the region is black
$\frac{1}{2}$ of the region is black

$\frac{2}{4}$ of the dots are black
$\frac{1}{2}$ of the dots are black

The last two examples illustrate that $\frac{2}{4}$ of either a whole or a group is equal to $\frac{1}{2}$ of the whole or the group respectively.

e.g. $\frac{1}{3}$ is equivalent to $\frac{2}{6}$

$\frac{2}{3}$ is equivalent to $\frac{4}{6}$

$\frac{1}{4}$ is equivalent to $\frac{2}{8}$

LEVEL 8   Computations and Operations

Basic Curriculum	*Suggested Materials and Procedures*
THE ADDITION AND MULTIPLICATION OF NUMBERS	
Adding unequal groups or sets of numbers	Using expanded notation with regrouping

e.g.   44,491 = 44 thousands, 4 hundreds, 9 tens, 1 one

or

44 thousands, 48 tens, 1 ten, 1 one

or

44 thousands, 48 tens, 11 ones

Adding of 4 digit numerals in combination with 4, 3, 2, and 1 digit numerals, or combinations thereof

Combining equal groups or sets

e.g.   Without regrouping. Also use regrouping.

$$4 + 4 + 4 = 12$$
$$22 + 22 + 22 = 66$$
$$392 + 392 = 784$$

Adding of numerals containing 4, 3, 2, or 1 digits with various numbers of addends

THE SUBTRACTION AND DIVISION OF NUMBERS

Subtracting unequal groups or sets of numbers

e.g.

$$\begin{array}{r} 9762 \\ -6521 \\ \hline 3241 \end{array}$$

$$9762 - 6521 = 3241$$

Subtracting of 4 digit numerals in combination with 4, 3, 2, and 1 digit numerals, or combinations thereof

Separating equal groups or sets

e.g.

$$\begin{array}{r} 28 \\ -\ 7 \\ \hline 21 \\ -\ 7 \\ \hline 14 \\ -\ 7 \\ \hline 7 \\ -\ 7 \\ \hline 0 \end{array}$$

or

$$7\overline{)28}^{\,4}$$

Using repetitive subtraction or dividing by using the number in the equal group as the divisor

LEVEL 8   Computations and Operations *(continued)*

Basic Curriculum	*Suggested Materials and Procedures*
THE BASIC LAWS OF OPERATIONS	
Commutative property of addition and multiplication	e.g. $9 + 2 = 2 + 9$ $9 + 2 = 11$ $2 + 9 = 11$ e.g. $4 \times 5 = 5 \times 4$ $4 \times 5 = 20$ $5 \times 4 = 20$
Associative property of addition and multiplication	e.g. $3 + 9 = \square$ $3 + (7 + 2) = \square$ $(3 + 7) + 2 = \square$ $10 + 2 = 12$ e.g. $20 \times 30 = (2 \times 10) \times 30$ $= 2 \times (10 \times 30)$ $= 2 \times 300$ $= 600$

LEVEL 8   Geometry

Basic Curriculum	*Suggested Materials and Procedures*
Review previous work	Recognition of geometric figures, ideas of points, lines, line segments, angles, circles.
Develop concept of a closed plane figure	Have the students see the difference between a closed plane figure and a series of lines that is not a closed figure. Use diagrams.

Not closed plane figures

Closed plane figures

Introduce the general concept of perimeters, areas, and volume of plane and solid geometric figures and shapes	Stress that the measurement of perimeter is lineal measure (along a line): feet, yards, miles, etc. Area measurement is in square measurement and has to do with how much space is *covered* by any particular figure or shape. Volume measure is how much something *contains* and is measured in cubic measure.

LEVEL 8 Measurement

It is important to recognize that the process of measurement involves comparing and counting. At the fourth grade level, measurement concepts should be developed intuitively. Measurement concepts can be explored best through physical activities using various materials. Develop concepts of measuring by using small squares and cubes. Through planned exercises, the children will discover some basic formulas for finding area and volume; however, no attempt is made to formalize and use these in computation.

Basic Curriculum	*Suggested Materials and Procedures*
PROVIDING EXPERIENCE IN WORK WITH LENGTH, AREA AND VOLUME	Re-emphasize that we count segments to find length; square units to find area; cubes to determine volume.
	Demonstrate measurement concepts through counting of discrete objects.
	Allow children to handle and examine various physical objects that can be used as units for measurement, such as a straight piece of wire or stick for finding length, a cardboard square or a tile for finding area, and some kind of block for finding volume.
Providing experiences in working with concepts of length	Use rulers with inches and rulers with centimeters or have children construct rulers to measure lengths of various objects.
	Introduce the idea of measuring to the nearest half inch and nearest half centimeter. Have children measure objects in the room.
Providing experiences in work with area	Provide sets of squares and allow children to decide on area to be measured. They then count discrete (separate and distinct), objects in a given set to determine the area.
	Work with square-inch and square-centimeter units.
	Measure the areas of rectangles.
	Give children opportunity to discuss methods they use to arrive at the area for various types of figures. (Some may determine the standard formula for the area of a rectangle.)
Providing experiences in work with volume	Give children opportunity to work with sets of blocks stacked in particular patterns.
	Allow them to form different types of figures.
	Include metric system in working with length, area and volume.

Example 4   LEVELS OF PROGRESS IN MATHEMATICAL ELEMENTS *(continued)*

LEVEL 11 Language and Nature of the Number System

Basic Curriculum	*Suggested Materials and Procedures*
THE ORDER AND PATTERN SEQUENCE OF THE NUMBER SYSTEM	

Reinforcing the concept developed previously of cardinal numbers and numerals through nine hundred ninety-nine thousand, nine hundred ninety-nine

Reinforcing the concept of zero as a place holder

	hundred thousands	ten thousands	thousands	hundreds	tens	ones
*	7	5	0	0	0	0
**	6	0	8	1	9	3

The location (or place) of a digit within a numeral tells what the digit means.

*Seven hundred fifty thousand
$(7 \times 100,000) + (5 \times 10,000) + (0 \times 1000) +$
$(0 \times 100) + (0 \times 10) + (0 \times 1)$
$700,000 + 50,000 + 0000 + 000 + 00 + 0 = 750,000$

**Six hundred eight thousand, one hundred ninety-three
$(6 \times 100,000) + 0 \times 10,000) + (8 \times 1000) +$
$(1 \times 100) + (9 \times 10) + (3 \times 1)$
$600,000 + 00,000 + 8000 + 100 + 90 + 3 = 608,193$

Reinforcing the concept of zero as a starting point

Use rulers, yard sticks, tape measures, etc.

Introducing zero as an arbitrary constant

e.g.   Number line

$$-3 \quad -2 \quad -1 \quad 0 \quad 1 \quad 2 \quad 3$$

e.g.   Introduce negative numbers through the use of Centigrade scale and Farenheit scale thermometers

LEVEL 11 Language and Nature of the Number System *(continued)*

Basic Curriculum	*Suggested Materials and Procedures*

THE 1–10 RELATION-SHIP OF THE NUMBER SYSTEM
 	
Continuing the understanding of the relationships between and among digits
 	
   Developing and building understanding of place value concepts
	e.g.
	
	   1000 1000 1000 100 100 100 100 10 10 1 1 1 1 1
	
	(3 × 1000) + (4 × 100) + (2 × 10) + 5 = 3425
	
	e.g. Provide experiences using the abacus.
	
	Devise several kinds of abaci—horizontal, vertical. Stress the abstract idea of place value and its concrete relationship.
	
	   The use of an abacus and a place-value chart strengthens the pupils' concepts of place value. Labeling the places on the abacus and on the chart in different ways extends these concepts for use later to help pupils understand each step in an algorithm. For instance, the places on an abacus are labeled ones, tens, hundreds, etc., to hundred millions. The abacus is then used to explain reading and writing of numerals in order to build concepts of periods in numerals and to show that a digit has a value that depends upon its place in the numeral. Place-value charts are similarly labeled.

Continuing to emphasize grouping by tens	Pupils must have a clear understanding of ones' place, tens' place, etc. They should know that a number such as 4,265 can be thought of in many ways: 4,265 ones; 4,000 + 265; 4,000 + 200 + 60 + 5; 3,000 + 1,200 + 60 + 5, etc. They should understand that each place in a decimal numeral has a value ten times as great as the place at its right. These concepts need considerable attention.

LEVEL 11   Language and Nature of the Number System *(continued)*

Basic Curriculum	*Suggested Materials and Procedures*

SYMBOLS USED IN ESTABLISHING THE RELATIONSHIP BETWEEN AND AMONG NUMBERS LEADING TO SENTENCES OR STATEMENTS

Reinforcing the meaning of = and ≠

The meaning of = is reinforced along with the fact that if a mark is drawn through the sign ≠, the sign means "not equal to".

Reinforcing the meaning of > and <

The symbol > means that the number named on the left is greater than the number named on the right.

e.g. $4 \times 3 \; \boxed{>} \; 3 \times 2$ $25 - 2 \; \boxed{>} \; 9 + 4$

$7 - 3 \; \boxed{>} \; 4 - 2$ $9 + 4 \; \boxed{>} \; 5 + 6$

The symbol < means that the number named on the left is less than the number named on the right.

e.g. $2 + 9 \; \boxed{<} \; 9 + 3$ $8 + 4 \; \boxed{<} \; 18 - 4$

$4 - 1 \; \boxed{<} \; 2 + 6$ $64 \div 8 \; \boxed{<} \; 3 \times 4$

Note the fourth grade curriculum for fuller explanation.

FRACTIONS

Understanding that a fraction is part of a whole

$\frac{1}{2}$ of the circle is shaded

$\frac{3}{4}$ of the square is shaded

$\frac{1}{4}$ of the bar is shaded

Understanding that a fraction is connected with a given whole

Are all $\frac{1}{2}$'s equal?

$\frac{1}{2}$ $\frac{1}{2}$ $\frac{1}{2}$ $\frac{1}{2}$ $\frac{1}{2}$ — NO

Are all $\frac{1}{4}$'s equal?

$\frac{1}{4}$ $\frac{1}{4}$ $\frac{1}{4}$ $\frac{1}{4}$ $\frac{1}{4}$ — NO

LEVEL 11 **Language and Nature of the Number System** *(continued)*

Basic Curriculum	*Suggested Materials and Procedures*

Realizing that a fraction must be related to a measurable or countable thing or group	When speaking of $\frac{1}{2}$ of a necktie—this would make sense only if discussing $\frac{1}{2}$ the surface area of the tie
	
	  $\frac{1}{2}$ a person might make sense if referring to the person's weight
	
	  $\frac{1}{2}$ a room might make sense if referring to the cubic measure

MATERIALS: colored sticks

Blue sticks   Black sticks

Children should say two blue, five in all, therefore, two-fifths are blue.

e.g.   Number pairs and fractions

A  B   C   D

The exercises in the table below will help you think about number pairs and fractions. Each row of the table refers to one of the letters above. Supply the missing information.

Letter	Number Pair		Fraction of the region shaded
	Part shaded	Parts in all	
B	2	3	$\frac{2}{3}$
A		5	
	1		$\frac{1}{3}$
C			$\frac{1}{4}$

LEVEL 11   Computations and Operations

Basic Curriculum	*Suggested Materials and Procedures*
THE ADDITION AND MULTIPLICATION OF NUMBERS	
Adding unequal groups or sets of numbers	
Adding of 6 digit numerals in combination with 5, 4, 3, 2, and 1 digit numerals, or combinations thereof	Using expanded notation with regrouping e.g. 444,491 = 4 hundred thousands, 4 ten thousands, 4 thousands, 4 hundreds, 9 tens, 1 one or 444 thousands, 4 hundreds, 9 tens, 1 one or 400 thousands, 40 thousands, 4 thousands, 4 hundreds, 8 tens, 1 ten, 1 one
Determining sums through 999,999 with and without renaming	Using number sentences, open and closed, direct or indirect e.g. $8 + 3 = 11$ closed $7 + 3 = \square$ direct $8 + 3 = \square$ open $7 + \square = 10$ indirect
Adding unequal fractions	e.g. $\frac{1}{4} + \frac{1}{2} = \frac{1}{4} + \frac{2}{4} = \frac{3}{4}$ Put things together into the same set. You find an equivalent set into which these can fit.
Combining equal groups or sets	
Adding numerals containing 5, 4, 3, 2, or 1 digits with various numbers of addends	e.g. Without regrouping. Also use regrouping. $4 + 4 + 4 = 12$ $22 + 22 + 22 = 66$ $392 + 392 = 784$ $4,444 + 4,444 = 8,888$
Multiplying using the number of addends as the multiplier	e.g. $4 + 4 + 4 = 3 \times 4 = 12$ $22 + 22 + 22 = 3 \times 22 = 66$ $392 + 392 = 2 \times 392 = 784$ $4,444 + 4,444 = 2 \times 4,444 = 8,888$

LEVEL 11 Computations and Operations *(continued)*

Basic Curriculum	*Suggested Materials and Procedures*
Addends of 4, 3, 2, or 1 digits	
Multiplier of 1, 2, or 3 digits	e.g. Regrouping using 3 digit multiplier
Other ways of multiplying	e.g. Reverse multiplier and multiplicand. Use the addends of the multiplier as multipliers and add the partial products.

e.g.

$$
\begin{array}{cc}
2 & 10 \\
\times 5 & \times 5
\end{array}
\qquad
\begin{array}{cc}
2 & 10 \\
\times 10 & \times 10
\end{array}
\qquad \text{or} \qquad 12 \times 10 + 12 \times 5
$$

$$
\begin{array}{r}
12 \\
\times 15 \\
\hline
60 \\
12 \\
\hline
180
\end{array}
\qquad \text{or} \qquad
\begin{array}{r}
15 \\
\times 12 \\
\hline
30 \\
15 \\
\hline
180
\end{array}
$$

e.g.   A multiplier of 16 could be divided into the addends 9 and 7. Use 9 and 7 as multipliers, then combine the products.

$$
\begin{array}{r}
13 \\
\times 16 \\
\hline
78 \\
13 \\
\hline
208
\end{array}
\quad \text{or} \quad
\begin{array}{r}
13 \\
\times 9 \\
\hline
117
\end{array}
\; + \;
\begin{array}{r}
13 \\
\times 7 \\
\hline
91
\end{array}
\; = \;
\begin{array}{r}
117 \\
+91 \\
\hline
208
\end{array}
$$

Use the factors of the multiplier as multipliers in successive order.

e.g.   A multiplier of 24 has the factors of 2, 3, and 4 ($2 \times 3 \times 4 = 24$). Use 2, 3, and 4 as multipliers in successive order.

$$
\begin{array}{r}
57 \\
\times 2 \\
\hline
114 \\
\times 3 \\
\hline
342 \\
\times 4 \\
\hline
1368
\end{array}
\qquad \text{or} \qquad
\begin{array}{r}
57 \\
\times 24 \\
\hline
228 \\
114 \\
\hline
1368
\end{array}
$$

| Learning multiplication facts with products through 100 | |
| Adding equal fractions | e.g. $\frac{1}{4} + \frac{1}{4} = \frac{2}{4} = \frac{1}{2}$ |

LEVEL 11 Computations and Operations *(continued)*

Basic Curriculum	*Suggested Materials and Procedures*
THE BASIC LAWS OF OPERATIONS These laws are important only as development of understandings, not unto themselves. Commutative property of addition and multiplication	 Two numbers may be added in either order to give the same sum. e.g. $\qquad 9 + 2 = 2 + 9$ $\qquad\qquad 9 + 2 = 11$ $\qquad\qquad 2 + 9 = 11$ Two numbers may be multiplied in either order to give the same product. e.g. $\qquad 4 \times 5 = 5 \times 4$ $\qquad\qquad 4 \times 5 = 20$ $\qquad\qquad 5 \times 4 = 20$

LEVEL 11 Geometry

Basic Curriculum	*Suggested Materials and Procedures*
Review previous work	Stress the ideas of points, lines, line segments, angles, circles. Particular emphasis should be placed on the concept of the closed plane figure and on the idea of perimeter in common plane figures without the use of formulas. Also include the difference between linear, area, and volume measurement.
Sets of points. Concept of a point, segment, ray and plane	Demonstrate the difference between: a point segment ray plane Discuss some physical objects that are examples of points, segments, rays, or planes, i.e.: pencil point beam of light table top Review work involving intersecting and parallel lines can be reintroduced with this work.

LEVEL 11 Geometry *(continued)*

Basic Curriculum	Suggested Materials and Procedures
The use of the compass	Construct line segments, circles, and triangles of varying sizes. Use the compass to compare the size of various lines and angles. Demonstrate the use of the compass to bisect a line segment. Demonstrate the use of the compass to bisect an angle.

LEVEL 11 Measurement

Basic Curriculum	Suggested Materials and Procedures
REVIEW OF LENGTH	Have the children cut a piece of string equal to the length of a certain part of their body. For example, have a child come before the class and stretch a string as far as he can reach from his nose to the tip of his fingers and then cut the string according to this distance.
	Have the children use this piece of string to measure such things as the width of the room, the length of the blackboard, and so on.
	Emphasize the fact that we can select any unit we please for measurement so long as the unit is appropriate to what we are measuring. It is helpful if we select units that are known to people with whom we wish to communicate our measurements.
	Re-emphasize that we use segment units to find length.
	Have the children mark a segment that is the width of their index finger. Use this segment to make a ruler that is at least 16 units long. Use this ruler to measure various lengths.
	Have the children mark on their papers a segment that is as long as their shoes. By folding the paper, divide the shoe unit into 8 parts of the same size. Let each of these smaller parts be a unit called a "toe". Have the children measure various lengths and widths to the nearest "toe".
	In addition, the children should have various experiences in using inch and centimeter units. Allow them to compare the many different units they have used.

LEVEL 11   Measurement *(continued)*

Basic Curriculum	*Suggested Materials and Procedures*

REVIEW PERIMETER

Exhibit on the board several polygons and mark the lengths of the sides.

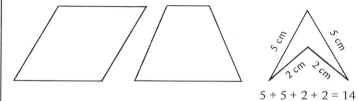

$$5 + 5 + 2 + 2 = 14$$

Review the definition of perimeter by using a string to measure objects.

Exhibit the addition equation for each polygon which will yield its perimeter.

Have the children write these equations.

Stress the word *perimeter*.

Have the children attempt to give a definition of *perimeter*.

Allow children to determine the perimeter of various polygons. When the lengths of the sides of a polygon are not whole numbers, it may be difficult for the children to find the perimeter by measuring the sides and adding. The perimeter of a polygon may be found by rolling the polygon along a ruler.

  (a)   Draw a line. Cut out the polygon and mark on this line the length of the first side.

  (b)   Roll the polygon along the line and mark the length of the second side.

  (c)   Continue to roll the polygon along the line until you have marked the length of each side.

LEVEL 11 Measurement *(continued)*

Basic Curriculum	*Suggested Materials and Procedures*

Have the children measure various polygons to the nearest centimeter and inch.

Expose the children to the concept of the perimeter (circumference) of a circle. Continue this activity by using circles of different sizes and record on a chart the diameters and circumferences.

By sticking a pin through the center, you can roll the circle along the line. Note with the children that for each circle the circumference is just a little more than 3 times the diameter.

Example 4   LEVELS OF PROGRESS IN MATHEMATICAL ELEMENTS *(continued)*

LEVEL 13   Language and Nature of the Number System

Basic Curriculum	*Suggested Materials and Procedures*

THE ORDER AND PATTERN SEQUENCE OF THE NUMBER SYSTEM.

Continuing to read and write larger numerals; introduction of billions and trillions.

To make numerals easier to read, commas are used to separate them into periods. (A period is represented as groups of numerals, each containing three places.)

Periods	Trillions			Billions			Millions			Thousands			Units		
Place value	Hundreds	Tens	Ones	Hundreds	Tens	Ones	Hundreds	Tens	Ones	Hundreds	Tens	Ones	Hundreds	Tens	Ones
Digits: *					2	4	1	3	3	0	0	0	2	7	4
**			4	7	2	9	0	0	0	6	7	3	0	0	3

*Look at the first numeral in the table. How many billions are represented? How many millions? How many thousands? How many units?

**Look at the second numeral in the table. What is the first period you will name? Why will you not name millions? After you say "673 thousand" what will you say?

A numeral with four digits may or may not have a comma.

e.g.   Three thousand, four hundred and fifty-six   3456
/or
3,456

A numeral with five or more digits should have one or more commas.

e.g.   Four hundred fifty six thousand, four hundred and twenty-two   *Always* 456,422

Twelve million, twenty five thousand, two hundred and six   12,025,206

Continue to re-enforce concepts of zero.

e.g.   Write the numeral for each of the following:

Seventeen million, five hundred thousand, seventy-six.   _____

Thirty five billion, seven hundred million, sixty eight thousand, nine hundred and fifty-two.   _____

LEVEL 13   Language and Nature of the Number System *(continued)*

Basic Curriculum	*Suggested Materials and Procedures*
Factors and Factoring	
Exploring exponants	
(a) Reading the name of each exponant form.	(a) 3^2 is read "three to the second power" or "three squared" 5^3 is read "five to the third power" or "five cubed" 6^4 is read "six to the fourth power" 4^5 is read "four to the fifth power"
(b) Renaming each exponant form with a $(\times)$, multiplication expression	(b) $5^5 = (5 \times 5 \times 5 \times 5 \times 5)$
(c) Renaming each multiplication expression using exponant form	(c) $(2 \times 2 \times 2 \times 2) = 2^4$
A number that can be renamed as a number squared is a perfect square.	$4 = \quad 2^2$. , $9 = 3^2$. , $16 = 4^2$. , $81 = 9^2$ *Rename:* 25 _____ , 36 _____ , 49 _____ , 64 _____ , 100 _____
THE 1–10 PATTERN RELATIONSHIP OF THE NUMBER SYSTEM.	
Maintenance of abilities previously acquired in relation to counting, ordinals and money.	
Roman numerals through D and M	
Exploring and comparing the position of numerals in historical and Hindu-Arabic systems of numeration	
Reading and understanding Roman numerals	e.g. Stress that the Roman system does not use place value (which offers a contrast to base ten). When two Roman symbols are placed side by side, we add or subtract to determine the number represented.

LEVEL 13 Language and Nature of the Number System *(continued)*

Basic Curriculum	*Suggested Materials and Procedures*

Suggested Materials and Procedures:

When the smaller number is represented on the right, we add: XI means 10 + 1.

When the smaller number is represented on the left, we subtract: IX means 10 − 1.

e.g. Construct an addition-subtraction and a multiplication-division table in Roman numerals and Arabic numerals through 5 and make comparison between each pair.

+	I	II	III	IV	V
I	II	III	IV	V	VI
II	III	IV	V	VI	VII
III	IV	V	VI	VII	VIII
IV	V	VI	VII	VIII	IX
V	VI	VII	VIII	IX	X

X	I	II	III	IV	V
I	I	II	III	IV	V
II	II	IV	VI	VIII	X
III	III	VI	IX	XII	XIV
IV	IV	VIII	XII	XVI	XX
V	V	X	XV	XX	XXV

e.g. Contrast base-ten Arabic numerals and corresponding Roman numerals XXIII and 23, XIX and 19, XXX and 10 + 10 + 10

e.g. Introduce the use of a bar over Roman numerals to denote thousands

$$\overline{\text{XXIII}} = 23,000 \text{ (State Curr.)}$$

NOTE: Review Roman numerals through MM (2000) (State Curr.)

Comparing other systems

Egyptian and Greek

Point out that Egyptian and Greek systems did not use place value.

e.g. Give a number for each of the following exercises:

1 = 1	
10 = ∩	
100 = ?	
1000 = ▲	
1,000,000 = ⚓	

?∩∩∩ | | (132)

⚓ ▲ ▲ ? ? ? ∩∩ | | | (1,002,323)

LEVEL 13   Language and Nature of the Number System *(continued)*

Basic Curriculum	*Suggested Materials and Procedures*
SYMBOLS	

SYMBOLS

Continued use of the symbols $<$, $>$, and $=$

  In equalities and inequalities of whole numbers.

Complete the following with the proper notation ($<$, $>$, or $=$) in the space provided.

$$3^2 + 2^2 \underline{\quad} 12 \qquad\qquad 64 \div 8 \underline{\quad\cdot\quad} 2^3$$
$$4^2 + 2^3 \underline{\quad} 2^7 \qquad\qquad 5 \times 2^2 \underline{\quad} 5^2$$
$$\text{e.g.} \quad 4^2 \ (16) = 5^2 \ (25) - 3^2 \ (9)$$
$$16 \ = 16$$

  In equalities and inequalities of fractions

$$\frac{4}{4} = 1 \qquad \frac{2}{4} = \frac{1}{2} \qquad \frac{3}{4} > \frac{1}{4} \qquad \frac{3}{8} < \frac{5}{8}$$

  Using parentheses

Parentheses are a grouping symbol used to indicate which operations are to be performed first. In the example $7 - 4 - 1 = \square$, we might write $(7 - 4) - 1 = \square$ which means that we are to subtract 4 from 7 and then subtract 1 from that difference:

$$(7 - 4) - 1 = \square$$
$$3 - 1 = \square$$
$$2 = \square$$

or we might write $7 - (4 - 1) = \square$ which means that we are to subtract 1 from 4 first and then subtract that difference (3) from 7.

$$7 - (4 - 1) = \square$$
$$7 - 3 = \square$$
$$4 = \square$$

In either case the operation to be performed first is indicated within the parentheses.

Several sets of parentheses can be used in one equation, as $(7 + 2) - (2 + 3) = \square$. Again, the operations indicated within the parentheses are to be performed first. The sum of $2 + 3$ is to be subtracted from the sum of $7 + 2$.

$$(7 + 2) - (2 + 3) = \square$$
$$9 - 5 = \square$$
$$4 = \square$$

LEVEL 13 Language and Nature of the Number System *(continued)*

Basic Curriculum	*Suggested Materials and Procedures*
INTRODUCTION OF DECIMALS (Continued from level 12)	Fractions in base 10 can be expressed in two forms, common fractions and decimals. Decimals are an extremely convenient and efficient way to represent fractional parts. For this reason, decimals are widely used in industry and science and form the numerical basis of our monetary system. In order for pupils to understand decimals, they must know place value.
Using decimal names of tenths, hundredths, and thousandths	Carefully examine the following structural outline of the decimal system and then apply it to other bases if desired.

e.g.

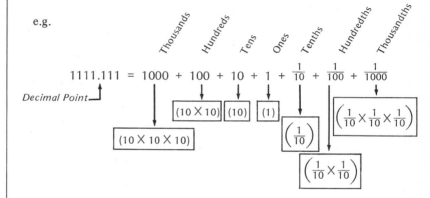

Note the way in which place value is expressed to the right of the decimal point.

e.g. $3.54 = (3 \times 1) + (5 \times \frac{1}{10}) + (4 \times \frac{1}{100})$

$= 3 + \frac{5}{10} + \frac{4}{100}$

$= 3 + \frac{50}{100} + \frac{4}{100} = 3 + \frac{54}{100}$ which reads as three *and* fifty four hundredths

e.g. $45.209 = (4 \times 10) + (5 \times 1) + (2 \times \frac{1}{10}) + (0 \times \frac{1}{100}) + (9 \times \frac{1}{1000})$

$= 40 + 5 + \frac{2}{10} + \frac{0}{100} + \frac{9}{1000}$

$= 40 + 5 + \frac{200}{1000} + \frac{0}{1000} + \frac{9}{1000}$

$= 40 + 5 + \frac{209}{1000}$ which reads as forty-five *and* two hundred nine thousand

---

LEVEL 13   Language and Nature of the Number System *(continued)*

Basic Curriculum	*Suggested Materials and Procedures*

FRACTIONS

Understanding that a fraction is a rational number and that each class of equivalent fractions can be considered as exactly one rational number and one point on the number line

Building the rational number concept from fractions (number pairs) is very much like building the cardinal-number concept from sets in earlier years. The cardinal number two is associated with the class of sets equivalent to:

$$2 = \left(\begin{array}{c} \triangledown \\ \square \end{array}\right) - - - \left(\begin{array}{c} \times \\ + \end{array}\right) - - - \left(\begin{array}{c} \circ \\ \diamond \end{array}\right) - - - \left(\begin{array}{c} \triangledown \\ \maltese \end{array}\right) - - - \left(\text{etc.}\right)$$

e.g.

For each set of equivalent fractions	we think of one rational number to represent the class of all fractions equivalent to the fractions	and one point on the number line.

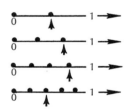

$$\left\{\frac{1}{2}, \frac{2}{4}, \frac{3}{6}, \frac{4}{8}, \frac{5}{10}\right\} \qquad \frac{1}{2}$$

$$\left\{\frac{2}{3}, \frac{4}{6}, \frac{6}{9}, \frac{8}{12}, \frac{10}{15}\right\} \qquad \frac{2}{3}$$

$$\left\{\frac{3}{4}, \frac{6}{8}, \frac{9}{12}, \frac{12}{16}, \frac{15}{20}\right\} \qquad \frac{3}{4}$$

$$\left\{\frac{2}{5}, \frac{4}{10}, \frac{6}{15}, \frac{8}{20}, \frac{10}{25}\right\} \qquad \frac{2}{5}$$

Exploring and understanding greater than, less than, and betweenness, with fractions

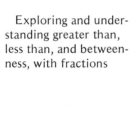

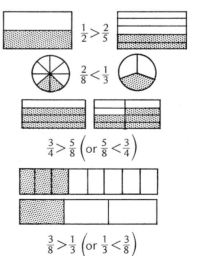

$$\frac{1}{2} > \frac{2}{5}$$

$$\frac{2}{8} < \frac{1}{3}$$

$$\frac{3}{4} > \frac{5}{8} \left(\text{or } \frac{5}{8} < \frac{3}{4}\right)$$

$$\frac{3}{8} > \frac{1}{3} \left(\text{or } \frac{1}{3} < \frac{3}{8}\right)$$

LEVEL 13   Language and Nature of the Number System *(continued)*

Basic Curriculum	*Suggested Materials and Procedures*

Fractional Parts of Sets

  Numerator represents fractional part of set.

  Denominator represents complete set.

(a) $= \frac{3}{4}$

(b) $= \frac{1}{10}$

(c) $= \frac{4}{5}$

(d) $= \frac{5}{12}$

Note: Dark or shaded area represents fractional part of set.

Draw symbols to represent:

$$\frac{3}{7} \qquad \frac{3}{5} \qquad \frac{5}{9} \qquad \frac{7}{10} \qquad \frac{3}{8}$$

  Extending competence through use of subsets.

$= \frac{4}{5}$

  Comparing subsets within a given set

$$\frac{2}{3} \qquad \frac{1}{3} \qquad\qquad \frac{4}{8} \qquad \frac{1}{2}$$

  Learning to make your own fractions and comparing the fractional parts

What fractions compare each of the following subsets to their respective sets?

LEVEL 13 Computations and Operations

Basic Curriculum	Suggested Materials and Procedures
ADDITION AND SUBTRACTION Maintenance and extension of abilities previously acquired. Emphasis on speed and accuracy.	Assist the children in a better understanding of the regrouping process in the addition and subtraction of large numbers.

Regroup

4643 =	4 thousands	6 hundreds	4 tens	3 ones
3588 =	3 thousands	5 hundreds	8 tens	8 ones
7054 =	7 thousands	0 hundreds	5 tens	4 ones
9879 =	9 thousands	6 hundreds	7 tens	9 ones
25,164 =	23 thousands	17 hundreds	24 tens	24 ones

Regroup

1,744 =	1 thousands	7 hundreds	4 tens	4 ones
24,220 =	24 thousands	2 hundreds	2 tens	
960 =		9 hundreds	6 tens	
26,924				

Regroup

4667 =	4 thousands	6 hundreds	6 tens	7 ones
−1289 =	1 thousands	2 hundreds	8 tens	9 ones
3378 =	3 thousands	3 hundreds	7 tens	8 ones

Note: Each column has been added or subtracted without regard to the column beside it; i.e., ones-column with seven borrows 10 ones from tens-column with six, it borrows 100 from the hundreds, column, etc.

MULTIPLICATION AND DIVISION OF NUMBERS

Multiplication

  Review of three methods of finding a product.

$3 \times 35 =$	35 $\times 3$	35 $\times 3$
$3 \times (30 + 5)$		
	15 (3×5)	105
$(3 \times 30) + (3 \times 5)$	90 (3×30)	
		Ans. 105
$90 + 15$	$15 + 90$	
Ans. 105	Ans. 105	

LEVEL 13 Computations and Operations *(continued)*

Basic Curriculum	*Suggested Materials and Procedures*

Extension of these
concepts to two-place
multipliers.

$$\begin{array}{r} 36 \\ \times 25 \\ \hline 180 \\ 72 \\ \hline 900 \end{array}$$

$5 \times (30 + 6)$
$5 \times 30 + 5 \times 6$
$\quad 150 + 30$
$2 \times (30 + 6)$
$2 \times 30 + 2 \times 6$
$\quad 60 + 12$

$180 \rightarrow *$
$\downarrow\downarrow$
$\downarrow\downarrow$
$72 \rightarrow **$
$\downarrow\downarrow$
900

*Multiplier (5) in 25 is in units place.

**Multiplier (2) in 25 is in tens place.

Division of numbers

Three-digit divisors

Copy exercise:

$$\begin{array}{r} 4.?? \\ 229\overline{)\$968.75} \end{array}$$

Begin by asking how many 2's there are in 9. Why do you write
the 4 in the hundreds place in the quotient?

Multiply 229 by 4 and complete the exercise.

Four-place quotients

To place the first digit of the quotient
in its correct place-value position, think:
Is 100 contained in 8? 89? 890? Where
will you write the first digit?

Think: How many 1's are there in 8?
Before you write 8 in the thousands place,
multiply 142 by 8 mentally. Is 8 too large?
Is 7 too large? Is 6? Write 6 and multiply;
then subtract.

Now think: How many 1's are in 4?
Before writing 4 in the hundreds place,
what should you do? Is 4 too large? Is 3?
Is 2? Write 2 and multiply; then subtract.

Before dividing the third time, think as
before. Continue the exercise. Is there a
remainder when you reach the end?

$$\begin{array}{r} ?\,?.?? \\ 142\overline{)\$8937.48} \\ \underline{852} \\ 41? \\ \underline{284} \\ 133? \\ \underline{1278} \\ ??? \end{array}$$

LEVEL 13 **Computations and Operations** *(continued)*

Basic Curriculum	*Suggested Materials and Procedures*
BASIC FACTS Mastery of multiplication facts through 9 X 9; maintenance of multiplication facts involving 10's, 11's, and 12's. 　Mastery of 90 division facts. **FRACTIONS** Maintenance and extension of abilities involved in addition and subtraction of fractions. 　Common fractions	
	(a)　$\overset{*}{\frown}$ $\frac{3}{6} + \frac{1}{6} = \frac{4}{6} = \frac{2}{3}$
	(b)　$\overset{*}{\frown}$ $\frac{5}{6} - \frac{1}{6} = \frac{4}{6} = \frac{2}{3}$
Using L.C.M.	(a)　$\frac{2}{3} + \frac{3}{4} + \frac{1}{2} = \left(\frac{\text{L.C.M.}}{12} \right)$
	(b)　$\frac{6}{12} + \frac{9}{12} + \frac{7}{12} = \frac{22}{12} = 1\frac{10}{12} = 1\frac{5}{6}$
Mixed numbers	(a)　$5\frac{2}{3} + 3\frac{1}{3} = 8\frac{3}{3} = 9$
	(b)　$5\frac{2}{3} - 3\frac{1}{3} = 2\frac{1}{3}$
	*Reduced

LEVEL 13 Geometry

Basic Curriculum	*Suggested Materials and Procedures*
CONTINUED USE OF GEOMETRIC FIGURES IN MEASURING PERIMETER AND AREA.	

Square = S^2

Rectangle = $l \times w$

Triangle = $\frac{1}{2}$ bh

Perimeter = Distance around

RECTANGULAR PRISM

Surface area
(Total surface area)

Total length
(Total edge)

$$TSA = 2 \times (lw + lh + wh)$$
$$= 2 \times (27 + 45 + 15)$$
$$= 2 \times 87$$
Ans. 174 sq.

$$TE = 4 \times (l + w + h)$$
$$= 4 \times (9 + 3 + 5)$$
$$= 4 \times 17$$
Ans. 68

VOLUME OF A PRISM

The number of cubic units in a solid geometric figure determines the volume of the figure.

To find the volume of a prism

$$V = (\text{Area of base}) \times h$$
$$V = (9 \times 3) \times 5$$
$$V = 27 \times 5$$
$$V = 135 \text{ cubic units}$$

LEVEL 13 Measurement

Basic Curriculum	Suggested Materials and Procedures
REVIEW THE CONCEPT OF VOLUME AND RELATE SOME CONCEPTS OF LIQUID MEASURE TO THOSE OF CUBIC MEASURE	We count cubic units to find volume. Use a set of blocks to construct several different figures. Allow the children to examine some cartons (such as a cereal box, ice cream carton, etc.) and measure the various dimensions to arrive at at least an approximation of the cubic-inch or cubic-centimeter content of each carton. Also have children determine how many quarts each container holds. For example, have them count to see how many times the contents of a quart container can be put into a gallon ice cream carton. They could discover that a gallon is approximately 230 cubic inches and that a gallon is 4 quarts. Have children determine the volume of various figures.
THE INTRODUCTION OF ANGLE MEASURE	Review the lessons in geometry that are concerned with the comparison of two angles with respect to size. The children must be aware that we do not determine the size of an angle by the amount of the ray shown. Tell children we count angle units to measure angles. We may use any unit we choose, but it is helpful if everyone agrees to use certain special units. Choose a specific unit. Call it your unit. Use your unit to construct other angles. For example, how many units $<$ will fit into this angle? $<$ There are two special angle units, a radian and a degree. Define protractor as having several angle units placed side by side to make it easier to measure angles. Have children make their own protractors by drawing a circle with $4\frac{1}{2}$ cm radius on a piece of tracing paper. Cut out half of this circle and trace units side by side. Have children measure various angles with their own protractors.

Basic Curriculum	Suggested Materials and Procedures

LEVEL 13 Measurement *(continued)*

THE CONVERSION OF STANDARD MEASURES

Converting the English measures

Review with the children the meanings of the more common units and then present on the board some exercises similar to these:

(a) 1 yd. = _____ ft.   (h) 1 qt. = _____ pt.
(b) 1 ft. = _____ in.   (i) 1 pt. = _____ cups
(c) 1 day = _____ hr.   (j) 1 wk. = _____ days
(d) 1 hr. = _____ min.   (k) 1 mi. = _____ ft.
(e) 1 min. = _____ sec.   (l) 1 mi. = _____ yd.
(f) 1 lb. = _____ oz.   (m) 1 ton = _____ lb.
(g) 1 gal. = _____ qt.   (n) 2 ft. 16 in. = 3 ft. 4 in.

Converting the metric measures

e.g. Convert within the metric system:

(a) 1 meter = _____ cm.
(b) 1 decimeter = _____ cm.
(c) 1 centimeter = _____ mm.
(d) 1 decimeter = _____ mm.
(e) 1 meter is _____ mm.
(f) 6 centimeters & 14 millimeters =
       7 centimeters and _____ mm.
(g) 10 decimeters = _____ meter
(h) .001 meter = _____ mm.
(i) .01 meter = _____ cm.
(j) .01 meter = _____ mm.
(k) .1 meter = _____ cm.
(l) .8 meter = _____ mm.
(m) .007 meter = _____ mm.
(n) 15 millimeters = _____ cm. & _____ mm.
(o) 10 millimeters = _____ centimeter
(p) 1000 grams = _____ kilogram
(q) 1 hectogram = _____ grams
(r) 1 decagram = _____ grams
(s) 1 kilometer = _____ meters
(t) .1 meter = _____ kilometer

DIAGNOSTIC INVENTORY OF THE
LEARNING DEVELOPMENT
INVENTORY

LEARNING DEVELOPMENTAL
PROFILE

INDIVIDUAL DIAGNOSTIC
INSTRUMENT FOR READING

MATHEMATICS DIAGNOSTIC
SURVEY

MATERIAL RELATED
TO CHAPTER 3

Diagnostic inventories can be made in several ways. Many school districts choose to select from sets of exercises already developed and to create relevant diagnoses of the material they would like to teach in relation to their pre-determined sequence. Other schools develop diagnoses from scratch. They feel that such diagnoses are more closely related to the learning developmental sequence they have themselves developed.

What follows in example 5 is a diagnostic inventory that was developed in the Design for Urban Education. It is also the one used in the John Gill School, Redwood City School District, Redwood City, California. Kenneth McCarthy, principal of the school, and his colleagues revised the instrument to some degree. Mr. McCarthy's point of view in regard to the inventory and its administration is shown in two statements that follow example 5. Reports from the school psychologist and the remedial reading teacher add further insights.

In addition to the above, selected items from the individualized reading program of the Orange Local School District are presented. It is appropriate in this instance to show the immediate tie-in between the Diagnostic Inventory and the Learning Developmental Profile, which is discussed more fully in the next section concerned with materials related to chapter 4.

The Learning Developmental Profile of an individualized reading program (levels 1 through 15) is shown in example 6. This set of checklists from level One A through Fifteen is maintained for each child from kindergarten through what traditionally is called the fifth grade. Allied with the Learning Developmental Profile is the material found under example 7. It consists of individual diagnostic instruments. (In addition there are other types of curriculum-related pupil exercise sheets.) The code at the beginning of each part relates to the learning developmental profile in example 6. These records are used in pretesting and posttesting, or in activities intended for reinforcement in day-to-day teaching. The record sheets are classified by level and coded in terms of a particular sheet related to that level. The capital letter E to the right of a code numeral means "easy", H means "hard." The easy and hard materials are also used as alternate forms of an item and can be either a first or a second attempt to inventory the quality of performance in a particular skill. By dovetailing examples 6 and 7 and relating them to the material in chapter 4, it is possible to get a clearer picture of the learning-profile diagnostic activities we feel are essential to developing continuous-progress programs.

Example 5   DIAGNOSTIC INVENTORY OF THE LEARNING DEVELOPMENT INVENTORY*

This is a diagnostic tool that should be administered at the beginning of the school year. The same inventory should be given at the end of May to ascertain the levels of growth in the specific skill areas found in the LDI.

The DI will show adjustments for each of the skill areas being diagnosed. Therefore, at the end of May, the DI should be rewritten and readapted for use in September.

Instructions to Teachers for Administering the DI:

The DI exercises are designed to show whether pupils have mastered, or partially mastered, skills necessary to progress in reading and language learning. Work through the exercises, page by page, with the pupils in a group. Some first- and some second-grade pupils may reach their limit at the end of section X, but all should attempt the work at least that far.

Each teacher who completes an LDI should refer to the exercises on the DI as she judges the pupil's abilities. The exercises are not to be graded (as is done to ascertain a letter grade), but simply marked to show weaknesses and strengths as they apply to the LDI.

Any discrepancies should be listed on a separate sheet of paper and returned to the office so they can be used in revisions of the DI and the LDI.

Please refer to the Minimum Attainment Section Scores (MASS) for the 22 sections of the DI to determine whether a plus or minus goes in the box attendant to the skill stated on the LDI.

LEVEL I

Directions: Place an X on the item that is different from the other items in each row.

oooo	ooooo	oooo	oooo	oooo		
DJ	DJ	DJ	JD	DJ	DJ	
look	look	look	book	look		
dropped	dropped	dropped	cropped	dropped		
held	help	help	help	help		
a A	a A	a A	q A	a		
Came	Came	Came	Came	Come	Came	Came

*(The DI was developed under the supervision of Maurie Hillson and Joseph Bongo by Mildred Dougherty and Beverly Tannis. Permission to reproduce any of this material should be obtained from the team of authors so that proper credit can be given. Only part of the DI is reproduced here.)

Example 5 DIAGNOSTIC INVENTORY OF THE LEARNING
DEVELOPMENT INVENTORY *(continued)*

LEVEL II

Directions: Join the capital letters to the small letters that mean the same thing. Do it like this. (Illustrate this on the chalkboard using two or more letters as follows):

A	u		B	v
F	p		G	g
K	f		L	l
P	a		Q	b
U	k		V	q
G	h		D	x
H	m		I	n
M	r		N	s
R	w		S	d
W	g		X	i

E	o
J	t
O	y
T	z
Y	e
Z	j

Example 5 DIAGNOSTIC INVENTORY OF THE LEARNING
DEVELOPMENT INVENTORY *(continued)*

LEVEL V

Directions: *Draw a line from the picture to the word that means the same thing as the picture.*

GIRL

BABY

HORSE

BOY

**Example 5   DIAGNOSTIC INVENTORY OF THE LEARNING
DEVELOPMENT INVENTORY** *(continued)*

LEVEL VII

Directions: (Draw a ball on the board. Put the letter b beside it.) Say, "Draw a line from the beginning sound to the picture of a thing that starts with that sound, like this." (Demonstrate with the ball and the b.)

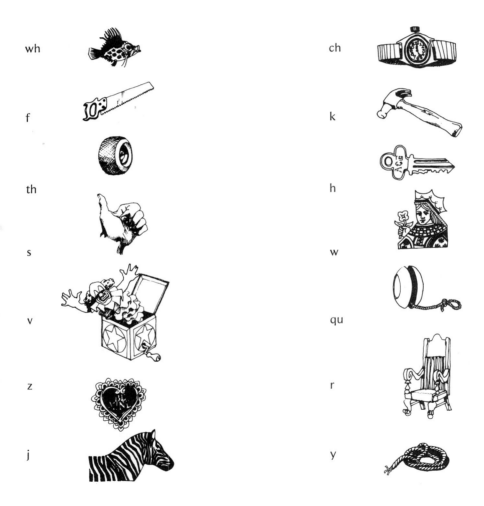

wh

f

th

s

v

z

j

ch

k

h

w

qu

r

y

Example 5   DIAGNOSTIC INVENTORY OF THE LEARNING
DEVELOPMENT INVENTORY *(continued)*

LEVEL VIII

Directions: (Draw a sock on the board and put a k *near it. Say, "Look at the picture and think of how it sounds at the end. How does* sock *sound at the end? You hear the* k *sound at the end of* sock. *On this page, write the ending sound in the space near each picture. The sounds you need are in the middle of the page."*

cu

ha

ba

pi

ja

p
b
t
d
ll
g
m
n
x
r

dru

cra

do

bo

be

Example 5 DIAGNOSTIC INVENTORY OF THE LEARNING
DEVELOPMENT INVENTORY *(continued)*

LEVEL IX

Directions: Say, "Draw a line to connect the pictures of things that rhyme." Help the children to identify things they cannot recognize.

Example 5   DIAGNOSTIC INVENTORY OF THE LEARNING
DEVELOPMENT INVENTORY *(continued)*

LEVEL X

Directions: Ask the children to tell you what Jane is doing in each picture. Then tell them that four *of the pictures tell a story. Say, "Number 1 is put in the right place for you. Put the number 2 in the box that tells the part of the story that comes after 1, the number 3 in what comes after box 2, the number 4 in the box that tells the end of the story."*

Example 5   DIAGNOSTIC INVENTORY OF THE LEARNING
DEVELOPMENT INVENTORY *(continued)*

LEVEL XIII

Directions: "In each word, draw a line through the vowels you do not hear." (Illustrate: place)

scare	leap	strange	peanuts	gate	before

noise	believe	certainly	anyone

Directions: "Draw a line through each silent consonant in these words." (Illustrate: light)

could	walked	whistled	tonight	kick

LEVEL XIV

Directions: Say "Put an X in front of each word that tells something that you can do."

tea	through	march
smile	eat	itself
prince	horse	obey

LEVEL XVII

Directions: Say "Draw a line to match words that have the same meaning." (synonyms)

big	saved
kept	huge
frightened	chew
gnaw	afraid

LEVEL XVIII

Directions: Say "Draw a line to match words that are opposite in meaning." (antonyms)

huge	free
straight	awake
trapped	small
sleeping	crooked

A Point of View

There are many sophisticated commercial reading diagnostic tests that diagnose reading difficulties. However, they all have one thing in common. They require the examiner to test one pupil at a time, which requires time and personnel.

The purpose of this test is to be able to identify reading problems early and screen all children at an early age. If problems can be quickly ascertained, proper techniques can be employed to quickly prevent problems from occurring, and if necessary a specialist can treat the specific problem. To give the proper kind of help immediately is imperative. Our current method allows many children to proceed through the sixth grade without the necessary screening techniques.

As this test is an experimental one, we will be using control groups to test its value. The test will cover levels 1 through 7 in reading.

Permission to use the original version of this instrument was given by Dr. Maurie Hillson, professor of education, Rutgers University, New Brunswick, New Jersey.

A revision of the test was completed by me with the help of the following people: Mrs. Lucille Andrews, primary consultant; Mrs. Bess Gilmore, remedial reading teacher; Mr. Jack Marchi, psychologist; and Miss Donna Turley, psychologist.

Kenneth McCarthy
Principal

Summary of Findings of Experimental Group Diagnostic Test in Reading at John Gill School

Presently we are testing all third-year children and are using all second- and fourth-year pupils as control groups. We are also testing all children who should be on level 2 in reading, but are now receiving special readiness work in kindergarten.

We are trying to determine if children have one of four problems that might interfere with reading:

1. visual-perceptual
2. emotional
3. low mental age
4. reading problems that need special emphasis or techniques.

Testing children in groups of 28 or less for third-year children takes about thirty to forty-five minutes, depending on the maturity of the group.

Mrs. Gilmore, remedial reading teacher, reports that an individual Spache Reading Diagnostic Test takes about twenty minutes to one hour per child. She also reports that interpretation of the group test measured by comparison with individual testing is about the same. Individual testing shows the area of reading difficulty, but the experimental group test shows this, plus several other important areas that influence reading. The group test shows:

1. visual-perceptual problems
2. possible emotional problems
3. mental age or IQ.

Test results of Mrs. Davis's class (levels 2, 3, and 4) where 26 children were tested. According to Miss Donna Turley, school psychologist, 14 of the 26 would indicate enough difficulty, with experimental testing to merit follow-up examinations. Where children selected by the experimental measure as needing follow-up consideration were compared with those evaluated by the teacher as being problems, there was a striking relationship. Eight of the 14 are in the low reading group.

Test results of Mrs. Hughes's class (levels 2, 3, and 4). Ten of the 29 children tested need further psychological testing to determine the specific nature of their difficulty. One of the ten screened would probably be a candidate for an E.H. class.

Test results of Mrs. Marcelli's class (levels 5 and 6). Five of the 29 children tested needed further psychological testing to determine the specific nature of their difficulty.

Special placement in kindergarten of seven first-year children. Children receiving special help in the afternoon in readiness and beginning reading. Possibly three students of the seven will require special testing. No definite plans have been made for these children.

Some children indicating real difficulty with the group test may prove to have significant disturbances, even though in class performance, at the present time, they may not be in jeopardy.

Many children are never referred for psychological evaluation, though they proceed through school hampered by unknown difficulties. The purpose of the present test is to identify *early* students who are unable to do maximum learning. Possible reasons for not identifying such children include:

1. The hope the child will mature and somehow catch up.
2. There may be a reluctance on the part of the teacher to turn problems over to an outside person.
3. Pressures and demands upon teacher and later upon guidance personnel may allow less demanding problems to be ignored.
4. Some people believe that extra reading after school and "homework" by the parent will somehow "catch him up."
5. Teachers will usually refer the aggressive acting-out child and often disregard the well-behaved child who has more severe problems.

6. The bright child who is not reading to capacity may not ever be recognized.
7. The history of reading has *not* been the prevention of reading difficulties.

By not having a proper evaluation in the first place, the majority of children who are having reading problems are placed in the remedial reading class where their problems may not ever be solved. In my opinion, this group test is a good one and merits serious consideration. It also implies that we are only "scratching the surface," if we are to have each youngster reach his optimum growth in reading. An increase in guidance personnel would be necessary, if we were to test all primary children.

Kenneth McCarthy
Principal

Findings of School Psychologist

Under the creative analysis of reading and learning problems and their lack of early identification and treatment, and John Gill School, under Principal Ken McCarthy, has chosen to experimentally search for a measure which would capably indicate problem students, as well as future reading problems students. This would facilitate making proper diagnosis and providing ways (yet to be determined) for the clearing of problems to pave the way for smoother maximum learning. With the experience and background of both the principal and his teachers involved, it would seem possible to arrive at more accurate tools of measurement, and more capable follow-up. The hope seems to be to learn to avoid reading problems by early identification and treatment, rather than by placing the emphasis upon remediation, as in the past.

As a beginning, a wide-ranging experimental test was devised. For the purpose of indicating emotional and visual-perceptual problems, it included drawing a person and the task of reproducing as exactly as possible some Bender-like drawings. It was hoped these two measures would indicate students who would likely have difficulty of an emotional or neurological nature, were they further tested.

To the present, the outcomes have been most interesting, in that lists of students having high difficulty scores, arrived at by combined analysis by the school counselor and psychometrist, have had a very high relationship with teacher suggested lists of students with difficulty. Of interesting future consideration will be the outcomes of not only these students, when further tested, but also the small group also further tested, who were not identified by teachers. Were we to find these unidentified students to have problems worthy of follow-up, there would be a reinforcement for the need to do this type of large-scale examining, rather than rely solely upon teacher referrals. We could say, undoubtedly, at present that such large-scale examination would identify the same students teachers see as having problems.

It would seem the basis for this study and experimentation is most sound, and, whether or not the present measure is found adequate, with continued careful analysis and evaluation, plus further creativity in planning, there might be produced a procedure for identifying and helping students with problems that would interfere with reading progress in early elementary school.

Donna Lee Turley
School Psychologist

Report from the Remedial Reading Teacher

The results of the Experimental Group Test given to the primary level of John Gill School have been placed on graph forms showing individual scores in each area of the test. The children in this group that are in Special Reading have been given the Spache Diagnostic Reading Test. There seems to be enough correlation between these results and the child's academic performance to justify continued use of this procedure in finding, diagnosing, and giving help to children with reading problems. The group test seems usable in the ungraded primary program in that greater numbers of children can be tested in less time. Continuance of this program would include refining of the Experimental Test, improvement in administering it, and a more comprehensive use of the results.

Bess Gilmore
Remedial Reading Teacher

Example 8 is a Mathematics Diagnostic Survey that relates to the sequences in math developed in the Madison Area Project, Syracuse, New York. This survey spans what was traditionally covered in grades 4 through 8.

Example 6   LEARNING DEVELOPMENTAL PROFILE

<u>READING LEVEL 1-A</u>

Name _____   Teacher _____

Date Beginning _____ Date Moved to Next Level _____

☐	1. Speaks in sentences
☐	2. Enjoys picture books
☐	3. Recognizes likenesses and differences: size, shape, quantity
☐	4. Comprehends listening activities
☐	5. Discriminates sounds
☐	6. Listens attentively for a short period of time
☐	7. Recognizes basic colors
☐	8. Has experienced left to right progression
☐	9. Enjoys participating in academic activities
☐	10. Prints name: capital/lowercase
☐	11. Prints other letters of the alphabet or words
☐	12. Reads some words
☐	13. Says the letters of the alphabet in order
☐	14. Names the letters of the alphabet out of order (some or all)
☐	15. Expresses himself well verbally
☐	16. Notes relationships in pictures
☐	17. Can finish stories
☐	18. Can classify items
☐	19. Uses simple picture clues successfully
☐	20. Participates in composing story charts

Comments:

(Complete when level is completed, child transfers, or at end of school year.)
Orange Primary School/Early Readiness/ Rev March 67

Example 6   LEARNING DEVELOPMENTAL PROFILE *(continued)*

READING LEVEL 1-B

Name _____   Teacher _____

Date Beginning _____   Date Moved to Next Level _____

	1. Demonstrates appropriate habits and attitudes
	2. Recognizes likenesses and differences in letters, words, and shapes
	3. Understands left to right
	4. Is skillful at rhyming
	5. Can express the main idea of a story
	6. Recalls details of a story accurately
	7. Can retell the story, poem, rhyme in proper sequence
	8. Can draw logical conclusions to familiar experiences
	9. Uses picture clues successfully
	10. Can match pictures and words to charts
	11. Knows top from bottom, left to right. Moves eyes from left to right.
	12. Is aware of differences in sounds in words: rhyme/beginning sounds
	13. Can direct attention at an activity for at least fifteen minutes
	14. Has developed general muscular control as readiness for writing
	15. Distinguishes initial consonant sounds
	16. Can match capital and small letters
	17. Recognizes differences between capital and small letters
	18. Is skillful at auditory imagery
	19. Understands some abstract words

Comments:

(Complete when level is completed, child transfers, or at end of school year.)
Orange Primary School/Early Readiness/Rev March 67

Example 6   LEARNING DEVELOPMENTAL PROFILE *(continued)*

READING LEVEL 2

Name _____ Teacher _____

Date Beginning _____ Date Moved to Next Level _____

	1. Can comprehend, interpret, and retell experience chart stories
	2. Associates meaning with the printed word; aware word has meaning
	3. Knows left from right; moves eyes left to right across a row
	4. Can tell or repeat short stories, poems, and rhymes in sequence
	5. Has visual discrimination of letters, words, and shapes
	6. Is aware of differences in sounds in words: rhyme/first sounds
	7. Can direct attention for fifteen minutes at worktime
	8. Has developed general muscular control as readiness for writing
	9. Can write his first name in manuscript letters
	10. Shows an interest in books and in acquiring information
	11. Can follow simple directions
	12. Can classify items

Comments:

(Complete when level is completed, child transfers, or at end of school year.)
Orange Primary School/Adv Readiness/Rev March 67

Example 6   LEARNING DEVELOPMENTAL PROFILE *(continued)*

READING LEVEL 3

Name _____   Teacher _____

Date Beginning _____   Date Moved to Next Level _____

	1. Sight vocabulary appropriate to level 3
	2. Uses context clues and word analysis to identify printed words
	3. Has visual-auditory perception of initial consonants
	4. Can substitute initial consonants in words
	5. Has visual-auditory perception of rhyme
	6. Recognizes words formed by adding *s* to known root words
	7. Is interested in books and has a desire to read them
	8. Understands and follows related independent reading activities
	9. Has good silent reading habits
	10. Can comprehend and interpret level 3 material
	11. Can match capital-letter words and small-letter words
	12. Can locate answers to questions

Comments:

(Complete when level is completed, child transfers, or at end of school year.)
Orange Primary School/Pre-Primer/Rev March 67

Example 6   LEARNING DEVELOPMENTAL PROFILE *(continued)*

<u>READING LEVEL 4</u>

Name _____   Teacher _____

Date Beginning _____   Date Moved to Next Level _____

	1. Sight vocabulary appropriate to level 4
	2. Has visual-auditory perception of initial and final consonants and digraphs
	3. Can write initial and final consonants and substitute them in words
	4. Understands structural changes made by adding *'s, ed,* or *ing* to known root words
	5. Uses context clues and word-analysis skills to identify unknown words
	6. Knows common word families
	7. Recognizes the possessive form
	8. Recognizes the speaker in quotations
	9. Can choose and read appropriate responses to questions
	10. Can recognize opposites

Comments:

(Complete when level is completed, child transfers, or at end of school year.)
Orange Primary School/Primer/Rev March 67

Example 6   LEARNING DEVELOPMENTAL PROFILE *(continued)*

<u>READING LEVEL 5</u>

Name _____ Teacher _____

Date Beginning _____ Date Moved to Next Level _____

	1. Sight vocabulary appropriate to level 5
	2. Uses context clues appropriate to level 5
	3. Uses phonetic and structural analysis in attacking new words and in word recognition
	4. Can blend consonant sounds (initial and final) in words
	5. Understands structural changes made by adding *er* (of comparison) to known words
	6. Recognizes and understands inflected forms made by adding *s, 's, ed, d, ing* to known root words
	7. Recognizes and understands compound words
	8. Can comprehend and interpret level 5 material
	9. Uses picture dictionary to find words for writing
	10. Uses the Table of Contents
	11. Recognizes capital and small letters
	12. Recognizes some vowel sounds
	13. Recognizes and understands contractions
	14. Recalls what has been read: silently/orally
	15. Locates answers to questions
	16. Is able to work independently

Comments:

(Complete when level is completed, child transfers, or at end of school year.)
Orange Primary School/1/Rev March 67

Example 6   LEARNING DEVELOPMENTAL PROFILE *(continued)*

<u>READING LEVEL 6</u>

Name _____ Teacher _____

Date Beginning _____ Date Moved to Next Level _____

	1. Has acquired basic sight vocabulary and previous skills
	2. Understands the use of soft *c* and *g*, hard *c* and *g*
	3. Understands three letter consonant blends
	4. Recognizes the vowel dipthongs *ou, ow, oi, oy*
	5. Understands the effect of final *e* on vowels
	6. Understands the effect of *r* on vowels
	7. Recognizes root words and the suffixes *y, en, es, est*
	8. Understands plurals (*y* to *i*, *f* to *v*, *es*)
	9. Recognizes singular possessives
	10. Begins dictionary and reference skills; alphabetizes to first letter
	11. Can use the Table of Contents effectively
	12. Can classify and organize information
	13. Can verify information
	14. Understands the main idea
	15. Understands the sequence of ideas or events
	16. Is able to work independently

Comments:

(Complete when level is completed, child transfers, or at end of school year.)
Orange Primary School/2-1/Rev March 67

Example 6   LEARNING DEVELOPMENTAL PROFILE *(continued)*

<u>READING LEVEL 7</u>

Name _____   Teacher _____

Date Beginning _____   Date Moved to Next Level _____

	1. Has acquired basic vocabulary and previous skills
	2. Knows the effect of *l, u,* and *w* on vowels
	3. Recognizes and knows the suffixes *ly, ful, ness, tion*
	4. Recognizes and knows the prefixes *a, be, un, re, in, dis*
	5. Has auditory recognition of syllables
	6. Expands dictionary and reference skills; alphabetizes to two letters
	7. Recognizes synonyms and homonyms
	8. Is sensitive to character traits and mood in stories
	9. Has comprehension skills appropriate to level 7
	10. Observes punctuation marks
	11. Reads orally with fluency and expression
	12. Recognizes quotation marks
	13. Is able to work independently

Comments:

(Complete when level is completed, child transfers, or at end of school year.)
Orange Primary School/2-2/Rev March 67

Example 6   LEARNING DEVELOPMENTAL PROFILE *(continued)*

READING LEVEL 8

Name _____ Teacher _____

Date Beginning _____ Date Moved to Next Level _____

☐	1. Vocabulary: basic sight words/basic level 8 vocabulary
☐	2. Applies structural-analysis skills: prefixes, suffixes, root words
☐	3. Able to supply synonyms and antonyms
☐	4. Can form plurals by adding *s, es, ies*
☐	5. Maintains visual-auditory perception of syllables
☐	6. Understands and uses beginning rules of syllabication
☐	7. Has comprehension appropriate to level 8
☐	8. Maintains oral reading skills
☐	9. Knows how to form contractions
☐	10. Has good listening skills
☐	11. Is able to work independently

Comments:

(Complete when level is completed, child transfers, or at end of school year.)
Orange Primary School/3-1/Rev March 67

Example 6   LEARNING DEVELOPMENTAL PROFILE *(continued)*

READING LEVEL 9

Name _____ Teacher _____

Date Beginning _____ Date Moved to Next Level _____

☐	1. Understands basic level 9 vocabulary
☐	2. Knows meaning of specific prefixes and suffixes
☐	3. Can supply homonyms
☐	4. Understands use of glossary to find word meaning
☐	5. Can form plurals by changing *f* to *v* and adding *es*
☐	6. Understands all basic rules of syllabication
☐	7. Can hyphenate words using syllable rules
☐	8. Understands use of primary accent
☐	9. Has comprehension appropriate to level 9
☐	10. Maintains oral reading skills
☐	11. Has good listening skills
☐	12. Is able to work independently

Comments:

(Complete when level is completed, child transfers, or at end of school year.)
Orange Primary School/3-2/Rev March 67

Example 6   LEARNING DEVELOPMENTAL PROFILE *(continued)*

READING LEVEL 10

Name _____ Teacher _____

Date Beginning _____ Date Moved to Next Level _____

	1. Mastery of independent word attack
	2. Selects main idea with skill
	3. Organizes ideas in sequence
	4. Perceives cause-effect relationships
	5. Can draw conclusions and state generalizations
	6. Can make critical evaluations
	7. Is sensitive to time, place, mood in story setting
	8. Identifies unfamiliar words and establishes meaning independently
	9. Selects variety of reading materials
	10. Adjusts reading rate and intensity to purpose and material
	11. Can proofread
	12. Has elementary outlining skills
	13. Uses dictionary to determine meaning and pronunciation
	14. Uses reference skills: encyclopedia/atlas
	15. Has basic library skills: card catalog/library organization
	16. Generally shows initiative, interest, responsibility in reading
	17. Is able to work independently

Comments:

(Complete when level is completed, child transfers, or at end of school year.)
Orange Primary School/Consol-St Sk /Rev March 67

Example 6 LEARNING DEVELOPMENTAL PROFILE *(continued)*

READING LEVEL 11

Name _____ Teacher _____

Date Beginning _____ Date Moved to Next Level _____

	1. Knows phonic skills developed in levels 1–10
	2. Comprehends basic fourth grade vocabulary (85 percent of test)
	3. Knows various spellings for the same consonant sound and the same vowel sound
	4. Identifies base or root word, verb tenses, compound words, plurals
	5. Increases knowledge of specific prefixes, suffixes, and formation of plurals
	6. Increases knowledge of homonyms, synonyms, antonyms and homographs
	7. Applies principles of syllabication in independent word attack, using vowel and consonant rules
	8. Knows four visual clues to accenting syllables
	9. Extends dictionary skills: uses pronunciation key, guide words, and as a source of other information (measurement, capitals, statistics)
	10. Analyzes multiple meanings of words
	11. Classifies words from lists and stories (specific to general)
	12. Classifies from general to specific
	13. Understands and follows directions, oral and written
	14. Is able to work independently

Comments:

(Complete when level is completed, child transfers, or at the end of school year.)
Orange Elementary Schools /4-1/ August 68

Example 6   LEARNING DEVELOPMENTAL PROFILE *(continued)*

READING LEVEL 12

Name _____   Teacher _____

Date Beginning _____   Date Moved to Next Level _____

	1. Arranges ideas and events in sequence
	2. Summarizes material read
	3. Maintains and refines outlining skills
	4. Outlines to precede giving a talk, and talks from an outline
	5. Develops group discussion skills using bridging phrases
	6. Uses main topic–subtopic type of index
	7. Develops skill in using cross references
	8. Maintains and refines listening skills: (1) appreciation, (2) sequence, (3) information, (4) main idea
	9. Develops eye-voice span of three words
	10. Develops choral reading skills: good enunciation, meaningful phrasing, pleasing voice
	11. Interprets punctuation marks and typographical clues
	12. Interprets figurative and idiomatic language
	13. Develops critical reading skills: checks validity of printed statement, inferences; evaluates actions of story characters
	14. Is able to work independently

Comments:

(Complete when level is completed, child transfers, or at end of school year.)
Orange Elementary Schools /4-2/ August 68

Example 6   LEARNING DEVELOPMENTAL PROFILE *(continued)*

<u>READING LEVEL 13</u>

Name _____ Teacher _____

Date Beginning _____ Date Moved to Next Level _____

	1. Maintains learned-word recognition skills and applies at new level
	2. Identifies and interprets root words, suffixes, and prefixes
	3. Develops word recognition in context areas
	4. Develops an understanding of primary and secondary accent patterns
	5. Understands vowel differences in open and closed syllables and in accented and unaccented syllables
	6. Notes effect of accent on meaning and part of speech (noun or verb)
	7. Increases knowledge of heteronyms, homographs, and synonyms
	8. Maintains and elaborates outline procedures
	9. Uses context clues to determine specific meanings
	10. Recognizes and interprets imagery and figurative language
	11. Interprets dialect and colloquial language
	12. Identifies and compares literary forms
	13. Restates main ideas in his own words
	14. Is able to work independently

Comments:

(Complete when level is completed, child transfers, or at end of school year.)
Orange Elementary Schools /5-1/ August 68

Example 6   LEARNING DEVELOPMENTAL PROFILE *(continued)*

<u>READING LEVEL 14</u>

Name _____ Teacher _____

Date Beginning _____ Date Moved to Next Level _____

	1. Understands and follows directions
	2. Distinguishes fact from opinion
	3. Reorganizes and rewrites a poor paragraph
	4. Develops correct speech, and interprets written language through oral reading
	5. Finds the details on a proposed item
	6. Interprets and organizes related facts from the reading of diagrams, maps, and charts
	7. Reviews and refines dictionary skills
	8. Skims for specific purposes
	9. Extends listening skills
	10. Takes notes on what he has read
	11. Refines outlining skills
	12. Enters into group discussion in a courteous manner
	13. Is able to work independently

Comments:

(Complete when level is completed, child transfers, or at end of school year.)
Orange Elementary Schools /5-2/ August 68

Example 6   LEARNING DEVELOPMENTAL PROFILE *(continued)*

<u>READING LEVEL 15</u>

Name _____ Teacher _____

Date Beginning _____ Date Moved to Next Level _____

	1. Maintains previously learned skills and applies at a higher level
	2. Increases recognition and understanding of prefixes, suffixes, and parts of speech
	3. Interprets typography
	4. Comprehends contemporary meanings of words in reference to outdated ones
	5. Begins instruction in *Reader's Guide to Periodical Literature*
	6. Uses newspapers, bulletins, and magazines for the latest news on a subject
	7. Reads and interprets bar graphs, diagrams, and maps
	8. Continues to improve conversational techniques in class discussion
	9. Analyzes relevancy, competency, and authenticity of reading materials
	10. Learns use of footnotes and captions
	11. Achieves effective oral interpretation
	12. Extends use of reference materials
	13. Determines literary form of a selection
	14. Interprets ideas, reads between the lines
	15. Applies reading skills in content subject areas
	16. Is able to work independently

Comments:

(Complete when level is completed, child transfers, or at end of school year.)
Orange Elementary Schools /Advanced 5/ August 68

Example 7   INDIVIDUAL DIAGNOSTIC INSTRUMENT FOR READING

Name _____   6:7–E

Directions: Add the suffix y to each word. Draw a line under the root part of the word. The first one is done for you.

1. windy
2. dust
3. rock

Directions: Add the suffix en to each word. Write the new word on the line. The first one is done for you.

eat   1. He had eaten his lunch.
beat   2. Our team was _____ today.
give   3. Tom had _____ his toys away.
fall   4. John had _____ out of the tree.

Directions: Write new words by adding er and est to these words.

	er	est
1. sweet	sweeter	sweetest
2. warm		
3. brave		
4. safe		

Directions: Use one of the words ending in est in a sentence.

1. _____

Use one of the words ending in er in a sentence.

2. _____

Name _____   6:7–H

Directions: Add the suffix y to each of these words. In some of them you will need to double the last letter. The first two are done for you.

1. trick   tricky
2. fog   foggy
3. star   _____
4. mud   _____
5. sun   _____
6. sand   _____

Example 7   INDIVIDUAL DIAGNOSTIC INSTRUMENT FOR READING *(continued)*

Directions: Write the correct form of the word given before the sentence. Write your own sentence for number 3.

short   1. Mother will _____ Susan's dress.
hard   2. The candy must _____ before we eat it.
fright   3.

Directions: Write new words by adding <u>er</u> and <u>est</u> to these words. For numbers 5 and 6, choose your own words.

	<u>er</u>	<u>est</u>
1. fresh	_____	_____
2. wild	_____	_____
3. ripe	_____	_____
4. wide	_____	_____
5. _____		
6. _____		

Name _____   6:12–E

Directions: Write each word under one of the headings given below:

work   peas   coat   talk
peaches   ham   pie   sing
hat   grapes   mittens   socks
jacket   oranges   smile   jump
apples   skip   beans   gloves

Things to Wear	Things to Eat	Things to Do

Directions: Write each word under one of the headings given below:

New York   ocean   city   pool
baby   radio   carrots   drum
trees   town   lake   kittens
horn   flowers   bells   apples
barnyard   zoo   store   grass

Places	Things That Grow	Things That Make Noise

Example 7   INDIVIDUAL DIAGNOSTIC INSTRUMENT FOR READING *(continued)*

Name _____   6:12–H

Directions: Circle the correct words or phrases.

1. Three good things to eat.

   (beans)   cord   (bread)   barns   (corn)   brick

2. Two things a boy can do.

   swim in the air
   ride a horse
   swim in the water
   drive a house

3. Three animals you can ride.

   cat   dog   donkey   monkey   camel   horse

4. Three things that men wear.

   suit   bonnet   skirt   tie   shirt   bats

Directions: In each row put a line under the word that does not belong.

1. red   blue   grass
2. man   dog   cat
3. fox   robin   wolf
4. potatoes   moved   wiggled
5. second   season   third

Name _____   7:4–E

Directions: Change the meaning of each underlined word by adding the given prefix.

un   1. Frisky is happy today.
         Frisky is unhappy today.
dis   2. The star will appear in the sky.
         The star will _____ in the sky.
un   3. John will load the truck.
         John will _____ the truck.
in   4. This answer is correct.
         This answer is_____ .
re   5. Patsy will fill the glass.
         Patsy will _____ the glass.

Directions: Write one word using the prefix un. Use the word in a sentence and underline it.

un   1. _____

Example 7 INDIVIDUAL DIAGNOSTIC INSTRUMENT FOR READING *(continued)*

Name _____ 7:4–H

Directions: From the list write new words and put them under the correct prefix. Draw a line under the root word. Four words have been done for you.

re	in	dis	un
recall	incomplete	disagree	unfriendly

complete   visible   appear   call
friendly   read   happy   agree

Directions: Write a word using each of these prefixes.

re   1.
in   2.
dis 3.
un 4.

Directions: Write a sentence using each word you just wrote.

1.
2.
3.
4.

Name _____ 8:9–E

Directions: Write the words that mean:

1. can't   _____can_____   _____not_____
2. wasn't   _____   _____
3. wouldn't _____   _____
4. we're   _____   _____
5. it's   _____   _____

Directions: Write the contraction that could be used in each of these examples.

1. He could not hear.   _____
2. Let us go home.   _____
3. I am going out.   _____
4. Do not walk fast.   _____
5. You must not talk.   _____

Directions: Write a sentence using a contraction in it.

Example 7   INDIVIDUAL DIAGNOSTIC INSTRUMENT FOR READING *(continued)*

Name _____   8:9–H

Directions: Write the complete words for each contraction on the line.

1. You can't take out books today.   _____
2. There aren't too many people here now.   _____
3. She couldn't go to the store.   _____
4. I'd like to meet her.   _____
5. I've read this before.   _____

Directions: In each row, draw a line under the two words that mean the same as the first word.

1. he's	<u>he is</u>	here is	there is
2. what's	where is	what is	will not
3. don't	do not	does not	can not
4. aren't	am not	will not	are not
5. it's	I am	it is	is not

Directions: Write a sentence using a contraction. Then write it again using the complete words.

1. _____
2. _____

_____

Name _____   9:3–E

Directions: Match each word in column A with a homonym in column B. Use the letter.

	Column A	Column B
g	1. would	a. meat
	2. pair	b. sea
	3. won	c. one
	4. cent	d. pear
	5. piece	e. scent
	6. sun	f. son
	7. meet	g. wood
	8. see	h. peace
	9. knew	i. their
	10. there	j. new

Directions: Write the correct homonym in each blank.

1. Mother keeps jars of fruit in the <u>cellar</u>.
2. The buyer will pay the <u>seller</u>.

Someone who sells something is a _____ .
A place underneath a house is a _____ .

Example 7   INDIVIDUAL DIAGNOSTIC INSTRUMENT FOR READING *(continued)*

1. The horse will <u>wait</u> at the gate.
2. John tried to <u>guess</u> the <u>weight</u> of the box.

       To stay in one place is to _____ .
       The number of pounds you are is your _____ .

Name _____   9:3–H

Directions: Match each word in column A with a homonym in column B. Use the letter.

Column A	Column B
_____ 1. forth	a. herd
_____ 2. so	b. hauls
_____ 3. beat	c. due
_____ 4. halls	d. sew
_____ 5. dew	e. beet
_____ 6. rein	f. rain
_____ 7. heard	g. road
_____ 8. rode	h. fourth
_____ 9. maid	i. made
_____10. plane	j. plain

Directions: Draw a line under the homonym in each sentence. Then write the correct word on the line in the third sentence.

A. The birds are over there.
   Their nest is finished.
   It was _____ nest.
B. Mother used a cup of flour in the cake.
   The vase held a single flower.
   The _____ was ground at the mill.
C. He put the reel of film in a drawer.
   The real reason was not known.
   The story is _____ , not make-believe.

Example 8   MATHEMATICS DIAGNOSTIC SURVEY

Name _____

Period _____

Date _____

Part I

Addition of Whole Numbers

1. 253   2. 965   3. 703   4. 897   5. 518 + 322 + 7 =
   +146   +375   809   469
                            608   856
                                         988
                                         835

Subtraction of Whole Numbers

6. 857   7. 862   8. 8032   9. 9000   10. 843 take away 144 =
   −342   −395   −2347   −3647

Multiplication of Whole Numbers

11. 304   12. 837   13. 27   14. 429   15. 257 × 26 =
    ×2   ×9   ×60   ×308

Division of Whole Numbers

16. $2\overline{)804}$ 17. $7\overline{)175}$ 18. $6\overline{)365}$ 19. $20\overline{)176}$ 20. 3922 ÷ 53 =

21. Draw a square   22. Draw a triangle   23. Draw a rectangle   24. Draw a circle

_____   _____   _____   _____

Addition of Fractions

25. $3\frac{3}{8}$ 26. $6\frac{3}{4}$ 27. $7\frac{1}{2}$ 28. $8\frac{3}{4}$
    $+1\frac{1}{8}$ $+5\frac{3}{4}$ $+2\frac{3}{4}$ $+5\frac{4}{5}$

Subtraction of Fractions

29. $3\frac{3}{4}$ 30. 5   31. $4\frac{3}{8}$ 32. $7\frac{1}{2}$
    $-1\frac{1}{4}$ $-2\frac{5}{6}$ $-2\frac{7}{8}$ $-4\frac{2}{3}$

Multiplication of Fractions

33. $3 \times \frac{3}{4} =$ 34. $\frac{1}{2} \times \frac{4}{5} =$ 35. $3\frac{3}{4} \times 4 =$ 36. $42\frac{1}{2}$ 37. 32
                                                                                              $\times\ 7$ $\times\ 4\frac{1}{4}$

Example 8   MATHEMATICS DIAGNOSTIC SURVEY *(continued)*

Division of Fractions

38. $4 \div \frac{3}{4} =$ 39. $6 \div 1\frac{1}{3} =$ 40. $2\frac{1}{2} \div 3\frac{3}{4} =$ 41. $\frac{3}{4} \div 2 =$

Addition and Subtraction of Decimals

42. $1.86 + 279.43 + .04 =$ 43. $2.2 + 18.63 + .008 =$

44. $37.56 - 1.48 =$ 45. $49.6 - 38.84 =$

Multiplication of Decimals

46. $\begin{array}{r} 12.7 \\ \underline{\times 4} \end{array}$ 47. $\begin{array}{r} 52 \\ \underline{\times .08} \end{array}$ 48. $\begin{array}{r} .43 \\ \underline{\times .2} \end{array}$ 49. $2.8 \times 80 =$

Division of Decimals

50. $3\overline{)4.59}$ 51. $.2\overline{).186}$ 52. $1.2\overline{)24}$

Part II   Reading and Writing Numbers

Write these numbers:

53. 97 _____

54. 423 _____

55. 8,970 _____

56. 200,000 _____

57. 4,004 _____

58. Twenty-six _____

59. Six hundred ten _____

60. Three thousand one hundred forty-two_____

61. Nine hundred thousand _____

62. Seven thousand fifty _____

Place Value

63. 13 = _____ tens + _____ ones

64. 648 = _____ hundreds + _____ tens + _____ ones

65. 1035 = _____ thousands + _____ hundreds + _____ tens + _____ ones

66. 973 = ___8___ hundreds + _____ tens + ___3___ ones

67. 67 = ___5___ tens + _____ ones

68. In 3064, _____ is in the hundreds' place

69. In 6345, _____ is in the thousands' place

70. In 821 _____ is in the tens' place

71. In 1827, _____ is in the one's place

72. In 426,825, _____ is in the ten-thousands' place

Example 8   MATHEMATICS DIAGNOSTIC SURVEY *(continued)*

Part II   **Reading and Writing Numbers** *(continued)*

Comparing Numbers

73. The number halfway between 10 and 20 is _____ .
74. One-third of 45 is _____ .
75. The number halfway between 240 and 360 is _____ .
76. Which number is nearest 56?   69   or   45   (circle correct answer)
77. Which number is farthest from 230?   213   or   244   (circle correct answer)

Understanding Fractions

Write a fraction to go with each picture:

78.   79.   80.   81.   82.

Place a circle around the right answer:

83. $\frac{1}{2}$ is the same as: $\frac{1}{8}, \frac{2}{8}, \frac{4}{8}, \frac{6}{8}$

84. $\frac{3}{4}$ is the same as: $.75, \frac{9}{15}, \frac{8}{12}$

85. $\frac{2}{5}$ is the same as: $.5, \frac{6}{9}, 40\%$

86. $\frac{2}{3} = \frac{}{15}$ 87. $\frac{18}{30} = \frac{}{10}$ 88. $\frac{3}{4} = \frac{15}{}$ 89. $\frac{35}{49} = \frac{5}{}$

90. $\frac{4}{5} = \frac{}{15}$ 91. $\frac{45}{60} = \frac{}{4}$ 92. $\frac{5}{9} = \frac{25}{}$ 93. $\frac{88}{121} = \frac{8}{}$

94. The school year is 180 days. If Eddie came only 90 days, what fraction would show the number of days he came to school?

Word Problems:

95. If Eddie went to Easy Bargain Center and bought a sweater for $3.50, a sportcoat for $12.75, and some shoes for $6.00, how much did Eddie spend all together?

96. Sadie went to the Record Shop on Salina Street and bought some records for $4.80, and gave the man a $10 bill. How much change did she get?

97. If six lemons cost 39¢, how much would two dozen lemons cost?

Example 8   MATHEMATICS DIAGNOSTIC SURVEY *(continued)*

Part II   **Reading and Writing Numbers** *(continued)*

98. If the distance from Madison Street to Genesee Street is 75 yards and the distance from Walnut Avenue to University Avenue is 195 yards, how far would you walk if you walked *all* the way around the block?

99. A bike is coasting down Madison Street at 15 miles an hour. How long would it take to go 5 miles?

100. On the thruway the distance from Syracuse to Buffalo is about 125 miles. A driver used 7 gallons of gas for this trip. How many miles did he get on a gallon of gas?

101. Ruby bought 2 lbs. of salted nuts at $1.49 a pound and paid for them with a $5 bill. How much money should she have received in change?

102. Isaac raked leaves last Saturday for 3 hours, and also walked the neighbor's dog. He was paid 35¢ for walking the dog and 50¢ an hour for raking leaves. How much did he earn that day?

103. Mrs. Johnson, during the month of August, spent $55.44 for groceries, $7.20 for the telephone bill, $65.00 for rent, $12.00 for the dentist and $18.20 for clothes for her children. How much did she spend all together that month?

MATERIAL RELATED TO CHAPTER 4

LEARNING DEVELOPMENTAL INVENTORY (LDI)

LEARNING DEVELOPMENTAL PROFILE

GUIDE FOR THE DI AND LDI RELATIONSHIPS

Developing learning profiles that screen out the elements of diagnoses and prototypes are easier to come by than the diagnostic inventories. This may be due to some misunderstanding of what the two devices are. We want to repeat our point of view that the *Learning Developmental Profile* is not a diagnostic instrument. It is an instrument or record keeping system that indicates, with precision, the learning status of an individual in relation to a sequence. Some people have mistakenly used the Learning Developmental Profile as a diagnostic activity. Actually it is a cumulative assessment of achieved competencies and skills related to the diagnosis. Example 9 is a Learning Developmental Inventory for reading that was created by the primary teachers of the Roosevelt School of Union City, New Jersey.

Example 9   LEARNING DEVELOPMENTAL INVENTORY (LDI)

Level 1

Name _____ Birth Date _____

School _____ Room _____ Boy _____ Girl _____

		Yes	No	Yes	No	
Note: Check every item below either yes or no.	Date Mo/Yr					*
1. Follows oral directions						2
2. Manipulates body normally						2
3. Works well in group						2
4. Works well independently						2
5. Listens to stories with attention and interest						2
6. Shows interest in books						2
7. Knows primary colors						1,2
8. Knows circle, square, rectangle, and triangle						1,2
9. Perceives likeness and difference in size and shape						1,2
10. Identifies familiar sounds						2
11. Follows left-to-right progression						1
12. Follows top-to-bottom progression						1
13. Gives simple sentences based on pictures						1
14. Gives simple sentences on life experiences						1
15. Shows vocabulary development						2
16. Recognizes and writes his own name						1
17. Picks out details in pictures						1

*1 represents an item that is measurable by paper-and-pencil tests or inventories. 2 represents an item of observable behavior that is readily noted by the teacher.

Level 1 *(continued)*

	Yes	No	Yes	No	
Date Mo/Yr					
18. Matches pictures					1
19. Matches letters					1
20. Can button and unbutton clothing					1,2
21. Can use scissors					1,2
22. Can recite nursery rhymes and short poems					1
23. Can learn words to songs					1
24. Recognizes and can name letters of the alphabet					1,2
25. Relates simple stories in sequence					1,2
26. Can recognize shapes with familiar objects					2
27. Shows leadership qualities					2

Total Yes Responses _____

Pupil progresses to next level only if _____ or more items are checked yes. If this number is reached, continue checking on next level.

Level 2

Name _____ Birth Date _____

School _____ Room _____ Boy _____ Girl _____

	Yes	No	Yes	No	
Date Mo/Yr					
Note: Check every item below either yes or no.					
28. Listens to and follows oral directions					2
29. Shows interest in learning to read					1,2

Example 9   LEARNING DEVELOPMENTAL INVENTORY (LDI) *(continued)*

Level 2 *(continued)*

	Yes	No	Yes	No	
Date Mo/Yr					
30. Gives evidence of ability to concentrate					2
31. Works well with group					2
32. Completes seatwork satisfactorily					1
33. Can carry on verbal exchange satisfactorily					1,2
34. Expresses thoughts well and in good form					1,2
35. Pronounces words correctly					1,2
36. Reads from left to right; top to bottom					1,2
37. Finds details, omissions, and misplaced objects in a picture					1
38. Knows consonants and vowels					2
39. Understands meaning of rhyming words					1,2
40. Discriminates between sizes					1
41. Discriminates between shapes					1
42. Discriminates between colors					1
43. Shows increased knowledge of auditory discrimination					1
44. Can spell simple words from dictation					1
45. Understands that words represent symbols					1
46. Understands that a sentence begins with a capital letter and ends with a period					1
47. Understands use of several sentences to tell a story					1,2
48. Knows correct use of period and question mark					1
49. Can read well on this level					1

Total Yes Responses _____

Pupil progresses to next level only if _____ or more items are checked. If this number is reached, continue checking on the next level.

Example 9   LEARNING DEVELOPMENTAL INVENTORY (LDI) *(continued)*

Level 3

Name _____ Birth Date _____

School _____ Room _____ Boy _____ Girl _____

	Yes	No	Yes	No	
Note: Check every item below either yes or no. Date Mo/Yr					
50. Begins to show fluency in reading					2
51. Can read with expression					2
52. Shows ability to maintain longer attention span					2
53. Shows growth in vocabulary					2
54. Associates meaning with printed form					1
55. Uses contextual clues in pictures associated with story					1
56. Recognizes vowels, short and long					1
57. Knows blends					1
58. Has built a knowledge of phonetic families					1
59. Can use families to build compound words					1
60. Spells words from dictation					1
61. Spells dictated sentences					1
62. Can write original sentences					1
63. Knows capital and small case letters					1
64. Knows days of week and months of year					1
65. Uses imagination in projection of self in story					2
66. Uses imagination in completing unfinished story					1,2
67. Is reading satisfactorily on this level					1,2
68. Can work independently from reading workbook					1
69. Completes seatwork assignments					1,2

Total Yes Responses _____

Pupil progresses to next level only if _____ or more items are checked yes. If this number is reached, continue checking on next level.

Example 9   LEARNING DEVELOPMENTAL INVENTORY (LDI) *(continued)*

Level 4

Name _____ Birth Date _____

School _____ Room _____ Boy _____ Girl _____

		Yes	No	Yes	No	
	Date Mo/Yr					
Note: Check every item below either yes or no.						
70. Displays enthusiasm about reading						2
71. Anticipates pleasure in reading a book						2
72. Selects and reads easy library books						2
73. Restates story episodes in the proper sequence						1,2
74. Reads with some expression						1
75. Perceives motives and cause and effect relationships in stories						2
76. Displays continuous growth in development of vocabulary						1
77. Displays mastery in sight vocabulary in basic readers						1
78. Uses certain structural clues as a help in identifying words						1,2
79. Recognizes simple family endings						1,2
80. Recognizes words formed by adding *s, 's, s', ed, er, ing,* to root words						1
81. Recognizes and identifies contractions in reading						1,2
82. Attacks easy unknown words through initial consonant substitution						1
83. Does simple classification of words into categories						2
84. Uses contextual clues as an aid in identifying words						1,2
85. Recognizes compound words						1
86. Displays a well-developed visual perception of initial consonant sounds						1
87. Displays a well-developed auditory perception of initial consonant sounds						1
88. Has a well-developed sense of rhyming						2
89. Succeeds on worksheets attendant to skills						2

Total Yes Responses _____

Pupil progresses to next level only if _____ or more items are checked yes. If this number is reached, continue checking on the next level.

Example 9   LEARNING DEVELOPMENTAL INVENTORY (LDI) *(continued)*

Level 5

Name _____   Birth Date _____

School _____ Room _____ Boy _____ Girl _____

	Yes	No	Yes	No	
Note: Check every item below either yes or no. Date Mo/Yr					
90. Shows continuous growth in sight vocabulary					1
91. Displays enthusiasm for reading; reads library books					2
92. Maintains a longer attention span					2
93. Reads more complex stories with expression					2
94. Uses table of contents					2
95. Recognizes alphabetical sequence					1
96. Restates a story in sequence					1
97. Displays ability to interpret a story					2
98. Has ability to distinguish fact from fantasy					2
99. Shows further development of classifying words into categories					1,2
100. Understands meaning of opposites					1
101. Demonstrates knowledge of consonant blends					1
102. Demonstrates knowledge of silent consonants in words					1
103. Applies structural analysis clues to unknown words					1
104. Substitutes initial and final consonants					1
105. Recognizes and identifies compound words					1,2
106. Recognizes that one word has several meanings					1,2
107. Has ability to recognize consonants and vowels					1,2
108. Recognizes short vowels					1,2
109. Recognizes family endings					1,2
110. Identifies long sounds of vowels					1, 2
111. Applies rule for words ending in *s, 's, ed, ing,* and *er* where there is no change in the root word					1
112. Identifies common contractions					1

Example 9   LEARNING DEVELOPMENTAL INVENTORY (LDI) *(continued)*

Level 5 *(continued)*

	Yes	No	Yes	No	
Date Mo/Yr					
113. Succeeds on teacher-made skill worksheets					2
114. Works independently with good work habits					2

Total Yes Responses _____

Pupil progresses to next level only if _____ or more items are checked yes. If this number is reached, continue checking on next level.

Comments:

Level 6

	Yes	No	Yes	No	
Date Mo/Yr					
115. Displays enthusiasm about reading and enjoys library books					2
116. Works independently with good work habits					2
117. Finds specific information through reading					1
118. Reads with comprehension					1
119. Interprets the main idea of a story					1
120. Makes judgments and draws conclusions about a story					1
121. Evaluates actions and traits of characters					1
122. Senses emotional reactions and infers motives of characters					2
123. Makes inferences about past and future actions					1
124. Compares and contrasts characters and story lines					2
125. Interprets figurative, idiomatic, and picturesque language					1,2
126. Continues to increase sight vocabulary where necessary					2
127. Displays continuous growth in development of vocabulary					1
128. Uses contextual clues as an aid in identifying words					1,2

Example 9   LEARNING DEVELOPMENTAL INVENTORY (LDI) *(continued)*

Level 6 *(continued)*

	Yes	No	Yes	No	
Date Mo/Yr					
129. Displays a well-developed visual perception of initial consonants					1
130. Displays a well-developed auditory perception of initial consonant sounds					1
131. Uses structural analysis as word attack method by adding *s, 's, es, d, ed, er, est, ing,* or *y* with no change in root words					2
132. Demonstrates an increased knowledge of consonant blends					1
133. Applies the rules governing vowel sounds					1
134. Recognizes words formed by doubling the final consonant, dropping final *e,* or changing *y* to *i* before endings or suffix					1
135. Demonstrates knowledge that single words have multiple meanings					1
136. Recognizes silent consonants					1,2
137. Can find the root word in a compound word					1
138. Classifies words by meanings or functions					1
139. Can identify units, chapters, titles in table of contents, and uses them					1,2
140. Organizes thoughts, uses complete sentences and expresses himself well in writing					1,2
141. Uses punctuation as a clue to meaning and oral expression					2

Total Yes Responses _____

Pupil progresses to next level only if _____ or more items are checked yes. If this number is reached, continue checking on next level.

Comments:

Example 9   LEARNING DEVELOPMENTAL INVENTORY (LDI) *(continued)*

Level 7

	Yes	No	Yes	No	
Date Mo/Yr					
142. Displays enthusiasm about independent reading					2
143. Works independently with good work habits					2
144. Reads with comprehension					1,2
145. Interprets main ideas of a story					1,2
146. Makes judgments and draws conclusions					1,2
147. Organizes and summarizes ideas					1,2
148. Identifies author's purpose or point of view					1,2
149. Knows the use of quotation marks and their use to identify speaker					1,2
150. Infers a logical pattern of nonstated events					1,2
151. Forms sensory images					2
152. Displays visual and auditory perception of all vowels and their variants					1
153. Identifies root words in compound words					1
154. Recognizes homonyms, antonyms, synonyms					1
155. Recognizes alphabetical sequence or alphabetical position in front, second, and third position					1
156. Shows continuous growth in sight vocabulary					1
157. Applies structural analysis clues on unknown words					1
158. Can substitute initial and final consonants					1
159. Applies words ending in *s, ed, ing, es, d, n, en, est,* and *er,* where there is no change in root word					1
160. Demonstrates the knowledge of silent consonants in words					1
161. Uses context clues					2
162. Maintains a longer attention span					2
163. Restates a story in sequence					1,2
164. Identifies the common contractions					1
165. Uses table of contents					2
166. Follows written directions					1

Example 9   LEARNING DEVELOPMENTAL INVENTORY (LDI) *(continued)*

Level 7 *(continued)*

	Yes	No	Yes	No	
Date Mo/Yr					
167. Knows two-letter blends					1
168. Demonstrates knowledge of three-letter blends					1
169. Recognizes multiple meanings of words					1
170. Applies rules governing silent vowels and their effect on other vowels such as *ae, oa, ea, ai*					1
171. Displays knowledge of use of prefixes and suffixes					1

Total Yes Responses _____

Pupil progresses to next level only if _____ or more items are checked yes. If this number is reached, continue checking on next level.

Comments:

_____

Level 8

	Yes	No	Yes	No	
Date Mo/Yr					
172. Reads with expression					2
173. Forms sensory images of ideas					2
174. Identifies and evaluates story character traits					1,2
175. Can demonstrate ability to organize and summarize ideas for purposes of remembering or story telling					1,2
176. Selectively rereads to find specific answer to verify an opinion, or prove an answer					1,2
177. Demonstrates ability to apply word meaning skills					1,2
178. Applies phonetic analysis in learning new words					2
179. Uses vowel clues to aid pronunciation					2
180. Applies the principles for determining syllables					1,2
181. Demonstrates knowledge of accent and its affect on vowel sounds					1,2

Example 9   LEARNING DEVELOPMENTAL INVENTORY (LDI) *(continued)*

Level 8 *(continued)*

	Yes	No	Yes	No	
Date Mo/Yr					
182. Recognizes and demonstrates an understanding of prefixes and suffixes					1,2
183. Uses pronunciation key to interpret dictionary symbols					1,2
184. Demonstrates knowledge that pronunciation of a word may depend upon its function in the sentence					1,2
185. Displays enthusiasm about reading					2
186. Enjoys library books					2
187. Works independently with good habits					2
188. Reads with comprehension					2
189. Interprets main idea of story					2
190. Senses emotional reactions and motives of characters					2
191. Draws inferences about past and future actions					2
192. Compares and contrasts characters and story lines					2
193. Interprets figurative and idiomatic language					2
194. Continues to increase sight vocabulary					1
195. Uses knowledge of word attack methods by adding endings such as *s, 's, es, d, er*					1
196. Shows increased knowledge of consonant blends					1
197. Recognizes words formed by doubling final consonants, dropping final *e*, or changing *y* to *i* before adding suffix					1
198. Recognizes words with final *le* preceded by consonant, as: tickle, whistle					1
199. Knows words of irregular spelling, as: caught, bought, enough					1
200. Knows suffixes *tion, ion, ation, ness, n, or, en, ful, less*					1
201. Demonstrates knowledge that single words have multiple meanings					1
202. Can find root word in compound words					1

Example 9   LEARNING DEVELOPMENTAL INVENTORY (LDI) *(continued)*

Level 8 *(continued)*

	Yes	No	Yes	No	
Date Mo/Yr					
203. Follows written directions					1

Total Yes Responses _____

Pupil progresses to next level only if _____ or more items are checked yes. If this number is reached, continue checking on the next level.

Comments:

Level 9

	Yes	No	Yes	No	
Date Mo/Yr					
204. Uses and reads books for pleasure and information					2
205. Creatively dramatizes stories or elements of a story accurately					2
206. Demonstrates enjoyment of many aspects of prose and poetry					2
207. Participates in choral reading activities					2
208. Creates original stories, compositions, and poems					1,2
209. Reads silently with comprehension					1,2
210. Demonstrates fluency and accuracy in reading					2
211. Independent reading yields facts and information					1,2
212. Applies knowledge of sequence of story; locates specific information to prove opinion					1,2
213. Reads according to punctuation as an aid to comprehension; knows use of quotation marks					1,2
214. Perceives relationships of time, place, and sequence					1,2
215. Analyzes and evaluates author's purpose and point of view					1,2
216. Demonstrates knowledge of various topics and subtopics in stories					1,2

Example 9   LEARNING DEVELOPMENTAL INVENTORY (LDI) *(continued)*

Level 9 *(continued)*

	Yes	No	Yes	No	
Date Mo/Yr					
217. Creates an outline of relevant ideas					1,2
218. Scans and skims a variety of materials for special information					1,2
219. Applies all phonetic skills in attacking unknown words; shows progress in structural analysis					1, 2
220. Attacks words independently while reading					1,2
221. Demonstrates understanding of items concerning words formed by doubling the consonant, dropping the final *e,* or changing *y* to *i, f* to *v,* before an ending or suffix					1, 2
222. Shows knowledge in use and understanding of synonyms, antonyms, homonyms, contractions					1,2
223. Displays vocabulary mastery of basic textual materials					1,2
224. Uses basic rules of syllabication and accent in vocabulary development					1,2
225. Applies research techniques in developing individual projects in a variety of ways					2
226. Uses title page, table of contents, glossary, and index as aids					2
227. Interprets main ideas of story					1,2
228. Makes judgments and draws conclusions					1,2
229. Infers a logical pattern of unstated events					1,2
230. Forms sensory images					2
231. Shows increase in sight vocabulary					1
232. Is capable of using context clues					2
233. Recognizes words formed by adding *s, es, n, en,* etc., with no change in root word					1
234. Displays total perception of vowels and their variants					1
235. Identifies root words in compound words					1
236. Knows alphabetical sequence in first, second, and third position					1

Example 9   LEARNING DEVELOPMENTAL INVENTORY (LDI) *(continued)*

Level 9 *(continued)*

	Yes	No	Yes	No	
Date Mo/Yr					
237. Knows three letter blends as *spr, str, scr, squ, thr, spl*					1
238. Recognizes silent consonants as in *wrong, ghost, lamb, knife, right*					1
239. Knows sound of *a* before *l* and *w*					1
240. Can identify How, Who, When, Where, and Why in stories					2
241. Knows common phonograms, long and short vowel types					1
242. Knows all vowel combinations and diphthongs					1
243. Recognizes that similar sounds have variant spellings such as *x* and *cks*					1
244. Discriminates between *ng* and *nk* sounds					1

Total Yes Responses _____

Pupil progresses to next level only if _____ or more items are checked yes. If this number is reached continue checking on next level.

School systems have, of course, developed mathematics programs in levels similar to those used for reading and language arts. For example, the Orange Local School District of Cleveland developed a mathematics program based on the Greater Cleveland Math Program (published by Science Research Associates, Chicago). Example 10 shows the Learning Developmental Profile as it was used for a student moving through the ten levels that cover the three years of the primary school. The references within the profile are to the Greater Cleveland Math materials and to the fully developed master-learning sequence that was created by the Orange Local School District. This is operationally defined and spelled out in much the same manner as in chapter 2.

Example 10   LEARNING DEVELOPMENTAL PROFILE

Primary Mathematics: Asides

Name_____   Teacher_____

Time	Date				Date		
Hour				Comparative values of sets			
Half hour							
Earlier and later				Addition of money			
Quarter hour				Subtraction of money			
Five minutes							
Minutes				Story problems			
Days of week				**Liquid Measure**			
Months				Cups			
Story problems				Pints			
Fractions				Quarts			
Halves				Half gallons			
Thirds				Gallons			
Fourths				Equivalent measures			
Fractions of a set				Story problems			
Story problems				**Linear Measure**			
Money				Inch			
Value of Penny				Nearest half inch			
Nickel				Nearest quarter inch			
Dime				Foot			
Quarter				Yard			
Half dollar				Conversion of units of measure			
Dollar				Story problems			

Orange Primary School/Rev. April '67

Example 10   LEARNING DEVELOPMENTAL PROFILE *(continued)*

Math Level "K"

Name _____   Teacher _____

Date Beginning _____   Date Moved to Next Level _____

Shapes:								
Circle								
Square								
Rectangle								
Triangle								
Vocabulary:								
Larger								
Smaller								
Greater								
Lesser								
Repeating Patterns								
Matching:								
Same object								
Different object								
Drawing objects								
Marks								
Numerals								
Ordinals								
Connecting Dots								
Joining Sets								
Counting in Sequence								
Recognizing Out of Sequence								
Calendar:								
Days of week								
Months								

Comments:

(Complete when level is completed, child transfers, or at end of school year.)

Example 10   LEARNING DEVELOPMENTAL PROFILE *(continued)*

Math Levels: Primary I

Name _____

Teacher _____

Date Beginning _____

Date Completed _____

Level 1					
Matching	17				
Numbers (1–5)	32				
Numbers (1–9)	58				
Numbers (1–10)	70				
Addition equations	80				
Story problems					
Unit Test	Date		Score		

Level 2					
Add, subtract (1–3)	87				
Add, subtract (1–4)	96				
Add, subtract (1–5)	106				
Place value	112				
Story problems					
Unit Test	Date		Score		

Level 3					
Add, subtract (1–6)	120				
Add, subtract (1–7)	127				
Place value (0–39)	130				
Add, subtract (1–8)	137				
Place value (0–49)	139				
Add, subtract (1–9)	156				
Place value: tens	166				
Add, subtract (1–19)	176				
Story problems					
Unit Test	Date		Score		

Level 4					
Add, subtract (11–12)	196				
Add, subtract (13–14)	203				
Add, subtract (15–16)	217				
Add, subtract (17–18)	226				
Two digits	246				
Story problems					
Unit Test	Date		Score		
PI Test	Date		Score		

Comments:
(Complete when PI is completed, child transfers, or at end of school year.)

Example 10   LEARNING DEVELOPMENTAL PROFILE *(continued)*

Math Levels: Primary II

Name _____   Teacher _____

Date Beginning _____   Date Moved to Next Level _____

Level 5					
Addition, subtraction (1–10)	36				
Addition, subtraction (1–19)	58				
Addition, subtraction (1–19)	94				
Add, subtract: 2-digit addends	119				
Story problems					
Unit Test	**Date**		**Score**		

Level 6					
Addition with carrying	143				
Subtraction with borrowing	147				
Borrowing, carrying	159				
3 digits: no borrowing or carrying	181				
3 digits: borrowing and carrying	188				
Borrowing, carrying	199				
Borrow, carry in two places	213				
Story problems					

Level 7					
Multiplication (0–5)	236				
Division, multiplication	247				
Story problems					
Unit Test	**Date**		**Score**		
PII Test	**Date**		**Score**		

Unit Test	**Date**	**Score**

Comments:

(Complete when PII is completed, child transfers, or at end of school year.)

Example 10   LEARNING DEVELOPMENTAL PROFILE *(continued)*

Math Levels: Primary III

Name _____   Teacher _____

Date Beginning _____   Date Completed _____

Level 8					
Addition and subtraction: review	27				
Add, subtract: two digits	57				
Add, subtract: carry, borrow to tens	74				
Add, subtract: three digits	90				
Add, subtract: carry, borrow to hundreds	107				
Story problems					
Unit Test	**Date**		**Score**		

Level 9					
Multiply (1–5)	121				
Multiply, divide (5X5)	126				
Multiply (0X5X9)	147				
Story problems					
Unit Test	**Date**		**Score**		

Level 10					
Multiply, divide (9X9)	155				
Add, subtr: borrow, carry in 2 places	170				
Multiply: carry to tens	192				
Division	198				
Add, subtract: four digits	222				
Add, subtract: seven digits	230				
Dictation test					
Multiply: three digits	240				
Division	249				
Story problems					
Unit Test	**Date**		**Score**		
PIII Test	**Date**		**Score**		

Comments:

(Complete when PIII is completed, child transfers, or at end of school year.)

Example 11 is another illustration of an item that relates to both a Diagnostic Inventory and the Learning Developmental Inventory. It is the kind of guide frequently designed by school systems, to use with both of the inventories listed above. The material in example 11, adapted from the Newark project, was developed by Kings Canyon Unified School District in the Fresno, California, area. It is an explanation of items in the Learning Developmental Inventory and their relation to sections of the Diagnostic Inventory. In our discussion of the Learning Developmental Profile we contended that it should be made handily and readily usable. The LDI and the DI guide make the relationship of the two items more clearly understood and lend a precision that is reflected in the more precise grouping that follows the assessment procedure.

Example 11   GUIDE TO THE DI AND LDI RELATIONSHIPS

(Diagnostic Sections—Developmental Items)

Introduction

The items on the Diagnostic Inventory (DI) levels 1 through 8 are for evaluating the specific ability of a child to perform those items found on the Learning Developmental Inventory (LDI). A quick survey of the 243 items on the LDI will indicate that frequently there are repetitions of particular items at various levels. Within the DI are items that relate to specified activities that underpin learning, and require maintenance. They are found in each of the levels of the inventory, although they are sometimes stated in different terms.

The DI is made up of 19 separate sections. Each of the sections represents a discrete set of activities.

An Analysis of Sections of the DI

The 19 sections of the DI relate to the particular items of the LDI in the following ways:

DI section I has to do with perceiving likenesses and differences. Each of the 7 items in section I indicate that a child can tell similarities in a group of items when one item is different from the rest. The ability to do this is a prerequisite skill in learning to read. Certain of these items are highly sophisticated, while others are basically gross. For instance, number 6 represents a gross-difference item by the use of the letter q in that line. However, in numbers 3 and 7 only one letter is changed in a whole word. This represents a finite ability to perceive with sophistication likeness and difference.

DI section II has to do with knowledge of upper and lowercase letters, letter recognition, and visual perception. The ability to see the relation between the upper and lowercase of the same letter is the skill being tested here.

DI section III is a visual perception as well as a cognitive perceptual activity. In this exercise, the child can not only pick out omissions, but also make cognitive decisions about various alternatives.

DI section IV covers perceiving of likenesses and differences through visual discrimination as well as using alternatives, and making certain kinds of discriminations such as selecting details in a given situation along with items having to do with motions, distances, and the like.

Example 11   GUIDE TO THE DI AND LDI RELATIONSHIPS *(continued)*

DI section V deals with the sight-sound-symbol relationship. Drawing a line to the correct picture indicates knowledge by the child that the word symbol does indeed represent an object, hence knowledge of the relationship between word and symbol.

DI section VI is a cognitive development exercise that shows whether a child can select the main idea of a story and respond to the story correctly in terms of that idea. This becomes a high-level intellectual comprehension skill.

DI section VII is a very simple beginning-sound exercise where a child draws a line to the beginning sound of a pictured item. This is a perceptual as well as an initial-consonant and initial-digraph sound-recognition activity that diagnoses ability to perceive these sounds.

DI section VIII relates to the ability to match pictures with ending sounds of selected letters, and the digraphs most frequently used in the ending position. The ability to do this is an immediate indication of readiness or performance in word-attack knowledge of final consonant sounds that in turn leads to final consonant substitutions.

DI section IX tests the ability of a child to understand rhyming. The teacher simply lets a child relate things that rhyme, after identifying all of the items on the page.

DI section X is a good example of sequence. There are six items, two of which are "screens." Item 1 is given. The ability to perform successfully on this section indicates knowledge of a sequence of events that is rational or reasonable. Sequence knowledge is an underpinning aspect of reading, necessary for success in reading growth. It appears very early in the LDI and continues through all levels. For instance, item 6, level 3, is a sequence item; item 17, level 5 is a sequence item. Growth in sequence continues through the whole program from pictured activities to basic-word activities.

DI section XI is a reading-comprehension activity. It allows children to use the context to make alternative decisions in terms of comprehension, and from that to make predictions as to what would be most correct.

DI section XII uses context to enhance reading comprehension by presenting present, past, and possible future situations. Choosing from among three titles the one that best fits, is the important point of this section. It is a rather long exercise, but it allows the pupil to demonstrate his power. In addition, activities at the end of this part of the inventory provide an opportunity for displaying knowledge of the alphabet and to show whether a child can alphabetize and comprehend a story by use of precise questions that call for a correct response from a group of responses.

DI section XIII is a phonetic item dealing with silent letters. It is a development of the concept of the final *e* sound which makes the vowel long, and the combination vowel sounds (the digraph), where only the first letter is sounded. The last item is an activity that deals with silent consonants and how various consonant sounds are used and understood.

DI section XIV is strictly a knowledge of vocabulary to indicate words that show action (verbs) as compared to words that indicate what things are (nouns).

DI section XV is a comprehension item that requires reading a story and selecting the best title, plus responding to items that concern comprehension.

DI section XVI is a continuation of section XV. It brings a pupil to a higher level of power, represented by the ability to make internal identification of particular items in a story, and the ability to selectively identify specified characters.

DI section XVII is a simple synonym exercise to indicate whether pupils have a knowledge of words that are similar in meaning.

Example 11   GUIDE TO THE DI AND LDI RELATIONSHIPS *(continued)*

DI section XVIII is an antonym exercise in which children indicate knowledge of words that are opposite in meaning.

DI section XIX is a basic exercise dealing with expression. In order to read with expression, one must understand punctuation. The ability to take an unpunctuated paragraph and apply correct punctuation is tested here.

Summary

By going back over each of the items in the LDI, a teacher can readily make associations of each item to the various sections of the DI. By noting the fact that the higher the level of the LDI, the more sophisticated the behavior (that is, sequence is low-level when pictures are used, and high-level with a jumbled story is put in order), a good diagnostic picture of a child can be obtained.

EXTENT-OF-APPLICATION
APPRAISAL FORM OF NONGRADED
THEORIES AND PRACTICES

IDENTIFIED CURRICULUM,
GROUPING, AND INSTRUCTIONAL
THEORIES IN NONGRADED
EDUCATION

FACTORS INFLUENCING SUCCESS
OF NONGRADED PROGRAM

SUMMARY: WHY OUR SCHOOLS
SHOULD BE NONGRADED

A MEMORANDUM FROM THE FIELD

SOME COMPARISONS OF SELECTED
DIMENSIONS RELATED TO
GRADEDNESS AND CONTINUOUS
PROGRESS

PLACES TO WRITE FOR
NONGRADED, CONTINUOUS-
PROGRESS PROGRAMS
AND PROCEDURES

ADDENDA

These items related to evaluation, self-inspection, and educational growth may prove helpful to anyone concerned with innovation in general. It is material against which progress and educational implementation can be measured. The items were devised by various people. For example, Juliet Beck developed an outstanding checklist for evaluating implementation of the curriculum theories of nongraded, continuous-progress education while she was involved in a research project at Bowling Green State University (1966–68). It was applied to several school districts purporting to be continuous-progress oriented, to indicate the extent to which they had moved along the continuum toward continuous-progress status.

EXTENT-OF-APPLICATION APPRAISAL FORM OF
NONGRADED THEORIES AND PRACTICES

Nongraded Theory or Practice Identified	Appraisal of Application or Use				
	Yes, to High Degree	Yes, to Minor Degree	Neg. Practice	Uncertain	No Mention
I. General Curriculum Considerations: The School System Gives Evidence of:					
A. A clear statement of objectives and philosophy					
B. Continuous curriculum study and planning					
II. Selection, Organization and Treatment of Learning Tasks: The School System Evidences and/or Makes Provision for:					
A. A longitudinal plan ensures continuity and sequence					
B. A differentiated treatment of curriculum areas					
C. The achievement of process goals					
D. An integration and balance of curriculum elements					
E. Specific curriculum objectives in behavioral terms					
III. Interpretation of Child Development and Learning Theories: The School System Recognizes and Makes Provision for:					
A. The total growth and development of children					
B. The uniqueness of each child					
C. Intra-individual differences among progress					

EXTENT-OF-APPLICATION APPRAISAL FORM OF
NONGRADED THEORIES AND PRACTICES *(continued)*

Nongraded Theory or Practice Identified	Appraisal of Application or Use				
	Yes, to High Degree	*Yes, to Minor Degree*	*Neg. Practice*	*Uncertain*	*No Mention*
D. Inter-individual differences among children					
E. The continuous, changing nature of growth and learning					
F. Continuity and progression within the learner					
G. The logical order of learning abilities					
H. The development of readiness for learning					
I. Integration and balance of learning					
J. Learning in meaningful context					
K. Application of learning					
L. The encouragement of the transfer of learning					
M. Proper motivation of learning through:					
1. Intrinsic motivation for truer learning					
2. Vivid initial experiences					
3. Continuity and positive reinforcement					
4. Success experiences					
5. Proper challenge and pressure					
6. Evaluation for guidance of learning					
7. Active involvement of the learner					
8. Experiences appropriate to learner's interest, learning, life style					

EXTENT-OF-APPLICATION APPRAISAL FORM OF
NONGRADED THEORIES AND PRACTICES *(continued)*

Nongraded Theory or Practice Identified	*Appraisal of Application or Use*				
	Yes, to High Degree	*Yes, to Minor Degree*	*Neg. Practice*	*Uncertain*	*No Mention*
IV. Grouping and Instructional Practices: The School System Practices and/or Provides the Following:					
A. Heterogeneous class groups with homogeneous subgroups					
B. Groupings determined by the nature of the learning tasks (grouping for specific goals disband when goal is met)					
C. Grouping on a variety of bases					
D. Flexibility in grouping procedures					
E. Grouping with a wide choice of alternatives:					
1. Use of team teaching					
2. Use of multi-age grouping					
F. Teachers operating in three-dimensional role					
G. Continual diagnosis and evaluation of learning					
H. Individualized instruction in terms of:					
1. Timing and pacing of learning					
2. Materials and resources used					
3. Instructional techniques used					
4. The kinds and sizes of groupings used					

EXTENT-OF-APPLICATION APPRAISAL FORM OF
NONGRADED THEORIES AND PRACTICES *(continued)*

Nongraded Theory or Practice Identified	Appraisal of Application or Use				
	Yes, to High Degree	Yes, to Minor Degree	Neg. Practice	Uncertain	No Mention
V. **The Reading Program:** The School System Evidences the Following Efforts, Provisions and Practices:					
1. Staff involvement in the curricular efforts					
2. Clearly defined learning and instructional objectives					
3. A clear understanding of the reading process					
4. A rethinking of reading and sub-skills—many sources					
5. A longitudinal view of the reading program					
6. An understanding of relationship of reading to other areas of curriculum					
7. Identification of relationship and phasing in of reading subskills					
B. Identification of skill sequences which have been placed on continuum					
C. Levels, if used, serve as guideposts in learning and insure:					
1. Individual progress, not progress by groups					
2. Curriculum differentiation					
3. Continuity and sequence of learning in reading					

EXTENT-OF-APPLICATION APPRAISAL FORM OF
NONGRADED THEORIES AND PRACTICES *(continued)*

	Appraisal of Application or Use				
Nongraded Theory of Practice Identified	*Yes, to High Degree*	*Yes, to Minor Degree*	*Neg. Practice*	*Uncertain*	*No Mention*
4. A plan based on rethinking of reading; not assigning of former materials to levels					
D. Reading instruction is increasingly individualized in terms of:					
1. Each child's timing and pacing of learning					
2. The instructional materials and resources used					
3. The instructional approaches and techniques used					
4. Kinds and sizes of groupings used					
E. Diagnosis, evaluation and reporting as integral elements of the reading program:					
1. Teaching is diagnostic					
2. Evaluation is continuous					
3. Reporting is comprehensive, specific, and individualized					
F. The maintenance of individual reading records					

IDENTIFIED CURRICULUM, GROUPING, AND INSTRUCTIONAL THEORIES IN NONGRADED EDUCATION

I. General Curriculum Considerations
    The school or school system evidences the following:
    A. Clear, written statement of curriculum philosophy and curriculum objectives, essential pre-requisites to curriculum study and planning.
    B. Provisions for continuous curriculum evaluation, study, revision, and planning involving persons representing various facets and levels of school program and organization.

II. Selection, Organization, and Treatment of Learning Tasks
    The curriculum design of the school or school system evidences and/or makes provisions for the following:
    A. Continuity and sequence in learning through a program that is arranged longitudinally through the identification of essential organizing elements.
    B. Differentiated treatment of curriculum areas determined by their nature: in broad content areas, key concepts are identified; in skill areas, sequences are identified and systematic mastery is encouraged.
    C. Achievement of process goals: development of skills of inquiry, evaluation, interpretation, application; the skills of "learning how to learn."
    D. Balance and integration of curriculum elements through identification or organizing centers and proper use of well-conceived curriculum guides and materials.
    E. Identification of specific learning and instructional objectives expressed in behavioral terms.

III. Interpretation of Child Development and Learning Theories
    The curriculum plan of the school or school system recognizes and makes provisions for the following:
    A. Total growth of children: social, emotional, and physical as well as intellectual and academic.
    B. Unique needs, interests, abilities, learning rates, styles, and patterns of each child.
    C. Intra-individual differences evident in progress of most children: child's varying progress in different areas of learning and in elements of a given area.
    D. Inter-individual differences present in a group of children; the ever-increasing varieties of needs, interests, and abilities existing between children.
    E. Continuous, changing nature of growth and learning of children: children are in constant state of becoming.
    F. Development of continuity and progression of learning within children; each child must internalize his learning; he must find order and meaning for himself.
    G. Logical order of learning: simple to complex; concrete to abstract.
    H. Encouragement and development of readiness for learning tasks.
    I. Integration and proper balance of learning; learning should not be atomized or haphazard.
    J. Presentation of learning in a meaningful context.
    K. Application and repetition of skills and concepts to ensure understanding and adequate mastery.
    L. Transfer of learning from one situation, or context, to another.

M. Proper motivation for learning; motivation that takes into account these crucial points:
   1. Intrinsic motivation ensures truer, longer-lasting learning.
   2. Nature and vividness of initial experiences are crucial to continued motivation.
   3. Motivation is sustained by continuity and reinforcements of learning experiences.
   4. Success is essential in sustaining motivation.
   5. Appropriate challenge and pressure are essential in sustaining motivation.
   6. Evaluation provides motivation and direction for further learning.
   7. Active involvement and effort on part of learner help sustain motivation.
   8. Experiences in keeping with interests and learning styles and patterns of learner help sustain motivation.

IV. Grouping and Instructional Policies and Practices
   School or school system implements nongraded philosophy through the following policies and practices:
   A. General grouping pattern for self-contained classrooms, multi-age groups, or team teaching units is heterogeneous for general class makeup with homogeneous subgrouping for a variety of purposes.
   B. Manner in which learners are grouped and regrouped for learning experiences is determined by nature of learning task: heterogeneous groupings for broad content areas where diversity enriches understanding; homogeneous groupings for specific and/or sequential tasks; homogeneous groups formed for attainment of specific educational goals and dissolved when goals have been achieved.
   C. Subgroups formed on basis of interest, friendships, and project tasks as well as on basis of academic progress.
   D. Grouping policies and practices are flexible so that changes can be made when needs of children or program warrant them.
   E. Grouping practices make available wide choice of alternatives in instructional programs and materials, styles of teaching, and peer groups, for each child. The following arrangements provide this wide choice of alternatives:
      1. Team teaching
      2. Multi-age grouping
   F. Teacher's role becomes increasingly that of a resource person and mobilizer of materials as he guides and advises students. Teacher evidences knowledge and expertise in following three dimensions:
      1. Relationship to learners
      2. Relationship to content of school program
      3. Pedagogy — art and science of instruction
   G. Careful, continuous diagnosis and evaluation of learning problems and progress seen as integral elements of the instructional program.
   H. Instruction is individualized in terms of variations in—
      1. Timing and pacing of learning
      2. Instructional materials and resources
      3. Instructional approaches and techniques
      4. Kinds and sizes of groupings

V. Reading Program of Nongraded Elementary School
   School or school system implements philosophy of nongrading in reading program through the following efforts, provisions, and practices:

A. Written curriculum materials that explain and guide reading program and give evidence of the following:
  1. Staff involvement in planning of reading program so that it is more uniformly understood and accepted by staff; program that more nearly fits unique needs of teachers, students, and community
  2. Clearly-defined set of learning and instructional objectives
  3. Clear understanding of total reading process
  4. Careful rethinking and complete understanding of reading process and subskills based on study of many sources
  5. Vertical, long-range view of reading program
  6. Clear understanding of relationship of reading to other areas of curriculum
  7. Clear identification of reading subskills with their relationships and phasing is clearly understood and indicated
B. Sequences in development of various subskills clearly identified and placed on continua; this promotes concept of continuous progress in learning, and means of plotting and evaluating pupil progress.
C. If levels have been identified, they are thought of as guideposts in child's continuous progress through the skills.
  Establishment of levels must insure:
  1. Progress on individual and not on group basis
  2. Differentiated treatment of curricular areas
  3. Continuity and sequence in learning
  4. Program based on rethinking of reading rather than assignment of former materials to levels
D. Instruction in reading increasingly individualized in terms of variations in—
  1. Each child's timing and pacing of learning
  2. Instructional materials and resources used with each child
  3. Instructional approaches and techniques used with each child
  4. Kinds and sizes of groupings for each child
E. Diagnosis, evaluation, and reporting are integral elements of reading program, and instruments that facilitate diagnosis, evaluation, and reporting have been carefully designed and are properly used. These aspects of the reading program are more specifically characterized as follows:
  1. Diagnosis is continuous, specific, and highly individualized.
  2. Evaluation is continuous, specific; involves use of commercially-prepared and teacher-made techniques and devices; and is carried on on group and individual basis.
  3. Reporting is regular, frequent, specific, comprehensive, highly individualized, and utilizes conferences and narrative reports. Checklists showing individual progress may accompany conferences and reports; comparative markings are not used.
F. Careful records are kept of each child's progress in acquiring reading skills so that continuous progress will be insured when child moves from one teacher to the next. Record indicates skills and understandings child possesses and is not merely a listing of reading materials that he has covered.

FACTORS INFLUENCING SUCCESS OF NONGRADED PROGRAM

The purpose of the following questionnaire is to assess characteristics that carry a continued importance to the stability of a nongraded program.
It is based on a document originally issued by John I. Goodlad and Robert H. Anderson.*

	Initially Important	Still Important	No Longer Important
Strong interest and desire on part of teachers			
Careful study by staff of other plans in existence; local research			
Effective use of PTA and other public-relations channels			
Staff concern about pupil retentions and related pupil adjustment problems			
Parent conferences; parent meetings			
Special interest and leadership shown by a teacher, principal, superintendent, or supervisor			
Continuous parent-education emphasis			
Successful efforts to explain and promote plan to parents			
Very careful step by step planning			
Help given by other school districts and college personnel			
Success of program in pilot school leading to more general adoption			
Friendly press and other publicity measures			
Cooperation and harmony among teachers			
Moving slowly			
Initiative shown by parents in promoting the idea			
Approval and support by the board of education			
Permanency of staff personnel			
Prospect of success for children and teachers			
Conservative admissions policy in first year; care in determining which children to admit to nongraded groups			
Help from central guidance and testing personnel			

List below any additional factors you feel have contributed to success of your program.

*John I. Goodlad and Robert H. Anderson, *The Nongraded Elementary School* (New York: Harcourt, Brace), pp. 170–71.

The following factors were found to be difficulties that had to be overcome by people establishing programs. The purpose of this section is to isolate factors that have continued importance related to the stability of nongraded program.

	Initially Important	Still Important	No Longer Important
Grade-level expectation habits of teachers			
Reluctance of traditionalists among teachers to try something different			
General problems of providing understanding to parents			
Problems of retaining or orienting new staff members to the plan			
Problems of designing appropriate report card or reporting procedure			
Grade-level expectation habits of parents			
Dealing with the parents whose children need more time in primary			
Continuous influx of new pupils and parents unfamiliar with plan			
Fears and doubts of teachers			
Students moving away who have been under the plan			
Problems of grouping and classifying children			
Insufficient materials for various achievement levels			
Leaders too impatient, not thoroughly informed			
Problem of being a pilot school among traditional schools			
Insufficient numbers of other schools in district using the plan			
Teachers violating operating rules			
Reticence or inability of staff to explain plan's basic values to parents			
Creating adequate nomenclature for new system			
Persuading board of education to approve plan			
State-mandated reports requiring grade designation			

List any additional factors that seem to present difficulties in relationship to the success of your nongraded program.

Summary: Why Our Schools Should Be Nongraded

(From an interpretation of surveys made on school systems using the nongraded plan, and by interpreting various articles written on this subject, the following compilation and summation of the main advantages of the nongraded elementary school were amassed.)

I. For Children—Nongraded continuous-progress education—

1. Reduces pressure because of less competition to meet predetermined standard
2. Stimulates cooperative attitude
3. Offers better chance of fitting slow-maturing child into group and being well accepted
4. Helps children to be more understanding and tolerant because more opportunities to help and be helped are provided
5. Stimulates younger children to want to do things older ones are doing
6. Diminishes bullying by older children
7. Stimulates superior child, since there is no grade average he can become self-satisfied with
8. Reduces tensions because idea of individual adequacy replaces personal rivalry
9. Provides unit span of years adaptable to lags and spurts that accompany growth
10. Provides progress levels that permit child to pick up after absence at point where he left off
11. Increases opportunities for leadership because of reduced grade-level stratification
12. Provides time range that permits some children of same chronological age to remain together while progressing at different academic rates suited to their particular capacities
13. Minimizes frustrations caused by failure
14. Contributes to sound mental health of slow learners
15. Does not hold up fast learners
16. Makes children more aware of progress
17. Provides for constant evaluation
18. Provides for continuous growth
19. Makes possible transfer at any time depending on child's needs
20. Provides for heterogeneous interest grouping and look-alike skill development grouping
21. Reduces pressure on child in regard to end-of-term goals
22. Increases teacher awareness of pupil individuality
23. Eliminates skipping and therefore reduces gaps in child's education
24. Creates opportunity for enrichment in depth for rapid and able learners

II. For Teachers—Nongraded continuous-progress education—

1. Contributes to teacher enthusiasm
2. Creates greater faculty-administration cooperation
3. Reduces pressure on teacher in regard to end-of-term goals
4. Evidences more teamwork on part of faculty members
5. Decreases teacher tensions
6. Allows fairer sharing of pupil load and better deployment
7. Reduces discipline problems
8. Diminishes boredom among students
9. Allows for better adaption to individual differences because of administrative framework for adjustment of curriculum and general overall flexibility
10. Lessens friction between teachers caused by encroachments on material reserved for next grade

III. For Parents—Nongraded continuous-progress education—

1. Better interprets philosophy of local school system
2. Explains how present graded philosophy does not square with the nongraded program. (Does philosophy of

education they want for children of their community fit graded educational pattern or call for nongraded one?)

3. Reveals what research reports concerning
   a) Retention
   b) Discipline
   c) Continuous progress
   d) Flexible placements based on—
      1. Reading growth and competence
      2. Intelligence potential
      3. Work habits
      4. Maturity factors—vis-a-vis stages of growth
      5. Social adjustment
      6. Chronological age
      7. Mental attitude
      8. Growth spurts and lags
6. Explains good reporting
7. Explains financial cost of education and burden of school costs due to nonpromotion, repetition, and dropouts

A Memorandum from the Field

To: Messers. Hillson and Bongo

From: Wanda Lister

Re: Observed changes in behavior and attitudes of pupils, teachers, and parents due to nongrading; needs for further implementations.

I. Pupils

1. The children now accept the responsibility of learning. They are growing more independent and less dependent on the teacher for their every move.
2. They are pleased that they can progress at their own rate without waiting until the whole group is ready.
3. The older remedial children are beginning to accept the challenge of wanting to learn how to read.
4. The children who never participated in a graded room, because of peer critics, are now offering their ideas.
5. They seem delighted to have more than one teacher. They are often heard comparing the traits and procedures of the various teachers.
6. The prescriptive teaching of reading skills has enabled many pupils to become more successful in reading.
7. The grouping at the readiness level has enabled 22 kindergarten pupils to be in formal reading instruction now, and all the others more advanced than ever before.
8. The multi-aging which naturally emerged by the placement of pupils according to their skill needs has enabled older slower students to be leaders in mechanical and manipulative areas to the younger brighter student.

II. Teachers

1. They have become more aware of the individual needs of pupils.
2. The Reading Levels Sequence has provided them with a specific framework for teaching reading.
3. The pressure of having to push pupils through a given text by a certain time has been removed.
4. The teachers now allow children to progress as rapidly as they can without the fear of using the next-grade teacher's texts.
5. The teachers are highly motivated and stimulated by participating in something new in education.
6. They are much more aware of reading skills and concepts, and now are teachers of skills rather than teachers of books.
7. They appreciate having another teacher able to evaluate, compare, and decide what is best for the child they are teaching.
8. The cooperation in sharing of materials and ideas has been tremendous among the teachers.

III. Parents

1. They are very pleased with the individualized attention being given their child.
2. They are delighted and impressed that the skills are being taught in their school.
3. They are pleased that their children like school and seem stimulated by the program.
4. They are volunteering to participate as classroom and clerical aids on a regular basis (fifty are now working at various times).
5. There are several parents who have taken the college course "The Nongraded School."

IV. Needs

1. Teachers—Classroom
   a) Classroom aides
   b) Listening posts; recorder; earphones
   c) Filmstrip viewers
   d) Paid time to develop tapes and materials
   e) Phonographs

2. Materials
   a) Printed skill packets (like IPI materials)
   b) Phonic skill tapes
   c) Skill filmstrips
   d) Plastic page protectors for reading kits
   e) Literature records and tapes
   f) Trade books for classroom use

SOME COMPARISONS OF SELECTED DIMENSIONS RELATED TO GRADEDNESS AND CONTINUOUS PROGRESS

Dimensions	Continuous-Progress Oriented	Grade-Level Oriented
Grouping and Deployment Procedures	Based on diagnosis; across ages; awareness of need and readiness. Workable groups used; size relates to need. Multiage groups naturally arise or are planned to insure diversity. Special needs groups; special skill intensity groups; ESL and FLES groups.	Subgrouping based on general ability or achievement to deal with reality. Intelligence quotients or reading achievement scores are used. Subject-matter groups usually within grades; planned for homogeneity based on standardized tests.
Pupil-Progress Procedures	Based on continuous teacher interaction, exchange and evaluation. Pupil-teacher evaluation in terms of interest and need. 3-year open block of time; no promotion or nonpromotion.	Based on year of chronology, usually in age groups. Teacher decision about progress, work, and evaluation. Annual or semiannual promotions used as stimulants. Nonpromotional practices govern rate of progress.
Curriculum Philosophy, Development, and Application	Content serves to teach skills. Interest areas with teacher guidance developed by contract. Emphasis on self-direction and independence. Small steps of growth reflected in sequences.	Hemmed in by philosophy and assignment of teachers or textbooks. Organized by subject-matter areas. Emphasis on covering content, on reading certain grade levels, acquisition of facts as evidence of learning.
Teacher-Role Orientations	Plan, teach, and evaluate cooperatively. Provide classroom climate to stimulate interest through differentiated resources and activities that fulfill needs based on diagnosis.	Divide up texts for coverage; follow curriculum guides; preplanned units. Assign work, hear recitation, test, evaluate learning and subgroup to meet needs. Provide additional resources for enrichment.

Places to Write for Materials for Nongraded, Continuous-Progress Programs and Procedures

It needs to be understood that many of these places report that they have continuous-progress, nongraded programs, or perceive themselves to be so oriented. The unevenness of the material will indicate that reality and rhetoric are often not the same. It is impossible to keep an up-to-date list, but a good collection of material can be gathered from many of these listings. A comment is added to certain places to indicate the nature of the material that is obtainable.

Unless otherwise indicated, it will be assumed that the programs are in public schools. Address correspondence to the superintendent of schools of the community. A fee may be charged.

Arizona
  Phoenix
  Tucson (Lulu Walker School)
California
  Basset (secondary school continuous-progress material)
  Barstow
  Berkeley (Columbus-University Lab School, reading-levels materials)
  Beverly Hills
  Corona
  Corte Madera (Granada)
  Emoryville
  Fowler
  Fremont (description of a secondary-school program)
  Fresno City Unified (an entire program booklet on their program)
  Garden Grove
  Hawaiian Gardens (Ferguson School)
  Kings Canyon
  Los Angeles (University Elementary School, UCLA)
  Millbrae

Oakland
Pleasanton
Poway (description of a secondary program)
Rowland Heights
Sacramento (descriptive booklet and collected research on their program)
San Jose
Southern Humboldt (Unified)
Terra Linda
Timber (Banyan Elementary School)
Torrance
Colorado
  Jefferson County Schools
  La Junta
  Meeker School District
Connecticut
  Avon (pamphlets and materials on their program)
  Bridgeport (Holy Rosary School)
  Bridgeport
  Norwalk
  South Glastonbury
  Suffield
  West Hartford (coordinated reporting and record-keeping system)
Florida
  Englewood
  Fort Lauderdale
  Gainesville
  Hillsborough County
  Melbourne (booklets describing nongraded secondary school phasing and cycling)
  Nova, Broward County (description of a secondary program)
  Palm Beach (bar-graph reporting forms)
  Tampa
Georgia
  Athens (Clark County schools)
  Atlanta
  Coffee County
  Savannah
Hawaii
  University of Hawaii Laboratory School

Illinois
  Barrington District No. 4
  Chicago (Tesla School)
  Chicago (Forestville Elementary)
  Cook County
  Evanston District No. 5 (secondary program materials)
  Glencoe
  Maywood
  Moline
  Park Forest
  Waukegan
Kentucky
  Fayette County
Kansas
  Wichita
Maryland
  Baltimore (Department of Catholic Education)
  Baltimore (City)
  Frederick (South Frederick Elementary School)
  Silver Springs
  Towson
Massachusetts
  Amherst (High School) (secondary school continuous-progress weighted marking procedures)
  Fayerweather Street School (Cambridge)
  Gloucester
  Lexington (Bridge School) (descriptive booklets on a school within a school)
  Lincoln
  Marblehead
  Newton (collection of many items related to their innovative programs)
Michigan
  Carson City (Crystal School)
  Chippewa Valley (description of a high school program)
  Dearborn
  Detroit
  Flint (description of the cycle plan)

Grand Rapids
Grosse Pointe
Highland Park (descriptive booklet on their grouping procedures)
Van Dyke (report forms and descriptions of a program used for many years)
Wayne
Minnesota
  International Falls
Missouri
  Cabool
  Labue Public School District
  St. Charles (complete description of their whole continuous-progress approach)
  St. Louis
  Tarkio
  University City
Montana
  Billings
  Broadview
Nevada
  Clark County
  Reno
New Mexico
  Los Alamos
New Jersey
  East Brunswick
  Glenridge
  Montclair
  Mountain Lakes, Board of Education (report on their continuous-progress program by Maurie Hillson)
  Newark (Camden Street School)
  South Brunswick
  South Orange (Montrose School)
  Teaneck
  Totowa
New York
  Amsterdam
  Bainbridge-Guilford (several booklets describing the plan and resulting research)
  Belmore
  Eastchester

East Irondequoit
East Williston
Elmira Heights (pamphlet on their program
and research)
Farmingdale
Glen Cove
Greele Central
Harborfields Central School District
Hastings-on-Hudson
Hewlett-Woodmere
Irvington
Ithaca
Marion
Maryvale
Middletown
Mineola (collection of items, including a
teacher evaluation)
Newfield
North Syracuse (directed parent-teacher con-
ference materials)
Plain Edge
Plain View–Old Beth Page
Port Washington
Rochester (Brighton District)
Rochester (Lewis H. Morgan School)
Rye (cumulative folder and record system)
Scottsville (Chili-Wheatland School) (many
items on a carefully developed secondary
program)
Setauket (a junior high school approach to
continuous progress)
Stony Point (Tomkins Cove School)
Suffolk County
Valhalla
Vestal
Wantagh
Williamsville-Maple (Maple School) (on loan:
A set of related materials on their non-
graded approach)
West Irondequoit, Rochester
Whitesboro
White Plains (Ridgeway Elementary School)
Yorktown Heights

Ohio
Cayton
Chagrin Falls
Cleveland
Leetonia
Orange Local School District, Cleveland
(many items on their program)
Salem
Shaker Heights
Tipp City (public-relations items related to
their program)
Western Springs
Youngstown
Oklahoma
Oklahoma City
Tulsa
Oregon
Alameda School, Ontario (brochures, photo-
graphs, and materials on their open plan
school and nongraded approach)
Hillsboro
Pennsylvania
Aliquippa
Lower Merion
Pittsburgh (Falk Lab School, University of
Pittsburgh) (descriptive materials)
Pittsburgh
Pittsburgh (Parochial schools)
Pittsburgh (Oakleaf Elementary)
Shamokin (reading levels booklet)
Rhode Island
Cranston
Middletown (booklet and report procedure at
the secondary level)
South Dakota
Douglas Air Force
Tennessee
Oak Ridge (a set of materials on a secondary
program)
Texas
Spring Branch
Utah
Provo

Randolph
Vermont
  Burlington
  Manchester
  Springfield
  Woodstock
Virginia
  Arlington County
  Charlottesville
  Hampton Institute Laboratory School,
    Hampton
  Richmond
Washington, D.C.
  The Model School Division School
Washington
  Aberdeen
  Bellevue
  Cedar Falls Community Schools
  Edmonds
  Seattle
West Virginia
  Charleston
  Huntington
Wisconsin
  Appleton (reporting procedures and explanations of their program)

Fond Du Lac
Green Bay
Milwaukee

A growing number of activities related to school reorganization, curriculum development, and innovation in general are taking place in Canada. The following is a very short list of places to write for materials concerning programs:

British Columbia Teacher's Federation 105—2235 Burrard St., Vancouver, 9, B.C.
Calgary, Alberta
Cartier Public School, London, Ontario
Hamilton, Ontario
Lakeshore Regional School Board, Montreal, Quebec
McKenzie Elementary School, Greater Victoria, British Columbia
North York, Mallow Road School, Don Mills, Ontario
Our Lady of Peace School, Fabreville, Quebec
Perth School, Toronto, Ontario
Scarborough, Ontario
St. Catherine's Separate Schools, Lincoln County, Ontario

BIBLIOGRAPHIC MATERIAL

The bibliographic material is in two sections. Section I is a partially annotated list of books that is divided as follows:

A. Trends in the elementary schools
B. The elementary nongraded movement
C. Secondary nongraded school programs
   1. Middle School Movement
   2. Other programs aimed at nongrading techniques
D. Team teaching
E. The Dual-Progress Plan
F. General basic references in education
G. Selected bibliographies for program development

Section II is a comprehensive list of articles (research-oriented and descriptive), pamphlets, and dissertations related to nongraded and other innovative programs in both elementary and secondary education.

Section I Annotated References

A. These are general references that give insight into movements and trends in elementary schools.

Anderson, Robert H. *Teaching in a World of Change.* New York: Harcourt, Brace & World, 1966.

Anderson, Vernon. *Curriculum Gudielines in an Era of Change.* New York: Ronald Press, 1969.

Bennis, W.G.; Benne, K.D.; and Chin, R., eds. *The Planning of Change.* 2d ed. New York: Holt, Rinehart & Winston, 1969.

Davis, Frederick B. *Modern Educational Developments: Another Look.* New York: Educational Records Bureau, 1966.

De Grazia, Alfred, John, and David, eds. Revolution in Teaching. New York: Bantam, Matrix edition, 1964.

Educational Testing Service. *New Approaches to Individualizing Instruction,* (report of a conference). Princeton, N.J.: ETS, 1965.

Franklin, Marian Pope. *School Organization: Theory and Practice.* Chicago: Rand-McNally, 1967.

Fraser, Dorothy M. *Deciding What to Teach.* Washington, D.C.: National Educational Association, 1963.

Frazier, Alexander, ed. *The New Elementary School.* Washington, D.C.: Association for Supervision and Curriculum Development, NEA, 1968.

Frazier, Alexander, ed. *A Curriculum for Children.* Washington, D.C.: Association for Supervision and Curriculum Development, NEA, 1969.

Goodlad, John I. *Curriculum and the Individual.*
Waltham, Mass.: Blaisdell, 1966.

Gross, Ronald, and Murphy, Judith, eds. *Revolution
in the Schools.* New York: Harcourt, Brace & World,
1964.

Guggenheim, Fred and Corrine L., eds. *New Frontiers
in Education.* New York: Grune & Stratton, 1966.

Hart, Leslie A. *The Classroom Disaster.* New York:
Teachers College Press, Columbia University, 1969.

Hays, David G., ed. *Britannica Review of American
Education.* Chicago: Encyclopaedia Britannica,
vol. 1, 1969.

Hillson, Maurie. *Change and Innovation in Elementary
School Organization.* New York: Holt, Rienhart &
Winston, 1965.

Hillson, Maurie. *Elementary Education: Current Issues
and Research in Education.* New York: The Free
Press, 1967.

Holt, John C. *How Children Fail.* New York: Pitman,
1964.

Holt, John C. *How Children Learn.* New York:
Pitman, 1967.

Leonard, George B. *Education and Ecstasy.* New York:
Dell, 1969.

Meierhenry, W. C. *Educational Media: Theory into
Practice.* Columbus, Ohio: Charles E. Merrill, 1969.

Michaelis, John; Grossman, Ruth; and Scott, Lloyd.
New Designs for the Elementary School Curriculum.
New York: McGraw-Hill, 1967.

Miles, Matthew B., ed. *Innovation in Education.* New
York: Bureau of Publications, Teachers College,
Columbia University, 1964.

Miller, Richard I. *Education in a Changing Society.*
Washington, D.C.: National Education Association,
1963.

Miller, Richard I. *Perspectives on Educational Change.*
New York: Appleton-Century Crofts, 1967.

Morgenstern, Anne, ed. *Grouping in the Elementary
School.* New York: Pitman, 1966.

Morse, Arthur D. *Schools of Tomorrow–Today.* New
York: Doubleday 1960. A report on educational
experiments prepared for the New York State
Education Department.

National Education Association. *Elementary School
Organization: Purposes, Patterns, Perspective.* The
National Elementary School Principals' Yearbook
41 (December 1961.)

National Society for the Study of Education.
"Individualizing Instruction." *In the Sixty-first
Yearbook of the Society,* Part I. Nelson, B. Henry
(ed.), Chicago: University of Chicago Press, 1962.

National Society for the Study of Education. "The
Changing American School," The Sixty-fifth Year-
book, Part II, John I. Goodlad (ed.), Chicago, Ill.:
University of Chicago Press, 1966.

Nesbitt, Marion. *A Public School for Tomorrow.* New
York: Dell, 1967.

Rogers, Carl R. *Freedom To Learn.* Columbus, Ohio:
Charles E. Merrill, 1969.

Rosenthal, Robert, and Jacobson, Lenore. *Pygmalion
in the Classroom.* New York: Holt, Rinehart &
Winston, 1968.

This is a study of teacher expectation and pupil
intellectual development that shows how one person's expectations for another's behavior can quite
unwittingly become a more accurate prediction of
development, simply for its having been made. If a
teacher expects a child to fail . . . he often does, but
if he is expected to do well he often succeeds.

*Schools for the Sixties: A Report of the National
Education Association Project on Instruction.* New
York: McGraw-Hill, 1963.

Snitzer, Herb. *Living at Summerhill: A Photographic
Documentary on A. S. Neill's Pioneering School.*
New York: Collier, 1968.

Thelen, Herbert A. *Classroom Grouping for Teach-
ability.* New York: Wiley and Sons, 1967.

*Washburne, Carleton Holsey, and Marland, Sidney P.
Jr. Winnetka: The History and Significance of an
Educational Experiment.* Englewood Cliffs, N.J.:
Prentice-Hall 1963.

Yates, A. *Grouping and Education.* New York: Wiley
and Sons, 1966.

B. The elementary nongraded school movement is of
course a strong one. The following basic books
present information which, if assimilated, could
readily be used as a base for change

Beggs, David W. III, and Buffie, Edward G. *Nongraded
Schools in Action: Bold New Venture.* Bloomington,
Indiana: Indiana University Press, 1967.

This book consists of articles by people well known
in the field of nongraded education. Part I is a discussion of the historical, philosophical, sociological,
and strategic approach to nongraded education.
Part II presents nongraded schools in action and the
"how-tos" of programs that include both the elementary and secondary movements in America. The
articles are precise and will help the reader understand the intensity of the movements. The material
is written by practitioners who tend to be specific.

Brown, B. Frank. *The Appropriate Placement School:
A Sophisticated Nongraded Curriculum.* West Nyack,
N.Y.: Parker, 1965.

This book emphasizes a program of mixed-aged

departmentalized classes, organized according to achievement levels, similar to the program of departmentalization suggested in this author's book on the nongraded high school. Discussion of the primary area is quite weak and offers few guidelines. The concept of appropriate placement as propounded by the author is worthwhile but in general is not too strong.

Dufay, Frank R. *Ungrading the Elementary School.* West Nyack, N.Y.: Parker, 1966.

This is the story of the establishment of a reading-levels program and the inherent instructional procedures. The process of moving from a traditional school to a nongraded school is also elaborated.

Glogau, Lillian, and Fessel, Murray. *The Nongraded Primary School: A Case Study.* West Nyack, N.Y.: Parker, 1967.

This is a case study of how a nongraded primary program was established under the direction of the coauthors who were principal and vice-principal of the school. This book is a worthwhile prerequisite to an understanding of some of the dimensions of nongrading and the attendant pitfalls.

Graves, William H. *Nongraded Schools: Elementary Principals' Guide.* College Station, Texas: Texas A & M Press, 1967.

A practical set of ideas that will help in avoiding some pitfalls in implementing a nongraded program.

Hillson, Maurie. *The Hillson Letters.* Chicago: Science Research Associates, 1966–67. Topics: various; all on the nongraded school. Also available in booklet form from SRA Ltd., Canada.

Howard, Eugene R.; Bardwell, Roger W.; and Gross, Calvin W. *How to Organize a Nongraded School.* Englewood Cliffs, N.J.: Prentice-Hall, 1966.

This small pamphlet is from the Successful School Management Series. The discussion is rather sparse but nonetheless precise in the areas that are helpful. There is also a fairly good set of addresses for procuring materials that would be helpful in setting up a program.

Miller, Richard I. *The Nongraded School: Analysis and Study.* New York: Harper & Row, 1967.

A helpful little book that brings together the major arguments concerning the nongraded school. Though there is an analysis, there is not very much in terms of implementation. However, it does give the reader some insights into the weaknesses and strengths of nongrading. Reading the book will help provide evidence to build a case for one's own school district.

Rollins, Sidney P. *Developing Nongraded Schools.* Itasca, Ill.: F. E. Peacock, 1968.

Some interesting points of view are presented but the concepts and the development of programs lack the dynamics of the area devoted to teacher preparation.

Tewksbury, John L. *Nongrading in the Elementary School.* Columbus, Ohio: Charles E. Merrill, 1967.

This little paperback is extremely worthwhile because of the down-to-earth discussion of the dimensions of various plans of nongrading. It is an attempt to describe in a simplified manner what nongrading is and how it works in the elementary school. The author deals with many practical questions and discusses many points that would be helpful in understanding the programs. For anyone working toward nongrading, the book will be an aid in answering some of the questions that constantly plague the innovator.

C. The secondary nongraded school movement is a growing one and there are various approaches to it.

 1. The "Middle School" movement in American education is part of one such activity that bridges the gap between the primary and secondary levels.

Alexander, William M.; Williams, Emmett L.; Compton, Mary; Hines, Vynce A.; Prescott, Dan; and Kealy, Roland. *The Emergent Middle School.* 2d enlarged ed. New York: Holt, Rinehart & Winston, 1969.

This is a most comprehensive survey of the status of the "middle school" movement. It is a compilation of insights rather than a specific point of view. Other texts listed here assume various points of view and are more detailed.

Grooms, Ann. *Perspectives on the Middle School.* Columbus, Ohio: Charles E. Merrill, 1967.

Kindred, Leslie W., ed. *The Intermediate School.* Englewood Cliffs, N.J.: Prentice-Hall, 1968.

Moss, Theodore C. *Middle School.* Boston, Mass.: Houghton Mifflin, 1969.

Popper, Samuel H. *The American Middle School: An Organizational Analysis.* Waltham, Mass.: Blaisdell, 1967.

 2. The high school is on the move and hopefully will fulfill trends that were started at earlier levels.

Brown, B. Frank. *The Nongraded High School.* Englewood Cliffs, N.J.: Prentice-Hall, 1963.

This is the original and most often referred to statement of secondary school nongraded education. There are other approaches (see Rollins above), but the ideas and philosophy come across clearly in this book.

Bush, Robert N., and Allen, Dwight W. *A New Design for High School Education.* New York: McGraw-Hill, 1964.

Bush, Robert N., and Allen, Dwight W. *A New Design for High School Education—Assuming a Flexible Schedule.* New York: McGraw-Hill, 1966.

Hamilton, Norman K., and Saylor, J. Galen. *Humanizing the Secondary School.* Prepared by the ASCD Council on Secondary Education. Washington, D.C.: Association for Supervision and Curriculum Development, NEA, 1969.

D. Team Teaching: There are few basic books in this area.

Bair, Medill, and Woodward, Richard G. *Team Teaching in Action.* Boston, Mass.: Houghton Mifflin, 1964.

This book concerns the experience of the Lexington Project and is pertinent to an understanding and knowledge of team teaching.

Beggs, David W. III, ed. *Team Teaching: Bold New Venture.* Indianapolis, Indiana: Unified College Press, 1964.

This set of articles indicates some of the demensions of team teaching. It is required reading for all who are considering some form of collaboration.

Davis, Harold S. *How to Organize an Effective Team Teaching Program.* Englewood Cliffs, N.J.: Prentice-Hall, 1966.

A practical "how-to" book that offers a solid point of view concerning teaming and ways to do it with success.

Hillson, Maurie, and Scribner, Harvey B., eds. *Reading in Collaborative and Team Approaches to Teaching and Learning, A SURED Project.* New York: Selected Academic Readings, 1965. (Available from Selected Academic Readings, Inc., 830 Broadway, New York.)

This set of articles is intended to give a broad insight into collaboration and organizing for teaming in both teaching and learning.

Shaplin, Judson T., and Olds, Henry F. Jr., eds. *Team Teaching.* New York: Harper & Row, 1964.

A set of articles by individuals who have had a close relationship with collaborative education.

E. The Dual-Progress Plan has received a good deal of attention. Two books on the subject are currently available.

Stoddard, George D. *The Dual Progress Plan: A New Philosophy and Program in Elementary Education.* New York: Harper & Row, 1961.

Heathers, Glen. *Organizing Schools for the Dual Progress Plan.* Danville, Ill.: Interstate Printers & Publishers, 1967.

Stoddard discusses the plan; Heathers tells how it has worked.

F. Certain general publications are of important value to everyone in education.

Encyclopedia of Educational Research. 4th ed. Edited by Robert L. Ebel. New York: Macmillan, 1969.

Several articles deal with nongrading, teaming, individualization and innovation. This is a recommended source for an educator's library. (See especially articles by Anderson, Heathers, Sowards, and Myers.)

Gage, N.L. *Handbook of Research on Teaching.* A Project of the American Educational Research Association, Chicago: Rand-McNally, 1963.

Gagne, Robert M., ed. *Learning and Individual Differences.* Columbus, Ohio: Charles E. Merrill, 1967.

Howes, Virgil M., et al. *Individualization of Instruction, A Search.* Los Angeles, Educational Inquiry, 1967.

G. The bibliographies listed here are resources that will aid in program development. *Starred* items are especially good because they are detailed and comprehensive.

Anderson, Robert H. *Team Teaching Bibliography.* CAPCI Bibliography No. 4, ASCD or NEA Research Division, 1201 Sixteenth Street, N.W., Washington, D.C. 20036.

Anderson, Robert H. *Bibliography (Selected Readings on Modern Education).* Chicago, Ill.: Science Research Associates, 1967.

*Anderson, Robert H. *Bibliography on Organizational Trends in the Schools.* Washington, D.C.: Center for the Study of Instruction, NEA, 1968.

Bernstein, Edna D. *Team Teaching: Selected References.* Curriculum Library Release Number 98, Board of Education of the City of New York, Bureau of Curriculum Research, 1966.

Davis, Harold S. ed. *Team Teaching Bibliography.* Staff Utilization Project, Cleveland, Ohio: Educational Research Council of Greater Cleveland.

Hillson, Maurie. *A Selected Bibliography on Organizational Innovation and Change Emphasizing the Nongraded Movement in American Education.* Curriculum Library Release Number 95, Board of Education of the City of New York, Bureau of Curriculum Development, 1966.

Hillson, Maurie. *Continuous Progress Education: A Selected Bibliography on the Nongraded School and Other Reorganizational Innovations.* Fresno, Calif: EDICT, Fresno County Regional Planning and Evaluation Center, 1967.

Jablonsky, Adelaide. *A Selected ERIC Bibliography on Individualizing Instruction* (ED027358), ERIC Document Reproduction Service (EDRS), The National Cash Register Company, 4936 Fairmont Avenue, Bethesda, Maryland 20014.

Herbert, John. *Team Teaching Bibliography.* Available from Teachers College, Columbia University, New York.

Hochstattler, Phyllis. *Team Teaching Bibliography.* Prepared for the Division of Education Development, Oregon State Dept. of Education, Salem, Oregon, 1964.

*McLoughlin, William P. *The Nongraded School: An Annotated Bibliography.* Albany, New York: The University of the State of New York, The State Education Department, Office of Research and Evaluation, 1967.

Oestreich, Arthur. Bibliography on *Nongraded Schools and Team Teaching.* Available from Arthur Oestreich, Director, Division of University Schools, Indiana University, Bloomington, Indiana.

Oregon State Department of Education, Division of Education Department. Selected Bibliography Related to *New Patterns of Staff Utilization.* Prepared by William Georiads and others, July 1965.

*Shinn, J., and Byron M. *A Bibliography (with selected annotations) On Nongraded Elementary Schools.* Urbana, Illinois, Bureau of Educational Research, College of Education, University of Illinois, 1967.

Note: All annotations are by the authors.

Section II Bibliography of Articles and Studies

Aaron, I.E. "Patterns of Classroom Organization." *Education* 80 (May 1960): 530–32.

"ACT Viewpoints." *Today's Education* 58 (March 1969): 60–61.

Ackerland, G. "Some Teacher Views on the Self-Contained Classroom." *Phi Delta Kappan* 40 (April 1959): 283–85.

Adams, M.A. "Continuous Growth: Report of Baltimore's Program." *Baltimore Bulletin of Education* 25 (April 1948): 258–64.

Airola, J.A. "Rummel Creek Goes Nongraded." *Texas Outlook* 48 (January 1964): 24–25.

"Albany Plan of Primary School Organization." *Elementary School Journal* 36 (February 1936): 413–16.

Alexander, M.K. "What Is the Junior Primary?" *School Director* 21 (December 1948): 6–7, 21.

Alexander, W. "What Educational Plan for the In-Between-Ager." *NEA Journal* 55 (March 1966): 30–32.

Alexander, W., and Williams, E.L. "Schools for the Middle School Years." *Educational Leadership* 23 (December 1965): 217–23.

Alexander, W.M. "A Survey of Organizational Patterns of Reorganized Middle Schools. Final Report." U.S. Office of Education Project, No. 7-D-026, University of Florida, Gainesville, 1968.

Alexander, W.M. "The New School in the Middle." *Phi Delta Kappan* 50 (February 1969): 355–57.

American Association of School Administrators. *A Climate for Individuality.* Statement of the Joint Project on the Individual and the School, Washington: A.A.S.A., 1965, p. 56.

Amidon, E.J.; Kiss, K.M.; and Palisi, A.J. "Group Supervision: A Technique for Improving Teaching Behavior." *National Elementary Principal* 45 (April 1966): 54–58.

Amidon, E., and Simon, A. "Teacher-Pupil Interaction." *Review of Educational Research* 35 (April 1965): 130–39.

Anastasiow, N.J., and Fischler, A.B. "A Proposal for Teaming Principals." *National Elementary Principal* 44 (November 1964): 59–64.

Anastasiow, N.J. "Comparison of Two Approaches in Ungrading Reading Instruction." *Elementary English* 45 (April 1968): 495–99.

Anastasiow, N.J., and Fischler, A.S. "Teaming of Principals Project After Three Years." *National Elementary Principal* 48 (February 1969): 17–23.

Anderson, D.D. "Personality Attributes of Teachers in Organizational Climates." *Journal of Educational Research* 62 (July-August 1969): 441–43.

Anderson, R.C. "The Case for Nongraded Homogeneous Grouping." *Elementary School Journal* 62 (January 1962): 193–97.

Anderson, R.H. "Ungraded Primary Classes: An Administrative Contribution to Mental Health." *Understanding the Child* 24 (June 1955): 66–72.

Anderson, R.H. "Ungraded Primary Classes." *Education Digest* 21 (November 1955): 47–50.

Anderson, R.H. "Ungraded Primary School as a

Contribution to Improved School Practices." In *Frontiers of Elementary Education II,* Syracuse: School of Education, Syracuse University, 1955: 28–29.

Anderson, R.H. "The Junior High School." *Architectural Record* 129 (January 1961): 126–31.

Anderson, R.H. "Team Teaching." *NEA Journal* 50 (March 1961): 52–54.

Anderson, R.H. "Three Examples of Team Teaching in Action." *Nation's Schools* 65 (May 1960): 62–65.

Anderson, R.H. "Organizational Character of Education: Staff Utilization and Deployment: Nongrading." *Review of Educational Research* 34 (October 1964): 460–61.

Anderson, R.H.; Hagstrom, E.A.; and Robinson, W.M. "Team Teaching in an Elementary School." *School Review* 68 (1960): 71–84.

Anderson, R.H., and Goodlad, J.I. "Self-appraisal in Nongraded Schools: A Survey of Findings and Perceptions." *Elementary School Journal* 62 (February 1962): 261–69.

Anderson, R.H., and Mitchell, D.P. "School Plant Design." *Nation's Schools* 63 (June 1960): 75–82.

Anderson, R.H. "Flexibility of School Administration and the Individualization of Instruction." In *The Computer in American Education,* edited by Donald D. Bushnell. New York: John Wiley and Sons, 1967.

Anderson, R.H. "Schools for Young Children: Organizational and Administrative Considerations." *Phi Delta Kappan* 50 (March 1969): 381–85.

Angrave, J. "Team Teaching and Nongrading: A Case for Individual Timetabling in Canadian Schools." *Canadian Education and Research Digest* 5 (March 1965): 48–59.

Apex: A Nongraded Phase-Elective English Curriculum. Trenton, Mich. Schools, 3rd ed., 1968.

Aretz, C.W. "Administration of a Program of Continuous Pupil Progress." *Elementary School Journal* 40 (May 1940): 679–87.

Armstrong, C.M., and Kowitz, G.R. "The Effect of Promotion Policy on Academic Achievement." *Elementary School Journal* 61 (1960–61).

Asbell, Bernard. "Cape Kennedy's High School for Sky-High Learning." *PTA Magazine* 58 (January 1964): 14–16.

Asbell, B. "The Primary School: Stop! Look! Evaluate!" Bulletin No. 61, Washington, D.C.: The Association, 1952.

Association for Supervision and Curriculum Development. *A Look at Continuity in the School Programs: 1958 Yearbook,* pp. 199–214. Washington, D.C.: The Association, 1958.

Atkins, T.A. "It's Time for a Change — Or Is It?" *National Elementary Principal* 48 (February 1969): 46–48.

Austin, K.C. "The Ungraded Primary School." *Childhood Education* 33 (February 1957): 260–63.

Austin, K.C. "The Ungraded Primary Unit in Public Elementary Schools of the United States." *Dissertation Abstracts* 19 (July 1958): 73. An Abstract of an unpublished doctoral dissertation, University of Colorado, 1957.

Ayers, J.B., and Powell, L.D. "What Can Young Children Learn — And When?" *Nation's Schools* 83 (May 1969): 82–83.

Bahner, J.M. "Grouping Within a School." *Childhood Education* 36 (April 1960): 354–56.

Bailey, B.H., and Dunkle, W. "The Kanawha Leadership Project." *West Virginia School Journal* 91 (January 1963): 13.

Bardwell, R. "Lock-Step Has No Place in Education." *Wisconsin Journal of Education* 92 (May 1960): 12–15.

Barnes, F.P. "Symptoms of Wheelphilia." *National Elementary Principal* 47 (November 1967): 31–39.

Barnickle, D.W., and Dagne, F.A. "Two Schools That are Nongraded." *Instructor* 77 (March 1969): 63–70.

Beaubier, E.W., and Hair, D. "Experiences with Differentiated Staffing." *Today's Education* 58 (March 1969): 56–58.

Beck, I.L., and Bolvin, J.O. "A Symposium, Language Arts in the Nongraded School: Part III, A Model for Nongradedness — The Reading Program for Individually Prescribed Instruction." *Elementary English* 46 (February 1969): 130–35.

Bell, D. "Continuous Progress." *Dimensions in Education* 2 (June 1968): 4–5.

Bergstrom, L.H. Section from an article on school reorganization in Saskatchewan. *Canadian Education and Research Digest,* September 1965.

Berman, L.M. "New School Organization, Same Old Curriculum." *National Elementary Principal* 47 (November 1967): 16–21.

Besvinick, S. "Secondary Education. The Effectiveness of a Nongraded School." *School and Society,* March 16, 1968, 181–84.

Bienenstok, T. "Resistance to an Educational Innovation." *Elementary School Journal* 65 (May 1965): 420–28.

Blackstock, C.R. "A Field Study to Initiate an Ungraded Primary School in Brazosport." *Dissertation Abstracts* 22 (January 1962): 2258. Unpublished doctoral dissertation, University of Houston, 1961.

Blain, M. "One Superintendent's Answer to a City's

Education Problems." *Phi Delta Kappan* 50 (January 1969): 274–79.

Bolt, R.H. "An Overview of Potentials of Computer-Assisted Instruction." Cambridge, Massachusetts: Bolt, Beranek and Newman. Paper presented at the First International Conference and Exhibit on the Impact of Educational Technology, American Management Association, July 15, 1965.

Boston, R.E., and Wendt, M.S. "Nongrading an Entire System." *Michigan Education Journal* 43 (January 1966): 21–22.

Bough, M. "Theoretical and Practical Aspects of the Middle School." *NASSP Bulletin* 53 (March 1969): 8–13.

Boyer, S. "Private Model for Public Schools." Part of the Monthly *Saturday Review* Supplement, "Education in America," sponsored by the Charles F. Kettering Foundation. *Saturday Review*, February 15, 1969, 99.

Brandt, R. "Middle School in a Nongraded System." *Journal of Secondary Education* 43 (April 1968): 165–70.

Brearly, H.C. "Are Grades Becoming Extinct?" *Peabody Journal of Education* 31 (March 1954): 258–59.

Brickall, H. M. *Organizing New York State for Educational Change.* Albany: New York State Education Department, December, 1961.

Briggs, L.J. *Sequencing of Instruction in Relation to Hierarchies of Competence.* American Institutes for Research, Pittsburgh, Pa., 1968.

Briggs, L.J., et al. *Instructional Media: A Procedure for the Design of Multi-media Instruction, A Critical Review of Research, and Suggestions for Future Research.* American Institutes for Research, Pittsburgh, Pa., 1967.

Brimm, R.P. "Middle School or Junior High? Background and Rationale." *NASSP Bulletin* 53 (March 1969): 1–7.

Brinkman, A. R. "The Tarrytowns Try Balanced Grouping." *Elementary School Journal* 59 (March 1959): 320–23.

Brinkman, A.R. "Now It's the Ungraded School." *PTA Magazine* 55 (June 1961): 24–26.

British Columbia Teacher's Federation. "Continuous Progress: A Collection of Articles and a Selective Bibliography on the Themes of Nongraded School Organization and Continuous Pupil Learning," December 1966.

British Columbia Teachers' Federation. "Continuous Progress: A Report on an Invitational Conference Sponsored by the British Columbia Teachers' Federa-

tion," February 1967.

British Columbia Teachers' Federation. "A Report of Some Continuous Progress Plans in British Columbia," March 1968.

British Columbia Teachers' Federation. *Involvement: The Key to Better Schools.* The Report of the Commission on Education of the British Columbia Teachers' Federation, September 1968.

Broadhead, F.C. "Pupil Adjustment in the Semi-Departmental Elementary School." *Elementary School Journal* 60 (April 1960): 385–90.

Brod, P. "The Middle School in Practice." *Clearing House* 43 (May 1969): 530–32.

Brooks, F.E. "A Faculty Meets the Needs of Pupils." *Educational Leadership* 11 (December 1953): 174–78.

Brown, B.F. "Ungraded Secondary School." *Bulletin of the National Association of Secondary-School Principals* 45 (April 1961): 349–352. Paper presented at the 45th Annual Convention of the National Association of Secondary-School Principals, Cobo Hall, Detroit, Michigan, February 11–15, 1961.

Brown, B.F. "The Non-Graded High School." *Phi Delta Kappan,* 44 (February 1963): 206–9.

Brown, B.F. "Nongraded School," *Bulletin of the National Association of Secondary-School Principals* 47 (May 1963): 64–72.

Brown, B.F. "An Answer to Dropouts: The Nongraded High School." The second article in a series on "Our Best High Schools," *Atlantic Monthly* 214 (November 1964): 86–90.

Brown, B.F., and Spinning, J.M. "Is Melbourne High School One Step Short of Utopia?" *Nation's Schools* 74 (December 1964): 10 ff.

Brownell, J.A., and Taylor, H.A. "Theoretical Perspectives for Teaching Teams." *Phi Delta Kappan* 43 (January 1962): 150–57.

Buckley, H.M. "Combatting the Problem of Failure." *Nation's Schools* 32 (November 1943): 105.

Budde, R. "Jump on the Nongraded Bandwagon? Stop! Think!" *National Elementary Principal* 47 (November 1967): 21–24.

Buechner, A.C. "Team Teaching in Elementary Music Education." *Music Educators Journal* 50 (November-December 1963): 31–35.

Buffie, E.G. "A Comparison of Mental Health and Academic Achievement: The Nongraded School vs. the Graded School." *Dissertation Abstracts* 23 (May 1963): 4255. Abstract of an unpublished doctoral dissertation, Indiana University, 1962.

Buford, F. "We Looked at Our Schools." *National Elementary Principal* 34 (December 1954): 20–22.

Burns, R.W. "Suggestions for Involving Teachers in Innovations." *Educational Technology* 9 (January 1969): 27–28.

Bushnell, D.D., and Allen, D.W. eds. *The Computer in American Education: Issues and Applications.* Preliminary papers for the AEDS-Stanford School of Education Invitational Conference sponsored by The Fund for the Advancement of Education, November, 1965. Note especially the position paper by Robert N. Anderson, "Flexibility of School Administration and the Individualization of Instruction," pp. 23–37.

Byron, G. "Teaching and Learning Through Inquiry." *Today's Education* 58 (May 1969): 40–42.

"Calgary's University Elementary School." *Education Canada* 9 (June 1969): 65–69.

Calhoun, L.S. "Chicago's Ben Bloom: All Can Learn." *Integrated Education* 7 (May-June 1969): 16–20.

Callaghan B. "Social Studies: The Flexible Content Approach." *Clearing House* 43 (February 1969): 368-70.

Carbone, R.F. "The Nongraded School: An Appraisal." *Administrator's Notebook* 10 (September 1961).

Carbone, R.F. "A Comparison of Graded and Nongraded Elementary Schools." *Elementary School Journal* 62 (November 1961): 82–88.

Carbone, R.F. "Nongraded School: Myth or Miracle?" *Montana Education* 39 (November 1962): 17–18.

Carle, D.S. "A Program of Pupil Progress Through the Primary Grades." *National Elementary Principal* 26 (December 1946): 15–18.

Carlson, R.O. *Adoption of Educational Innovations.* Eugene, Oregon: Center for the Advanced Study of Educational Administration, University of Oregon, 1965, p.84.

Carlson, W.B. "Interage Grouping." *Educational Leadership* 15 (March 1958): 363–68.

Carswell, E.M. "The Nongraded School: Planning for it, Establishing it, Maintaining it." *National Elementary Principal* 47 (November 1957): 11–16.

Carswell, E.M. "Physical Facilities for a Nongraded School." *National Elementary Principal* 46 (January 1968): 34–42.

Carr, S. "Where Learning Happens." *National Elementary Principal* 48 (April 1969): 44–51.

Chadwick, R. "Report Card in a Nongraded School." *National Elementary Principal* 45 (May 1966): 22–28.

Chadwick, R. "The Report Card in a Nongraded School." *National Elementary Principal* 46 (January 1968): 22–28.

"Changing Secondary Schools." *NASSP Bulletin* 47 (May 1963) the entire issue.

Central Michigan College. *A Cooperative Study for the Utilization of Teacher Competencies.* Mount Pleasant, Michigan: Central Michigan College, second printed report, 1955, p. 32.

Chittister, M. "Nongraded Educational System: An Analysis." *Catholic Educational Review* 65 (December 1967): 582-89.

Christensen, A. "Age-Graded Elementary School." *Educational Leadership* 18 (November 1960): 76–78.

Church, J.G. "Nongraded Programs from Shasta County to Beverly Hills." *California Education* 2 (March 1965): 25–26.

Cironi, C., and Emerson, P. "Slow Learner in a New Setting: A Continuous Progress Program." *New York State Education* 53 (January 1966): 19.

Claremont Graduate School. Claremont College, *The Claremont Teaching Team Program.* Claremont, California.

Coale, J.J. "The Mathematics Curriculum: An Opportunity for Innovation." Report of a speech delivered by W. Eugene Ferguson in a Subject-Field Meeting, Annual Conference of the National Association of Independent Schools, Feb. 1969. *Independent School Bulletin* 28 (May 1969): 79–81.

Cogan, M.L. "Clinical Supervision by Groups." Chapter 11, in *The College Supervisor*, 43rd Yearbook, The Association for Student Teaching. Dubuque, Iowa: William C. Brown Co., 1964.

Cohen, M. "Fill Out a Report Card on Your Child's School." *Pageant* 25 (October 1969): 93–101.

Coles, S.R., and Lewis, E.D. "Continuous Progress Plan Geared to Pupil's Ability." *School Progress*, February 1965.

Coles, S.R., and Lewis, Edward D. "Toward a Child-centered School." *Instructor*, May 1967.

Collier, C.L. "Nongraded Schools." *School and Society* 94 (January 22, 1966): 32.

Comeau, V. "Measuring Pupil Progress in the Nongraded School." *Educational Review*, May 1966.

Compton, M.F. "The Middle School." *Theory into Practice* 7 (June 1968): 108–110, and also in *Education Digest* 34 (April 1969): 22–24.

Conrad, M.J., et al. *School Plant Planning. An Annotated Bibliography.* School of Education, Ohio State University, Columbus, 1968, 70 p.

Cooper, J.M., and Seidman, E. "Helping New Teachers Focus on Behavioral Change." *Clearing House* 43 (January 1969): 301–306.

"Cooperative Teaching." *National Elementary Principal* 44 (January 1965), the entire issue.

Cook, A., and Mack, H. "The British Primary School." *Education Leadership* 27 (November 1969): 141–43.

Cox, D. "Learning on the Road." *Saturday*

Review 52 (May 17, 1969): 71.

Crittenden, J. "Effectiveness of a Nongraded School." *School and Society* 96 (March 1968): 181–84.

Cruthers, G.A. "The Nongraded Primary Unit." *Canadian School Journal*, November 1964.

Cunningham, L.L. "The Teacher and Change." *Elementary School Journal* 62 (December 1961): 119–29.

Cunningham, L.L. "Crisis in School Organization." *Educational Leadership* 26 (March 1969): 551–53.

Cunningham, R. "Implementing Nongraded Advancement with Laboratory Activities as a Vehicle: An Experiment in Elementary School Science." *School Science and Math* 67 (February 1967): 175–81.

Curcall, Mrs. J. "The Nongraded School and the Implications for Team Teaching." *Educational Record of the Province of Quebec*, September 1965.

Curriculum Materials. Association for Supervision and Curriculum Development, 1969, The Association, Washington, D.C.

Cutler, M.H. "This One-Room School Is Anything But Antiquated." *American School Board Journal* 156 (June 1969): 17–20.

Dagne, F. "Nongraded School." *Educational Leadership* 25 (November 1967): 122–23.

Dagne, F.A., and Barnickle, D.W. "Two Schools That Are Nongraded: How . . . What . . . Why." *Instructor* 78 (March 1969): 63–70.

Daniel, A.N. "An Example of Individual Instruction in Developmental Physical Education." From a special section, "Adapted Physical Education," *Journal of Health, Physical Education and Recreation* 40 (May 1969): 56.

Daniels, E.R. "Streaming or Continuous Progress Plans in the Elementary Grades." *Alberta School Trustee*, March 1, 1965.

Dean, C.D. "Continuous Growth Plan Replaces the Graded School in Billings." *Montana Education* 23 (February 1947): 12–13, 21.

Dean, C.D. "The Continuous Growth Plan." *Montana Education* 27 (November 1950): 23–24.

Dean, S.E. "Organization for Instruction in the Elementary Schools." *School Life* 42 (May 1960): 8–9.

Dean, S.E. "Pass or Fail." *Elementary School Journal* 61 (1960–61).

Dean, S.E. "Team Teaching: A Review." *School Life* 44 (September 1961): 5–8.

Dean, S.E., and Witherspoon, C.F. "Team Teaching in the Elementary School." *Education Briefs*, No. 38 (OE-23022), Washington, D.C.: U.S. Office of Education, Elementary Schools Section, January 1962.

Dean, S.E. "Elementary School Administration and Organization: A National Survey of Practices and Policies." Washington, D.C.: Department of Health, Education, and Welfare, 1963.

Dean, S.E. "Nongraded School." *School Life* 47 (December 1964): 19–23.

Dean, S.E. "Nongraded School." *Education Briefs*, No. 1 (OE-20009), Washington, D.C.: U.S. Department of Health, Education and Welfare, Division of Elementary and Secondary Education, July 1964.

Delaney, E.C. *The Case for the Ungraded Primary Unit.* Research Bulletin, 6, New Brunswick, N.J.: New Jersey School Development Council, Rutgers, The State University, December 1961.

De Long, V. "Primary Promotion by Reading Levels." *Elementary School Journal* 38 (May 1938): 663–71.

"Design for Team Teaching." *Instructor* 77 (May 1968): 65–76.

Diesner, R.H. "Continuous-Progress Approach in Biology." *Science Teacher* 36 (March 1969): 53–55.

Di Lorenzo, L.T., and Salter, R. "Cooperative Research on the Nongraded Primary." *Elementary School Journal* 65 (February 1965): 269–77.

Dinkel, M.R. "Rx for Classroom Spring Fever—Move the Chairs." *Grade Teacher* 86 (April 1969): 70–71.

Di Pasquale, V.C. "Schools Without Grades." *Better Homes and Gardens* 33 (September 1955): 28.

Di Pasquale, V.C. "The Relation Between Dropouts and the Graded School." *Phi Delta Kappan* 16 (November 1964): 129–33.

Docking, R., and Hogan, D. "Breaking Grade Barriers." *Michigan Educational Journal* 42 (January 1965): 16–17.

"Don't Step on Thumper." *School Progress*, August 1967.

Douglass, M.P. "Reading and Nongrading in the Elementary School." *Claremont Colorado Reading Conference Yearbook*, 1962, pp. 85–95.

Downey, L.W. "Direction Amidst Change." *Phi Delta Kappan* 45 (February 1961): 186–91.

Drumheller, S. "A Symposium, Language Art in the Nongraded Schools: Part I, Objectives for Language Arts in Nongraded Schools." *Elementary English* 46 (February 1969): 119–25.

Dufay, F.R. "The Development of Procedures for the Implementation of the Nongraded Primary School in Central School District No. 1, Plainview-Old Bethpage, New York." *Dissertation Abstracts* 25 (October 1964): 2311. Abstract of an unpublished doctoral dissertation, New York University, 1962.

Durrell, D.D. "Adapting Instruction to the Learning Needs of Children in the Intermediate Grades." *Journal of Education* 152 (December 1959): 2–9.

Durrell, D.D. "Implementing and Evaluating Pupil-Team Learning Plans." *Journal of Educational Sociology* 39 (April 1961): 360–65.

Durrell, D.D. "Team Learning." *Grade Teacher* 77 (June 1960): 20.

Durrell, D.D., and Scribner, H.B. "Problems and Possibilities in Differentiating Instruction in the Elementary School." *Journal of Education* 152 (December 1959): 72–73.

Durrell, D.D. "Looking Ahead," presentation made in connection with the 50th Anniversary of Boston University School of Education, May 1968. *Journal of Education* 151 (February 1969): 3–4.

Dyer, P. "A Symposium, Language Art in the Nongraded Schools: Symposium Introduction." *Elementary English* 46 (February 1969): 111–18.

Dyer, P., et al. "A Symposium, Language Arts in the Nongraded School: Part IV, A Telephone-Conference Discussion-Language Arts on the Elementary School, Nongraded Programs." *Elementary English* 46 (February 1969): 136–44.

Eastman, T.W. "Pupil Reaction to Nongrading." *School Progress,* August 1967.

Eddinger, J. "Report Cards . . . Who Needs Them?" *Grade Teacher* 86 (January 1969): 68–70.

Educational Facilities Laboratories, Inc. *The Cost of a Schoolhouse.* A report from Educational Facilities Laboratories, Inc., 477 Madison Avenue, New York, 1960, p. 144.

Educational Facilities Laboratories, Inc. *Design for ETV Planning for Schools with Television.* Prepared by Dave Chapman, Inc., Industrial Design, New York, 1960.

Educational Facilities Laboratories, Inc. *Relocatable School Facilities.* A report from Educational Facilities Laboratories, Inc., 477 Madison Avenue, New York, 1964, p. 61.

Educational Facilities Laboratories, Inc. *Middle School: A Report of Two Conferences on the Definition of Its Purpose, Its Spirit and Its Shape for the Consideration of the Board of Education of the Bedford Public Schools, Mount Kisco, New York.* New York: Educational Facilities Laboratories, January 1962.

Educational Facilities Laboratories, Inc. *Middle Schools.* A profile report from Educational Facilities Laboratories, Inc., 477 Madison Avenue, New York, 1965.

Educational Facilities Laboratories, Inc. *Schools for Team Teaching: Ten Examples.* A profile report available free from Educational Laboratories, Inc., 477 Madison Avenue, New York, February 1961.

Educational Facilities Laboratories, Inc. *The School Library: Facilities For Independent Study in The Secondary School.* A report available from Educational Facilities Laboratories, Inc., 477 Madison Avenue, New York, 1963.

Educational Facilities Laboratories, Inc. *Schools Without Walls: Profiles of Significant Schools.* A profile report available from Educational Facilities Laboratories, Inc., 477 Madison Avenue, New York, 1965.

Educational Facilities Laboratories, Inc. *To Build a Schoolhouse.* A 28-minute film available from Educational Facilities Laboratories, Inc., 477 Madison Avenue, New York, 1965.

Educational Facilities Laboratories, Inc. *Educational Change and Architectural Consequences. A Report on Facilities for Individualized Instruction.* Available from Educational Facilities Laboratories, Inc., 477 Madison Avenue, New York, 1969.

Eibler, H.J. "Characteristics for Innovation." *Clearing House* 43 (May 1969): 523–26.

Eisman, E. "What's Brewing in Bassett." *Audio-Visual Instruction* 8 (March 1963): 136–37.

Eldred, D.M., and Hillson, M. "The Nongraded School and Mental Health." *Elementary School Journal* 63 (January 1963): 218–22.

Eldredge, G.F. "The New School Day—A Search for More Individualization in Learning," report of a speech delivered by Dwight Allen in a General Meeting at the Annual Conference of the National Association of Independent Schools, February, 1969. *Independent School Bulletin* 28 (May 1969): 37–38.

"Elementary School Organization." *National Elementary Principal* 41 (December 1961), the entire issue.

Elliott, R.W. "New Problems in Articulation." *American School Board Journal* 142 (June 1961): 11.

Ellison, M. "Let's Ungrade and Upgrade the English Curriculum." *English Journal,* February 1967.

Elsbree, W.S. *Pupil Progress in the Elementary School,* Practical Suggestions for Teaching No. 5. New York: Bureau of Publications, Teachers College, Columbia University, 1943.

Elsbree, W.S. "Promotion and Failure Policies in the Graded School." *National Elementary Principal* 26 (December 1946): 7–9.

English, F. "Questions and Answers on Differentiated Staffing." *Today's Education* 58 (March 1969): 53–54.

Entwistle, H. "Practical and Theoretical Learning." *British Journal of Educational Studies* 17 (July 1969): 117–28.

Estvan, F.J. "Teaching the Very Young: Procedures

for Developing Inquiry Skills." *Phi Delta Kappan* 50 (March 1969): 389–93.

"Evaluation of Team Teaching in the Elementary Schools." Bureau of Educational Research, Board of Education of the City of New York, 1967.

Faith, E.F. "Continuous Progress at the Primary School." *Phi Delta Kappan* 30 (May 1949): 356–59. Also in *Education Digest* 15 (December 1949): 15–17.

Fearing, P. "Nongraded Foreign Language Classes." *Foreign Language Annals* 2 (March 1969): 343–47.

Feldhusen, J.F., and Szabo, M. "A Review of Developments in Computer Assisted Instruction." *Educational Technology* 9 (April 1969): 32–40.

Ferguson, D.A., and Neff, N. "Nongraded School Administers to the Dull-Normal Child." *School and Community* 47 (October 1960): 16–17.

Feurzcig, W. "The Computer as an Educator." Conference Proceedings, 8th International Convention on Military Electronics, Washington, D.C., 1964, pp. 354–56.

Filbin, R.L. "Continuous Progress for All: Implications for the High School." *American School Board Journal* 143 (October 1961): 11–14.

Finley, R.M. "A Study of a Self-contained Group of Third, Fourth, and Fifth Grade Children, Glencoe, Illinois, 1953–54." *Dissertation Abstracts* 17 (August 1957): 2347.

Fischer, B.B., and Fischer, L. "Toward Individualized Learning." *Elementary School Journal* 69 (March 1969): 298–303.

Fischler, A.S. "Use of Team Teaching in the Elementary School." *School Science and Mathematics* 62 (April 1962): 281–88.

Fischler, A.S., and Shoreman, P.B. "Team Teaching in the Elementary School: Implications for Research in Science Instruction." *Science Education* 46 (December 1962): 406–15.

Five Milwaukee Teachers. "We Plan for Living and Learning." *Childhood Education* 26 (September 1949), 19–23.

Flint, F.E. "The Right to Fail." *Today's Education* 58 (April 1969): 39–40.

Forbes, M.M. "So How Is A.V. Different in a Nongraded Program?" *Audio-Visual Instruction* 8 (October 1963): 578–79.

"Forest Hill Story; Part 2: How Staff and Parents React to Continuous Progress Program." *School Progress*, December 1967.

Franklin, M.P., and Perry, L. "Ungraded Elementary School." *Virginia Journal of Education* 55 (March 1962): 16–17.

Franklin, M.P. "Nongraded Organizational Patterns: Theory and Practice." *Virginia Journal of Education* 56 (April 1963): 11–12.

Franklin, M.P. "Nongraded Schools." *Educational Forum* 30 (March 1966): 331–34.

Friedlander, B.Z. "Today's Innovations in Teaching." *NEA Journal* 55 (March 1966): 10–14.

Fries, H.C. "A Continuous Progress School." *American School Board Journal* 119 (July 1949): 52.

Funaro, G.J. "Team Teaching: The Danger and the Promise." *Clearing House* 43 (March 1969): 401–3.

Funk, H.D. "Nonpromotion Teaches Children They Are Inferior." *Illinois Schools Journal* 49 (Summer 1969): 130–33.

Garvey, J.F. "Possible Over-Emphasis on Large-Group Instruction." *Education* 89 (February-March 1969): 213–14.

Geddes, C.L., and Kooi, B.Y. "An Instructional Management System for Classroom Teachers." *Elementary School Journal* 69 (April 1969): 337–45.

Gilbert, J.H. "Multigraded Developmental Plan Focuses on Pupil Achievement: Telsa School Breaks Through Traditional Graded Structure." *Chicago Schools Journal* 43 (February 1962): 209–14.

Gilbert, J.H. "Telsa School Breaks the Lock-Step." *Elementary School Journal* 64 (March 1964): 306–9.

Gilbert, V.K. "The Ungraded Secondary School." *Ontario Secondary School Teachers Federation Bulletin*, March 1967.

Gillis, J.C. Jr. "Performance Contracting for Public Schools." *Educational Technology* 9 (May 1969): 17–20.

Ginther, J. "Sloganism in Education." *Elementary School Journal* 62 (February 1962): 240–42.

Glaser, R. "The Design of Instruction." Chapter 9 in *The Changing American School*, 1966 Yearbook, Part II, edited by John I. Goodlad. Chicago, Illinois: The Society, 1966, pp. 215–42.

Glaser, R., and Reynolds, J., eds. *Teaching Machines and Programmed Learning, Volume 2: Date and Directions.* Washington, D.C.: National Education Association, 1201 Sixteenth Street, N.W., 1965.

Glaser, R. "The Design and Programming of Instruction." In *The Schools and the Challenge of Innovation,* Committee for Economic Development, New York, 1969, pp. 156–215.

Glass, R., and Murphy, J. *Educational Change and Architectural Consequences: A Report on Facilities for Individualized Instruction.* Educational Facilities Laboratories, Inc., 477 Madison Avenue, New York, 1968, 90 p.

Glasser, W. "Schools Without Failure." *Instructor* 78 (January 1969): 60–61.

Glasser, W.E. "The Effect of School Failure." *National Elementary Principal* 49 (September 1969): 8–18.

Glogau, L. "Make Me A Nongraded School." *National Elementary Principal* 44 (May 1965): 51–54.

Goldman, B.A. "War Is On: Graded vs. Nongraded; A Parody." *Peabody Journal of Education* 45 (July 1967): 9–10.

Goldstein, W. "Team Planning: Heart Transplant in Teaching." *Clearing House* 43 (January 1969): 272–74.

Goodlad, J.I. *The Summer Children.* A film on a summer session with disadvantaged children. University Elementary School, UCLA, Los Angeles 90024.

Goodlad, J.I. *This is a Laboratory School.* Film. University Elementary School, UCLA, Los Angeles 90024.

Goodlad, J.I. "More About the Ungraded Plan." *NEA Journal* 44 (May 1955): 295–96.

Goodlad, J.I. "Ungrading the Elementary Schools." *NEA Journal* 44 (March 1955): 170–71.

Goodlad, J.I. "Developmental Reading in the Upgraded Plan." In *Reading in the School of Tomorrow*, Kent State University Bulletin, November 1957, 12–17.

Goodlad, J.I. "In Pursuit of Visions." *Elementary School Journal* 59 (October 1958): 1–17.

Goodlad, J.I. "Illustrative Programs and Procedures in Elementary Schools." In *The Integration of Educational Experiences*, Fifty-seventh Yearbook of the National Society for the Study of Education, Pt. III, Chicago: University of Chicago Press, 1958, 173–93.

Goodlad, J.I. "The Elementary School of the Future." In *Education in Transition*, edited by Frederick C. Gruber, Philadelphia: University of Pennsylvania Press, 1960, 99–109.

Goodlad, J.I. "Classroom Organization." In *Encyclopedia of Educational Research*, 3rd ed., 1960, pp. 221–26.

Goodlad, J.I. "Revamping Elementary Education," *Elementary School Journal* 61 (December 1960): 119–26.

Goodlad, J.I. "What About Nongrading Our Schools?" *Instructor* 70 (May 1961): 6.

Goodlad, J.I. "Promising Practices in Nongraded Schools." *Midland Schools* 75 (May 1961): 15–16. Also printed in *Education Digest* 27 (October 1961): 8–10.

Goodlad, J.I. "Toward Improved School Organization." *National Elementary Principal* 41 (December 1961): 60–127.

Goodlad, J.I. "Reading in the Reorganized Elementary School." *Claremont Colorado Reading Conference Yearbook*, 1961, pp. 36–44.

Goodlad, J.I. "The Nongraded School: An Evalua-Evaluation." In *Tomorrow's Teaching*, Oklahoma City: Frontiers of Science Foundation of Oklahoma, 1962, pp. 90–93.

Goodlad, J.I. "Inadequacy of Graded Organization— What Then?" *Childhood Education* 39 (February 1963): 274–77.

Goodlad, J.I. *Planning and Organizing for Teaching.* Washington, D.C.: National Education Association, 1963, p. 190.

Goodlad, J.I. *School Curriculum Reform in the United States.* New York: The Fund for the Advancement of Education, 1964, p. 96.

Goodlad, J.I. "Meeting Children Where They Are." *Saturday Review* (March 20, 1965): 57.

Goodlad, J.I. "The Future of Learning and Teaching." *AV Communication Review* 16 (Spring 1968): 5–15.

Goodlad, J.I. "The Schools vs. Education." *Saturday Review* 52 (April 19, 1969): 59–61.

Goodlad, J.I. "Educational Change: A Strategy for Study and Action." *National Elementary Principal* 48 (January 1969): 6–16.

Goodlad, J.I. "How Do We Learn?" From the monthly *Saturday Review* Supplement, "Education in America," sponsored by the Charles F. Kettering Foundation. *Saturday Review* 52 (June 21, 1969): 74. Adapted from a longer essay, "Schooling and Education," published in the 1969 edition of *The Great Ideas Today.*

Goodlad, J.I., and Anderson, R:H. "The Nongraded Elementary School: 1958 Progress Report." *NEA Journal* 47 (December 1958): 642–43.

Goodlad, J.I., and Anderson, R.H. "Educational Practices in Nongraded Schools: A Survey of Perceptions." *Elementary School Journal* 43 (October 1962): 33–44.

Goodlad, J.I., and Rehage, K.J. "Unscrambling the Vocabulary of School Organization." *NEA Journal* 51 (November 1962): 34–36.

Goodlad, J.I., and Sand, O. "Patterns of School Organization." Fifty-five minute tape recording, Washington, D.C.: National Education Association, Department of Elementary School Principals, 1962.

Goodlad, J.I., et al. "Reading Levels Replace Grades in the Nongraded Plan." *Elementary School Journal* 57 (February 1957): 253–56.

Goodman, Kenneth S. "Reading: A Wealth of New Materials and Approaches." From a special report, "What's New In Curriculum," *Nation's Schools* 84 (August 1969): 38–40.

Gordon, I.J. "Determining Teacher Effectiveness."

Educational Leadership 20 (November 1962): 119–25.

Gore, L.L. "The Nongraded Primary Unit." *School Life* 44 (March 1962): 9–12.

Gore, L.I., and Koury, R.E. *A Survey of Early Elementary Education in Public Schools, 1960–61.* Washington, D.C.: U.S. Department of Health, Education, and Welfare, 1965.

Gores, H.B. "The Congenial School." *Educate* 2 (March 1969): 24–31.

Gorman, C.J. "The University of Pittsburgh Model of Teacher Training for the Individualization of Instruction." *Journal of Research and Development in Education* 2 (Spring 1969): 44–46.

Gorman, C.J. "Annual Reassignment of Teachers: An Important Ingredient of Nongrading." *Elementary School Journal* 69 (January 1969): 192–97.

Gorton, R.A. "Parental Resistance to Modular Scheduling." *Clearing House* 43 (March 1969): 392–95.

"The Gradeless School." *Newsweek* 52 (September 15, 1958): 76.

Gran, E.E. "Why Not an Ungraded Intermediate Program. Douglas School at Ellsworth Air Force Base . . . ." *Instructor* 72 (January 1963): 48 ff.

Greig, J., and Lee, R.R. "Cooperative Administration." *National Elementary School Principal* 44 (January 1965): 71–76.

Gross, R., and Watt, R. "Staff Involvement and Structural Change." *Journal of Secondary Education* 44 (March 1969): 112–15.

Grossman, R. "Problem-Solving Activities Observed in British Primary Schools." *Arithmetic Teacher* 16 (January 1969): 34–38.

Haas, A. "First Year Organization of Elmcrest Elementary School: A Nongraded Team-Teaching School." *American School Board Journal* 151 (October 1965): 22.

Hall, D.C. "Continuous Progress: An Elementary School Program Determined by Child's Needs and Abilities." *Kentucky School Journal* 29 (January 1951): 10–14.

Haller, E.J., and Anderson, B.D. "Contextual Effects on Educational Aspirations: Some Canadian Evidence." *Administrator's Notebook* 17 (March 1969).

Halliwell, J.W. "A Comparison of Pupil Achievement in Graded and Nongraded Primary Classrooms." *Journal of Experimental Education* 32 (Fall 1963): 59–64.

Hamilton, W., and Rehwoldt, W. "By Their Differences They Learn." *National Elementary Principal* 37 (December 1957): 27–29.

Hammond, R.A., and Forsythe, H. "Should Any Child Skip Kindergarten?" *Instructor* 78 (May 1969): 60.

Harris, B.H. "Helping to Read: A Proposal." *Phi Delta Kappan* 50 (May 1969): 530–33.

Hart, H.C. "Classroom Structures Rapidly Changing." *Education* 86 (December 1965): 195–201.

Hart, L.A. "The New Breed of School Critic." *Educational Leadership* 26 (April 1969): 671–73.

Hart, L.A. "Learning at Random." *Saturday Review* 52 (April 19, 1969): 62–63.

Hart R.H. "The Nongraded Primary School and Arithmetic." *Arithmetic Teacher* 9 (March 1962): 130–33.

Harvey, J.M. "On Your Mark, Set Set, Whoa!" *Argus* (July–August 1966).

Haye, M. "The Testing Program in the Ungraded Primary." *School and Community* 47 (October 1960): 14.

Hazlett, J.A. "The Need for Perspective." Paper presented at the North Central Association Annual Meeting, March 25, 1969. *North Central Association Quarterly* 43 (Spring 1969): 321–27.

Hearn, N., and Reid, G. "The Webster Story." *Michigan Educational Journal* 32 (December 1954): 179–85.

Heathers, G., and Pincus, M. "Dual Progress Plan in the Elementary School." *Arithmetic Teacher* 6 (December 1959): 302–05.

Heathers, G. "The Dual Progress Plan." *Educational Leadership* 18 (November 1960): 89–91.

Heathers, G. "The Role of Innovation in Education." *National Elementary Principal* 43 (September 1963): 9–14.

Heathers, G. "Team Teaching and the Educational Reform Movement." In *Team Teaching*, edited by Judson T. Shaplin and Henry F. Olds, Jr., pp. 345–75. New York: Harper and Row, 1964.

Heathers, G. "Research on Implementing and Evaluating Cooperative Teaching." *National Elementary Principal* 44 (January 1965): 27–33.

Heese, E. "Do You Believe in Lesson Plans?" *Clearing House* 43 (April 1969): 492–93.

Heffernan, H. et al. "What Research Says About Nonpromotion." *California Journal of Elementary Education* 21 (August 1952): 24.

Heller, R.W., and Hansen, J.C. "The Middle School and Implications for the Guidance Program." *Peabody Journal of Education* 46 (March 1969): 291–97.

Hester, K.B. "Every Child Reads Successfully in a

Multiple-Level Program." *Elementary School Journal* 53 (October 1952): 86–89.

Hickey, P. *Classification of Primary School Children.* Research and Survey Series, No. 12, *St. Louis Public School Journal* 6 (July 1953).

Hickey, P. "Discarding Traditional Grade Organization Is Better for Slow, Average and Rapid Learners." *School and Community* 44 (March 1958): 14–16.

Hilfiker, L.R. "Interpersonal Characteristics and Innovativeness in School Systems." *Journal of Applied Behavioral Science* 5 (July, August, September, 1969): 441–45.

Hillson, M. "The Nongraded School." In *New Frontiers in Education,* New York; Grune and Stratton, 1966.

Hillson, M., et al. "A Controlled Experiment Evaluating the Effects of a Nongraded Organization on Pupil Achievement." *Journal of Educational Research* 57 (July–August 1964): 548–50.

Hillson, M. "Continuous Progress Education." *Pact Magazine* 7, Provincial Association of Catholic Teachers of Quebec (December 1968): 12–19 ff.

Hillson, M. "Teacher Concerns and Commitments." *OECTA Review* 28 (March 1969): 8–16.

Hines, V.A., and Alexander, W.M. "Evaluating the New Middle School." *National Elementary Principal* 48 (February 1969): 32–36.

Hoban, P.F., and McManus, B.J. "How to Nongrade a Small High School: Cycling Courses in Social Studies and English." *School Management* 9 (September 1965): 78–81.

Hoffa, H., and Fawcett, T. "Team Teaching and Art Teaching." *School Arts* 62 (February 1963): 18–20.

Hoflich, J.E. "Ungraded Primary." *National Catholic Education Association Bulletin* 57 (November 1960): 8–25.

Holloway, G.E. "The Nongraded School: A Decision." In *News Exchange.* Buffalo, N.Y.: The Western New York School Study Council, State University of New York at Buffalo, June 1961.

Holmes, M. "I Reject Ungrading." *Monday Morning* 2 (November 1967): 21–24.

Hopkins, Kenneth D.; Oldridge, O.A.; and Williamson, M. "An Empirical Comparison of Pupil Achievement and Other Variables in Graded and Ungraded Classes." *American Educational Research Journal* 2 (November 1965): 207–15.

Hoover, W.F. "Patterns of Organization for Learning." *Audio-Visual Instruction* 13 (June 1968): 588–90.

Horowitz, M. "MacDonald College Dual Progress Plan: A Study in Curriculum Development and School Reorganization." *Canadian Education Research Digest* 8 (March 1968): 60–67.

Housego, Dr. B. E. J. "The Nongraded Elementary School: Selected Problems." *Canadian Education and Research Digest,* September 1968.

Houts, P.L. "Profile of the Nongraded Child." *National Elementary Principal* 46 (January 1968): 4–10.

Howard, E.Z. "A Look at Specialization." *Educational Leadership* 26 (March 1969): 547–50.

"How Forest Hill Got into its Continuous Progress Plan." *School Progress,* November 1967.

Howell, B. "The Middle School—Is It Really Any Better?" *North Central Association Quarterly* 48 (Winter 1969): 281–87.

Howsam, Robert B. "New Designs for Research in Teacher Competence." Joint Committee on Personnel Procedures of the California School Boards Association and the California Teachers Association, 1960.

Hunter, M. "Dimensions of Nongrading." *Elementary School Journal* 65 (October 1964): 20–25. Also printed in *Education Digest* 30 (November 1964): 35–37.

Hunter, M. "Teachers in the Nongraded School." *NEA Journal* 55 (February 1966): 12–15.

Hutchinson, J. "Ungraded Primary School." In *Toward Effective Grouping,* Washington, D.C.: Association for Childhood Education International, 1962.

Huus, Helen, ed. *Education and the National Purpose: 49th Annual Schoolmen's Week Proceedings.* Philadelphia: University of Pennsylvania Press, 1962.

Huus, H., ed. *Contemporary Issues Here and Abroad: 50th Annual Schoolmen's Week Proceedings.* Philadelphia: University of Pennsylvania Press, 1963, p. 311.

Huus, H., ed. *Freedom and Education: 51st Annual Schoolmen's Week Proceedings.* Philadelphia: University of Pennsylvania Press, 1965, p. 274.

Imhoff, M.M. *The Primary Unit.* Selected References, No. 1. Washington, D.C.: U.S. Office of Education, May 1957.

Ingram, V. "Flint Evaluates Its Primary Cycle." *Elementary School Journal* 59 (November 1960): 76–80.

Ithaca City School District. *The Glenwood Plan for Continuous Progress Education.* Ithaca, N.Y.: The Schools, 1964.

Ivey, D.L. "Nongraded English Program." *English Journal* 54 (February 1965): 115–17.

Jackson, L. "To Become Good Readers." *American Education* 5 (December 1969): 9–10.

Jarvis, G.M., and Fleming, R.C. "Team Teaching as Sixth Graders See It." *Elementary School Journal* 66 (October 1965): 35–39.

Johnson, G.R. "An Investigation of the Classroom Activities in a Selected Number of Nongraded Elementary School Classrooms." Doctoral thesis, Teachers College, Columbia University, New York, 1968.

Johnson, L.V., and Bardenstein, M.A. "The Ungraded Elementary School." *Delta Kappa Gamma Bulletin* 26 (Spring 1960): 46–50.

Jones, D.M. "A Feasible Plan for Continuous Admission." *Education* 89 (February-March 1969): 195–202.

Jones, J. "A Comparison of Pupil Achievement After One and One-half and Three Years in a Nongraded Program." *Journal of Educational Research* 61 (October 1967): 75–77.

Journal of Educational Sociology, 34, April 1961.

Kaplan, J.D. "Twin Revolutions: Mathematics Reform and PI." *Educational Product Report* 2 (March 1969): 10–11.

Kaufman, B., and Behune, P. "Nova High, Space Age School." *Phi Delta Kappan* 46 (September 1964): 9–11.

Kauth, P., and Brown, B.F. "Nongraded High School in Melbourne, Fla." *Bulletin of the National Association of Secondary School Principals* 46 (January 1962): 127–34.

Kayfetz, I. "The Emerging Pattern of Promotional Policy." *National Elementary Principal* 26 (December 1946): 2–7.

Kelly, F.C. "Doing Away With Grade Levels." *NEA Journal* 37 (April 1948): 222–23.

Kelly, F.C. "Ungraded Primary Schools Make the Grade in Milwaukee." *NEA Journal* 40 (December 1951): 645–46.

Kelly, F.C. "Ungraded Primary School." *Educational Leadership* 18 (November 1960): 80 ff.

Kierstead, R. "A Comparison and Evaluation of Two Methods of Organization for the Teaching of Reading." *Journal of Educational Research* 56 (February 1963): 317–21.

King, A.R. "Ungraded Primary Extended to Full Six-Year School." *School Management* 3 (February 1959): 58.

Kingdon, M. "Grades or Levels? Perspectives on the Ungraded Primary Plan In Michigan." *Michigan Education Journal* 39 (April 1962): 514–17.

Klemm, E. "Appropriate School Programs: The Nongraded Primary." *Education* 85 (April 1965): 488.

Klohr, P.R. "Studies of the Teaching Act: What Progress?" *Educational Leadership* 20 (November 1962): 93–96.

Knight, L.E. "A Study of Double Grades in New Haven City Schools." *Journal of Experimental Education* 7 (September 1938): 11–18.

Kohl, J.W. "Adoption, Adoption Stages and Perceptions of the Characteristics of Innovations." *California Journal of Educational Research* 20 (May 1969): 120–31.

Kopp, O.W. "Grouping Pupils in the Elementary Schools." *New York State Education* 54 (May 1957): 540–42.

Kopp, O.W. "The School Organization Syndrome vis-à-vis Improved Learning." *National Elementary Principal* 48 (February 1969): 42–45.

Kowitz, Gerald T. "The Change and Improvement of School Practices." *Phi Delta Kappan* 45 (February 1961): 216–19.

Labels and Fingerprints. Washington, D.C.: National Education Association, 1960.

Lambert, P.D. "Student Perception of Failure." *Phi Delta Kappan* 50 (February 1969): 353–54.

Lambert, P.; Goodwin, W.L.; and Wiersma, W. "A Study of the Elementary School Teaching Team." *Elementary School Journal* 66 (October 1965): 28–34.

Lamers, W.M. "Milwaukee's Ungraded Primary Plan." *American School Board Journal* 145 (November 1962): 11–13.

Lane, H.A. "Moratorium on Grade Grouping." *Educational Leadership* 4 (March 1947): 385–95.

Lane, R.H. "Organizing the Primary School." *Childhood Education* 14 (November 1937): 110–13.

Lane, R.H. "Experiments in Reorganizing the Primary School: A Symposium." *Childhood Education* 15 (February 1939): 262–71.

Languis, M.L., et al. "Teaming: Innovation in Teacher Education." *Educational Leadership* 26 (May 1969): 806.

Law, H. "This School was Built for Continuous Progress." *School Progress,* December 1967.

Leavitt, W. "Individuals, Front and Center." *American Education* 5 (February 1969): 4–6.

Lee, B. "Not a Solitary Seeking for Individual Glory; Touring the Nongraded Schools of Dade County, Florida." *Kentucky School Journal* 46 (March 1968): 27–28.

Lee, J.P. "Time Utilization for Optimum Learning." *Secondary Education* 44 (February 1969): 58–61.

Leith, G.O.M., et al. "Individual Versus Co-operative

Learning I: Influence of Intelligence and Sex." *Educational Research* 11 (February 1969): 95–103.

Levine, R.H. "They Made a Better School." *American Education* 5 (November 1969): 8–10.

Lewin, D. "Go Slow on Nongrading." *Elementary School Journal* 67 (December 1966): 131–34. Also printed in *Educational Digest* 32 (February 1967): 8–10.

Lewis, P. "Movable Doors and Partitions." *Nation's Schools* 84 (July 1969): 65–66.

Lierheimer, A.P. "Cast Off the Bowline!" *Today's Education* 58 (March 1969): 62.

Lindsey, J.F. "Non-graded Programs—Which One?" *Elementary School Journal* 68 (November 1967): 61–62.

Lindvall, C.M., et al. *Meeting the Needs of the Able Student Through Provision for Flexible Progression.* Pittsburgh: Coordinated Education Center, University of Pittsburgh, 1962.

Lippitt, P. "Children Can Teach Other Children. Changing Roles of the Teacher, Number 9." *Instructor* 78 (May 1969): 41.

Locus of Change: Staff Utilization Studies. Reprinted from the January 1963 issue of *The Bulletin*, a publication of the NASSP.

Lormier, Dr. W.C. "Why Nongrading Requires a Rethinking of Practices." *School Progress*, February 1967.

Mathews, Dr. A. "The Nongraded School." *Educational Review*, March 1966.

McBeath, A.G. "The Nongraded System." *Educational Review*, January 1966.

McBeath, R.J. "Is Education Becoming?" *AV Communication Review* 7 (Spring 1969): 36–40.

McCallum, C. "Non-graded Team Teaching." *Science and Children* 6 (September 1968): 42.

McCarthy, C.J. "Nongrading." *School Progress*, February 1967.

McCarthy, G. "The New Youth and the New Schools." *Education Canada* 9 (March 1969): 10–21.

McCarthy, R. "A Nongraded Middle School." *National Elementary Principal* 46 (January 1968): 15–21.

McDaniel, W.P. "Lemasters Elementary School Changes to Workable Nongraded System." *School and Community* 51 (May 1965): 14–15.

McLeod, D. "What Is a Nongraded School?" *Canadian Education Research Digest* 8 (March 1968): 38–45.

McLoughlin, W.P. *The Nongraded School: A Critical Assessment.* Albany, New York: The University of the State of New York, The State Department of Education, Office of Research and Evaluation, September 1967.

McLoughlin, W. "The Phantom Nongraded School."

Phi Delta Kappan 49 (January 1968): 248–50.

McMurtry, J. "Frank Brown and the Gradeless School." *Monday Morning* 2 (November 1967): 24–25.

McNally, H.J. "So It's Not Nongraded, But What Is It?" *National Elementary Principal* 47 (November 1967): 43–47.

McNally, H.J. "The Nongraded School—Some Current Questions." *National Elementary Principal* 46 (January 1968): 2–4.

Mercills, M.G. "The Primary School Unit." In *Bulletin of School of Education* 25. Bloomington, Ind: Indiana University, January 1949, 13–18.

Meyer, J.A. "Teaming a First Step for Interdisciplinary Teaching." *Clearing House* 43 (March 1969): 406–10.

Meyer, J.A. "Do Teachers Promote Change?" *Secondary Education* 44 (March 1969): 107–11.

"Middle Schools in Theory and in Fact." *NEA Research Bulletin* 47 (May 1969): 49–52.

Miller, J. "Designing Educational Environments." *Science Teacher* 36 (February 1969): 24–25.

Mineola Public Schools. *The Nongraded Primary School.* Mineola, N.Y.: The Schools, n.d.

Misner, P. "The Primary Unit Plan in Glencoe." *Schoolmen's Week Proceedings* 33 (June 1946): 100–101.

Moore, E.C.L. "Individualizing the Early Elementary Classroom." Report of a General Meeting at the Annual Conference of the National Association of Independent Schools, February 1969, in *Independent School Bulletin* 28 (May 1969): 43–45.

Moore, S., and Mizuba, K. "Innovation Diffusion: A Study in Credibility." *Educational Forum* 33 (January 1969): 181–85.

Morse, A.D. "Schools Without Grades: The Elementary Schools of Appleton, Wisc." In *Schools of Tomorrow—Today*, pp. 27–40. Albany, N.Y.: State Education Department, University of the State of New York, 1960.

Moss, T.C. "The Middle School Comes—And Takes Another Grade or Two." *National Elementary Principal* 48 (February 1969): 37–41.

Mouat, L. "An Unusual Lab School." *Southern Education Report* 4 (April 1969): 24–28.

Muchnik, M.M. "Joy, Frustration, and Excedrin: The Institute Paradigm." *Audiovisual Instructor* 14 (May 1969): 51–52.

Muessig, R.H. "Change—The Only Constant." *Educational Leadership* 26 (March 1969): 543–46.

National Education Association. *Focus on Change.* A 23-minute recording filmstrip narrated by Howard K. Smith.

National Education Association. *Deciding What to*

Teach and *Planning and Organizing for Teaching.* Filmstrips, stock nos. 281-11692 and 381-11696, respectively. Available at $7 each or $10 together from the Center for the Study of Instruction, National Education Association, 1201 Sixteenth St., N.W., Washington, D.C.

National Education Association. "Elementary School Organizational Purposes, Patterns, Perspectives." *The National Elementary School Principals Yearbook* 41 (December 1961): 157.

National Education Association. *Administrative Practices in Urban School Districts, 1958–59.* Research Report 1961–R10. Washington, D.C.: Research Division, National Education Association, 1961.

National Education Association. *The Principals Look at the Schools.* Washington, D.C.: Project on the Instructional Program of the Public Schools, The Association, 1962.

National Education Association, NASSP. *Focus on the Individual—A Leadership Responsibility.* Filmstrip by J. Lloyd Trump and Lois S. Karasik, 1965.

National Education Association. "Nongraded School Organization." *Research Bulletin of the National Education Association* 43 (October 1965): 93–95.

National Education Association. "Individualizing Instruction." A special issue of *NEA Journal* 54, November 1966.

National Education Association, Department of Elementary School. Principals. "The Nongraded School: Part 1." *National Elementary Principal* 47 (November 1967): 2–51.

National Education Association, Department of Elementary School Principals. "The Nongraded School: Part 2." *National Elementary Principal* 47 (January 1968): 2–45.

National Association of Secondary School Principals' Bulletin 66, January 1962. The entire issue prepared by the Committee on Staff Utilization. See also the January issue of each year for an annual report of the Staff Utilization Studies.

Nelson, T.L. "Pupil Progress Plan in Berkeley." *Elementary School Journal* 50 (February 1950): 315.

"New Directions for the American School." *School and Society* 97 (March 1969): 156–58.

"New Trends in School Building." *School Management* 13 (July 1969): 51–56, 58–63, 76–85.

"New York City Inaugurates a Continuous Progress Plan." *Elementary School Journal* 44 (September 1943): 9–10.

Nichols, N.J. "Interclass Grouping for Reading Instruction: Who Makes the Decisions and Why?" *Educational Leadership* 26 (March 1969): 588–92.

Nielsen, P., and Keropian, R. "How to Gain Instruc-

tional Time Without Additional Cost." *Journal of Secondary Education* 44 (January 1969): 25–30.

Niess, C. "A Nongraded Program for the Small High School." *Bulletin of the National Association of Secondary-School Principals* 50 (February 1966): 19–27.

Noall, M.F., and Nuttall, M. "Hurricane, Utah, High School Ungraded English Project." *National Association of Secondary School Principals Bulletin*, January 1962.

Noble, G. "Individual Differences and Intrinsic Programmed Instruction." *Programmed Learning Educational Technology* 6 (January 1969): 40–57.

"No Child is Failing in This School." *Grade Teacher* 86 (January 1969): 70–71.

"A Nongraded High School Gets Underway." *School Progress*, June 1968.

"Nongraded Schools." N.E.A. Research Division, Washington, D.C., May 1965.

"The Nongraded School." Department of Elementary School Principals, Washington, D.C., 1968.

"Nongraded Trimester Plan Makes High School Unique." *School Progress*, January 1965.

"Nongrading." *Review of Educational Research*, October 1964.

"Nongrading: You Can't Fit People Into Groups." *School Progress*, February 1967.

Norwalk Plan of Team Teaching, Third Report, 1960–61. Available from the Connecticut Board of Education, 105 Main Street, Norwalk.

Norwalk School Improvement Program, Fourth Report, April 1962–August 1963. Available from the Connecticut Board of Education, 105 Main Street, Norwalk.

Nussel, E.J., and Johnson, M. "Who Obstructs Innovation? A Study of Teacher Perception of Possible Obstacles to Innovation." *Journal of Secondary Education* 44 (January 1969): 3–11.

O'Beirne, G. "An Ungraded Early Elementary School Program." *Educational Methods* 21 (January 1942): 178–80.

O'Brien, G.E. "Leadership in Organizational Settings." *Journal of Applied Behavioral Science* 5 (February-March 1969): 45–63.

O'Connell, S. "Innovators must also be Tacticians." *Monday Morning*, January 1968.

Oehmig, E. "Lost in Nashville, Three Grades." *Nation's Schools* 18 (September 1966): 29.

Ogletree, E. "Homogeneous Ability Grouping—British Style." *Peabody Journal of Education* 47 (July 1969): 20–25.

Olson, C.E. "The Way It Looks to a Classroom Teacher." *Today's Education* 58 (March 1969): 59.

Olson, W.C. "Implications of the Dynamics of Instructional Groups." In *The Dynamics of Instructional Groups,* the 59th Yearbook of the National Society for the Study of Education, 268–80. Chicago: University of Chicago Press, 1960.

Oregon State Department of Education. "A Computer-Developed Modular Flexible Schedule." A Progress Report on an Oregon Program Acitivity at Marshall High School in Portland, Oregon, issued by the Division of Education Development, Oregon State Department of Education, Salem, 1964.

"Organizing for Effective Learning." *Educational Leadership* 17 (April 1960): 402–38.

Owen, J.G. "Strategies of Curriculum Innovation." *Journal of Curriculum Studies* 1 (November 1968): 19–26.

Palmer, D.S. "Advancing Each at His Own Speed: The Ungraded Program at Maple Park." *Washington Education* 71 (December 1959): 48–53.

Parker, J.R. "A Comparison of Organizational and Instructional Practices in Graded and Nongraded Schools." Doctoral thesis, University of California, Berkeley, 1967.

Patterson, G.J. "Unit Promotion System in the Hamilton Public Schools." *Canadian Educational Research Digest* 3 (March 1963): 48–53.

Peake, G.J. "Team Teaching, An Experiment in American Education." *Education Gazette,* March 1964: 132–35. Published by the Department of Education, New South Wales, Australia, Box 33, G.P.O., Sydney.

Pearce, L. "Exploration–Innovation: The New Learning Environment." *Science Teacher* 36 (February 1969): 20–23.

Peck, D. "The 8mm in Team Teaching." *Instructor* 78 (January 1969): 125–27.

Perkins, B. "Factors Which Have Influenced the Development of the Role of the Para-Professional in the Public Elementary Schools of Norwalk, Connecticut." Doctoral dissertation, New York University, 1961. Available at $2.00 from the Norwalk Board of Education, 105 Main Street.

Perkins, B., and team members of the Norwalk Plan. "Teamwork Produces Audio-Visual Techniques." *Grade Teacher* 71 (June 1960): 55–72.

Perkins, H.V. "Nongraded Programs: What Progress?" *Educational Leadership* 19 (December 1961): 166–69, 194.

Peters, K.L. "Achievement Levels Are a Comfortable Half-Step to a Nongraded Plan." *Nation's Schools* 74 (July 1964): 22–23.

Peterson, D.L. "Non-graded High School Challenges Slow, Average and Gifted Students at Melbourne, Fla." *School and Community* 49 (September 1962).

Phillips, E.L. "Team Teaching: Where Do We Begin?" *Clearing House* 43 (March 1969): 404–05.

Plunkett, W.T. "Independent Study at Syosset High School." *California Journal of Educational Research* 20 (March 1969): 63–68.

Polkinghorne, A.R. "Parents and Teachers Appraise Primary-Grade Grouping." *Elementary School Journal* 51 (January 1951): 271–78.

Polkinghorne, A.R. "Grouping Children in the Primary Grades." *Elementary School Journal* 50 (May 1959): 502–08.

Polos, N.C. "Flexible Scheduling–Advantages and Disadvantages." *Education* 89 (April-May 1969): 315–19.

Potter, G.L. "Making Continuity Possible." *Childhood Education* 25 (November 1948): 128–31.

Powers, A.E., and Schillo, R.J. *A Comparison of the Achievement of Children in Graded and Ungraded Primary Classes.* Pilot Studies, Richmond, Va.: Division of Educational Research, State Department of Education, n.d.

"Principal Would Change the Elementary Teaching System." *The Mail Star,* December 24, 1968.

"Principal Enns Tells How his Project R.O.B.L. Probes Change." *School Progress,* December 1968.

Provus, M.M. "Ability Grouping in Arithmetic." *Elementary School Journal* 60 (April 1960): 391–98.

"Pupil Progress in the Elementary Schools of New York State." Bulletin No. 1297, Albany, N.Y.: University of the State of New York, July 16, 1945.

Ramsey, W. "Which School Systems Get the Best Results in Reading?" *Journal of Reading Behavior* 1 (Summer 1969): 74–80.

Rand, J.J., and English, F. "Towards a Differentiated Teaching Staff." *Phi Delta Kappan* 49 (January 1968): 264–68.

Reid, J.L., et al. "A Special Kind of Middle School." A design prepared by Reid and Tarics, architects and engineers, San Francisco. *Nation's School* 83 (May 1969): 76–79.

"Report Pushes for Continuous Progress Plan." *Mail Star,* December 27, 1968.

"Reporting to Parents." *National Elementary Principal,* the entire issue, May 1966.

Rhoades, W.M. "Erasing Grade Lines." *Elementary School Journal* 67 (December 1966): 140–45.

Richardson, R.J. "An Information System for Individualized Instruction in an Elementary School." *Educational and Psychological Measurement* 29 (Spring 1969): 199–201.

Rimmington, G.T. "The Education of the Individual: An Evaluation of the Non-graded School." *Nova Scotia Journal of Education,* February 1965.

Ritzenhein, B.A. "Survey of Personal Perceptions of Selected Factors in Non-graded Programs in Eight Detroit Elementary Schools." *Dissertation Abstracts* 25 (March 1965): 5645. Abstract of an unpublished doctoral dissertation, Wayne State University, 1963. (#9)

Robbins, G.D. "The Impact of Current Educational Change Upon Teacher Education." *Journal of Teacher Education* 20 (Summer 1969): 182–87.

Robbins, M.P., and Miller, J.R. "The Concept School Structure: An Inquiry into its Validity." *Educational Administration Quarterly* 5 (Winter 1969): 37–49.

Roberts, G.M. "Two Non-graded Elementary School Programs: Facility Requirements and Utilization." *Dissertation Abstracts* 25 (November 1964): 2830. Abstract of an unpublished doctoral dissertation, The University of Tennessee, 1964. (#4)

Rodgers, F.A. "How Much Sequence?" *Instructor* 78 (March 1969): 43, 146, 148.

Rogers, E.M. "What are Innovators Like?" In *Change Process in the Public Schools*, by Richard O. Carlson, et al. p. 55. Eugene, Oregon: The Center for the Advanced Study of Educational Administration, University of Oregon, 1965.

Rogers, V.R. "Individualization Plus." *Instructor* 78 (January 1969): 88–89.

Rogers, V.R. "Nongraded Social Studies." *Instructor* 78 (May 1969): 73–74.

Rollins, S.P. "High School Where No One Fails." *School Management* 6 (May 1962): 77–79.

Rollins, S.P. "Ungraded High Schools: Why Those Who Like Them Love Them." *Nation's Schools* 73 (April 1964): 110 ff.

Roosa, J. "A Study of Organizational Climate, Leader Behavior, and Their Relation to the Rate of Adoption of Educational Innovations." Doctoral thesis, State University of New York, Albany, 1968.

Ross, G.A. "A Comparative Study of Pupil Progress in Ungraded and Graded Primary Programs." Doctoral thesis, Indiana University, Bloomington, 1967.

Russell, D.H. "Inter-class Grouping for Reading Instruction in the Intermediate Grades." *Journal of Educational Research* 39 (February 1946): 462–70.

Ryan, W.C. "The Ungraded Primary Class." *Understanding the Child* 24 (June 1955): 65.

Ryan, W.J. "Multimedia Learning Spaces Through Renovation." *Audiovisual Instructor* 14 (April 1969): 86–87.

Rylander, C.C. "Broadview Ungraded System." *Montana Education* 40 (April 1964): 16.

Salter, R. "Cooperative Research on the Nongraded Primary." *Elementary School Journal* 65 (1964–65).

Sanders, D.C. "Patterns of Organization." In *Elementary Education and the Academically Talented Pupil.* Washington, D.C.: National Education Association, 1961.

Sartain, H. "Applications of Research to the Problem of Instructional Flexibility." *Conference on Reading, University of Pittsburgh Report* 22 (1966), 97–113.

"Saskatchewan Plans all Ungraded Schools." *Teachers Magazine,* March 30, 1964.

"School of the Month: L.E. Berger Middle School, West Fargo, North Dakota." *Nation's Schools* 83 (March 1969): 108–109.

"School of the Month: Broken Arrow Elementary, Lawrence, Kansas." *Nation's Schools* 83 (May 1969): 108–110.

"School of the Month: Shadow Lake Elementary, Maple Valley, Washington." *Nation's Schools* 83 (June 1969): 82–84.

"Schools Can Change Grouping." *Childhood Education* 30 (October 1953): 64–66.

Scriven, E.G., and Harrison, A. Jr. "Let's Individualize Learning Skills." *Peabody Journal of Education* 46 (March 1969): 265–67.

Shane, H.G. "Grouping in the Elementary School." *Phi Delta Kappan* 41 (April 1960): 313–19.

Shaplin, J.J. "Team Teaching." *Saturday Review,* May 20, 1961: 54–55, 70.

Shearron, G. "Nongraded Schools." *National Elementary Principal* 47 (November 1967): 39–43.

"Should a School Have Fewer Specialists In Order to Reduce Class Size?" *Instructor* 78 (March 1969): 41.

Shuman, R.B. "Toward Reorganizing Secondary School English." *School and Society* 97 (February 1969): 97–98.

Shuman, R.B. "The Department Chairman and Innovation." *Peabody Journal of Education* 46 (January 1969): 194–99.

Shuster, A.H. "Principals and Teachers For Nongraded Schools: Pre-Service and In-Service Education." *National Elementary Principal* 46 (January 1968): 10–14.

Simon, S.B. "Down With Grades." *Today's Education* 58 (April 1969): 24.

Sister Clara Francis and Sister Mary Loretta Rose. "Ungraded School System Offers Greater Advantages Than the Graded School System: Debate." *National Catholic Education Association Bulletin* 61 (August 1963): 429–36.

Sister Josephine. "Student Reaction to the Ungraded Primary." *Peabody Journal of Education* 40 (March 1963): 291–95.

Sister Mary Alice. "Administration of Nongraded

Schools." *Elementary School Journal* 61 (1961–62).

Sister Mary Alice and D'Heurle, A. "New Ventures in School Organization: The Ungraded School and Use of Teacher Aids." *Elementary School Journal* 57 (February 1957): 268–71.

Sister M. Cordula. "Lowering the Grade Barriers." *Catholic Educational Review* 63 (February 1965): 111–17.

St. Mary, M.E. "The Administrative Team in Supervision." *National Elementary Principal* 45 (April 1966): 59–61.

Skapski, M.K. "Ungraded Primary Reading Program: An Objective Evaluation." *Elementary School Journal* 61 (October 1960): 41–45.

Sloan, F.A. Jr. "A Nongraded Social Studies Program for Grades Four, Five, and Six." *National Elementary Principal* 45 (January 1966): 25–29.

Smallwood, L.H. Jr. "Ungraded Elementary School: Reply." *Virginia Journal of Education* 60 (May 1962): 19–20.

Smith, L. "Continuous Progress Plan." *Childhood Education* 37 (March 1961): 320–23.

Smith, O.B. "A Concept of Teaching." *Teachers College Record* 61 (February 1960): 229–41.

Smith, R.J. "First Steps Toward an All-School Reading Program." *Journal of Reading* 12 (April 1969): 569–74.

Smith, R. "A Symposium, Language Arts in the Nongraded School: Part II, Language Arts Program in Nongraded Schools, Problems Arising." *Elementary English* 46 (February 1969): 126–29.

Smitter, F. "What Is a Primary School?" *California Journal of Elementary Education* 17 (February 1949): 139–45.

Snipes, W.T. "Promotion and Moving." *Elementary School Journal* 65 (1964–65).

Sommer, R. "Classrooms Are For Students." *American Education* 5 (June-July 1969): 18–21.

Spinning, J.M. "Is Melbourne High School One Step Short of Utopia? Review of the Nongraded High School." *Nation's Schools* 74 (December 1964): 10.

Splawn, R. "Nongraded Enterprise at Seminole High." *Texas Outlook* 52 (January 1968): 36–37.

Spohn, C.L. "Individualizing Instruction Through New Media Research." *Journal of Research in Music Education* 17 (Spring 1969): 94–99.

Sponberg, R.A. "New Kind of School Day." *Instructor* 78 (December 1968): 14–15. Also printed in *Educational Digest* 34 (April 1969): 46–48.

Sponsler, V., and Wagner, G. "The Primary School Plan." *Midland Schools* 75 (January 1961): 19–34.

Stauffer, R. "Is Cross-Class Grouping Effective? Joplin Plan." *Instructor* 77 (April 1968): 25.

Stenberg, V.A. "The Ungraded Primary School." *Encyclopedia Britannica.*

Stendler, C.B. "Grouping Practices," *Those First School Years,* 1960, the Yearbook of the Department of Elementary School Principals, National Education Association, *National Elementary Principal* 11 (September 1960): 147-65.

Stenquist, J.L. "How Baltimore Handles Pupil Promotion." *Nation's Schools* 27 (January 1941): 41–44.

Stoddard, G.D. "Dual Progress Plan in Elementary Education." *Educational Forum* 25 (March 1961): 271–76.

Story, M.L. "Let's Give Winnetka Another Chance." *Educational Forum* 27 (November 1962): 99–102.

Strickland, J.H. "Who Goes to School? Is the Child Really There?" *Educational Leadership* 26 (February 1969): 459–63.

Strickland, J.A., and Alexander, W. "Seeking Continuity in Early and Middle School Education." *Phi Delta Kappan* 50 (March 1969): 397–400.

Sturgeon, D.R. "Continuous Promotion in Elementary Schools." *School Administration,* March 1966.

Taylor, J.L.; Bryce, M.; and Moury, R.E. *Space and Facilities for Art Instruction,* U.S. Department of Health, Education and Welfare. For sale by the Superintendent of Documents, U. S. Government Printing Office, Washington, D.C. 20402–price 65¢.

Team Teaching at the Elementary School Level. Report of an Invitational Workshop sponsored by Perkins and Will Partnership, Architects, 309 W. Jackson Blvd., Chicago, Illinois, 60606, May 1964. Guest speakers were R.H. Anderson and E. McBeth, Ford Foundation.

Theman, V. "Continuous Progress in School." *Childhood Education* 18 (September 1941): 21–23.

Thomas, J.I. "From Kindergarten to What?" *National Elementary Principal* 46 (January 1968): 44–45.

Thomas, J.I. "Individualizing Instruction in the Social Studies." *Social Studies* 60 (February 1969): 71–76.

Thomas, J. "Reconciling Theory and Practice in the Elementary School." *Elementary School Journal* 68 (April 1968): 349–52.

Thompson, E. "The Ungraded Plan Helps Provide for Continuity of Learning." *NEA Journal* 48 (January 1958): 16–18.

Thompson, Mr. and Mrs. J.F. *The Nongraded Elementary School: The Continuous Progress Program.* A report of the New Mexico Western States Small Schools Project, Santa Fe, N.Mex: The State Department of Education, n.d.

"Three Slants on Curriculum: Dearborn Innovations Hailed." *Michigan Education Journal* 41 (January 1964): 11.

"Topics of Current Interest: Continuous Progress Primary." *Education* 84 (January 1964): 313.

"Toward Improved School Organization." *Elementary School Organization: Purposes, Patterns, Perspective,* the Yearbook of the Department of Elementary School Principals, National Education Association, *National Elementary Principal* 12 (December 1961): 60–127.

"Trimester Plan Makes Move Novel," an illustrated plan. *Nation's Schools* 73 (April 1964): 84–88.

Tschippert, O.B. "The Primary School: General Philosophy and Plan," Aliquippa, Pa.: Aliquippa Public Schools, (1960).

Tucker, M.B. "The Shoes Didn't Fit." *NEA Journal* 45 (March 1956): 159–61. Also printed in *Education Digest* 22 (September 1956): 27–29.

Turnbaugh, R.C. "Middle School: A Different Name or a New Concept?" *Clearing House* 43 (October 1968): 86–88.

Turner, E. "Ungraded Primary Room at Kremlin." *Montana Education* 42 (April 1966): 19.

Turner, W.E. "A Plan to Appraise Individual Progress for Continuous Learning." *Elementary School Journal* 69 (May 1969): 426–30.

Turney, D.T. *The Instructional Secretary as Used by Classroom Teachers.* Nashville, Tennessee: George Peabody College for Teachers 1959, p. 361. See also by D. Turney, *Secretaries for Teachers,* Nashville, Tennessee: George Peabody College for Teachers, 1962, available for $1.50.

Ultican, T. "Blue Springs Reports on First Year Experiences with the Ungraded Primary Plan." *School and Community* 48 (October 1961): 22, 46.

"Ungraded Primary: Has Your Staff Considered It?" *School Management* 3 (November 1959): 40.

University of Oregon. *Change Processes in the Public Schools.* Center for the Advanced Study of Educational Administration, 1965, p. 92.

Voege, R.B. "Innovating? Involve the Student." *Clearing House* 43 (May 1969): 543–46.

Wagner, G. "What Schools Are Doing in Developing the 'Continuous Growth Program'." *Education* 78 (May 1959): 595–96.

Wagoner, R.H.A. "Symposium, Language Arts in the Nongraded School: Riposte, A Review." *Elementary English* 46 (February 1969): 145–46.

Waller, E.A. "Ungraded Primaries." *Wisconsin Journal of Education* 81 (January 1949): 8–9.

Walters, H.G. "Pupil Progress in the Richmond Schools." *Teachers College Journal* 20 (December 1948): 47–55. Terre Haute, Ind.: Indiana State Teachers College.

Warren, J.W. "Travel With Apache: A Tour of Nongraded Schools." *National Elementary Principal* 46 (January 1968): 29–33.

Washburn, C.W., and Raths, L.E. "The High School Achievement of Children Trained Under the Individual Technique." *Elementary School Journal* 28 (1927): 214–24.

Weaver, J.F., "A Non-Grade-Level Sequence in Elementary Mathematics." *Arithmetic Teacher* 7 (December 1960): 431.

Webster, S.W. "The Case for a Federal Demonstration School System. Current Trends in Negro Education and Shorter Papers, Section D." *Journal of Negro Education* 38 (Spring 1969): 182–84.

Welch, J. "ILMOK Thursday." *National Elementary Principal* 48 (January 1969): 21–22.

West, L.C. "A New Partnership is Needed!" *School Libraries* 18 (Winter 1969): 31–32.

"What Schools are Doing." *Nation's Schools* 83 (April 1969): 76–82.

"What's the Case for Nongraded Secondary Schools?" *School Progress,* November 1966.

"What is Innovation?" *Educational Technology* 9 (February 1969): 35–36.

Wheat, L.B. "The Flexible Progress Group System." *Elementary School Journal* 38 (1937): 175–83.

Wilcutt, R.E. "Individual Differences—Does Research Have Any Answers for Junior High Mathematics Teachers?" *School Science and Mathematics* 69 (March 1969): 217–25.

Wilklow, L.B. "New York State Middle School Practices—1969." *Educational Horizons* 47 (Spring 1969): 117–21.

Wille, L. "Room for Miracles." *American Education* 5 (August-September 1969): 7–10.

Williams, A.B. "Adjusting Library Scheduling to Continuous Development Plan: Unscheduled Periods Increase Library Use." *Chicago Schools Journal* 46 (February 1965): 201–205.

Williams, W. "Academic Achievement in a Graded School and in a Nongraded School." *Elementary School Journal* 67 (December 1966): 135–39. Also printed in *Education Digest* 32 (January 1967): 41–43.

Wilson, A.T. "The Ungraded Primary School: How One City Has Adopted It." *American Teacher Magazine* 43 (February 1959): 5–6, 20.

Wolfson, B.J. "Look at Nongradedness." *Elementary English* 42 (April 1965): 455–57.

Woodbury, R.M., ed. *Organization of the Elementary School in Terms of Pupil Progress.* Cambridge, Mass.: New England School Development Council, April 1952.

Woodring, P. "Reform Movements from the Point of View of Psychological Theory." In *Theories of Learning and Instruction,* National Society for the Study of Education, 1964 Yearbook, Part 1. Chicago: University of Chicago Press, 1964, pp. 286–303.

Wrightstone, J.W., "Classroom Organization for Instruction. What Research Says to the Teacher." Bulletin No. 13. Washington, D.C.: Department of Classroom Teachers and American Educational Research Association, (May 1957).

Wyman, R. "Let's Try the One-Room School Again." *American School Board Journal* 149 (July 1964): 9–10.

Yates, D.P. "Flexibility in School Plant Development and Utilization." Doctoral thesis, University of Tennessee, Knoxville, 1968.

Yeomans, E. "Adapting Leicestershire Techniques (Report of a General Meeting at the Annual Conference of the National Association of Independent Schools, February, 1969)." *Independent School Bulletin* 28 (May 1969): 43.

Zahorik, J.A. "Individual Instruction and Group Instruction." *Journal of Educational Research* 62 (July-August 1969): 453–55.

Zerby, J.R. "Comparison of Academic Achievement and Social Adjustment of Primary School Children in the Graded and Nongraded School Program." *Penn State Review of Education Research* 13 (May 1961): 33. Unpublished doctoral dissertation, Pennsylvania State University, 1960.

EPILOGUE

If one thing is dramatically clear at this point, it is that continuous-progress-oriented education is child-oriented education. The attempt to make the child central to all our educational endeavors offers a greater hope for success if it concerns his total life. We can think of no better way of ending this book than by sharing some ideas of CBS News Correspondent Harry Reasoner from his network radio series, "The Reasoner Report":

A lady, writing in the *Reader's Digest* recently, said some things that needed to be said on the general theme that we should let children be children. She gave a horrible example that would sound contrived if all of us hadn't observed similar incidents: a woman in a park, bending over a baby carriage, making soft meaningless sounds to the baby, who is chuckling and making soft sounds right back. Then another lady with a baby carriage comes over and says, "Don't you know you shouldn't make meaningless sounds to a baby? It interferes with their early formation of proper speech patterns."

There are a lot of people like that. Their kids go to extra classes on Saturday when they get bigger, and when they get a lot bigger they go to psychiatrists; they grow up and write books like *The Mystery of Being a Woman*. These people eat their own young. The only problem is they want to eat ours too. The lady, writing in the *Reader's Digest*, says she thinks this may be the worst time in history to be a child, especially a kid in some social group or community where early learning is the fad; she is probably right.

I was glad to read there is no evidence that a child who learns to read early is a better reader by sixth grade than a child who learns to read when he is ready—which is a highly variable age. Sometimes the whole process of forcing learning on a youngster becomes ridiculous, as in the old story of the man who was bragging about how well he had done in his speedreading course. "I've increased my reading speed a hundred times", he told a friend. "Why just last night I read *War and Peace* on the train going home. It was about Napoleon and some other people." This kind of thing also happens with kids. For example, an eight-year-old I knew was exposed to a third-grade classroom discussion based on events at the UN during a period of tension. She was able to parrot a lot of names and phrases, but she had no more idea of what was really going on at the UN than a clam. You may say that she sounds like a senator, but that's irrelevant. Rote learning of facts or abilities before you are able to use them with imagination, or before you *want* them, produces people who can pass college boards, but not creative or happy men.

Another thing about people who don't want kids to be kids is that they limit children to *their* concept of a child's abilities. Programmed teaching, for example, pushes a child along at a set pace that may be too fast for him in terms of what we've been talking about. At the same time it seldom gives any surprises or huge jumps either. There is also a horrible kind of children's book that brags of having only 200, or 800, or whatever, different words in it, suitable for different reading levels. The people who publish such stuff are under the impression that the whole world shares their mediocrity; that it is important for readers to know what the words mean. Of course, as a child discovers the wonders of reading, it's important *not* to know what all the words mean. And no fair looking them up, either. Guess!

There ought to be something we could do about people who want to take the fun out of life; people who rewrite the Bible and change the names of holidays and warn about talking baby talk to your babies. Perhaps we could find some pleasant but uninhabited island and put them all on it, without a boat. They could then educate and reform each other, and leave the rest of us, particularly the kids, alone.

Amen! (the authors)

INDEX

The text of this book was composed
on a Magnetic Tape Selectric Composer
(MTSC) in 10 point Bodoni and the
illustrative matter in 10 point Optima
by Associated Techdata, Inc., of Palo
Alto.

Bodoni is one of a family of modern
typefaces based on a style developed
by G. Bodoni shortly before the French
Revolution. Optima, which lies
between a classic roman and a sans
serif, was designed by the German type
designer Hermann Zapf in 1958.

Printing and binding were done by
Kingsport Press, Inc., Kingsport,
Tennessee.